W9-AFS-128

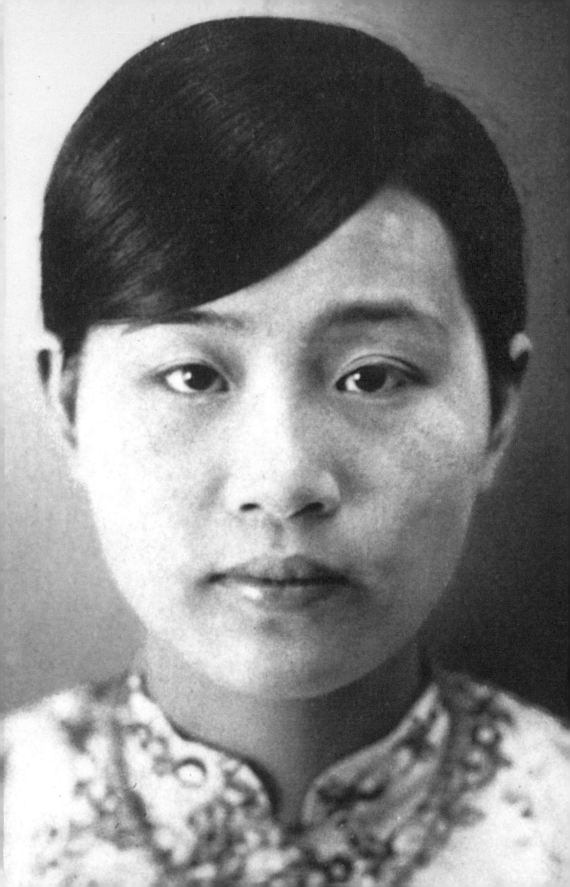

AT AMERIC

CHINESE IMMIGRATION DURING

The University of North Carolina Press CHAPEL HILL AND LONDON

AT AMERICA'S GATES

THE EXCLUSION ERA, 1882-1943

ERIKA LEE

Designed by Kristina Kachele
Set in Monotype Walbaum with Heliotype & Serlio display
by Tseng Information Systems, Inc.

The paper in this book meets the guidelines for permanence and durability of
the Committee on Production Guidelines for Book Longevity of the Council on
Library Resources.

Library of Congress Cataloging-in-Publication Data

Lee, Erika.
At America's gates: Chinese immigration during the exclusion era, 1882–1943 /
Erika Lee.
p. cm.
Includes bibliographical references and index.
ISBN 0-8978-2775-4 (alk. paper)—ISBN 0-8078-5448-4 (pbk.: alk. paper)
1. Chinese Americans—Social conditions—19th century. 2. Chinese Americans—
Social conditions—20th century. 3. Chinese Americans—Legal status, laws,
etc.—History. 4. Immigrants—United States—History—19th century.
5. Immigrants—United States—History—20th century. 6. United States—
Emigration and immigration—History. 7. China—Emigration and immigration—History. 8. United States—Emigration and immigration—Government
policy. 9. United States—Race relations. I. Title
E184.C5L523 2003
325'.2351073—dc21

2002013375

cloth   07 06 05 04 03   5 4 3 2 1
paper   07 06 05 04 03   5 4 3 2 1

Portions of Chapter 5 appeared earlier, in somewhat different form, in Erika Lee,
"Enforcing the Borders: Chinese Exclusion along the U.S. Borders with Canada
and Mexico, 1882–1924," *Journal of American History* 89, no. 1 (June 2002):
54–86 (© 2002 by the Organization of American Historians; reprinted by
permission).

In memory of my grandparents,
Ben Huie (Hui Bing Gee) and Gladys Huie (Moy Sau Bik)
and
Wallace Lee (Lee Chi Yet) and Mary Lee (Wong Lan Fong)

CONTENTS

ILLUSTRATIONS

TABLES

AT AMERICA'S GATES

INTRODUCTION

AMONG THE THOUSANDS of gold seekers who flocked to California in the mid-nineteenth century was Moy Dong Kee, my maternal great-great-great-grandfather.[1] A twenty-year-old farmer from Sun Jock Mee village in the Pearl River delta of southern China, he arrived in California in 1854 with big dreams of *Gum Saan,* or Gold Mountain, as the Chinese called the United States. Like many other immigrants, he came as a sojourner intending to work in America for a short time and then return home to his family and village. Instead, his initial trip to San Francisco stretched into a fifty-two-year stay that took him all across the United States. The opportunities in America were plentiful, and Moy found that he could provide much more for his wife and three children by staying in the United States. Eventually, he earned enough money to move to New York City and he opened Kwong Wah Tai & Co., a small Chinese goods store in the heart of Chinatown. He was also able to make at least three trips to visit his wife and children, who remained in China. This was not unusual. Chinese — and other immigrants — were customarily "transnational," maintaining families and socioeconomic, political, and cultural ties across international borders. Moy's son, my great-great-grandfather Moy Shai Quong, eventually came to America in 1873. Together, father and son opened up two more stores in Philadelphia, and both learned to speak, read, and write a little English. In 1906, Moy Dong Kee returned to China to retire at the age of seventy-two. Moy Shai Quong remained in the United States and eventually brought his own son, my great-grandfather Moy Wah Chung, to join him in 1907. Finally, my grandmother Moy Sau Bik, the fourth generation (and the first woman) of her family to immigrate to the United States, arrived in 1933 with my grandfather Huie Bing Gee and my aunt Mai Ling.[2]

Sixty-four years after Moy Dong Kee first sailed into the port of San Francisco, my paternal grandfather, Lee Chi Yet, came to the United States in 1918. Orphaned at a young age in Poon Lung Cheung village in Toisan, Grandfather quit school early and worked as a farmer in the village and then as a day laborer in the city of Toisan. For him and many others, the belief that the United States was a land of wealth and opportunity remained a strong and compelling reason to migrate abroad. Economic, social, and political instability in the Pearl River delta worsened during the late nineteenth and early twentieth centuries. The situation in Grandfather's village became particularly desperate. Coming to the United States was nothing less than a means of survival. As he recounted years afterward, "My eye just looking for a way to get out. I want to live, so I come to the United States."[3]

In the intervening years between Moy Dong Kee's first arrival in the United States in 1854 and Lee Chi Yet's landing in San Francisco in 1918, Chinese immigration to the United States had changed dramatically. Entry into the country in 1854 was relatively uncomplicated, because immigration to the United States was generally free and unrestricted. America welcomed immigrants from around the world to "settle" the land and provide the labor for its newly industrializing economy. Although some states regulated migration across their borders, federal policies—for the most part—promoted and encouraged immigration. Moy Dong Kee thus probably packed his bags, said good-bye to his wife in China, booked passage on a ship in Hong Kong, arrived in San Francisco, and simply disembarked. No gates barred his entry; no gatekeepers demanded immigration documents or subjected him to rigorous interrogations.

By the time Lee Chi Yet arrived in San Francisco, however, new laws had severely limited Chinese immigration into the United States. The Chinese Exclusion Act, passed in 1882, barred all Chinese laborers from entering the country for ten years and prohibited Chinese immigrants from becoming naturalized citizens. It expressly allowed only a few specific classes of Chinese to

Moy Dong Kee, the author's great-great-great grandfather, and his business card, 1901. At the time this photograph was taken, Moy was sixty-five years old and applying for re-admission into the United States. He had been migrating between China and the United States since 1854. His business card clearly demonstrated his status as a merchant in New York City. Courtesy of the National Archives, Northeast Region, New York, New York.

KWONG. WAH TAI & CO.

Importers and Dealers in

紐約埠

Chinese Groceries,

also General Merchandise.

No. 14 MOTT STREET, N. Y.

廣華泰號

NEW YORK,

continue to immigrate to the United States.[4] While laborers were prohibited, merchants, teachers, students, diplomats, and travelers were "exempt" from exclusion. Court cases later initiated by the Chinese in America secured the right of families of merchants and native-born citizens of the United States to apply for admission (or readmission) into the country as well. A product of the anti-Chinese movement that had begun in the West, the Exclusion Act marks the first time in American history that the United States barred a group of immigrants because of its race and class. The act also set the terms for the first large-scale deportation of an immigrant group. Later legislation renewed and strengthened the original act, and the exclusion of Chinese was made a permanent part of U.S. immigration policy until its repeal in 1943.

Thus, when Lee Chi Yet sailed into San Francisco, immigration to the United States was no longer an uncomplicated matter. His ship, the SS *Korea*, was met by a corps of uniformed U.S. immigration officials. While most non-Chinese immigrants were allowed to disembark after only a cursory examination, all new and some returning Chinese immigrants were rounded up and ferried to the eight-year-old immigration station on Angel Island, located in the middle of the San Francisco Bay. Once on the island, Lee and the other Chinese were escorted by guards for thorough medical examinations and interrogations. Chinese immigrants were believed to be contaminated with parasitic diseases and other ailments considered dangerous and contagious. They were also suspected of using false papers and identities to evade the exclusion laws. Grandfather was subjected to a particularly humiliating physical examination as part of government authorities' attempts to prove or disprove that he was indeed the age he claimed to be. He was stripped naked, and physicians meticulously examined his teeth, skin, hair, sexual organs, and bones and noted their findings in his immigration file. While immigrants were undergoing their medical examinations, immigrant inspectors searched their suitcases, trunks, and other possessions and stored them away. Personal letters and other belongings thought to be important to the case at hand were frequently confiscated. The Chinese were then sent to the crowded detention barracks to await further investigation.

Returning immigrants usually did not have to wait too long, especially if their papers were in order. But Lee Chi Yet was a new arrival and his admission into the country depended upon his ability to prove that he was exempt from the exclusion laws. A farmer all of his life, Grandfather did not qualify as one of the exempt classes, so he had purchased papers from another immigrant who agreed to claim him as his son. This "paper son" system was a common strategy that had evolved among the Chinese in response to the restrictive parameters of the exclusion laws. In order to immigrate to the United States, Grandfather gave up his identity as Lee Chi Yet and became Yee Shew Ning, son of merchant Yee Yook Haw. With his new identity came a new family history that he studied and memorized, including the names, ages, whereabouts, and other details of his "mother," two "brothers" and one "sister," his "grandparents," and "aunts" and "uncles." The real test came when both "father" and "son" were called before immigration officials and subjected to the extensive interrogations that had become routine over the course of the government's enforcement of the exclusion laws. Interviewed separately, they were asked detailed questions about their family and village life and their departure for America. "How many rows in your home village?" asked Inspector A. S. Hemstreet on July, 10, 1918. "Who lives in the third house from the head of the village?" "Give the names of husband, wife, and children who all live there." In total, the inspector asked Grandfather 145 questions. Fortunately, his answers agreed with his paper father's for the most part, and Grandfather was released from Angel Island after a stay of two weeks.[5]

The differences between Moy Dong Kee's pre-exclusion arrival in the United States and Lee Chi Yet's experience illustrate the enormous effects that the exclusion laws had on Chinese immigrants and American immigration. By the 1920s, a hierarchy of admissible and excludable immigrants had been codified into law, reinforcing ideas of "fitness" that were measured by an immigrant's race, ethnicity, class, and gender. Immigrants became keenly aware of how these new laws affected their lives. Decisions about who could still enter the country as well as when and how it could be accomplished had to be carefully weighed and planned. Even resident aliens and native-born Chinese American citizens faced potential exclusion if they left the United States and tried to return. The risks were glaringly apparent as immigrants were thrust into direct confrontations with a newly centralized and bureaucratic American state machinery. Borders, gates, and walls that were open to some while closed to others became a reality of immigration to the United States. Edward Steiner, an early scholar of immigration, observed that by 1905, it was "a hard, harsh fact [that the] grinding machinery of the law . . . sifts, picks, and chooses; admitting the fit and excluding the weak and helpless."[6]

I have long been interested in the Chinese exclusion laws, the anti-Chinese movement that led to their passage, and the debates surrounding Chinese immigration in the late nineteenth and early twentieth centuries. But I did not learn about these things from my own family. One grandmother refused to talk about the "old days" — times that were full of pain and wounds that never healed. When I could coax her into talking about her past, I had to take surreptitious notes under the dining room table. Other relatives also placed a premium on secrecy, preferring — like many Chinese Americans — to keep the years of exclusion buried. I thus turned to the historical record to examine two distinct but interrelated questions: How did the Chinese exclusion laws affect the Chinese in America? And how did they transform the United States into a gatekeeping nation, in which immigration restriction — largely based on race and nationality — came to determine the very makeup of the nation and American national identity? The result is a book that illustrates just how large a shadow the exclusion laws cast upon every aspect of Chinese American life. Chinese immigrant families were forced apart. Immigrants were placed under an immense amount of government scrutiny and were often unfairly excluded from the country. Stereotypes left over from the anti-Chinese movement portrayed Chinese men and women as degraded, dangerous menaces and helped to shape immigration officials' decisions about whom to admit and whom to exclude. Both newly admitted immigrants and even native-born Chinese American citizens were at constant risk of government surveillance and expulsion. This book also emphasizes how the Chinese in America responded to and resisted the exclusion laws and the constraints on their liberties, freedom of movement, and civil rights. Individually and collectively, Chinese immigrants and Chinese Americans vehemently protested against the injustice of the racist exclusion laws in court, in public, in the press, and in petitions sent to government officials in both the United States and China. They also responded by simply evading the exclusion laws altogether through illegal immigration or by successfully adapting their migration strategies to conform to the demanding immigration system that the exclusion laws set in motion.

The exclusion laws marginalized and constrained generations of Chinese immigrants and the Chinese community in America.[7] But the consequences of exclusion extended far beyond the confines of their community and ushered in a completely new era in U.S. history. Beginning in 1882, the United States stopped being a nation of immigrants that welcomed foreigners without restrictions, borders, or gates. Instead, it became a new type of nation, a gatekeeping nation. For the first time in its history, the United States began to exert federal control over immigrants at its gates and within its borders, thereby setting standards, by race, class, and gender, for who was to be welcomed into the country. Immigration patterns, immigrant communities, and racial identities and categories were significantly affected. In the process, the very definition of what it meant to be an "American" became even more exclusionary. Subsequent immigration laws — even those directed at restricting southern and eastern European immigrants — allowed for whites to become full-fledged members of the American nation. On the other hand, the Chinese exclusion laws and other government legislation excluding all other Asian immigrants reflected and maintained an exclusionary and racialized national identity that marked Asians, African Americans, Latinos, and Native Americans as outsiders.[8] Although the Chinese Exclusion Act was repealed in 1943, its legacy continued to shape immigration control and race relations throughout the entire twentieth century. The system of immigration restriction and exclusion based on race was formally abolished in 1965. But in the late twentieth century, militarized efforts to enforce U.S. borders, a revitalized anti-immigrant campaign, and new gatekeeping policies based on race echoed earlier policies and practices from the Chinese exclusion era.

As symbols of immigration restriction, the themes of America's gates and gatekeeping organize this study. San Francisco, the main port of entry for Chinese and the home of the largest Chinese American community in the United States during the exclusion era, serves as the main gateway around which the book is centered. The Chinese exclusion laws are important historical markers that open this investigation, but the emphasis in this book is on the encounters between the Chinese in America and the politics, processes, and consequences of immigration restriction and exclusion. I define Chinese exclusion as an institution that produced and reinforced a system of racial hierarchy in immigration law, a process that both immigrants and immigration officials shaped, and a site of unequal power relations and resistance. Immigration law thus emerges as a dynamic site where ideas about race, immigration, citizenship, and nation were recast. Chinese exclusion, in particular, reflected, produced, and reproduced struggles over the makeup and character of the nation itself.

At the heart of this book are the stories of outspoken critics of the exclusion policy, of "illegal" immigrants who posed as paper sons or surreptitiously crossed the northern and southern borders into the United States, of wives and children remaining in China, of immigration officials who struggled with an anti-Chinese public as well as with the bureaucratic demands of the government, and of Chinese American citizens who found their citizenship status threatened because of their race. Through these many voices and perspectives, it becomes clear that the consequences of Chinese exclusion were felt not only on the personal, individual level but on the national and international levels as well.

Until recently, we have known very little about how the policies of Chinese exclusion actually worked in practice or how Chinese immigrants and returning residents responded and adapted. Historian Sucheng Chan has characterized the exclusion era as the "dark ages" of Chinese American history, "a deplorable lacuna in American historiography."[9] To be sure, there is a rich scholarly record on the anti-Chinese movement. Historians have studied the politics behind the passage of the Chinese Exclusion Act, and the law has been widely recognized as a significant watershed in immigration and American history.[10] These works, however, focus almost all their attention on the actions and motives of the "excluders" rather than the "excluded" and often end in the year 1882, when this book begins.[11] They have little to say about the impact of exclusion on the Chinese in America, the interactions between Chinese immigrants and U.S. immigration officials, or the broader transformation of the United States into a gatekeeping nation.

Legal historians have begun to fill in some of these gaps by mining little-used sources to document legal doctrine shaping the exclusion laws and their enforcement. Lucy Salyer, in particular, was the first to demonstrate Chinese exclusion's importance to the shaping of modern immigration law.[12] Others have also documented the significant ways in which Chinese successfully used the American judicial system to challenge discriminatory legislation.[13] Legal scholars' primary interest in the legal debates, statutory architecture, judicial rulings, and enforcement procedures, however, have kept the law, rather than the Chinese, at the center of the story.[14] Conversely, social historians have focused their attention on explaining the internal social structures, labor patterns, organizations, institutions, and identities of the Chinese in America.[15] Most recently, scholars have adopted an explicitly transnational framework to highlight the ongoing trans-Pacific migrant networks and allegiances and economic, social, and political ties that existed between the Chinese in America and their families and villages in southern China as well as with other Chinese communities throughout the Americas and Southeast Asia.[16] Abandoning purely nation-centered analyses of migration, these works have expanded our understandings of the complex, global circumstances under which Chinese lived and labored during the exclusion era. Their emphasis on the transnational rather than the national, however, has obscured the impact of the American nation-state and the exclusion laws in particular in structuring and circumscribing transnational migration, networks, and identities.[17] Transnational interpretations of twentieth-century migration cannot merely replace national ones. Nations and nation-states remain central elements shaping and explaining both the processes of migration and the lives of migrants themselves.[18]

The Chinese exclusion era has previously been analyzed within the confines of separate subfields of history—social, immigration, Asian American, legal, Chinese, political, labor, or western. This book illustrates how Chinese immigration and American exclusion can best be understood only at the intersections of these subfields rather than within their boundaries. To make sense of the complex relationships, migration patterns, and political processes transformed by Chinese exclusion, one must consider several interrelated issues. *At America's Gates* first reconstructs the lives and relationships of exclusion-era Chinese and documents the various strategies they used to adapt to exclusion. But it also examines the centrality of race in immigration restriction and the ways in which the Chinese exclusion laws set in motion drastic political and legal changes in American immigration regulation. Combining the social history of Chinese Americans with a critical analysis of race, immigration law, and the state, this book offers a strikingly different narrative from the usual story of immigration and settlement, one that identifies the implementation of the Chinese exclusion laws as the main catalyst that transformed the United States into a gatekeeping nation.

While historians routinely refer to the Chinese exclusion era as one uniform period spanning from 1882 to 1943, this study emphasizes the importance of change over the course of the exclusion period. Chinese immigration patterns and the terms of the exclusion laws and the ways in which they were enforced evolved in many ways over the sixty-one years of exclusion. Part I of this book encompasses the first two decades of the exclusion era. The actual parameters and application of the laws were unclear, and it was not certain who would enforce the laws or how exclusion would be accomplished. Even the permanence of exclusion was not firmly established. Nevertheless, it was in these years that the United States developed into a gatekeeping nation, one which sought to control the number, race, ethnicity, and class of immigrants admitted into the country and eligible for American citizenship.

Scholars have characterized the anti-Chinese movement as "tangential" to larger patterns of twentieth-century American nativism, or anti-immigrant sentiment. They identify the debates over immigration and race in the 1920s—when a national-origins quota system was established—as the most significant period of American immigration restriction.[19] Chapter 1 suggests, however, that the Chinese exclusion era beginning in the 1870s and 1880s is in fact the critical starting point. Chinese exclusion not only set an important precedent in immigration law, it changed the ways Americans viewed and thought about race, immigration, and the United States' identity as a nation made by immigration. New understandings and definitions of race and racial categories were constructed in these debates and laws—a process that sociologists Michael Omi and Howard Winant have called "racial formation."[20] And new forms of regulation and identification were created to control Chinese—and, later, all—immigration to the United States.

The American gatekeeping ideologies, policies, and practices that originated in Chinese exclusion were at the center of the reshaping of America, and especially the growth of the federal government at the turn of the twentieth century. This new level of expansion, centralization, and bureaucratization, or "state-building," came in the form of regulating both foreigners arriving into the United States and foreigners and citizens already residing there. Political historians have ignored the role of race in the state-building processes of the late nineteenth and early twentieth centuries, but *At America's Gates* insists that race—and Chinese exclusion in particular—was a central agent of change.[21] In Chinese exclusion, the active role of the "state"—a term that political scientists and other scholars use to describe governmental systems and policies that attempt to structure not only the relationships between people and their government but also relationships and identities *among* individuals and groups—becomes clear. Chinese exclusion reinforced the important part that the federal government was beginning to play in controlling race relations, immigration and immigrant communities, and citizenship.[22] State mechanisms used to regulate immigration, enforce national borders, and distinguish U.S. citizens, legal immigrants, and illegal immigrants, such as the U.S. Immigration and Naturalization Service, U.S. passports, "green cards," and illegal immigration and deportation policies, can all be traced back to the Chinese exclusion era. Chinese immigration and exclusion are thus particularly important to our understanding of how nations are formed, challenged, and reconstituted from within and without.[23]

If American gatekeeping can be traced back to the 1870s and the debates over Chinese immigration, its origins can also be situated specifically in the American West, where arguments in support of Chinese exclusion arose and had the greatest political impact throughout the early twentieth century. By being the first to call for the closing of America's gates, westerners set in motion changes in national immigration policy. Anti-immigrant politics, immigration regulation, and border enforcement ceased to be the exception and instead became the rule.[24] To examine how the West shaped American gatekeeping, Chapter 2 turns to the local immigrant inspectors and interpreters based in San Francisco, their federal counterparts in Washington, D.C., and their methods of interpreting and enforcing the exclusion laws. These self-proclaimed "keepers of the gate" influenced the development of the U.S. immigration service both locally and nationally, making "gatekeeping" in the West the model for the entire nation. The Chinese exclusion laws might have been passed in Washington, D.C., but they were implemented at various ports of entry around the country, where the laws' meanings and consequences were constantly in flux. A narrow focus on legal statutes or judicial decisions obscures our understanding of how government officials, immigrants, and citizens interpreted, enforced, and challenged the law.[25] Instead, studying "law at its bottom fringes" — and the ways in which Chinese exclusion was actually enforced and contested at the local and federal levels — challenges traditional scholarship on immigration law that focuses primarily on changing patterns of nativism or the legislative battles behind the passage of American immigration policy.[26]

Parts II and III explore the years from 1910 to 1924, a period marked by growing nativism, a rise in Chinese illegal immigration, and increased government regulation. By 1910, the enforcement of the exclusion laws had become centralized, systematic, and bureaucratic. All decisions regarding Chinese immigration moved out of the federal courts (which immigration officials believed gave too much advantage to the immigrants) and into the hands of the immigration service exclusively.[27] The political and legal challenges to exclusion brought by the Chinese were largely ineffectual, as illustrated by the establishment, in 1910, of the immigration station on Angel Island. Perceived by Chinese to be a symbol of America's racist immigration policies, Angel Island marked a new chapter in the government's enhanced control and containment of Chinese immigration. Illegal immigration began in this period but flourished in the next. The question of immigration restriction reached center stage, as the United States grappled with additional "floods" of allegedly inferior and unassimilable immigrants from other parts of Asia, Mexico, and southern and eastern Europe. The 1924 Immigration Act, which perfected Asian exclusion and placed restrictions on immigration from southern and eastern Europe, marked what historians have characterized as the "triumph of nativism."[28]

Part II probes the dynamic interaction between Chinese immigrants and immigration officials in San Francisco and on Angel Island, exploring how Chinese immigrants understood, experienced, and challenged their exclusion from the United States as well as why and how so many continued to immigrate. Despite its intent, the 1882 Chinese Exclusion Act failed to end Chinese immigration altogether. From 1882 to 1943, an estimated 300,955 Chinese successfully gained admission into the United States for the first time or as returning residents and native-born citizens. In fact, the number of exclusion-era Chinese admissions is greater than that during the pre-exclusion era, from 1849 to 1882, when 258,210 Chinese entered the United States.[29] The fact that so many managed to enter the United States in spite of the exclusion laws is truly significant. It raises questions about the efficacy of restrictive immigration laws and demonstrates the power of immigrant resistance and agency. In reconstructing the world that these individuals and groups inhabited and shaped, this section takes as a central starting point two primary goals of Asian American history to focus on both the excluded and the excluders and on the acts of resistance as well as the acts of exclusion.[30] Chapter 3 explains how the enforcement of the exclusion laws by American immigration officials not only resulted in additional exclusion acts that further hindered Chinese immigration but also helped to define and reinforce understandings of Chinese as "Orientals" and foreign "others" who endangered the American nation.[31] The Chinese adapted to the increasing number of barriers they encountered by drawing upon a wide range of legal, political, and migration strategies. Increasingly, they also articulated and insisted upon claiming their own place in America.

Many of the effects of the exclusion laws were felt outside of the United States, and the transnational nature of Chinese immigration was a major factor shaping the entire exclusion era. As Chapter 4 demonstrates, Chinese migrants did maintain significant socioeconomic, cultural, and political ties with their families and homeland despite the legal barriers that placed limitations on Chinese immigration. Scholars have pointed out that Chinese "lived their lives across international borders."[32] However, it is also clear that the exclusion laws and the growing power and efficacy of American immigration regulation strained these transnational linkages. Recent studies have overemphasized the centrality of transnationalism for the Chinese in America during this period and have largely ignored the structural forces that limited or stunted frequent movement back and forth. They have also failed to consider how class and legal status might have affected the extent to which Chinese lived transnationally.[33] During an era of increased regulation of international migration by nation-states, the maintenance of transnational migration patterns, ties, and networks was certainly possible, but only under certain prescribed limitations.

Part III traces the growth of illegal immigration during the exclusion era and shows its consequences for both the Chinese community and U.S. immigration policy and border enforcement. Chinese continued to challenge their exclusion from the United States, but they often did so covertly, as illegal immigrants. Illegal immigration has proved to be one of the most significant consequences of the Chinese exclusion era. But while contemporary illegal immigration to the United States has been the focus of much attention, illegal immigration during the exclusion era has been largely ignored.[34] Chinese became, in effect, the country's first "illegal immigrants," entering the country through the back doors of Canada or Mexico or engaging in a highly organized interracial, transnational business of fraudulent immigration documents. Although Chinese were just one of the immigrant groups entering the country illegally during this time period, they nevertheless became the primary public symbol of the "illegal immigrant." As a result, U.S. immigration officials focused a disproportionate amount of time and resources on preventing Chinese entries and arresting Chinese suspected of being in the country unlawfully. These policies laid the foundation for later government campaigns to control other illegal immigrants. Moreover, U.S. immigration policies and prerogatives "migrated" across U.S. borders and had significant repercussions both outside of the United States and beyond the issue of Chinese exclusion.

From 1924 to the repeal of the exclusion laws in 1943, Chinese immigrants and the U.S. government became locked into an interdependent cycle. The more Chinese adapted to the changing contours of exclusion enforcement, the harder the government made it to enter the country. Increasingly, the futility and folly of the Chinese exclusion laws became apparent. Chinese lived with the consequences of exclusion long after they had passed through America's gates, and immigration officials increasingly argued that the exclusion laws were "probably the most difficult piece of legislation to enforce ever placed upon the statute books."[35] The futile system of exclusion would remain unchanged, however, until 1943, when the laws were repealed once and for all.

Part IV addresses the consequences and legacies of exclusion during this last period and beyond. Chapter 7 illustrates how American gatekeeping moved from the gates and borders into interior cities and towns, thereby affecting the entire Chinese American community. The epilogue examines how Chinese exclusion cast a shadow upon the entire United States during the twentieth century, in the form of gatekeeping policies that admitted, deported, and monitored immigrants based on their race.

This is the first study to use local, national, and transnational frameworks as well as the vantage points of both Chinese immigrants and U.S. immigration officials to examine the Chinese exclusion era. It is also the first to systematically analyze an incredibly rich and diverse body of government records on Chinese immigration and exclusion that was made publicly available only in the late 1980s and early 1990s. The immigration arrival files of the U.S. Immigration and Naturalization Service document every single Chinese immigrant who applied for admission or re-admission into the country or was deported from the United States during the exclusion era. The records reveal who immigrated, under which classes and categories, with which family members, and with what results. They include entry and reentry documents and visas; supporting business, school, and organizational records; notarized affidavits; translated letters and writings; correspondence from attorneys, acquaintances, and enemies; photographs; family histories; and extensive interviews with applicants and their family members and other witnesses. They capture the lives of ordinary people, their problems and acts of resistance, under the extraordinary circumstances of exclusion in ways that no other set of historical records have. There are an estimated 100,000 individual files of Chinese immigrants who entered the country through San Francisco alone, the busiest port of entry for Chinese. The immigration service at other ports of entry, such as New York, Seattle, Boston, and Philadelphia, created and maintained additional sets of files. Their sheer volume, breadth, and depth make these records the richest primary sources on Chinese immigration and the Chinese in America.

When I began research for my doctoral dissertation in the fall of 1993, most of these records had yet to be processed by the staff at the San Bruno, California, branch of the National Archives. Aside from Chinese American genealogists, local students researching their roots, and a few others, few people had used the records, and no scholar had yet worked with them as a whole. During my first trip, I experienced one of those fantastic "Eureka!" moments that excite historians. In each dusty box I examined, forgotten lives, journeys, secrets, hardships, and triumphs unfolded before my eyes. Faces looked out at me from yellowed INS forms—men and women, young and old, rich and poor, legal and illegal. Among them were the faces of my grandparents, whose files I found after some detective work. My grandfather's photograph showed a confident young man with slicked back hair wearing a traditional Chinese tunic. My grandmother's file included their wedding portrait, which immigration officials had confiscated in 1927 to include in the government's official record. Realizing that my grandparents represented only two of the thousands

The author's grandparents, Wong Lan Fong and Lee Chi Yet, on their wedding day in 1926. Submitted as proof of the couple's marriage, this photograph was confiscated by the Immigration and Naturalization Service to be used as evidence in Wong Lan Fong's case for admission in 1927. The numbers written on the photograph are Wong's immigration case file number. Courtesy of the National Archives, Pacific Region, San Bruno, California.

of lives and stories to be unearthed in these documents overwhelmed me. So did a newfound sense of responsibility to share all of their stories.

The immigration records allow us to understand the Chinese exclusion era in a way that has not been possible before. They provide a unique lens through which to see not only the everyday lives of Chinese immigrants and the roles of immigration officials in enforcing immigration law but also the enormous impact that the Chinese exclusion laws had on immigration, race, and the nation as a whole. In an attempt to create some type of system that would allow me to analyze immigrant arrival files from the entire exclusion period, I surveyed and collected data from more than 600 immigrant files from 1884 to 1940, selected by random sample. Following the extensive paper trails that each file contained, I reviewed several dozen other files as well. Much of the statistical information that appears in the book was eventually compiled from other sources, such as the annual reports of the U.S. Bureau of Immigration (precursor to the U.S. Immigration and Naturalization Service). But my survey of the San Francisco files allowed me to track larger changes in immigrant composition, transnational migration patterns and networks, enforcement practices, immigration service personnel, immigrant strategies (such as the use of lawyers), and the complex relationship between immigration officials and Chinese, as well as the changing terrain of exclusion over its sixty-one years of existence. Most important, the files brought to life the actual experiences of Chinese under exclusion and demonstrated the unique ties that bound Chinese to each other and to the nation-state.

Rich as they are, these records — like all sources — are problematic in some ways. First, the documents were created in the language of immigration law and within the context of government regulation. They also privilege the perspective and prerogative of immigration officials. The level of detail, the questions asked, the manner of questioning, and the presentation of testimony were all determined by the government officials recording and processing the information. References in officials' diaries and personal correspondence hint at an immense anti-Chinese bias that informed the nature and scope of their work. Because the reliability of the government's translation of Chinese voices and sources into English changed over the years, the accuracy of the translations should also be considered, especially during the first decade of the exclusion era, when the government banned the hiring of interpreters of the Chinese race. But by the 1900s, the quality and consistency of translations in the San Francisco office improved, due in large part to civil service reforms in the immigration service. Lastly, the reliability of the testimony itself must also be questioned in many cases. Because of the proliferation of illegal immigration and the false names and identities that the exclusion laws produced, much of the personal information recorded in the files can be considered unreliable.

Through the course of my research, I learned how to work around these flaws. I used the government perspective to tease out enforcement practices, attitudes, and biases among immigration officials. I read behind and between the lines for the Chinese voice and used sources originating from the immigrants themselves as much as possible. The white lies told in the course of establishing a false identity for the purposes of immigration did not necessarily affect the integrity of the larger narrative because I was interested in capturing general patterns and strategies rather than recreating true family genealogies. It was also fairly easy to determine which immigrants were using false names and fraudulent papers. Some immigrants had been rejected out of hand; others made an admission of guilt themselves as part of the so-called anti-Communist Confession Program of the 1960s, when government officials encouraged and coerced illegal Chinese immigrants to come forward to legalize their status and denounce Communism. These statements were also included in the files. To protect the privacy of individuals, all names of persons who were found to have entered the country illegally or who arrived in the United States after 1926 have been changed.

In addition to the immigrant arrival files in San Francisco, I also mined the voluminous personal and official correspondence and papers of local and federal immigration officials to understand the motivations and rationales behind their decision making. Because Chinese were such active and vocal critics of the exclusion policy, their petitions, protests, and letters are also part of this voluminous public record. Lastly, I interviewed Chinese immigrants and Chinese Americans who immigrated to and lived in America during the exclusion era, and I relied heavily upon studies and oral histories done by other scholars.

Taken together, these chapters document and bring alive thousands of voices that had been virtually erased from the historical record. They explain the significance of Chinese exclusion for both Chinese Americans and American history. Throughout the researching and writing of this book, I have taken as my guide a poem written by an anonymous male detainee in the immigrant barracks on Angel Island who pleaded with readers to remember and recover this history. Carving deeply into the wooden walls, the author who identified himself only as "One from Xiangshan" wrote:

There are tens of thousands of poems composed on these walls.
They are all cries of complaint and sadness.
The day I am rid of this prison and attain success,
I must remember that this chapter once existed.[36]

This book does more than merely remember and document the history of Chinese exclusion. It captures the struggles of a community and a nation during one of this country's most divisive and destructive eras and explains how and why the United States became transformed from a nation of immigrants into a gatekeeping nation.

PART I

CLOSING THE GATES

The twin metaphors of "gates" and "gatekeepers" have commonly been used to describe American efforts to control immigration. By the end of the twentieth century, the metaphor had become embedded in academic and public discourses on immigration, reflecting a renewed restrictionist ideology and mood. A wide range of scholars and journalists have written about "guarding the gate," the "clamor at the gates," "the gatekeepers," the "guarded gate," "closing the gate," etc.[1] Perhaps the best-known and most recent use of the term "gate" is the U.S. Immigration and Naturalization Service's Operation Gatekeeper, a militarized campaign initiated in 1994 to restrict the illegal entry of Mexican immigrants into the United States near San Diego, California.[2] Following the terrorist attacks in New York and Washington, D.C., on September 11, 2001, new calls to establish tighter gatekeeping measures have also received much media attention and broad public support. Although journalists, policy makers, and academics use the gatekeeping metaphor widely, there has been little serious inquiry into how the United States first came to define itself as a gatekeeping nation or what that definition has actually meant for both immigrants and the nation. While much has been written explaining how changing patterns of American nativism have led to the restriction and exclusion of immigrants, we know very little about the consequences of immigration laws themselves. Several questions remain: What effects do immigration policies have at America's gates and within the nation itself? How is gatekeeping related to domestic race relations, racial identities, and state-building? How have immigrants responded and resisted? What are the legacies of American gatekeeping policies for contemporary immigration and immigration law? This section defines American gatekeeping, places its origins in the debates over Chinese immigration in the American West during the late nineteenth century, and suggests it be used as a paradigm to reconsider American immigration history.

The Chinese Exclusion Act was passed at the federal level in 1882, but it was in the distinct regional context of 1870s California that politicians and anti-Chinese activists began to talk about closing America's gates for the first time.[3] Explicit in the arguments for Chinese exclusion were several elements that would become the foundation of American gatekeeping ideology: racializing Chinese immigrants as permanently alien and even inferior on the basis of their race, class, culture, and gender relations; controlling them through limitations on economic and geographic mobility and prohibitions on naturalization; and protecting the nation by using the power of the state to exclude and restrict new immigrants and track and deport foreigners already in the United States.

Making and enforcing U.S. immigration policy have always involved several overlapping concerns, goals, and variables.[4] Immigrants have been excluded and restricted on the basis of their race, ethnicity, class, gender, sexuality, moral standing, health, and political affiliation, among other factors. Some of these justifications for exclusion and restriction were more important during certain historical periods than others. But they often intersected with each other, working separately and in concert to regulate not only foreign immigration and immigrant communities but also domestic race, class, and gender relations. Immigrant laborers who were considered a threat to American white working men were summarily excluded on the basis of class. Restriction laws targeting immigrants suspected of immoral behavior or those "likely to become public charges" affected female immigrants disproportionately.[5] Efforts to exclude immigrant groups on the basis of their alleged menace to U.S. public health constituted what Alan Kraut has called "medicalized nativism," and the diseases considered most dangerous were explicitly tied to racialized assumptions about specific immigrant groups.[6] Homosexuals were denied entry beginning in 1917 under clauses in general immigration laws related to morality and the barring of "constitutional psychopathic inferiors."[7]

Race was thus not the only factor shaping immigration law, but it was the most important one. Even today, domestic race relations and fears that certain immigrants (especially immigrants of color) are not as assimilable or desirable as others have reinforced the role of race in immigration policies. In turn, immigration laws have shaped the very meanings of race and racial identities. Federal immigration laws became the means to achieve restrictionists' goals and reflected and reinforced the existing racial hierarchy in the country, leaving America's gates open to some and closed to others.[8] Understanding the racialized origins of American gatekeeping provides a powerful counternarrative to the popular "immigrant paradigm" that celebrates the United States as a "nation of immigrants" and views immigration as a fulfillment of the "promise of American democracy." As many critics have pointed out, this popular conception of the nation ignores the very real power of institutionalized racism in excluding immigrants and people of color from full and equal participation in American society, economy, and polity. Explicitly barred from the country, Asian immigrants do not fit easily into the immigrant paradigm and offer a different narrative highlighting the limits of American democracy.[9] Viewing immigration history within a gatekeeping framework shifts our attention from traditional issues such as assimilation or cultural retention to the consequences of restriction, exclusion, and deportation for both immigrant and non-immigrant communities.

Reconceiving the United States as a gatekeeping nation thus offers an especially suitable framework for Asian and Latino immigrants, two groups that not only have been among the largest immigrant populations in the twentieth century but also have caused the most debate and inspired new regulations.[10] European immigrants were, in general, protected from the harsher exclusion and deportation laws that targeted Asians and Mexicans, but they were not entirely free from the impact of gatekeeping laws.[11] As nativism increased in the 1920s, southern and eastern European immigrants came to be racialized as threats to the nation, often along the same lines as Asians. And once the gates of immigration law were built, the bureaucratic machinery established to admit, examine, deny, deport, and naturalize immigrants was applied to all groups.

Gatekeeping, through the legislation it entailed, also served as an important impetus to American state-building at the end of the nineteenth century, a force that both political and immigration historians have largely ignored.[12]

In the United States, the great migrations of Asians, Europeans, and Mexicans from the 1880s to 1924 coincided with and helped instigate an expansion of the modern administrative state. They inspired the establishment of a state bureaucracy to enforce laws and to protect the nation's geographic borders as well as its internal borders of citizenship. Gatekeeping was also inextricably tied to the expansion of U.S. imperialism at the end of the nineteenth century. At the same time that the United States began to assert its national sovereignty by closing its gates to unwanted foreigners, it was also expanding its influence abroad through military and economic force, and it extended some of its immigration laws to its new territories.[13]

Closing America's gates to various "alien invasions" was additionally instrumental in articulating a definition of American national identity and belonging at the turn of the twentieth century.[14] Americans learned to define "American-ness" by excluding and containing foreign-ness. Through the admission and exclusion of foreigners, the United States both asserted its sovereignty and reinforced its identity as a nation.

Immigration patterns and immigrant communities were profoundly changed by the new laws and the ways in which they were enforced. The ideology and administrative processes of gatekeeping dehumanized and criminalized immigrants, defining them as "unassimilable aliens," "unwelcome invasions," "undesirables," "diseased," "illegal." But gatekeeping is not only a form of state action. It is a result of interactions between immigrants and the state. Even those groups who were most affected by immigration restriction played active roles in challenging, negotiating, and shaping the new gatekeeping nation. In both their overt challenges and their everyday acts of resistance, immigrants defied their exclusion from the United States by moving around the barriers designed to exclude them while simultaneously staking their own claims to America.

In this section, Chapter 1 locates the roots of American gatekeeping in the debates, racialized discourses, and regulations surrounding Chinese immigration and exclusion. Chapter 2 focuses on the federal immigration officials charged with interpreting and enforcing the exclusion laws, demonstrating how they shaped the development of the U.S. immigration service locally and nationally.

CHAPTER ONE

THE CHINESE ARE COMING. HOW CAN WE STOP THEM?

Chinese Exclusion and the Origins of American Gatekeeping

IN 1876, H. N. CLEMENT, a San Francisco lawyer, stood before a California State Senate Committee and sounded the alarm: "*The Chinese are upon us. How can we get rid of them? The Chinese are coming.* How can we stop them?"[1] Panicked cries such as these and portrayals of Chinese immigration as an evil, "unarmed invasion" had been shared by several witnesses before the committee, which was charged with investigating the "social, moral, and political effects" of Chinese immigration. Testimony like Clement's was designed to reach a broad audience, and the committee hearings themselves were part of a calculated political attempt to bring the question of Chinese immigration to a national audience.[2] Many Californians had long felt beleaguered by the influx of Chinese immigrants into the state and now believed that it was time that the federal government took action. As the committee's "Address to the People of the United States upon the Evils of Chinese Immigration" stated, the people of California had "but one disposition upon this grave subject . . . and that is an open and pronounced demand upon the Federal Government for relief."[3]

At the time of the committee hearings, the United States was just beginning to exert federal control over immigration. Its first efforts had begun one year earlier in response to the California lobby to exclude Asian contract labor and women (mostly Chinese) suspected of entering the country for "lewd or immoral purposes." The resulting Page Law, passed in 1875, represented the country's first—albeit limited—regulation of immigration on the federal level and served as an important step toward general Chinese exclusion.[4] The U.S. Congress eventually heeded the call of Californians and other westerners to protect them from the so-called Chinese invasion with the 1882 Chinese Exclusion Act.

Historians have often noted that the Chinese Exclusion Act marks a "watershed" in U.S. history. Not only was it the country's first significant restrictive immigration law; it was also the first to restrict a group of immigrants based on their race, nationality, and class. As Roger Daniels has written, the Chinese Exclusion Act was "the hinge upon which the legal history of immigration turned."[5] This observation has become the standard interpretation of the anti-Chinese movement, but until recently, most accounts of Chinese exclusion have focused more on the anti-Chinese movement preceding the Chinese Exclusion Act rather than on the six decades of the exclusion era itself.[6] Moreover, there has been little attempt to explain the larger impact and legacies of Chinese exclusion. For example, how did the effort to exclude Chinese influence the restriction and exclusion of other immigrant groups? How did the racialization of Chinese as excludable aliens contribute to and intersect with the racialization of other Asian, southern and eastern European, and Mexican immigrants? What precedents did the Chinese Exclusion Act set for the admission, documentation, surveillance, and deportation of both new arrivals and immigrant communities within the United States?

When the Page Law and the Chinese Exclusion Act serve as the beginning rather than the end of the narrative, we are forced to focus more fully on the enormous significance of Chinese exclusion. It becomes clear that its importance as a "watershed" goes beyond its status as one of the first immigration policies to be passed in the United States. Certainly, the Page Law and the Chinese Exclusion Act provided the legal architecture for twentieth-century American immigration policy.[7] Chinese exclusion, however, also introduced gatekeeping ideology, politics, law, and culture that transformed the ways in which Americans viewed and thought about race, immigration, and the United States' identity as a nation of immigrants. It legalized the restriction, exclusion, and deportation of immigrants considered to be threats to the United States. It established Chinese immigrants—categorized by their race, class, and gender relations as the ultimate example of the dangerous, degraded alien — as the yardsticks by which to measure the desirability (and "whiteness") of other immigrant groups. Lastly, the Chinese exclusion laws not only provided an example of how to contain threatening and undesirable foreigners, they also set in motion new modes and technologies of immigration regulation, including federal immigration officials and bureaucracies, U.S. passports, "green cards," and illegal immigration and deportation policies. In the end, Chinese exclusion forever changed America's relationship to immigration.

The Anti-Chinese Movement and the Passage of the 1882 Chinese Exclusion Act

Chinese immigrants began to arrive in the United States in significant numbers following the discovery of gold in California in 1848. Most came from the Pearl River delta region in Guangdong, China, and, like the majority of newcomers to California, the Chinese community was comprised mostly of male laborers. They were only a small fraction of the total immigrant population of the United States. From 1870 to 1880, a total of 138,941 Chinese immigrants entered the country, 4.3 percent of the total number of immigrants (3,199,394) who entered the country during the same decade.[8]

Their small numbers notwithstanding, Chinese immigrants were the targets of racial hostility, discriminatory laws, and violence. This racism was grounded in an American Orientalist ideology that homogenized Asia as one indistinguishable entity and positioned and defined the West and the East in diametrically opposite terms, using those distinctions to claim American and Anglo-American superiority. Americans first learned to identify Chinese through reports from American traders, diplomats, and missionaries in China. Their portrayals of Chinese as heathen, crafty, and dishonest "marginal members of the human race" quickly set Chinese apart. At first seen as exotic curiosities from a distant land, Chinese immigrants came to be viewed as threats, especially as Chinese immigration increased throughout the gold rush period.[9]

Orientalist fears of the Asian "other" intersected and overlapped with domestic fears about American race, class, and gender relations. During the 1870s, massive population growth, coupled with economic dislocation in California in general, and San Francisco in particular, helped fan the fires of early anti-Chinese sentiment. By 1871, historians estimate, there were four workers for every job, but Chinese laborers were producing 50 percent of California's boots and shoes. By 1882, Chinese made up between 50 and 75 percent of the farm labor in some California counties.[10] Blaming Chinese workers for low wages and the scarcity of jobs, anti-Chinese leaders first charged that the Chinese were imported under servile conditions as "coolies" and were engaged in a new system of slavery that degraded American labor.[11] Chinese immigrants' purported diet of "rice and rats" was also cited as a clear sign that they had a lower standard of living, one that white working families could not (and should not) degrade themselves by accepting.[12] Samuel Gompers, president of the American Federation of Labor, framed this issue explicitly by asking, "Meat vs. Rice—American Manhood vs. Asiatic Coolieism. Which Shall Survive?"[13] Such rhetoric heightened the appeal of groups like the Workingmen's Party of California. Founded in 1877 and headed by Irish immigrant Denis Kearney, the party's rallying cry was "The Chinese Must Go!" Local and national politicians alike used race- and class-based economic arguments to nationalize the Chinese question. As Gwendolyn Mink has illustrated, the anti-Chinese movement in California was a "building block of national trade-union politics" that "transposed anti-capitalist feeling with anti-immigrant hostility."[14]

Many of the arguments in favor of restricting Chinese immigrants also hinged explicitly on gender and sexuality. As Sucheta Mazumdar argues, a specific kind of Orientalism emerged in the West, with Chinese women symbolizing some of the most fundamental differences between the West and the "Far East."[15] The almost 900 Chinese prostitutes in California in 1870 came to represent a sexualized danger with the power to subvert both the domestic ideal and the existing relations between white heterosexual men and women. Their mere presence made possible the crossing of racial and class lines and renewed fears of "moral and racial pollution."[16] Chinese prostitutes were also believed to carry more virulent strains of venereal disease that had the power to "poison Anglo-Saxon blood." They allegedly not only threatened the morals of the larger society but, as exclusionists argued, could also cause its downfall.[17]

Historian Karen Leong reminds us that the ways in which both American and Chinese masculinity were constructed in the anti-Chinese debates were also central arguments for Chinese exclusion. Exclusionists claimed that Chinese men exploited women (by supporting the Chinese trade in prostitution) and immigrated alone, failing to establish families. Both actions, they argued, pointed to their lack of manhood.[18] Chinese men also did not abide by the rules that divided labor by gender in American society. Expelled from mining camps, excluded from industrial and agricultural labor, Chinese men had established an economic niche for themselves in laundries, restaurants, and domestic service, all occupations traditionally assigned to women.[19] Their physical appearance and choice of clothing also disturbed American perceptions of proper gender roles. Prior to the Chinese Revolution in 1911, Chinese men shaved their foreheads and wore their hair in a queue as a symbol of loyalty to the Qing Empire. The loose garments that Chinese men often wore were also cause for scrutiny. In 1901, a California agricultural journal complained that "the good dollars which ought to be going into a white man's pocket" were instead going to the "Chinaman" and "that garment of his which passes for 'pants.'" Both the queue and the garments were seen as sexually ambiguous at a time when strict gender codes generally dictated short hair and pants for men, long hair and dresses for women.[20]

Such class- and gender-based arguments for Chinese exclusion merged with charges that Chinese were racially inferior and would worsen America's existing race problems. Underlying the anti-Chinese movement was a larger campaign to impose and sustain white supremacy in the West. Californians had long envisioned their state to be an Edenic, unspoiled land where free labor might thrive. This image was disrupted by the "Chinese Problem."[21] Alexander Saxton has demonstrated how the heirs to the Jacksonian Democratic Party—committed to territorial expansion, defense of slavery, and a belief in the racial inferiority of Africans and Native Americans—systematically nourished and exploited anti-Chinese sentiment and turned the Chinese immigration question into a centerpiece of California politics.[22] When Chinese immigrants began arriving in America, the conquest of American Indians and Mexicans in the West had been accomplished only recently. Moreover, white anti-Chinese residents of California and other Pacific Coast states felt that the future of "their society" was particularly endangered because of their proximity to Asia.[23] In order to highlight the alleged racial threat that Chinese posed, the similarities between African Americans and Chinese immigrants were drawn most explicitly. Both the "bought" Chinese prostitute and the "enslaved" Chinese coolie were conflated with African American slaves. Racial qualities commonly assigned to African Americans were used to describe Chinese immigrants. Both were believed to be heathen, inherently inferior, savage, depraved, and lustful.[24] Chinese, like African Americans, were "incapable of attaining the state of civilization [of] the Caucasian." And while some believed the Chinese were "physiologically and mentally" superior to African Americans, they were more of a threat, because they were less assimilable.[25]

Anti-Chinese activists' charges that Chinese were unwilling and, in fact,

A STATUE FOR *OUR* HARBOR.

"A Statue for Our Harbor," from *The Wasp*, Nov. 11, 1881. This well-known cartoon published in the *Wasp* in 1881 captured all of the themes of class-based economic competition, racial and health menace, conquest, and gender ambiguity explicit in the Chinese exclusion movement. Featuring a stereotypical image of the Chinese male coolie in place of the Statue of Liberty, the cartoon suggests that while New York's statue represented the promise of (European) immigration, California's statue symbolized how Chinese immigration would overrun the West and destroy the nation itself. Courtesy of the San Francisco History Center, San Francisco Public Library.

incapable of assimilating were repeatedly used to introduce and support the idea of closing America's gates to Chinese immigration. Chinese immigrants were first set apart from both European immigrants and native-born white Americans. One witness before the 1876 California State Committee on Chinese Immigration described Chinese immigration as an unwelcome "invasion" of "new" and "different" immigrants, while the earlier classes of (European) immigrants were "welcome visitors." In this way, the country's immigrant heritage and identification as a nation of immigrants was largely preserved. Even more important, the witnesses continued to emphasize how Chinese were "permanently alien" to America, unable to ever assimilate into American life and citizenship.[26]

These interrelated threats justified that legal barriers be established and that metaphorical gates be built and closed against the Chinese in order to protect Americans. Western politicians effectively claimed the right to speak for the rest of the country and to assert American national sovereignty in the name of Chinese exclusion. They argued that it was nothing less than the duty and the sovereign right of Californians and Americans writ large to exclude the Chinese for the good of the country. H. N. Clement, the San Francisco lawyer, explicitly combined the themes of racial difference, the closed gate/closed door metaphor, and national sovereignty to articulate this philosophy. "Have we any right to *close our doors* against one nation and open them to another?" he asked. "Has the Caucasian race any better right to occupy this country than the Mongolian?" He answered with an emphatic "Yes." Citing contemporary treatises on international law, Clement argued that the greatest fundamental right of every nation was self-preservation, and the Chinese immigration question was nothing less than a battle for America's survival. "A nation has a right to do *everything* that can secure it from threatening danger and to *keep at a distance* whatever is capable of causing its ruin," he continued. "We have a great right to say to the half-civilized subject from Asia, '*You shall not come at all.*'"[27]

Both the West's history of extending and reinforcing white supremacy in the region and its unique relationship with the federal government paved the way toward Chinese exclusion and the larger development of a gatekeeping nation. The language and politics of the anti-Chinese movement closely followed other western campaigns of territorial expansion, expropriation of Native American lands, and the subjugation of African Americans and Mexicans. The exclusion of Chinese immigrants became a "natural" progression in the region's history of racial oppression and segregation, but because immigration was recognized as a federal, rather than state or regional, issue, westerners could not achieve their directives alone. As one of the best examples of what historians have identified as a "quintessentially western story" of westerners relying upon the federal government to solve the region's racial and class problems, anti-Chinese activists designed a special plea for assistance to the U.S. Congress.[28] Their message was clear: Chinese immigration was both a "local grievance" and a "national question," the "darkest cloud" not only on California's horizon but on the republic's as well.[29] The threats, pleas, and cajoling worked. In 1880, unrelenting lobbying resulted in a revision of the Burlingame Treaty that had protected Chinese immigration since 1868. By March of 1882, midwestern congressman Edward K. Valentine (R-Nebraska) had articulated western exclusionists' message perfectly. "In order to protect our laboring classes," he proclaimed in the halls of Congress, "*the gate must be closed.*"[30] With the passage of the Chinese Exclusion Act in 1882, the federal government rode to the rescue of the West once again. The exclusion of Chinese became yet one more chapter in the region's consolidation of white supremacy, but with enduring, national consequences.

The Example of Chinese Exclusion: Race and Racialization

One of the most significant consequences of Chinese exclusion was that it provided a powerful framework to be used to racialize other threatening, excludable, and undesirable aliens. After the Chinese were excluded, calls to restrict or exclude other immigrants followed quickly, and the rhetoric and strategy of these later campaigns drew important lessons from the anti-Chinese movement. For example, the class-based arguments and restrictions in the Chinese Exclusion Act were echoed in campaigns to bar contract laborers of any race. Southern and eastern European immigrants — like Chinese — were denounced as "coolies, serfs, and slaves." Such connections were persuasive. In 1885, the Foran Act prohibited the immigration of all contract laborers.[31]

The gender-based exclusions of the Page Act were also duplicated in later government attempts to screen out immigrants, especially women, who were perceived to be immoral or guilty of sexual misdeeds. The exclusion of Chinese prostitutes led to a more general exclusion of all prostitutes in the 1903 Immigration Act.[32] Signifying a larger concern that independent female migration was a moral problem, other immigration laws restricted the entry of immigrants who were "likely to become public charges" or who had committed a "crime involving moral turpitude."[33] As Donna Gabaccia has pointed out, such general exclusion laws were theoretically "gender-neutral." In practice, however, "any unaccompanied woman of any age, marital status, or background might be questioned" as a potential public charge. Clauses in the 1891 Immigration Act excluded women on moral grounds. Sexual misdeeds such as adultery, fornication, and illegitimate pregnancy were all reasons for exclusion. Lastly, echoes of the "unwelcome invasion" of Chinese and Japanese immigration were heard in nativist rhetoric focusing on the high birthrates of southern and eastern European immigrant families. Immigrant fecundity, it was claimed, would cause the "race suicide" of the Anglo-American race.[34]

Race clearly intersected with these class- and gender-based arguments and played perhaps the largest role in determining which immigrant groups were admitted or excluded. The arguments and lessons of Chinese exclusion were resurrected over and over again during the nativist debates over the "new" immigrants from Asia, Mexico, and southern and eastern Europe, further refining and consolidating the racialization of these groups. David Roediger and James Barrett have suggested that African Americans provided the racial model for southern and eastern European immigrants. The terms "guinea," to refer to Italians, and "hunky," to refer to Slavic immigrants, were especially connected to these two groups often laboring in industries and jobs previously dominated by African Americans.[35] In terms of immigration restriction, however, new immigrants were more closely racialized along the Chinese immigrant model, especially in the Pacific Coast states. There, whiteness was defined most clearly in opposition to Asian-ness or "yellowness."[36] The persistent use of the metaphor of the closed gate, combined with the rhetoric of "unwelcome invasions," most clearly reveals the difference. African Americans, originally brought into the nation as slaves, could never really be "sent back" despite their alleged inferiority and threat to the nation. Segregation and Jim Crow legislation was mostly aimed at keeping African Americans "in their place." Chinese, who were racialized as polar opposites to "Americans," also clearly did not belong in the United States and were often compared to blacks. But unlike African Americans, they could be kept at bay through immigration laws. Later, immigration restrictions were expanded to include southern and eastern European and Mexican immigrants but never applied to African Americans.

As early-twentieth-century nativist literature and organization records illustrate, the language of Chinese restriction and exclusion was quickly refashioned to apply to each succeeding group. These connections—though clear to contemporary intellectuals, politicians, and nativists — have not been made forcefully enough by immigration historians, who too often study European, Asian, or Latino immigrants in isolation from one another. John Higham, the leading authority on American nativism, has claimed that the anti-Asian movements were "historically tangential" to the main currents of American nativism. Edith Abbott, who authored one of the first comprehensive studies of immigration, argued that "the study of European immigration should not be complicated for the student by confusing it with the very different problems of Chinese and Japanese immigration." Carl Wittke, considered a founder of the field, devoted much attention to Asians in his important survey of American immigration history but argued that their history was "a brief and strange interlude in the general account of the great migrations to America."[37] Continued intellectual segregation within immigration history is a fruitless endeavor.[38] In the case of immigration restriction, it is now clear that anti-Asian nativism was not only directly connected to American nativist ideology and politics in the early twentieth century; it was in fact their dominant model.

Following the exclusion of Chinese, Americans on the West Coast became increasingly alarmed about new immigration from Asia, particularly from Japan, Korea, and India. Californians portrayed the immigrants as comprising another "Oriental invasion," and San Francisco newspapers urged readers to "step to the front once more and battle to hold the Pacific Coast for the white race."[39] Like the Chinese before them, these new Asian immigrants were considered threats because of their race and labor. The Japanese were especially feared because of their great success in agriculture. Moreover, unlike the Chinese community, which had a large proportion of single male sojourners, Japanese tended to settle and start families in the United States. The political and cultural ideology that came to be used in the anti-Japanese movement immediately connected the new Japanese threat with the old Chinese one. Headlines in San Francisco newspapers talked of "another phase in the Immigration from Asia" and warned that the "Japanese [were] taking the place of the Chinese." Similar charges that the Japanese were unassimilable and exploitable cheap labor were made. And because the Japanese were supposedly even more "tricky and unscrupulous," as well as more "aggressive and warlike," than the Chinese, they were considered even "more objectionable."[40] Political leaders made the connections explicit. Denis Kearney, the charismatic leader of the Workingmen's Party, which spearheaded the anti-Chinese movement in San Francisco during the 1870s, found the Chinese and Japanese "problems" to be synonymous. A Sacramento reporter recorded Kearney in 1892 berating the "foreign Shylocks [who] are rushing another breed of Asiatic slaves to fill up the gap made vacant by the Chinese who are shut out by our laws. . . . Japs . . . are being brought here now in countless numbers to demoralize and discourage our domestic labor market." Kearney rousingly ended his speech with "The Japs Must Go!"[41] In 1901, James D. Phelan, mayor of San Francisco, spearheaded the Chinese Exclusion Convention of 1901 around the theme "For Home, Country, and Civilization." Later, in 1920, he ran for the U.S. Senate under the slogan "Stop the Silent Invasion" (of Japanese).[42]

The small population of Asian Indian immigrants also felt the wrath of nativists, who regarded them as the "most objectionable of all Orientals" in the United States.[43] In 1905, the San Francisco–based Japanese-Korean Exclusion League renamed itself the Asiatic Exclusion League in an attempt to meet the new threat. Newspapers complained of "Hindu Hordes" coming to the United States. Indians were "dirty, diseased," "the worst type of immigrant . . . not fit to become a citizen . . . and entirely foreign to the people of the United States." Their employment by "moneyed capitalists" as expendable cheap labor and India's large population "teeming with millions upon millions of emaciated sickly Hindus existing on starvation wages" also hearkened back to the charges of a cheap labor invasion made against Chinese and Japanese immigrants.[44]

Racialized definitions of Mexican immigrants also referred back to Chinese immigration. Long classified as racially inferior, Mexican immigrants often served as replacement agricultural laborers following the exclusion of Asian immigrants.[45] Although their immigration was largely protected by agricultural and industrial employers through the 1920s, Mexican immigrants were long-standing targets of racial nativism, and many of the arguments directed toward Mexicans echoed earlier charges made against the Chinese. Because the legal, political, and cultural understandings of Chinese immigrants as permanent foreigners had long been established, nativists' direct connections between Chinese and Mexicans played a crucial role in racializing Mexicans as foreign. As Mae Ngai has shown for the post-1924 period, the characterization of Mexicans as foreign, rather than as the natives of what used to be their former homeland, "*distanced* them both from Anglo-Americans culturally and from the Southwest as a region" and made it easier to restrict, criminalize, and deport Mexicans as "illegal."[46]

Nativists used the Chinese framework to characterize Mexicans as foreign on the basis of two main arguments: racial inferiority and racial unassimilability. George P. Clemens, the head of the Los Angeles County Agricultural

Department, explained that Asians and Mexicans were racially inferior to whites because they were physically highly suitable for the degraded agricultural labor in which they were often employed. The tasks involved were those "which the Oriental and Mexican due to their crouching and bending habits are fully adapted, while the white is physically unable to adapt himself to them."[47] While Chinese were considered to be biologically inferior because of their status as heathens and their alleged inability to conform to an Anglo-American mold, Mexicans were degraded as an ignorant "hybrid race" of Spanish and Native American origin.[48] As Mexican immigration increased, fears of a foreign invasion of cheap, unassimilable laborers similar to the Chinese one permeated the nativist literature. Major Frederick Russell Burnham warned that "the whole Pacific Coast would have been Asiatic in blood today except for the Exclusion Acts. Our whole Southwest will be racially Mexican in three generations unless some similar restriction is placed upon them."[49] (Burnham, of course, conveniently ignored the fact that the Southwest—as well as most of the American West—had already been "racially Mexican" long before he himself had migrated west.) V. S. McClatchy, editor of the *Sacramento Bee*, warned that the "wholesale introduction of Mexican peons" presented California's "most serious problem" in the 1920s.[50] Increased Mexican migration to Texas was an especially contested issue, and nativists there pointed to the example of California and Chinese immigration to warn of their state's future. "To Mexicanize Texas or Orientalize California is a crime," raged one nativist.[51] Chester H. Rowell argued that the Mexican invasion was even more detrimental than the Chinese one because at least the "Chinese coolie"— "the ideal human mule"—would not "plague us with his progeny. His wife and children are in China, and he returns there himself when we no longer need him." Mexicans, he argued, might not be so compliant or easy to send back.[52]

Other nativists extended the racial unassimilability argument to Mexicans by claiming that they "can no more blend into our race than can the Chinaman or the Negro."[53] Anti-Mexican nativists increasingly called for restriction by framing the new Mexican immigration problem within the old argument for Chinese exclusion. Major Burnham blamed the reliance on cheap Mexican labor on the immigration promoters of the 1920s, just as Denis Kearney had blamed the capitalists and their "Chinese pets" during the 1870s. "It is the old Chinese stuff, an echo of the [18]70s, word for word!" wrote Burnham. Moreover, Burnham believed that immigration law—and specifically the same types of exclusionary measures used against the Chinese—were the only remedy: "Let us refuse cheap labor. Let us restrict Mexican immigration and go steadily on to prosperity and wealth just as we did after the Asiatic Exclusion Acts were passed."[54]

At the same time, some of the race- and class-based theories and arguments used against Asians and Mexicans were being applied to certain European immigrant groups, especially in the northeastern United States, where most European immigrants first landed and settled. The sense of "absolute difference" that already divided white Americans from people of color was extended to certain European nationalities. Because distinctive physical differences between native white Americans and European immigrants were not readily apparent, nativists "manufactured" racial difference. Boston intellectuals like Nathaniel Shaler, Henry Cabot Lodge, and Francis Walker all promoted an elaborate set of racial ideas that marked southern and eastern Europeans and others as different and inferior, a threat to the nation. In 1894, they formed a new nativist group, the Immigration Restriction League (IRL), in Boston.[55]

Both Italians and French Canadians, for example, were often compared with Chinese immigrants. Italians were called the "Chinese of Europe," and French Canadians were labeled the "Chinese of the Eastern States." As Donna Gabaccia has argued, Chinese and Italians "occupied an ambiguous, overlapping and intermediary position in the binary racial schema." Neither black nor white, both were seen as in-between, or "yellow," "olive," or "swarthy." Their use as cheap labor also linked the two together. Italians were often called "European coolies" or "padrone coolies."[56] French Canadians were compared to Chinese immigrants because of their alleged inability to assimilate to Anglo-American norms. An 1881 Massachusetts state agency report charged that French Canadians were the "Chinese of the Eastern States" because "they care nothing for our institutions. . . . They do not come to make a home among us, to dwell with us as citizens. . . . Their purpose is merely to sojourn a few years as aliens."[57] In 1891, Henry Cabot Lodge opined that the Slovak immigrants—another threatening group—"are not a good acquisition for us to make, since they appear to have so many items in common with the Chinese."[58] Lothrop Stoddard, another leading nativist, went even further by arguing that eastern Europeans were not only "like the Chinese"; they were, in fact, part Asian. Eastern Europe, he explained, was situated "next door" to Asia and had already been invaded by "Asiatic hordes" over the past two thousand years. As a result, the Slavic peoples were mongrels, "all impregnated with Asiatic Mongol and Turki blood."[59]

Such explicit race- and class-based connections to Chinese immigration were effective in defining and articulating nativists' problems with newer immigrants. The old Chinese exclusion rhetoric was one with which Americans were familiar by the 1910s, and it served as a strong foundation from which to build new nativist arguments on the national level. The Immigration Restriction League used this tactic masterfully. In a 1908 letter to labor unions, the organization affirmed that Chinese immigration was the ultimate evil but warned that the Orient was "only one source of the foreign cheap labor which competes so ruinously with our own workmen." The IRL charged that the stream of immigrants from Europe and western Asia was "beginning to flow," and without proper measures to check it, it would "swell, as did the coolie labor, until it overwhelms one laboring community after another."[60]

In a letter to politicians, the IRL defined the issues and the sides even more clearly. The letter asked congressmen and senators across the country to identify the "classes of persons" who were desired and not desired in their state. The IRL made this task simple by offering them pre-set lists of groups they themselves deemed "desirable" and "undesirable." The politicians needed only to check the groups in order of preference. In the "desired" categories, "Americans, native born," topped the list. The generic category of "persons from northern Europe" came second. Then, the specific groups of British, Scandinavians, and Germans followed. Asiatics, southern and eastern Europeans, illiterates, and the generic "foreign born" were all lumped together in the second list of supposed unwanted and excludable immigrants.[61] The IRL could make no clearer statement: the new threat from Europe and the old threat from Asia were one.

Because of different regional politics and dynamics of race relations, divergent opinions about the connections between the old Asian immigration problem and the new European one existed on the West Coast. On the one hand, the parties behind the virulent anti-Asian campaigns broadened their appeals to preserve "America for all Americans" and called into question just who was a "real American." The San Francisco–based Asiatic Exclusion League implied that all aliens were dangerous to the country and passed a resolution that required aliens to disarm in order to prevent insurrection.[62] Other nativists in California expressed fears of the degraded immigrants entering the country from both Asia and Europe. Homer Lea, the author and leading proponent of the Yellow Peril theory of Japanese domination of America, warned that the growing immigration from Europe augmented the Japanese danger by "sapping America's racial strength and unity."[63] The California branch of the Junior Order of United American Mechanics, a well-established nativist group, allied itself with the Asiatic Exclusion League and announced that southern Europeans were semi-Mongolian.[64]

On the other hand, western nativists continued the West's campaign to preserve a "white man's frontier" by emphasizing the differences between Europeans and Asians and by privileging whiteness at the expense of people of color. Significantly, many of the leading nativists were European immigrants and second-generation Americans themselves.[65] Denis Kearney, leader of the anti-Chinese Workingmen's Party, was an Irish immigrant. James D. Phelan, leader of the anti-Japanese movement, was Irish American. By leading racist campaigns against Asian immigration, Kearney and Phelan reaffirmed their own status as whites. In the multiracial West, such consolidations of whiteness were central to sustaining the existing racial hierarchy. The best expression of this sentiment occurred during the 1901 Chinese Exclusion Convention, an event organized to lobby for the permanent exclusion of Chinese immigrants. While attendees rallied around the convention theme of protecting the American "home, country, and civilization," keynote speakers strongly defended an open-door policy toward all European immigrants. In an impassioned speech, A. Sbarboro (an Italian immigrant/Italian American himself), president of the Manufacturers' and Producers' Association, declared that in California,

> we want the Englishman, who brings with him capital, industry and enterprise; the Irish who build and populate our cities; the Frenchmen, with his vivacity and love of liberty; the industrious and thrifty Italians, who cultivate the fruit, olives, and vines—who come with poetry and music from the classic land of Virgil; the Teutonic race, strong, patient, and frugal; the Swedes, Slavs, and Belgians; we want *all good people from all parts of Europe*. To these, Mr. Chairman, we should never close our doors, for although when the European immigrant lands at Castle Garden he may be uncouth and with little money, yet soon by his thrift and industry he improves his condition; he becomes a worthy citizen and the children who bless him mingle with the children of those who came before him, and when the country calls they are always ready and willing to defend the flag to follow the stars and stripes throughout the world.[66]

Sbarboro, by explicitly including Italians and Slavs, indeed, all immigrants from all parts of Europe, with the older stock of immigrants from France, Sweden, Germany, and Belgium, made clear that the distinction to be made was not among European immigrants but between European and, in this case,

Asian immigrants. Membership in the white race was tantamount. Southern and eastern European immigrants had the potential to become worthy citizens. Even the European immigrant's children would be American patriots some day. The belief that second-generation Chinese would do the same was unimaginable.

An increasing number of politicians and policy makers across the country disregarded Sbarboro's pleas to keep America's doors open to Europeans and instead supported restrictions on immigration from southern and eastern Europe. Nevertheless, Sbarboro's attempts to distinguish European immigrants from Asians pointed to significant differences in the ways in which European, Asian, and Mexican immigrants were racially constructed and regulated by immigration law. First, southern and eastern European immigrants came in much greater numbers than did the Chinese, and their whiteness secured them the right of naturalized citizenship, while Asians were consistently denied naturalization by law and in the courts. Whiteness permitted European immigrants more access to full participation in the larger American polity, economy, and society. Although they were eventually greatly restricted, they were never excluded. As Mae Ngai has shown, the 1924 Immigration Act restricted European immigrants according to their "national origins" (rather than race), presuming their shared whiteness with white Americans and separating them from non-Europeans. The act thus established the "legal foundations . . . for European immigrants [to] becom[e] Americans." Chinese, Japanese, Korean, Filipino, and Asian Indian immigrants were codified as "aliens ineligible to citizenship."[67]

Mexican immigration differed from both southern and eastern European and Asian immigration on several levels. First was Mexico's proximity to the United States and the relatively porous U.S.-Mexican border, which facilitated migration to and from the United States. As historians have shown, Mexican immigrants were treated differently, even considered "safe" from mainstream nativism, because of their status as long-term residents and their propensity to be "birds of passage," returning home after the agricultural season ended rather than settling in the United States permanently.[68] In addition, Mexico's contentious history with the United States and the latter country's "legacy of conquest" aggravated already tense U.S.-Mexican relations, racialized Mexicans as inferiors, and structured Mexican immigrant and Mexican American life within the United States in ways that contrasted sharply with the lives of other immigrant groups. In the post-1924 period, Mexicans were categorized as "illegal," an all-encompassing racial category that not only negated any claim of Mexicans belonging in a conquered homeland but also extended to both Mexican immigrants and Mexican Americans.[69]

The significant differences in the ways that these immigrant groups were viewed functioned to shape both immigration regulation and immigrant life in distinct ways. Still, the rhetoric and tools of gatekeeping were instrumental in defining the issues for all immigrants and set important precedents for twentieth-century immigration. Each group held its own unique position within the hierarchy of race and immigration, but all eventually became subjected to an immigration ideology and law designed to limit their entry into the United States. By the early twentieth century, the call to "close the gates" was sounded in relation not only to Chinese immigration but to immigration in general. Thomas Bailey Aldrich, poet and former editor of the *Atlantic Monthly*, reacted to the new immigrants from southern and eastern Europe arriving in Boston in 1892 by publishing "The Unguarded Gates," a poem demonizing the new arrivals as a "wild motley throng . . . accents of menace alien to our air."[70] Just as H. N. Clement had suggested "closing the doors" against Chinese immigration in 1876, Madison Grant, the well-known nativist and leader of the Immigration Restriction League, called for "closing the flood gates" against the "new immigration" from southern and eastern Europe in 1914.[71] At the same time, Frank Julian Warne, another nativist leader, warned that unregulated immigration from Europe was akin to "throwing open wide our gates to all the races of the world."[72]

The solution, all agreed, lay in immigration policy, and a succession of federal laws were passed to increase the control and regulation of threatening and inferior immigrants. The Immigration Act of 1917 required a literacy test for all adult immigrants, tightened restrictions on suspected radicals, and, as a concession to politicians on the West Coast, denied entry to aliens living within a newly conceived geographical area called the "Asiatic Barred Zone." With this zone in place, the United States effectively excluded all immigrants from India, Burma, Siam, the Malay States, Arabia, Afghanistan, part of Russia, and most of the Polynesian Islands.[73] The 1921 and 1924 Immigration Acts drastically restricted immigration from southern and eastern Europe and perfected the exclusion of all Asians, except for Filipinos.[74] In 1934, Filipinos were also excluded, and both Filipinos and Mexicans were singled out for massive deportation and repatriation programs during the Great Depression.[75] By the 1930s, exclusion, restriction, and deportation had been extended to other immigrant groups and codified into law and immigration service practices. The cycle that had begun with Chinese exclusion was completed.[76]

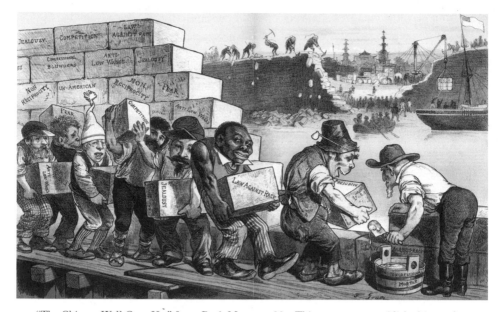

"The Chinese Wall Goes Up," from *Puck*, Mar. 29, 1882. This cartoon was published just a few months before the Chinese Exclusion Act was passed by Congress. Symbolizing the existing racial and ethnic threats already plaguing the United States, the builders of the wall are European immigrant and African American men drawn in stereotypical fashion. The irony here is that while the United States builds a wall to exclude Chinese, immigrants and African Americans considered to be racially inferior threaten the nation from within. Prejudice, jealousy, competition, and fear are the building blocks of Chinese exclusion. Demonstrating the wide national appeal of the movement, the wall is held together with "congressional mortar" being doled out by President Grover Cleveland. Courtesy of the University of Minnesota Library.

The Example of Chinese Exclusion: Immigration Regulation

The concepts of race that developed out of Chinese exclusion provided the ideological structure within which other immigrant groups were compared and racialized. The passage of the Chinese Exclusion Act also ushered in drastic changes in immigration regulation and set the foundation for twentieth-century policies designed not only for the inspection and processing of newly arriving immigrants but also for the control of potentially dangerous immigrants already in the country. Written into the act itself were several major changes in immigration regulation. All would become standard means of inspecting, processing, admitting, tracking, punishing, and deporting immigrants in the United States. First, the Exclusion Act paved the way for the appointment of the country's first federal immigrant inspectors. Years before a federal immigration agency was established in 1891, the inspectors of Chinese immigrants (under the auspices of the U.S. Customs Service) were the first to be authorized to enforce U.S. immigration law on behalf of the federal government.[77] Prior to the passage of the Page Law and the Chinese Exclusion Act, there was neither a trained force of government officials and interpreters nor the bureaucratic machinery with which to enforce the new law. The U.S. collector of customs and his staff had been granted the authority to examine Chinese female passengers and their documents under the Page Law, but the Chinese Exclusion Act extended the duties of these officials to include the examination of all arriving Chinese.[78] Under the new act, inspectors were also required to examine and clear Chinese laborers departing the United States.[79]

Second, the enforcement of the Chinese exclusion laws set in motion the federal government's first attempts to identify and record the movements, occupations, and familial relationships of immigrants, returning residents, and native-born citizens. Because of the complexity of the laws and immigration officials' suspicions that Chinese were attempting to enter the country under fraudulent pretenses, the government's enforcement practices involved an elaborate tracking system of registration documents and certificates of identity and voluminous interviews with individuals and their families.[80] Section 4 of the Exclusion Act also established "certificates of registration" for departing laborers. Such certificates were to contain the name, age, occupation, last place of residence, and personal description of the Chinese laborer. This information was also recorded in specific registry books kept in the customhouse. The certificate entitled the holder to "return and reenter the United States upon producing and delivering the [document] to the collector of customs." The laborer's return certificate was the first document of its kind issued to an immigrant group by the federal government, and it served as a passport facilitating reentry into the country. Chinese remained the only immigrant group required to hold such reentry permits (or passports) until 1924, when the new immigration act of that year issued — but did not require — reentry permits for other aliens.[81]

The documentary requirements established for Chinese women emigrating under the Page Law and for exempt-class Chinese (merchants, teachers, diplomats, students, travelers) applying for admission under the exclusion laws also set in motion an "early . . . system of 'remote control' involving passports and visas" through which U.S. consular officials in China and Hong Kong verified the admissibility of immigrants prior to their departure for the United States. The Exclusion Act of 1882 placed this responsibility in the hands of Chinese government officials alone, but an 1884 amendment gave U.S. diplomatic officers the responsibility of verifying the facts on the so-called Section 6 certificates required of exempt-class Chinese so that the documents could be considered "*prima facie* evidence of right of reentry."[82]

Eventually, in an effort to crack down on illegal entry and residence, the Chinese exclusion laws were amended to require all Chinese already in the country to possess "certificates of residence" and "certificates of identity" that served as proof of their legal entry into and lawful right to remain in the country. The rules regarding these precursors to documents now commonly known as green cards were first outlined in the 1892 Geary Act and 1893 McCreary Amendment, which required Chinese laborers to register with the federal government. The resulting certificates of residence contained the name, age, local residence and occupation of the applicant (or "Chinaman," as the act noted), as well as a photograph. Any Chinese laborer found within the jurisdiction of the United States without a certificate of residence was to be "deemed and adjudged to be unlawfully in the United States" and would be vulnerable to arrest and deportation.[83] The Bureau of Immigration used its administrative authority to demand a similar "certificate of identity" for all exempt-class Chinese, including merchants, teachers, travelers, and students, beginning in 1909. Although such certificates were supposed to serve as "indubitable proof of legal entry," they failed to protect legal immigrants and residents from government harassment. The requirement that all Chinese possess the certificates subjected the entire community — including immigrants and residents who were supposed to be exempt from the exclusion laws — to the same system of registration and scrutiny governing Chinese laborers. Apparently, the plan was an extension of an existing system of registration used for Chinese Americans entering the mainland from Hawaii.[84] No other immigrants were required to hold documents proving their lawful residence until 1928, when "immigrant identification cards" were first issued to any new immigrants arriving for permanent residence. These were eventually replaced by the "alien registration receipt cards" (that is, "green cards") after 1940.[85]

The institution of these documentary requirements verifying Chinese immigrants' rights to enter, reenter, and remain in the country codified a highly organized system of control and surveillance over the Chinese in America. Much of the rationale behind them stemmed from the prejudiced belief that it was, as California congressman Thomas Geary explained, "impossible to identify [one] Chinaman [from another]."[86] This unprecedented method of processing and tracking immigrants eventually became central to America's control of all immigrants and immigration in the twentieth century.

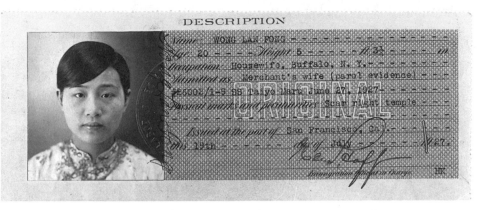

Certificate of Identity of Wong Lan Fong, the author's grandmother, 1927. Beginning in 1909, all persons of Chinese descent, including U.S. citizens, were issued certificates to identify them as having been legally admitted into the country. No other immigrants were required to hold documents proving their lawful residence until 1928, when "immigrant identification cards" were first issued to new immigrants arriving for permanent residence. After 1940, these were replaced by the "alien registration receipt cards," or "green cards." Courtesy of the National Archives, Washington, D.C.

The Chinese Exclusion Act set another precedent by defining illegal immigration as a criminal offense. It declared that any person who secured certificates of identity fraudulently or through impersonation was to be deemed guilty of a misdemeanor, fined $1,000, and imprisoned for up to five years. Any persons who knowingly aided and abetted the landing of "any Chinese person not lawfully entitled to enter the United States" could also be charged with a misdemeanor, fined, and imprisoned for up to one year.[87] Defining and punishing illegal immigration directly led to the establishment of the country's first modern deportation laws as well, and one of the final sections of the act declared that "any Chinese person found unlawfully within the United States shall be caused to be removed therefrom to the country from whence he came."[88] These initial forays into federal regulation of immigration would be even further codified and institutionalized seven years later in the Immigration Act of 1891.[89]

The Closed Gate: Renewing and Expanding Chinese Exclusion, 1882–1904

The first result of exclusion was that Chinese immigration dropped dramatically. In 1882, before the Chinese Exclusion Act went into effect, 39,579 Chinese rushed to enter the United States. Thereafter, the numbers fell to an all-time low in 1887, when immigration officials admitted only ten Chinese immigrants into the United States.[90] Other immigrants gained admission through the courts, but over all, Chinese exclusion was extremely effective in limiting Chinese immigration in the first two decades of the exclusion era. The number of Chinese departing from the United States also greatly increased (probably a result of a burst of anti-Chinese violence throughout the West after 1882). Statistics for most years are not available, but the Chinese Bureau in San Francisco recorded a total of 11,434 departures of Chinese residents in the first fourteen months after the Exclusion Act was passed, and the trend apparently continued throughout the 1880s.[91] For the period from 1888 to 1890, the bureau's records indicate a total of 11,312 departures of Chinese residents.[92] In 1888, the number of departures was still extremely high, and S. J. Ruddell, the chief inspector at the port, remarked that the excess of departures was "very noticeable." "The number of stores [in Chinatown] are decreasing every day," he testified before a congressional committee in 1890. The passage of the Exclusion Act, he continued, had made a "very marked difference" among the Chinese population, and if the trend continued, he predicted, the community might "completely disappear."[93] While some of the departing immigrants might have reentered the United States at a later date, immigration officials overwhelmingly agreed that the Chinese Exclusion Act itself prevented most Chinese from even attempting to immigrate to the United States.[94]

The Chinese Exclusion Act was clearly successful in reducing Chinese immigration to the United States. Californians and other proponents of exclusion, however, believed that the 1882 act was a failure. Chinese immigration was not completely halted, and many believed that employers, the Chinese, and the federal courts took advantage of loopholes in the laws that, in their minds, made a mockery of the exclusion laws. As Lucy Salyer has shown, until 1903, federal district courts were indeed much more lenient in enforcing the exclusion laws than were the immigration officials at the ports of entry.[95]

Calls to amend the laws were almost immediate. One and a half years after President Arthur had signed the Chinese exclusion bill, San Franciscans clamored for more laws and outlined a registration policy for all Chinese immigrants. In December 1884, the San Francisco Board of Supervisors unanimously passed a resolution that explained that while the Chinese Exclusion Act had "to some extent prevented the Chinese hordes from coming into this State as heretofore, . . . the ingenuity of these people in contriving means to land on our shores is almost incredible." The resolution called upon California senators and representatives to pass legislation instituting a strict registration and deportation system in order to "protect our people."⁹⁶ (Significantly, the registration provisions were later adopted by the federal government as part of the Geary Act of 1892.) In response, Congress passed a bill in 1884 that strengthened the existing exclusion law. Chinese laborers from any foreign country (not just China) were excluded, and immigration officials were required to record extensive identification information for all Chinese immigrants. The documentary requirements and the terms of criminal punishment for illegal immigration were also affirmed.⁹⁷

In 1888, Congress refined the terms of exclusion. Instead of explicitly prohibiting only Chinese laborers, the new provisions excluded *all* Chinese except "teachers, students, merchants, or travelers for pleasure or curiosity." The law also prohibited any returning Chinese laborer from entering the country unless he had a lawful wife, child, or parent in the United States, or had property or debts due him worth at least $1,000. This aspect of the 1888 act was particularly harsh because it stipulated that the returning laborer's marriage had to have taken place at least a year prior to the laborer's application to depart and return to the United States and that the marriage had to be characterized as a "continuous cohabitation of the parties as man and wife."⁹⁸ The Scott Act of the same year nullified 20,000 return certificates already granted and immediately denied entrance to returning Chinese laborers.⁹⁹ Some California exclusionists even introduced legislation that called for the exclusion of all Chinese except for diplomatic officials.¹⁰⁰ Although these bills failed, they reflected the long-range goals of exclusionists.

The original Chinese Exclusion Act suspended the immigration of Chinese laborers for a period of ten years. When the act came up for renewal in 1892, Congress readily passed the Geary Act, sponsored by Thomas Geary, a California Democrat in the U.S. Senate. The amended act renewed the exclusion of laborers for another ten years.¹⁰¹ By 1898, the original Chinese Exclusion Act was extended to Hawaii. In 1901, the Chinese Exclusion Convention brought together 2,500 anti-Chinese delegates who represented not only laboring men but also business and professional groups united by the desire to "prevent the threatened invasion of Mongol hordes to the peril and degradation of American labor."¹⁰² The expiration of the Geary Act was a major topic of discussion. One of the stars of the convention was San Francisco mayor James Phelan, who highlighted California's citizens' role in "sounding the alarm" and serving as the "wardens of the Golden Gate" in the face of an onslaught of undesirable and dangerous Chinese immigrants.¹⁰³ Again, the metaphor of the gate—both as a San Francisco geographical landmark and as a symbolic barrier against

Chinese immigration—remained central to exclusionists' arguments. In 1902, Congress passed a bill that renewed the exclusion of Chinese laborers and extended exclusion to all insular possessions of the United States, including the Philippines.[104] In 1904, the Chinese Exclusion Act was extended without time limit, and it remained in effect until its repeal in 1943.[105]

Conclusion

For Chinese immigrants, the year 1882 marked the end of one chapter in history and the beginning of a new one. From 1882 to 1904, the exclusion laws were expanded in scope and across geographic regions. Chinese immigrants felt the effects of these laws immediately, and Chinese immigration dropped dramatically. However, as later chapters will show, Chinese immigrants challenged and evaded the exclusion laws throughout the exclusion era.

The United States' relationship with immigrants reached a similar turning point. The Chinese Exclusion Act instituted the first of many restriction and exclusion laws, but its significance goes far beyond the legal realm. Chinese exclusion helped redefine American politics, race, class, and gender relations, national identity, and the role of the federal government in controlling immigration. The result was a nation that embraced the notion of building and guarding America's gates against "undesirable" foreigners in order to protect white Americans. Rooted in a western American desire to sustain white supremacy in a multiracial West, gatekeeping became a national reality and was extended to other immigrant groups throughout the early twentieth century. Both the rhetoric and the tools used to exclude the Chinese were repeated in later debates over immigration. In many ways, Chinese immigrants became the models against which others were measured. Nativists repeatedly pointed to ways in which other Asians, Mexicans, and Europeans were "just like" the Chinese and argued that similar restrictions should be extended to them as well. By the 1930s, immigration inspections, passport and other documentary requirements, the surveillance and criminalization of immigration, and the deportation of immigrants found to be in the country illegally all became standard operating procedures in the United States. Nativists no longer needed to ask "*how* can we stop immigrants?" They had found the answer in Chinese exclusion.

CHAPTER TWO

THE KEEPERS OF THE GATE

U.S. Immigration Officials and Chinese Exclusion

ONCE THE UNITED STATES passed the Chinese Exclusion Act, it faced the daunting task of interpreting and enforcing the law. The gate had been built and closed, but the new law introduced several pressing questions: who would enforce the laws, and how could the government ensure that they were administered correctly? Because the Chinese exclusion laws represented the government's first attempts to process immigrants arriving at American shores, the ways in which it answered these questions mattered not only for the Chinese in America but for immigration regulation in general. Both U.S. immigration officials and the federal district courts played important roles in the enforcement of the Chinese exclusion laws. As legal historians have demonstrated, until 1905, the courts provided an important channel through which Chinese immigrants successfully gained admission into the country after being first denied entry by immigration officials. Between 1882 and 1905, the federal district court for northern California and the state circuit court heard over 9,600 Chinese habeas corpus cases, which alleged that the Chinese petitioners (many of whom claimed U.S. citizenship) were indeed entitled to land and that they were being unlawfully detained. On average, the court overturned the immigration officials' decisions to deny entry in over 50 percent of the cases.[1] Nevertheless, the courts reviewed the applications of only a fraction of the total number of Chinese immigrants seeking admission into the United States. While the courts admitted fewer than 5,000 Chinese in the first twenty-three years of the exclusion era, at least 53,162 Chinese immigrants and returning residents were processed and admitted into the country by immigration officials from 1894 to 1905.[2] In addition, after the Chinese were prohibited from using the courts in admission cases in 1905, all Chinese immigrants were processed through administrative channels. The vast majority of Chinese cases were thus not decided in the courtrooms but on the decks of arriving steamers, in the detention sheds built especially for Chinese, and later, at the immigration station on Angel Island in the San Francisco Bay.

As the self-proclaimed "keepers of the gate" at the port of San Francisco—by far the largest port of entry for Chinese and other Asian immigrants during the late nineteenth and early twentieth centuries—federal immigration officials controlled the fate of many, if not most, Chinese arriving in and returning to America. But the impact of their decisions was felt on a larger scale as well and directly shaped American gatekeeping at the local and national levels.[3] The immigration officials in San Francisco fit the model of lower-level government workers or "street-level bureaucrats" who became "de facto policy makers," as described by political scientist Michael Lipsky. As he argues, public policy is best understood by how it is implemented in "the crowded offices and daily encounters of street-level workers," not by how it is created in the legislatures or "top-floor suites" of high-ranking administrators. Left to themselves, the early immigration officials in San Francisco had the power to decide how to implement laws and to establish specific regulations and procedures. These decisions in effect became public policy. Taken together, the individual actions of these officials added up to an agency policy.[4]

Revealing the long-established connection between anti-immigrant politics and immigration law enforcement, many of the policies and procedures developed by these first immigration officials were expressly designed in response to the anti-Chinese politics permeating San Francisco at the end of the nineteenth century. Many local and federal immigration officials were notoriously biased against the Chinese, and anti-Chinese racism became institutionalized in official culture, correspondence, and hiring practices. Over time, efforts at reform did alter the makeup of the immigration service and some of the worst abuses were banned, but a deep-rooted suspicion of Chinese remained ingrained throughout the exclusion era.

The United States Customs Service, a department with no previous experience enforcing immigration laws, was called upon to enforce the exclusion
laws because it already had a trained corps of government officials in place at
the nation's ports, where immigrants first disembarked. It also had experience
working with international steamship companies.[5] Yet, the Customs Service
received no clear instructions on how to enforce the law. The only attempt by
the federal government to clarify its newfound role came in the form of a new
official post known as the "Chinese inspector." Chinese government officials
were supposed to screen prospective Chinese immigrants first to make sure
that they were eligible to immigrate to the United States. A certificate, known
as a Section 6 certificate (which referred to the provision in the 1882 Exclusion
Act that stipulated which categories of Chinese were exempt from exclusion),
was issued to each immigrant found eligible. Shipmasters were then supposed
to create a list of all Chinese passengers aboard with a notation of their immigrant status. Once the ship arrived in the United States, the Chinese inspector
was charged with giving final approval to those claiming a right to enter, but
the guidelines he was given regarding the method and means of determining the veracity of immigrant claims were vague at best.[6] Almost two weeks
after the passage of the Chinese Exclusion Act, the secretary of the treasury,
who supervised the Customs Service, issued a circular informing the collectors
of customs at each port of the terms of the Exclusion Act and of the general
ways in which the certificates for departing laborers should be handled. However, as the day approached when free immigration of Chinese laborers was
supposed to cease, no further guidance from the secretary was forthcoming.
The Chinese consulate in San Francisco actually took the initiative to meet
with the collector of customs at that port to issue certificates of identification
and collector's certificates that would allow departing laborers to reenter. Not
until three months after the Exclusion Act was passed did the Treasury Department provide more direction to the local collectors of customs.[7] In later
years, little improved. Only when new situations and questions arose did the
inspector of customs request instructions from the Treasury Department.

The administration of the Chinese exclusion laws evolved in a piecemeal
fashion, and by the 1890s, a general framework for the administration of the
immigration laws had been established. At the top was the secretary of the
treasury. Directly below him was the commissioner-general of immigration,
who headed the Bureau of Immigration, which was established in 1891. In-

spectors were in place at each port of entry. Instructions from the Treasury Department in addition to court decisions and the provisions of the laws themselves constituted the primary enforcement regulations. But the loose administrative structure of the Customs Service and the absence of a strong and centralized immigration agency allowed the customs officials in San Francisco to develop local policies and interpret the exclusion laws in their own fashion during the first two decades of the exclusion era.[8]

Although they might have lacked a clear mandate from federal officials in Washington, D.C., the immigrant inspectors of the San Francisco Chinese Bureau received definitive directions from local politicians and labor leaders eager to exclude the Chinese. In August 1882, just three months after the Exclusion Act had been passed, in response to constituent complaints that the laws were not being enforced strictly enough, California congressman W. S. Rosencrans appealed to U.S. Treasury secretary Charles G. Folger. "Assure our people of the Pacific that your Department [can] provide for an effective surveillance over the execution of the law against Chinese immigration!" he pleaded.[9] Politicians continued to keep in close contact with immigration officials throughout the exclusion era.[10] Local newspapers also fanned the fires of anti-Chinese sentiment in California by consistently reporting on the routine work of the immigration officials and the arrivals of Chinese in San Francisco. They scrutinized the actions of the Chinese Bureau and were quick to launch their own investigations to expose leniency or corruption in the service. These sensationalist news stories sustained the anti-Chinese movement throughout the state of California and the Pacific Coast region well after the passage of the 1882 act.[11]

San Francisco immigration officials, California politicians, and the larger anti-Chinese public developed close and reciprocal relationships. Because the position of collector of customs was filled through a political appointment, he and the Customs Service found it politically expedient to act upon the will of the people and to comply with public demands for strict enforcement. Many of the lower-level officials in the service also owed their positions to local and state politicians.[12] In turn, San Francisco officials were routinely called upon to give their expert testimony and support to amendments to the exclusion laws in Washington, D.C. Acting as such dutiful public servants at the expense of Chinese, immigration officials in San Francisco could expect the necessary support from state congressmen and senators in their appointments and reappointments.[13]

The effect of anti-Chinese politics on enforcement procedures was clear. Enforcement of the exclusion laws tended to follow the strictest interpretation possible. Immigration officials argued that the laws expressly allowed only five exempt classes of Chinese to immigrate—merchants, teachers, students, travelers, and diplomats. Any other Chinese would be excluded. Despite the fact that they were clearly not laborers, accountants, doctors, etc., as well as spouses and children of exempt-class immigrants, were to be excluded, for example. As the 1901 official regulations for the service stated, "The true theory is not that all Chinese persons may enter this country who are not forbidden, but that only those who are entitled to enter are expressly allowed."[14] Moreover, decisions that might arouse public anger were not made lightly. When Treasury Department officials in Washington ordered the collector of customs in San Francisco to reverse his decision to deny entry to two Chinese students in 1885, the collector wrote back that such actions might incite violence. "The people of this coast are very sensitive in regard to Chinese immigration," he warned. Public outcry over Chinese immigration was even "more pronounced" than in previous periods, and mass meetings were being held all over the coast to drive Chinese immigrants out of the area. "In San Francisco," he continued, "there is a subdued undercurrent of hostility to this race," and unless federal officials were willing to encourage violence and riots, "the Government should use any endeavor to see [the exclusion laws] faithfully enforced."[15]

By 1896, San Francisco had earned the reputation as the most difficult processing center for both newly arriving Chinese immigrants and departing Chinese residents. Members of the latter group were required to deposit their statements and register their certificates forty-eight hours prior to their departure from the United States, for example. Thus, many residents had to arrive in San Francisco at least three days before their steamer was scheduled to sail for China. This what not a requirement at other ports. It appears that new Chinese immigrants chose more distant entry points like those in upstate New York, Vermont, and Maine, specifically because they were known to have higher admission rates. R. P. Schwerin, vice president of the Pacific Mail Steamship Company, the main steamer line traveling between China and the United States, complained to the Treasury Department in 1899. While 15 percent of all applicants had been refused landing in San Francisco during the previous year, the northeastern ports had not denied any.[16]

The public's anti-Chinese sentiment only partly explains the strict interpretations of the exclusion laws in San Francisco. Immigration officials in the Chinese Bureau were often participants, even leaders, of the Chinese exclusion movement and brought their own prejudices to bear on Chinese immigration cases. John H. Wise, collector of customs in San Francisco from 1892 to 1898, had been actively involved in the anti-Chinese movement leading up to exclusion. Originally a southerner from Virginia, Wise migrated to California in 1853 when President Franklin Pierce appointed him inspector of customs in San Francisco. By 1875, Wise had established a successful wool commission business and was serving on the San Francisco Board of Supervisors when it passed some of the most notorious anti-Chinese ordinances in the state and nation.[17] A prominent Democrat, Wise was eventually appointed the collector of customs by President Grover Cleveland in 1892.

Wise described himself as a "zealous opponent of Chinese immigration," and he established a siege mentality among his subordinates.[18] In 1895, he warned them to be on guard lest the "cunning of the Chinese defeat the vigilance of the Government officers."[19] Wise's term as collector of customs was marked by an increasingly strict interpretation and enforcement of the laws that targeted all Chinese, even those who were supposed to be exempt. Wise began by establishing administrative procedures that made it more difficult for Chinese to enter and reenter the United States. In fact, as one historian has noted, Wise required more evidence from Chinese immigrants than "mandated by either Congress or the secretary of the treasury." For example, while the Chinese Exclusion Act had specifically stated that a "Chinese person other than a laborer could be admitted upon presentation of a certificate from the Chinese government certifying his right of admission," Wise required additional proof of status from exempt-class Chinese.[20] Beginning in 1893, he required every departing Chinese merchant to file with the customs office a photograph of himself and a sworn statement giving the name of each partner in the firm to which he belonged, the value of each partner's interest and the aggregate capital invested, the location and character of the business, and a photograph of the business headquarters. Upon his return, any merchant who claimed to be a partner in a certain firm was interrogated. His statements were then checked against the data already on file. If any discrepancies were found, the application was refused. This policy was Wise's alone and was not shared by other collectors in the country. As Wise wrote in one letter, "I cannot, of

John H. Wise, U.S. collector of customs at the port of San Francisco from 1892 to 1898, c. 1910. Describing himself as a "zealous opponent of Chinese immigration," Collector Wise instituted increasingly strict interpretations and enforcement of the exclusion laws during his term. He discouraged Chinese men in the United States from sending for their wives and made it much more difficult for all exempt-class Chinese, including native-born American citizens, from gaining admission or re-admission into the country. Because the port of San Francisco was the point of entry for the vast majority of Chinese immigrants, Wise's policies helped make gatekeeping in the West a model for the nation. Reprinted from George Meyer, *Municipal Blue Book of San Francisco*, 1915. Courtesy of the San Francisco History Center, San Francisco Public Library.

course, tell you what interpretation of the law other Collectors may make, but this is mine."[21]

The integration of Wise's own anti-Chinese attitudes into his work as the chief immigration official in the country is notably revealed in the case of Wong Fong, whose fate was determined by Collector Wise in 1895. A longtime resident of the United States, Wong had traveled to China for a brief stay in the early 1890s. When he returned to San Francisco in 1895 to be reunited with his fiancée, Wise denied him entry into the country for reasons that are unclear. Wong was forced to spend time in the detention barracks by the wharf and grew ill. He requested traditional Chinese medicine and herbs in lieu of the poor-quality food given to detainees, but his requests were denied. Wong Fong then hired an attorney to persuade Wise to reverse his deportation decision, but Wise apparently was unmoved. The collector ordered Wong to be deported and even seemed to gloat at the prospect. In a letter to Wong's attorney, H. A. Ling of Los Angeles, Wise included the following poem that not only mocked Wong's predicament but also perpetuated stereotypes about Chinese diets, to which exclusionists often referred to support claims that Chinese were racially inferior.

Now poor Wong Fong, he feels quite ill,
As I am told by Ling
And won't eat any nice birds' nests
Nor even will he sing.

So just to make this poor Wong Fong
Feel very good and nice
I've sent him back to China
Where he can eat his mice.

And poor Wong Fong, he had to leave
Behind his fiancee
And go back to China
Across the dark blue sea.

And Mr. Ling was left behind
And did'nt [*sic*] get his fee
Because the cruel Collector
Sent Wong across the sea.[22]

Wise's mocking attitude regarding the deportation and unfortunate circumstances of Wong Fong aptly reflects how deeply embedded anti-Chinese sentiment was in the early immigration service. Wise candidly told inquirers that he would look for any reason to exclude a Chinese and that "if proof [was] not of the most convincing kind, landing [would] be refused."[23] Such an approach to Chinese exclusion earned Wise enormous popularity and respect in California. As sociologist Mary Roberts Coolidge observed in 1909, Wise's methods were sound politics. "In California, an invariable symptom of official ambition for political preferment has been zeal in administering the exclusion laws," she wrote. "The sword hanging over the head of every officeholder for twenty-five years past has been leniency to the Chinaman."[24] Wise was so popular for his zealous enforcement of the exclusion laws that a majority of the members of the California state legislature attempted to draft him to be the Democratic nominee for governor.[25]

Wise's less vigilant successors faced constant scrutiny. Collector Frederick

Smith Stratton, the last collector of customs to preside over the enforcement of the exclusion laws before the Bureau of Immigration took over in 1900, was criticized for addressing complaints raised by Chinese immigrants.[26] Both the local press and Stratton's superiors in Washington, D.C., also took exception to what they and the public believed to be his lax attitude. "Stratton has appeared reluctant to face the music in enforcing the Chinese exclusion act," an official in the Treasury Department told a reporter. "Now he has got to do that, as the law requires, or be ready to stand aside for somebody who will."[27] Fortunately for Stratton, his duties inspecting Chinese immigrants lasted only one year.

If John H. Wise represented anti-Chinese politicians, James R. Dunn, who became the chief inspector in the San Francisco office on May 15, 1899, represented the anti–Chinese labor contingent. Like Wise, Dunn possessed what sociologist Mary Roberts Coolidge called "extreme anti-Chinese prejudices" that resulted in "a sort of reign of terror" against the Chinese.[28] His biases likely originated from his strong connections with organized labor, one of the most vociferous sectors of the anti-Chinese movement. Described as a longtime ally of Terence V. Powderly, the former Knights of Labor leader and U.S. commissioner-general of immigration, Dunn enjoyed the full support of labor organizations throughout his tenure in San Francisco. In these circles, he was known as "an energetic and resourceful leader in the crusade against the Chinese."[29]

Much of Dunn's motivation came from his frustration with the exclusion laws, which he thought were hopelessly weak and full of loopholes. Dunn especially resented the interference of the courts, which often overturned immigration officials' decisions to deny entry. Such rulings, he felt, made "monkeys" of the immigration officials and "let down the bars" that anti-Chinese exclusionists had worked so hard to erect.[30] To make matters worse, Dunn's superiors in the Treasury Department sometimes upheld the decisions by the courts. As a result, Dunn took it upon himself to enforce the laws and regulations to the very limits of technicality. He also instituted new rules aimed at hindering Chinese applicants. Dunn was even known to misrepresent the testimony of Chinese applicants and their witnesses in order to prevent their entry and to seize important papers and documents without returning them.[31]

During Dunn's tenure as chief inspector, Chinese immigrants found it harder to enter the country than ever before. Their certificates were doubly scrutinized, their witnesses were called into question, and their investigations took longer. According to Dunn's own estimates, the changes he instituted doubled the number of Chinese immigrants forced to use attorneys when applying for admission. This need for outside help, Dunn observed, showed there was "no better proof of the strictness" of the Chinese Bureau's new system of enforcement.[32] His superior, Commissioner-General of Immigration Terence Powderly, praised him. In his 1901 annual report, Powderly described Dunn as being "energetic, intelligent and capable" because nearly two-thirds of all Chinese applicants for the previous fiscal year had been denied admission.[33] In fact, the collector of customs in San Francisco found Dunn to be such an effective enforcer of the Chinese exclusion laws that in 1900 he urged the Treasury Department to allow Dunn to "be properly clothed with authority to determine *all* [Chinese] cases [without having to get the collector's final authorization] subject only to the appeal to the Department."[34]

While his colleagues and superiors praised Dunn, Chinese immigrants and their supporters complained of increased hardship. In 1900, Reverend Ira Condit, a missionary and frequent spokesperson on behalf of the Chinese community in San Francisco, charged that Dunn's treatment of Chinese was dehumanizing and cruel. "When they do arrive," Condit explained, "merchants, laborers are all alike penned up, like a flock of sheep, in a wharf-shed, for many days, and often weeks, at their own expense, and are denied all communication with their own people, while the investigation of their cases moves its slow length along. A man is imprisoned as a criminal who has committed no crime."[35]

The Chinese community also accused Dunn of misconduct in two highly publicized cases. One involved Chinese merchant Ho Mun, who arrived in San Francisco from the Portuguese colony of Macao in September 1899. Ho carried with him the proper certificates issued by the Portuguese authorities and the visa issued by the American consul at Hong Kong, but he was rejected on a minor technicality.[36] Ho was kept in the detention shed set up by the Pacific Mail Steamship Company. He became seriously ill, but Inspector Dunn refused medical care for him for over two months. Ho's lawyers finally succeeded in moving him to the county jail, but he died a few days later. Nothing Ho had done justified his long detention or his being refused basic medical attention.[37] Another case involved Lew Lin Gin, a child who was ordered deported by Inspector Dunn and then lost while under the care of the immigration service. Despite a thorough search of the steamer and the Chinese quarters, the child was never found.[38]

These two cases enraged both Chinese and many Americans, and the publicity generated by the cases was used by immigrant advocates to call for

Dunn's transfer. The inspector, however, remained popular among the labor groups in San Francisco, and they began their own campaign to retain him. Twenty-four labor organizations rallied to his defense by sending a document defending Dunn, titled "Resolution in Favor of James R. Dunn," to both Congress and the president. Resurrecting the anti-Chinese rhetoric used in the 1870s, the resolution portrayed Dunn as a "fearless" champion of labor who had made "powerful enemies" among "those interested in the coming of Chinese to this country" (presumably large corporate employers).[39] Dunn received an outpouring of support from his fellow staff as well, but despite this goodwill, he was transferred to St. Louis in 1901.[40]

Although Dunn was removed from the bureau in San Francisco, the spirit of his labor-friendly, restriction-minded approach to the enforcement of the Chinese exclusion laws remained intact and deeply embedded in the immigration service at all levels. At the core of this approach was the need for the "right type" of men to be employed as immigration inspectors. Politicians and anti-Chinese leaders believed that it was imperative that employees of the service have the right sort of background and frame of mind (that is, anti-Chinese views) in order to effectively enforce the exclusion laws. Therefore, California politicians lobbied for fellow Californians and Pacific Coast residents to be given "preference" over other candidates for immigration service jobs. U.S. senator George C. Perkins of California went so far as to suggest to Commissioner-General of Immigration Frank Sargent that candidates from the "interior states" would not be familiar with "the class of Chinamen who come to this country." Californians, on the other hand, had a lifetime's worth of "experience hav[ing] to deal with the Chinese" and were thus highly qualified. Just as white southerners insisted that their "special relationship" with African Americans made them the natural choice in solving the "negro problem," Californians argued that they knew best how to take care of the "Chinese problem."[41]

Descriptions of Chinese in official government correspondence and documents both reflected and reinforced the anti-Chinese racism that permeated the immigration service at large. On various forms and in correspondence and internal memoranda, immigration officials often referred to Chinese in derogatory terms such as "Chinaman," "coolie," or "Chink."[42] The attitudes behind the use of these terms often translated into the physical mistreatment of Chinese immigrants. In 1899, a Treasury Department investigator found that the Chinese inspector in charge of detained Chinese often pushed the Chinese around, "useing [sic] force [that] is wholly unnecessary."[43] In 1909,

Mary Roberts Coolidge, sociologist and critic of the Chinese Bureau's enforcement of the exclusion laws, observed that the early immigration service "had been filled up with ignorant, narrow-minded men whose idea of effective enforcement was simply to shut out more Chinamen, no matter of what class, by greater severity, suspicion, and intimidation."[44]

Successive heads of the San Francisco Chinese Bureau thus inherited a system in which biases against Chinese were built into all levels of enforcement procedures. At the same time, they continued to be affected by their own prejudices. John P. Jackson, who had been a former army official during the Civil War, succeeded John H. Wise as collector for the port of San Francisco in 1898. Although he generally adopted more lenient standards than those established by Wise, he also admitted to insiders that it would relieve him greatly "to deny them [Chinese immigrants] all in a body, as fast as they arrive."[45] He also admitted that in his view, the goal of the Chinese Bureau was simply to "reduce the number of Chinese in this country [so that] this country has one less Chinaman."[46] Moreover, Jackson continued to implement procedures and documentary requirements that were not required by law but were used to "terrorize" the Chinese. In a letter to fellow collector David G. Browne, Jackson conceded that the affidavits required by the Chinese Bureau as proof of exempt status served no real purpose except to inflict a sense of fear into the Chinese. "The requiring of affidavits in these cases is more of a moral terror held over the makers thereof than of any legal validity," Jackson explained. "Of course we never say anything of this outside, but leave the impression upon these Chinese applicants and their friends that the making of an affidavit in their cases has all the sanctity of the law."[47]

Chinese Interpreters

Anti-Chinese prejudices were so institutionalized within the Chinese Bureau that they affected hiring decisions as well. In 1896 the Treasury Department instructed Collector John Wise in San Francisco to discharge all of his Chinese interpreters and to hire only white men in the future.[48] The same policies applied toward Japanese immigration as well.[49] Government officials believed that Chinese could not be trusted in immigration work. Many claimed that it was almost impossible to find an "honest Chinaman." In 1900, the special deputy of customs for the port of Plattsburg, New York, pointedly told an inspector at another port, "I suppose we want an honest Chinaman for inter-

Pacific Mail Steamship Company detention shed, 1899. Prior to the establishment of the Angel Island Immigration Station, Chinese applying for admission into the United States were detained in the Pacific Mail Steamship Company shed located at Pier 40 in San Francisco. Courtesy of the National Archives, Washington, D.C.

preter and if so I reckon we would have to go to Heaven to find him and I doubt whether there are any there or not."[50]

These attitudes created immense problems in the government's ability to correctly interpret Chinese immigrant testimony. In addition, a lack of funding, a scarcity of qualified white interpreters, and the variety of Chinese dialects all resulted in inconsistent translations and haphazard spellings of Chinese names. In 1904, Commissioner-General of Immigration Frank Sargent admitted that "the Bureau has noted for years that frequently in papers made up by its officers, all of which relate to certain Chinamen, the names, or pho-

U.S. immigration officials of the U.S. Customs Service inspecting newly arriving Chinese at the Pacific Mail Dock, 1899. Before 1910, immigrant inspections and interrogations took place at the Pacific Mail Steamship Company's dock. The procedures first established by these immigrant inspectors and interpreters laid the foundation for the zealous enforcement of the exclusion laws across the country throughout the exclusion era. Courtesy of the National Archives, Washington, D.C.

netic monosyllables representing such names in English, will be spelled in two, three, and sometimes six or seven different ways."[51]

Under the government's restrictive and racist hiring guidelines, the ideal Chinese Bureau interpreter was expected to be white, to have some proficiency in Chinese, and to possess a flawless reputation for honesty and integrity. Whites who were affiliated in any way with Chinese were automatically excluded for their suspicious ties and assumed tendency toward corruption. For example, Tim Cox, an applicant for the interpreter's position in the San Francisco bureau in 1896, was found to be ineligible because of his "affiliations with the Chinese." Fannie B. Watson, a white woman, applied for the post of Chinese interpreter in 1896 but was deemed completely disqualified "first because she is a woman, second because she is married to a Chinaman named Chew Mot . . . and [because] her affiliations with the Chinese still further disqualify her for the position."[52] "Chineseness" apparently tainted whites in ways that made them as suspicious and dangerous as Chinese themselves.

The Chinese Bureau did hire a few white individuals who were apparently somewhat capable in translating Chinese testimony and documents. One was Carlton Rickards, one of only two white interpreters in the entire immigration service who knew Chinese in 1890. During fourteen years of study, Rickards had learned various Chinese dialects in San Francisco and was reportedly considered a reliable interpreter by both the service and the Chinese community. As he told a congressional committee, "I have been very often interpreter in the United States courts, and the statements I take on board the steamers from the Chinese are never questioned in the courts; the attorneys always admit them as true, and the Chinese have never questioned a statement that I have ever heard of."[53] In 1902, T. H. Gubbins became another white interpreter for the service. Gubbins, an American whose parents lived in Hong Kong at the time of his birth, had spoken both English and Chinese while he was growing up.[54] Immigration officials looked for other recruits among returning missionaries to China.[55]

Individuals like Rickards and Gubbins were rare, and until the immigration service consented to hiring nonwhite interpreters, it was constantly plagued with an interpreter shortage.[56] Moreover, the immigration service was disappointed to find that white interpreters could not be trusted either. In 1899, Carlton Rickards was dismissed on charges that he had been involved in smuggling hundreds of Chinese into the United States through Port Townsend, Washington, three years earlier. As an agent for the department explained, smugglers used Rickards as the interpreter in cases where "it was necessary to admit a DUMB Chinaman," knowing that Rickards would insert the correct answers into the testimony in exchange for a bribe.[57]

When the immigration service resumed hiring nonwhite interpreters, officials nationwide continued to distrust their Chinese staffs.[58] Collector Jackson of San Francisco was loath to hire Asian interpreters even when it was clear that the white interpreters available to the service had weak language skills.[59] In 1899, the acting secretary of treasury complained that it was "extremely difficult to secure the services of reliable and trustworthy Chinese interpreters."[60] The collector of customs in Plattsburg, New York, agreed. "I prefer a white to be the Chinese interpreter if possible," he wrote to the commissioner-general of immigration in 1901.[61] Since only a few Chinese interpreters were hired by the immigration service, they were extremely busy. Chinese interpreter Jin Fuey Moy, for example, was in demand all over the Northeast in 1899 and traveled from port to port. When he was not available, the business of examining Chinese applicants came to a standstill. In New York, a group of Chinese merchants was detained because no one was available to record the merchants' testimonies and conduct their exams.[62]

One of the most curious and revealing examples of the immigration service's deep-rooted suspicion of Chinese interpreters involved John Endicott Gardner. He fulfilled both needs of the Chinese Bureau in San Francisco: not only was he able to speak and read Chinese and English fluently, he was white. Gardner, who grew up in Hong Kong, was hired as an interpreter and inspector in 1896 and later became one of the most influential officials in the country. He was recommended by the city's most prominent clergymen and politicians, among them the Reverend Ira Condit and a clerk of the U.S. District Court. Treasury Department agents found him to be the "best Chinese interpreter and translator on the Pacific Coast and one of the best in the country." He was also experienced, having served as an interpreter for the governments of both the United States and Canada, and his integrity was beyond question.[63]

Gardner's initial acceptance into the service was less than certain, however, because he was only half-white, his mother being Chinese. At the time of his hiring in 1896, Collector of Customs John H. Wise was still under orders to prohibit the employment of interpreters of the Chinese race even though the service badly needed an able interpreter. The Treasury Department launched an investigation. Reliable sources informed the treasury agents that Gardner's father was English and his mother was "a native of China and a subject of the Emperor of that country." In his initial communication on the subject, Special Agent Moore wrote that this fact "would seem to bring Mr. Gardner within the prohibition of the Department that no Chinese be employed." On further investigation — and creative interpretation of the department regulations — the Treasury Department found a loophole that allowed it to hire Gardner. Although he had been born in China to a Chinese mother and an English father, he later became a United States citizen when his widowed mother remarried John Vrooman, an American missionary and later U.S. consul in China.[64] After Gardner's mother died, Vrooman adopted him and brought him to the United States. Encouraged by Reverend Condit, the Treasury Department finally ruled that Gardner was an American citizen and of American parentage.[65] The Treasury Department's ruling in Gardner's case — that Gardner's Chinese blood was *not* a liability and thus did not subject him to the department's prohibition on Chinese employees — was evidence of a double standard. It would not apply to biracial Chinese immigrants and residents who desired to enter the United States.[66]

Gardner was appointed as a Chinese interpreter, but his biracial status continued to hinder him in his initial years in the service. His superiors conceded that Gardner's intelligence and his knowledge of the Chinese language were beyond dispute, but because of his Chinese blood, he was not fully trusted. As Collector J. P. Jackson confided to the secretary of the treasury, "There are racial characteristics in Inspector Gardner's temperament (he being himself half Chinese, and having been born in China) that seriously impair his efficiency as an impartial and unbiased interpreter."[67] Gardner found himself vulnerable to charges of a more personal nature as well. E. Percivale Baker, a stenographer in the bureau who was later discharged for collaborating with lawyers to admit Chinese immigrants, attacked Gardner as a "half-breed Chinese . . . [whose] mother was from one of the lowest classes of prostitutes."[68] In 1899, a committee of Chinese merchants charged Gardner with mistreatment and sent a list of grievances to the Chinese consulate. The Chinese consul rejected the petition on the grounds that it contained trumped-up complaints designed to injure Gardner's reputation.[69] Despite such setbacks, Gardner endured the fits and starts of his early career in the San Francisco office and became an invaluable asset to the Bureau of Immigration.

Western Gatekeeping: San Francisco as the Model for the Nation

Western politicians' calls that the nation must "close its doors" to Chinese immigrants began the United States' transformation into a gatekeeping nation. The anti-Chinese politics within the Chinese Bureau in San Francisco, the numbers of Chinese it inspected (from 1899 to 1901 alone, three-fourths of all new and returning Chinese were reported to have been processed in San Francisco[70]), and the effectiveness with which it enforced the exclusion laws gave the regional office a national reputation. Consequently, San Francisco immigration officials had an important impact on national policies and procedures, in some cases directly contributing to the administration of the exclusion laws across the country. San Francisco immigration officials were often called upon as Chinese experts in Washington, D.C., and it was not uncommon for collectors and immigration officials at other ports to send difficult cases to the

San Francisco office for advice on procedures.[71] Chief Inspector James R. Dunn played a prominent role in regularizing enforcement procedures across the nation, and he routinely used San Francisco practices as the model to which all other ports should conform. In 1901, the collector of customs in Port Townsend, Washington, invited Dunn to advise him on enforcement procedures. Soon thereafter, Dunn traveled to Santa Barbara and San Diego to give advice. In 1901 and 1902, Dunn visited all of the other ports on the Pacific Coast, as well as Illinois and Ohio, to lend his expertise. Dunn was also regularly called to Washington, D.C., to express his opinions to the nation's leaders. As the "recognized expert of the Bureau of Immigration," he addressed Congress when it began to debate the permanent extension of exclusion in 1901, and he gave advice on certain features of the exclusion policy. He also met with President Theodore Roosevelt, who strenuously supported continuing and strengthening Chinese exclusion.[72]

By the turn of the century, the official policy emanating from Washington clearly echoed the San Francisco ideology: the government should "facilitate the departure [of Chinese] and keep them from coming back."[73] Collectors of customs were instructed by their superiors in the Treasury Department that they "should be guided by the policy of our law . . . that Chinese are an undesirable addition to our society; that their presence is a disturbing element that tends only to evil and corruption, and that every presumption, every technicality and every intendment should be held against their admission and their testimony should have little or no weight when standing alone."[74]

Vigilant Enforcers in Washington, D.C., 1882–1910

Exclusionists and the more vigilant officials in the Chinese Bureau in San Francisco found great allies in Washington, D.C., one of whom was Terence Vincent Powderly, who served as the U.S. commissioner-general of immigration from 1898 to 1902.[75] Powderly used the post to further the cause of labor in issues relating to immigration. He sought to restrict the number of immigrant laborers who he believed would take jobs away from the white workingmen of America and thereby endanger American values and civilization. Though he disclaimed animosity toward any race, class, or creed, Powderly's strict application of immigration laws arose not only from his pro-labor sentiments but also from a virulent strain of racism, especially against the Chinese and Japanese. In a New Year's message in 1902, Powderly proclaimed that European immigrants—"those sturdy men of Scotland, Germany, Ireland"—would always

Terence V. Powderly, U.S. commissioner-general of immigration from 1898 to 1902, c. 1915. Under his supervision, the Bureau of Immigration became more centralized and restrictionist. Powderly was successful in establishing tighter controls over the U.S.-Canadian and U.S.-Mexican borders and in extending the policy of Chinese exclusion to Hawaii and the Philippines. Courtesy Archives of the Catholic University of America (ACUA), T. V. Powderly Papers.

be welcomed, but "the others we must exclude for our own good." "Whatever is done," Powderly concluded, "the Chinese will be kept out."[76] Perpetuating the view that Asian immigration represented an invasion of racially inferior peoples, he wrote of his determination to "check the advancing hordes and whores who seek our shores in search of wealth and—if pressed—work." He also referred to the Japanese as the "syphilis-tainted, minions of the Mikado, the almond-eyed, pigeon-toed, pig-tailed, hen-faced legions of the celestial empire [who] might storm the citadel at San Francisco."[77] "I am no bigot," Powderly claimed, "but I am an American, and believe that self-preservation is the first law of nations as well as nature."[78]

Throughout his tenure, Powderly consistently worked to strengthen enforcement of the Alien Contract Labor laws, and he remained an ardent supporter of Chinese and Japanese exclusion.[79] His goal was to exclude all undesirable—especially Asian—immigrants from the United States, and the Bureau of Immigration proved to be easily adapted to this task. Although the small budget allocated to immigration matters limited the efforts of immigration officials, Powderly allied himself with the many California politicians eager to strengthen the enforcement of the Chinese exclusion laws and successfully campaigned for more funds and more power for the Bureau of Immigration.

The relationship between Powderly and the Pacific Coast interests was an enduring one. As historian Delber McKee put it, with Powderly's appointment, "the spirit of [anti-Chinese leader] Denis Kearney took over the young bureau . . . and Californians soon realized their fondest hopes." The changes brought on under Powderly's administration were not sanctioned by any specific legislation but were implemented through internal administrative policies, a sign of the immense power he wielded on his own.[80]

When Powderly entered office, he began to put into effect what one scholar has coined the "Powderly Exclusion Policy," immigration legislation and rules that would exclude *all* Chinese, save diplomats.[81] His plan followed a concept outlined by journalist J. M. Scanland in 1900. "The exclusion policy does not exclude," Scanland wrote. "The only way to check this flow [from loopholes in the laws] is to repeal the favored clause excluding all except diplomats."[82] When a June 1900 act of Congress shifted control of Chinese immigration to the commissioner-general of immigration, Powderly viewed the move as a clear mandate to expand the scope of exclusion.[83] Powderly's plan had three significant features that greatly curtailed remaining Chinese immigration and increased the deportation of illegal immigrants already in the United States. First, he sanctioned raids and harassment of Chinese communities. Second, he increased border enforcement along the U.S.-Canadian border to prevent Chinese illegal immigration. Finally, he sanctioned the geographical extension of the exclusion policy to Hawaii and the Philippines, two newly acquired American territories in which a sizable number of Chinese immigrants had settled. Powderly was particularly concerned about this last aspect of Chinese immigration, describing Hawaii as "a dumping ground of aliens."[84]

Powderly filled the bureau with employees friendly to American labor and hostile to the Chinese.[85] He also instructed all immigration officials to base their decisions on only the most incontrovertible evidence. If an official had any doubt whatsoever regarding an applicant's right of entry, he was told to "relieve yourself . . . by rejecting the applicant, leaving him to his own recourse by appeal to the Department."[86] Because the Bureau of Immigration tended to uphold the rulings of the port officials, Chinese who appealed were usually turned down. The only recourse left to them was to then appeal to the courts, but this option was expensive, and as later sections discuss, Chinese immigrants' access to the courts was eventually barred.

Powderly's tenure as commissioner-general of immigration came to a humiliating end when President Roosevelt dismissed him in the spring of 1902. The cause was a controversy involving Powderly and his subordinates at Ellis

Island.[87] His policies regarding the enforcement of the Chinese exclusion laws, however, remained unchallenged.

Frank P. Sargent, former president of the Brotherhood of Locomotive Firemen, replaced Powderly and served as commissioner-general from May 1902 until his death in 1908. Under Sargent, the bureau continued to refine its anti-Chinese policies. He explained to staff that he had been selected to "bring the enforcement of the immigration and Chinese exclusion laws up to the highest possible standard of excellence and efficiency."[88] As was the case with his predecessor, Sargent's interpretation of "excellence and efficiency" was the continued exclusion of Chinese on all possible fronts. Sargent was welcomed by the supporters of exclusion across the country who cited his long service in the labor movement, as well as his close relationship with labor leader Samuel Gompers. The *Peoria Journal* announced that since Sargent was a "true friend of labor," the exclusion laws would be enforced as they should be. "Commissioner Sargent is getting right after John Chinaman and is adopting more stringent measures to bar him out of the United States," the editor predicted.[89] He was especially welcomed in San Francisco, where one newspaper editor pointed out that Sargent was taking the restrictive stance that "California wants and needs."[90] Sargent himself pledged an energetic response to any attacks on the exclusion policy in the face of the "difficulties inherent in the character of the Mongolian race to be met and surmounted."[91]

Under Sargent's leadership, the numbers of Chinese denials and deportations increased, a fact that the commissioner considered one of his greatest achievements. In 1898, 7,195 exempt-class Chinese and returning laborers were admitted into the country, 280 were denied, and an additional 756 were arrested for being in the country illegally. Two hundred and twenty of those arrested were eventually deported back to China, making the ratio of admissions to denials and deportations 100:7. By 1904, the ratio changed to 100:57, with 2,676 exempt-class Chinese and returning laborers admitted into the country, 736 denied entry, 1,793 arrested, and 783 eventually deported.[92] With such figures, Sargent could boast that the work of his administration was "highly beneficial." He pushed the exclusion movement forward by barring new entries and expelling Chinese already in the country.[93]

Another active ally in the bureau's efforts to strengthen the Chinese exclusion laws was Californian Victor H. Metcalf, who was appointed secretary of commerce and labor (and supervisor of the Bureau of Immigration) by President Theodore Roosevelt in 1904. Known as a pro-labor, anti-Chinese politician, Metcalf was praised by the *San Francisco Chronicle* for his "clear judgment" and "thorough knowledge of Chinese character" as exemplified in his anti-Chinese decisions.[94] The San Francisco papers noted in particular Metcalf's decision to limit the rights of returning Chinese American citizens who were born in the United States but had been taken to China by their parents and raised there. Individuals who had been absent from the United States for so long, Metcalf argued, should not be able to claim birthright citizenship.[95] Together, Sargent and Metcalf continued the work begun by Terence Powderly and the zealous immigration officials of the customs service in San Francisco.

Changes in the government's administration of the exclusion laws also helped to centralize and strengthen their enforcement. In 1900, Congress transferred the administration of Chinese exclusion to the commissioner-general of immigration, but the everyday enforcement of the law still remained with immigration officials in the Customs Service.[96] In 1903, all Chinese immigration matters were placed under the control of the Bureau of Immigration and its parent department, the newly created Department of Commerce and Labor.[97] In 1905 the *Ju Toy* Supreme Court ruling barred all Chinese, including those claiming U.S. citizenship, from appealing the bureau's decisions in the courts. This ruling gave the bureau unprecedented power that exceeded that of most federal agencies.[98] By 1905, then, both local and national officials had made the gates of exclusion bigger and stronger, further limiting Chinese immigration to America.

The New Gatekeepers on Angel Island, 1910–1940

While the transfer of power from the Customs Service to the Bureau of Immigration was meant to strengthen enforcement—a move that might automatically put the immigrant at a disadvantage—it also brought significant changes that cleansed the system of some of the most explicit anti-Chinese biases. By 1910, when the immigration station on Angel Island opened, a significantly different breed of immigration official was processing Chinese immigrants. Immigration officers had fewer direct ties to anti-immigrant movements, and civil service reforms instituted across the federal government had ended the system of political patronage in employment.[99] By 1910, the bureau had been transformed from a decentralized corps of officers scattered across the country and vulnerable to local politics into a powerful, centralized agency of career civil servants. Unlike earlier immigrant inspectors whose appointments were often politically motivated, the officials in the new bureau were selected by merit and promoted if they adhered to standards of expertise and efficiency.

Appointments to the immigration service were based on results of civil service examinations that tested mental ability and knowledge of immigration laws and rules. By the early 1930s, 35 percent of the inspectors had completed high school, 15 percent had some college education, and 4 percent had legal training. One-third had previously been employed as clerks, interpreters, guards, or messengers in the immigration service before being appointed to the position of inspector. Another third had worked in other departments in the federal government.[100] Unlike earlier immigration inspectors who had received little training, early-twentieth-century inspectors were required to take courses in immigration law, criminal law, and court procedure.[101]

Some of these changes reflected a larger transformation in civil service in the federal government during the early twentieth century, but, as Lucy Salyer has shown, the vocal protests of Chinese and other immigrant groups against the unchecked power of the Bureau of Immigration also motivated the agency to reform itself.[102] As a means of placating immigrant groups, President Theodore Roosevelt appointed Oscar S. Straus, a Jewish immigrant, as secretary of commerce and labor in 1907. Entering the office on the heels of the Chinese boycott of American goods from 1905 to 1906, in which Chinese merchants in the United States and China charged the United States of discriminating against the Chinese, Straus was publicly sympathetic to Chinese demands and called for a less stringent enforcement of the Chinese exclusion laws. He advocated that admission should be the rule in Chinese cases and "exclusion the exception."[103] Straus also handled general immigration matters differently from his predecessors and offset the restrictionist character of the bureau. He consistently fought attempts to impose greater restrictions on immigrants, including the literacy test proposed by nativist groups like the Immigration Restriction League.[104]

The agency's attempts at reform were considered a success by outsiders. In 1904, the *Chicago Herald* observed that under the treasury and customs officials, "the people of China have been treated as if it were a crime to seek an education in the United States, or to travel in this country, or to attempt to trade here." Government officials had considered it their "duty to find reasons for the exclusion of as many Chinese as possible." Since the transfer of the Bureau of Immigration to the Department of Commerce and Labor, the newspaper approvingly reported, there had been "a decided change in the policy and the practice of the officials."[105]

Hart Hyatt North, then commissioner of immigration in San Francisco, carefully cut out the newspaper clipping and kept it in his scrapbook. Five

Hart Hyatt North (far right), commissioner of immigration, with employees of the U.S. Immigration Service at Angel Island, c. 1910. North served as commissioner at San Francisco from 1898 to 1909 and oversaw the construction of the immigration station on Angel Island. The new escape-proof island facility was credited with greatly increasing the rejection rates of Chinese immigrants. Courtesy of the Bancroft Library, University of California, Berkeley.

years later, when the Angel Island immigration station opened, North could boast of even more significant changes. In a letter to the commissioner of immigration in Philadelphia, he wrote, "the personnel of our force is better than almost ever before; most of the dead timber has been eradicated and we have additional new men who bid fair to be first rate."[106] North himself represented the new breed of official. A former lawyer and state congressman, North became commissioner of immigration in 1898 and was reappointed in 1905 and 1909 to the same post.[107] Chinese leaders like newspaper editor Ng Poon Chew described North as "the most honest, just and fair-minded man in the whole service at this port."[108]

North's successor, Luther Steward, also demonstrated a commitment to hiring fair-minded officials. He candidly admitted that the early enforcement of the Chinese exclusion laws had often been unjust. "There was a great deal of prejudice involved," Steward told visitors to the Angel Island immigration station in 1911. And while "some of the sore spots in the administration years ago [had] left their scars," Luther continued, "the present administration is devoid of any such [prejudice]. . . . We have striven earnestly to get broad-minded men who will not take any stand either for or against the applicant."[109] Steward might have been thinking of immigrant inspector John Birge Sawyer, who represented a new type of career bureaucrat that the Bureau of Immigration was now attracting.

Sawyer first entered the Chinese Bureau in Portland in 1902. He was a graduate of the University of California at Berkeley and had passed the civil service examination easily. He exemplified a new kind of government bureaucrat who viewed his work not as a stepping stone to an elected political office but as a career. Upon his appointment to the bureau in 1902, Sawyer recorded in his diary that he had "high hopes of the opportunity in government work."[110] Unlike many of his predecessors who had been active in the anti-Chinese movement, Sawyer sought to enforce the exclusion laws without bias. While stationed in the Portland office, he even came to the rescue of a Chinese man being harassed by an unruly mob.[111] Sawyer's attitude and approach were apparently not anomalies in the new immigration service. After transferring to Angel Island, Sawyer observed that Chief Inspector Charles Mehan also "maintained a very sympathetic attitude toward . . . every Chinese coming before the office." In 1918, Sawyer left the immigration service, but he continued to work on Chinese immigration matters in his new post as the U.S. vice consul in Shanghai, China.[112]

Notably, immigrant inspectors continued to be predominantly male. A few women were employed to serve in other positions, especially as "matrons" who supervised female detainees. In 1910, the commissioner of immigration in San Francisco hired the first Chinese woman to look after the Chinese women in detention on Angel Island. Tye Leung, who had been affiliated with the Presbyterian Mission in San Francisco since 1902, was recommended for her reliability and good character. Leung was expected to not only serve as an interpreter for the Chinese women but to also keep an eye out for Chinese prostitutes attempting to immigrate. One of her specific duties was to gather "definite evidence of the intentions" of the women arriving in San Francisco. Women were also regularly employed as stenographers, but none seems to have worked as an immigrant inspector during the period of this study.[113]

By 1910, the immigration service had undergone a quiet transformation. In 1915, officials within the bureau admitted that the agency had to be more uniform in its procedures and had to adopt a higher standard of fairness. To some extent, more formal procedures were adopted. A law division was established at the national level to integrate judicial procedures into the administration of the immigration laws.[114] Nevertheless, reform did not mean the end of racism in either immigration policy or the immigration service itself. Officials on Angel Island maintained much of the enforcement system that had developed in earlier years. The exacting medical examinations and aggressive interrogations and cross-examinations continued and increased in intensity as officers attempted to cope with growing illegal immigration. As later chapters will discuss, many of the procedures continued to reveal an institutionalized suspicion of all Chinese and unfairly hindered the entry of legal immigrants. Moreover, the immigration service's efforts to reform itself coincided with the great resurgence of nativism that continued to target Chinese and other Asians, as well as Mexicans and southern and eastern Europeans. As anti-immigration sentiment spread and gained momentum throughout the country, the relationship between nativists and immigration officials strengthened and the voices of immigrant rights groups were drowned out.[115]

Despite claims of reform, many immigration officials still held prejudiced views that affected their handling of Chinese cases. One Chinese observer recalled that some of the new immigrant inspectors on Angel Island were known to "proceed on the premise [to] do everything . . . to trip you up, and deny you admission."[116] Moreover, anti-Asian exclusionists in San Francisco continued to put pressure on officials to uphold the strictest standards of exclusion. In 1910, a scandal erupted in the San Francisco office over corruption among Chinese inspectors. When San Francisco commissioner of immigration Hart Hyatt North decided to remove the offenders, two inspectors who were particularly favored by the local press because they were "feared" by the Chinese, the *San Francisco Call* sarcastically praised him for taking "down some more bars on the exclusion gate," naming him "Idol of Chinatown."[117] The following year, North was forced to resign because of pressure from Californians, and the Asiatic Exclusion League in particular, which attacked him for his allegedly lax enforcement policies regarding Asian Indians.[118]

Additionally, distrust of Chinese employees within the service continued to influence hiring decisions. Chinese who applied for interpreter positions on Angel Island were not hired on the basis of their application and credentials alone. They were also required to obtain a letter of recommendation from a reputable white person who could vouch for their characters. If they were hired, Chinese interpreters were not trusted to be alone with the immigrants for long periods of time and they were regularly shifted around during interrogations. Interpreter Edwar Lee explained the bureau's rationale: "They were afraid of collusion between the interpreters and the applicants coming in. So in order to play it safe, one case may have two to three [interpreters]. You hear a portion of the testimony, say from the father. All right when it come to the applicant, they ask for change in interpreter."[119] Because interpreters might be taken away from cases midway through their processing, immigrant inspector John Birge Sawyer found that the system "paralyzed" the work of the entire office and caused "interruptions, delay, and confusion."[120] Despite such inconveniences the practice of separating Chinese interpreters from Chinese immigrants remained standard policy throughout the station's history.

The national headquarters of the Bureau of Immigration also reverted back to hiring outspoken nativists. No other immigration official promoted the nativist agenda more than Commissioner-General of Immigration Anthony Caminetti, who served from 1913 to 1920. A second-generation Italian American and the first commissioner in sixteen years who was not affiliated with the trade union movement, Caminetti was nonetheless a strong opponent of unrestricted immigration, especially from Asia.

A native Californian, Caminetti had been involved in both the anti-Chinese and anti-Japanese movements even before his political career began. In 1876, he was an officer in an anti-Chinese group in Jackson, California, which later became known as the Order of Caucasians. As a state congressman from 1890 to 1894, Caminetti called for an anti-Chinese mass meeting to rally support around the renewal of the Chinese Exclusion Act.[121] In 1913, when he served in the California State Senate, Caminetti called for a constitutional amendment to disfranchise American citizens of Chinese ancestry.[122] Caminetti used his position as commissioner-general to emphasize the western nativist theme of the Yellow Peril. In his annual reports, Caminetti consistently declared that Asian immigration continued to be a real threat to the United States.[123] In his 1916 annual report, for example, Caminetti recommended a ban on allowing Chinese American citizens to sponsor their foreign-born children. He wrote, "A Chinese who is a citizen of the United States merely by the 'accident of birth'" should not "be permitted to use his citizenship, especially when not cherished for any other purpose [other than] as a foundation upon which to introduce here one or more Chinese laborers, born to him abroad in his family village."[124] Caminetti's prejudices against the Chinese were deep-rooted and enduring. As his biographer put it, whether as a state congressman or the commissioner-general of immigration of the United States, Caminetti was "consistently anti-Chinese."[125] Even in 1920, when only 2,148 Chinese applied for admission into the country, Caminetti argued that exclusion was absolutely necessary "for the protection of our own people and our own institutions."[126]

The Chinese were not Caminetti's only targets. During his tenure, the bureau lobbied for the passage of the literacy test over the second veto of President Woodrow Wilson, as well as for the exclusion of Asian Indians and other Asian immigrants not already excluded by law. Caminetti also worked closely with Attorney General A. Mitchell Palmer during the Red Scare of 1919–20 to arrest and deport suspected alien radicals.

Conclusion

By the time that the immigration station on Angel Island opened its doors in 1910, the immigration service locally and nationally had been transformed from a corps of untrained Chinese inspectors under the Customs Service's jurisdiction to a centralized and highly bureaucratic agency under the Department of Commerce and Labor. The Chinese exclusion laws and their enforcement by the first keepers of the gate were central to this transformation. The policies created in San Francisco became the models for the rest of the nation, revealing the important role that San Francisco and California played in shaping the country's immigration laws and agenda. The Chinese exclusion laws themselves also extended the state's power into new realms of immigration regulation, including deportation of immigrants and immigrant documentation, interrogations, and investigations. Likewise, the bureau's efforts to formulate policy and procedures coincided with the rise of the regulatory state in general and the movement to centralize and strengthen the U.S. Bureau of Immigration in particular.

One of the primary influences on the decisions of both the San Francisco and the Washington, D.C., offices of the Bureau of Immigration was a deeply rooted and institutionalized anti-Chinese racism that was reinforced by public sentiment and political pressure. As this chapter makes clear, the immigration service did attempt reform. Nevertheless, the nativist and anti-Chinese impulses remained entrenched in both the letter of the exclusion laws and the Bureau of Immigration's own practices. With the triumph of nativism in the 1920s, the bureau further solidified its role as an ally of nativists and exclusionists.

PART II

AT AMERICA'S GATES

Throughout the Chinese exclusion era, the immigration station on Angel Island was widely recognized as "the main gateway" into the United States from Asia. Indeed, no other place symbolizes the Chinese immigrant experience during the exclusion era better than Angel Island. From 1910 to 1940, an estimated 175,000 Chinese immigrants were processed and detained in the station's barracks. While popularly called the "Ellis Island of the West," the immigration station on Angel Island was in fact very different from its counterpart in New York. Ellis Island, mainly a processing center for European immigrants, was governed by American immigration laws that restricted but did not exclude European immigrants. Angel Island, on the other hand, was the chief port of entry for Chinese and other Asian immigrants and represented American exclusion policies. Immigrants on Ellis Island usually spent only a few hours or at most a few days at the island depot, whereas Asians, and particularly Chinese, on Angel Island counted their detention time in weeks, months, and even years. Ellis Island was a processing station of entry, but Angel Island's purpose was to keep immigrants out. It became a symbol of exclusion, or, as historian Him Mark Lai has written, a "half-open door at best."[1] It both embodied and reinforced the racist immigration policies that singled out Chinese.

The "gateway to the Orient," Angel Island served as a physical manifestation of the Chinese exclusion laws. Chinese were not the only immigrants to be processed and detained at the island, but over the course of the exclusion era, they made up the majority. Not only were Chinese, Japanese, and European immigrants subject to separate systems of immigration restriction and regulation, they were also physically segregated by race (Japanese and European immigrants in the upstairs barracks; Chinese below) and by gender, with separate barracks for women and men of each race. Now a National Historic Landmark, Angel Island remains the most significant monument to Chinese immigration and exclusion. The poems written and carved into the station's walls by angry, frustrated, and homesick immigrants are especially powerful reminders of the costs and hardships of immigration under such a discriminatory regime. However, they are also evidence of immigrant resistance and perseverance, and it is this embodiment of the immigrant spirit that draws hundreds of thousands of visitors to the island every year.

This section focuses on the dynamic interaction of the excluders and the excluded in San Francisco and on Angel Island. Chapter 3 shifts our attention from the exclusion laws themselves to the ways in which exclusion enforcement institutionalized popular beliefs and stereotypes about Chinese. Procedures like those designed to counter the allegedly "natural" cunning and deceit of Chinese applicants or those based on the assumption that Chinese women were potential prostitutes and that Chinese Americans were fraudulent or inferior citizens further racialized Chinese as dangerous threats to the nation. Such government practices served as additional exclusion acts, making it even more difficult for Chinese to enter the country. Enforcement of the exclusion laws also drew upon — and in turn strengthened — the very meanings of race, class, gender, sexuality, and citizenship in America.

Chapter 4 explores Chinese immigration patterns and changing strategies of resistance to explain why Chinese continued to come to the United States and how they managed to get in while the exclusion laws were in effect. Transnational migration patterns and legal, political, and economic challenges to the exclusion laws all facilitated immigration and allowed additional classes of immigrants to apply for admission. Nevertheless, the policy of exclusion remained intact and largely unchanged. After 1910, in the midst of increasing nativism and immigration restriction, Chinese were most successful by learning how to negotiate their way through the exclusion laws instead of dismantling the policy altogether.

CHAPTER THREE

EXCLUSION ACTS

Race, Class, Gender, and Citizenship in the Enforcement of the Exclusion Laws

IN 1890, CARLTON RICKARDS, a San Francisco Chinese inspector, testified before a congressional committee on Chinese immigration and explained the methods he used to enforce the exclusion laws. "Of course I try to get evidence not for the Chinaman but against him, and then he has got to make his own proof," Rickards explained. "My examination is taken for the collector [of customs] and is as much against the case as it can be."[1] That Rickards used his powers as an inspector to favor the exclusion rather than the admission of Chinese immigrants was not contrary to government policy. Indeed, Rickards was merely following the Bureau of Immigration's written rules and regulations, which clearly stated that Chinese were to be judged "excludable until they could be proven otherwise."[2] Chinese immigrants confirmed that the exclusion laws were commonly enforced with a restrictionist mind-set. In 1908, Ng Poon Chew, the editor of the *Chung Sai Yat Po,* San Francisco's daily Chinese-language newspaper, wrote that in the twenty-six years of its existence, the Chinese exclusion policy had "steadily increased in stringency. [It] has been carried out with such vigor that it has almost become an extermination law."[3]

Rickards's and Ng's statements reveal that the ways in which immigration laws were interpreted and enforced were just as important—if not more—than the actual laws themselves.[4] Once passed, the exclusion laws raised significant questions about the policy of exclusion and the role of the government in controlling immigration. As the first federal immigration laws to require the screening of new arrivals, Chinese exclusion forced the United States into a new role of defining and distinguishing between admissible and excludable immigrants. Immigration officials were required to determine who was a member of the so-called exempt classes and who was not. The original Chinese Exclusion Act had provided exempt status for merchants, students, teachers, diplomats, and travelers. Additional court challenges brought by Chinese extended the exempt categories to include American citizens of Chinese descent and the wives and children of merchants. Such legal decisions and federal laws provided important guidelines. But the Chinese arriving in San Francisco were a diverse group of individuals who did not always fit into neat legal categories. Indeed, Chinese exclusion functioned on multiple, intersecting levels and raised significant questions that lawmakers had not anticipated: Who was Chinese? Who was a laborer, a merchant, a merchant's wife? What defined an American citizen of Chinese descent? And what were the standards of proof for all of these categories? The ways in which immigration officials answered these questions served as subsequent exclusion acts that further restricted Chinese immigration. Nineteenth-century stereotypes depicting Chinese as coolies, prostitutes, and pollutants and devious, unassimilable aliens merged with the new realities of exclusion and informed every aspect of admission and exclusion decisions.[5] And by defining "Chineseness," "merchant," "merchant's wife," "prostitute," and "citizen," the exclusion laws and their enforcement helped to forge not only Chinese American identities, but also the concepts of race, class, gender, sexuality, and citizenship for Americans in general.[6]

A "Chinaman" Is a "Chinaman": Exclusion and "Chineseness"

By singling out Chinese alone for exclusion, the exclusion laws meant that Chinese, regardless of class, immigration, citizenship, or residency status, were treated differently from other immigrant groups. From the time that immigration officials boarded an arriving steamship to the time an immigrant or returning resident was finally "landed," or officially admitted into the country, Chinese were subjected to longer examinations, interrogations, and detentions than were immigrants from any other country. Exclusion based on race and the identification of who was or was not Chinese, however, was problematical for immigration officials and created difficulties for Chinese, and for mixed-race Chinese in particular. Beginning in 1888, the Chinese exclusion laws were applied to "all persons of the Chinese race, whether subjects of China or other foreign power," as well as to "persons of Chinese descent."[7] But how the government determined who was a person of Chinese descent reveals how Chinese racial identity, or "Chineseness," continued to be socially constructed. "Chineseness" was determined mostly by socially defined physical markers of race, but immigration officials also depended on symbols of actual or perceived common descent such as language, association, class, and behavior.[8] These markers and symbols were more obvious to some officials than others, and thus the determination of who was or was not Chinese could be inconsistent.

One of the most notable cases illustrating this inconsistency involved Lawrence Klindt Kentwell, a Honolulu businessman and a student at Columbia University Law School in New York City who had an English father and Chinese mother. On several overseas trips in the 1890s and early 1900s, immigration officials in San Francisco and New York failed to recognize Kentwell as Chinese. His passport photo revealed a light-skinned, neatly groomed young man in suit and tie and hairstyle consistent with white American middle-class norms. According to Kentwell, immigration officials repeatedly "landed him like any other [non-Chinese] passenger."[9] Perhaps trained to identify "Chineseness" primarily through physical traits that were emphasized in popular culture — dark, yellow skin, and slanted eyes — these immigration officials did not recognize Kentwell as Chinese.[10] Class most certainly played an important role in their mistake. Kentwell traveled in the first-class cabin, unlike the majority of Chinese, who came in steerage. Moreover, his dress suggested that he was an American — or at least an Americanized — gentlemen; most Chinese, it was believed, wore the "traditional" Chinese-style tunics and loose-fitting pants, as well as a queue. Though he was half Chinese and thus subject to the Chinese exclusion laws, Kentwell did not conform to assumed standards of "Chineseness" and was not detained or questioned during these early trips.

In February 1904, however, when Kentwell returned from the Philippines to his home in Honolulu, where immigration officials knew him to be of mixed race, he was treated quite differently. According to Kentwell, immigration inspector Robert Brown immediately singled him out on board the steamship and insulted and embarrassed Kentwell in front of fellow passengers, demanding to see his papers. Brown "hinted sarcastically" that he knew Kentwell "had Chinese blood in his veins," and, according to Kentwell, treated him like a "common criminal."[11] Kentwell began a personal campaign protesting the government's classification of him as Chinese. "Race" and "Chineseness," Kentwell suggested, were not clearly defined and their meanings were applied inconsistently. He demanded clarification. In San Francisco and New York, he had been admitted without delay along with the white passengers on the ship. "Is it because the Chinese strain in my make up does not dominate the Anglo-Saxon, or perhaps my Chinese strain was not known to the mainland officers . . . that I did not meet the same fate as I did at the port of Honolulu?" Kentwell asked.[12] In letters to President Theodore Roosevelt, Commissioner-General of Immigration Frank Sargent, and Secretary of Commerce and Labor Victor Metcalf, Kentwell further contended that he should not even be classified as Chinese in the first place. "My father is an Englishman, and as I was born in British territory and under the law of nations, I am English, the Exclusion Act notwithstanding," he wrote.[13]

Immigration officials in Honolulu and Washington, D.C., did not agree. Kentwell was half Chinese by blood, they pointed out, and he was thus subject to Chinese exclusion. Moreover, they emphasized that Kentwell possessed other markers of "Chineseness." As Honolulu officials explained, Kentwell's association with the local Chinese community in Honolulu confirmed his Chineseness. Indeed, Inspector Robert Brown reported, Kentwell was "known to the Chinese people of Hawaii as Kam Duck Won" rather than by his English name.[14] The Honolulu officers consistently referred to Kentwell in internal correspondence in the same manner as they did other Chinese: simply as another "Chinaman."[15] Victor Metcalf also explained to Kentwell that his political allegiance to England was irrelevant. The Chinese exclusion laws "do not refer to Chinese in the political sense but as a race," he wrote. The government's inconsistent treatment of him was "undoubtedly due to such officials' ignorance of your being a person of Chinese descent."[16] For Kentwell, the sting of racial discrimination had a highly politicizing affect. After being "officially" classified as Chinese and subjected to the exclusion laws, Kentwell dropped his protest over his individual treatment and began to lecture on the injustices of the Chinese exclusion laws in general.

As Kentwell's case illustrates, the exclusion laws forced immigration officials to refine their definitions and categories of "Chineseness." Blood and descent were ultimately used as the primary markers of racial identity, but immigration officials also learned how to use language, association, and appearance to identify Chinese persons as well. Kentwell's case was far from unique. As the government grew more adept at racial identification, other Chinese of mixed descent found themselves similarly scrutinized by officials. The case of Mrs. J. Morton Riggs, a wealthy biracial resident of Honolulu and wife of a U.S. Marine Corps officer, for example, made headlines in 1904 when she was detained in San Francisco. Although Riggs was reportedly "attired in a conventional American gown" and had "no trace of the Asiatic in her features," she was still subjected to the same harsh treatment accorded all Chinese in San Francisco.[17] Unlike her fellow first-class passengers who were allowed to disembark as soon as the steamer reached San Francisco, Mrs. Riggs was grilled by immigration inspectors and her papers were heavily scrutinized before she was allowed to land.

Race and exclusion intersected not only in the construction of "Chineseness" but also in the creation of race-based immigration procedures designed for Chinese only. This separate treatment meant that Chinese were singled out as soon as they arrived in port. Whenever a steamer with Chinese passengers arrived in San Francisco, an inspector and an interpreter boarded it and separated all Chinese passengers from non-Chinese passengers. They then gathered any documents, photographs, and papers they might have and interrogated each Chinese individually.[18] Customs Service agents also kept track of all Chinese departing the United States. When a vessel with Chinese passengers departed San Francisco, the inspectors herded all of them into a specially erected corral and registered their names, ages, occupations, and former places of residence. These lists were kept by the Chinese Bureau and used when incoming steamers arrived.[19]

When the Angel Island immigration station officially opened on January 21, 1910, Europeans were separated from other races, and Chinese immigrants were kept apart from Japanese and other Asians. Men and women, including husbands and wives, were separated as well. They were not allowed to see or communicate with each other until they were admitted into the country. Children under age twelve were left with their mothers. The Chinese holding satisfactory papers, usually returning residents who had undergone a preinvestigation before departing the United States, were released. The others were ferried to Angel Island for further examination.[20]

Once on Angel Island, immigrants underwent medical examinations by officers of the U.S. Public Health Service, who acted on and reinforced the belief that Chinese constituted a greater health menace than other immigrant groups. Illustrating what historian Alan Kraut has called the "medicalization of preexisting nativist prejudices," medical exams were used to detect any "dangerous or loathsome" infectious diseases among immigrants. On Ellis

Immigrants walking toward the administration building of the Angel Island Immigration Station, c. 1916. When immigrants arrived in San Francisco, Chinese were separated from non-Chinese. Some returning immigrants were processed upon disembarkation, but most were ferried to the immigration station on Angel Island, where the average detention lasted two weeks. In contrast, most European immigrants arriving at Ellis Island were usually processed in a matter of hours. Courtesy of the California Department of Parks and Recreation.

Island, each arrival was examined in a line inspection that sought to determine the general health of the immigrant, as well as to detect any signs of trachoma, mental illness, contagious diseases, or other maladies.[21]

Immigrant inspectors and physicians on Angel Island looked for many of the same ailments as their counterparts on Ellis Island. However, acting on the belief that Chinese as a race were more diseased than European immigrants (and therefore both racially threatening and racially inferior), officials also kept an eye out for parasitic diseases common among the Chinese, seeking to use them as grounds for exclusion. These so-called Oriental diseases, such as uncinariasis (hookworms) and filariasis (round worms), were treatable and posed no serious health threat to the American population, but Chinese

TABLE 1. APPLICATIONS FOR ADMISSION TO THE UNITED STATES
AT ANGEL ISLAND, PORT OF SAN FRANCISCO, 1910–1924

Year	Chinese	Japanese	Other[a]	Total
1910	4,626 (53.6%)	N/A	N/A	8,620
1911	N/A	N/A	N/A	N/A
1912	N/A	N/A	N/A	N/A
1913	3,750 (42%)	3,477 (39%)	1,708 (19%)	8,935
1914	3,832 (38)	3,944 (39)	2,362 (23)	10,138
1915	4,548 (31.5)	4,982 (34.5)	4,896 (34)	14,426
1916	4,035 (29.4)	4,712 (34.4)	4,957 (36.2)	13,704
1917	3,558 (28)	4,218 (34)	4,708 (38)	12,484
1918	5,316 (30)	5,403 (31.7)	6,852 (39)	17,571
1919	3,792 (25)	N/A	N/A	14,913
1920	8,594 (38)	6,267 (27.5)	7,892 (34.5)	22,853
1921	4,707 (21)	N/A	N/A	22,751
1922	4,908 (35)	N/A	N/A	14,056
1923	5,009 (35)	N/A	N/A	14,348
1924	5,438 (33)	N/A	N/A	16,263
Total	62,113	33,003	33,375	191,062

Sources: U.S. Department of Commerce and Labor, *Annual Reports of the Commissioner-General of Immigration* (Washington: GPO, 1910–11); U.S. Department of Labor, *Annual Reports of the Commissioner-General of Immigration* (Washington: GPO, 1912–24).
Note: N/A = figures not available.
[a] The Immigration and Naturalization Service did not keep regular statistics on the nationalities of other immigrants applying for admission at San Francisco. Some immigrant groups that were known to have been processed on Angel Island were Asian Indians, Mexicans, Spanish, Portuguese, Russians, and South and Central Americans.

afflicted with them were still detained. After 1917, clonorchiasis (liver fluke) was added to the list.[22] As Nayan Shah has illustrated, such practices served as "medical borders" on Angel Island. They were justified as national necessities and perpetuated the long-standing notion that the Chinese were associated with particularly intolerable diseases.[23] Chinese leaders charged that the governmental regulations were discriminatory and arbitrary barriers erected to thwart the entry of Chinese immigrants. This distrust of American officials ran so deeply among Chinese that many believed that some diseases and afflictions that were grounds for exclusion were not bona fide ailments but just additional means to unfairly exclude the Chinese. One American diplomat observed in 1907 that "many Chinese who have to do with American immigration officials do not believe that there is such a disease as trachoma, but believe that it is a device to keep them out."[24] As Mr. Jow, a former detainee on Angel Island in 1918 explained, "They examined you for everything. They just wanted to give us trouble."[25]

Because the exclusion laws legitimized discriminatory treatment of Chinese immigrants, the way in which they were enforced supported underlying suspicions about Chinese held over from the anti-Chinese movement. Portrayals of Chinese as crafty, dishonest, cunning, and intelligent that were first made popular in the 1870s gained even more currency as anxiety over Chinese illegal immigration increased and took root in state policy.[26] Customs collectors in San Francisco complained that every steamer from Asia brought "vast numbers of the most cunning and prolific in desire to deceive the Customs officers of any race of people."[27] Journalists remarked that tracking Chinese immigration gave government officials "plenty of trouble" and required "all the ingenuity that a white man always requires in dealing with a Chinaman."[28] Commissioners-general in Washington, D.C., reported annually of the "natural difficulties" arising from dealing with the Chinese. They "looked alike," and immigration officials had great difficulty in "distinguishing [one] Chinese person from another." Charges that Chinese traded places with one another were also highlighted in government reports. Moreover, "all Chinese" possessed "totally different standards of morality" from whites and used their great "mental acuteness and ingenuity" to defeat the government. The exclusion laws, Commissioner-General Terence Powderly proclaimed, were thus "no match for the Chinese."[29]

Immigration officials first responded with procedures designed to keep better identification records of Chinese immigrants and residents in the country. Written physical descriptions and photographs had been made part of the admission procedures during the very early years of exclusion enforcement. The Bureau of Immigration under Commissioner-General Frank Sargent instituted more drastic measures, most notably the Bertillon system, which the treasury secretary had recommended in 1902 and was approved by Congress and put into practice by immigration inspectors in 1903. The method, invented by French scientist and criminal detective Alphonse Bertillon in the 1880s, relied upon detailed body measurements as a means of identifying criminals.[30] Believing that photographs were not reliable tools of identification, Bertillon recorded the length and width (or circumference) of subjects' forearms, feet, fingers, ears, heads, teeth, hair, and genitalia, claiming that these measurements alone provided exact identification markers. Commissioner-General Sargent was enthusiastic about using the Bertillon system on Chinese immigrants because he was confident that it would assist the government not only in distinguishing one Chinese applicant from another but also detect fraudulent entries. Inspectors were instructed to photograph all newly arriving and departing Chinese laborers and to conduct exhaustive physical examinations in accordance with Bertillon's methods. After the boycott of American goods in China, the system was dropped.[31] Although the bureau was supposed to restrict the use of this humiliating system to the identification of Chinese laborers only, historian Delber McKee notes that in practice, "any Chinese person suspected of being a laborer — and most Chinese were — had to undergo the examination."[32] Nativists and immigration officials alike connected all Chinese with criminals and criminal behavior. The Chinese considered the use of the Bertillon system one of the most objectionable features of Chinese exclusion enforcement. As an editor of a Chinese daily newspaper told an immigration service investigator in 1906, the Chinese regarded the system of minute measurement as "a great humiliation." "In their judgment," he explained, "it places them on par with criminals, and they lose face among their fellows when it is known that they have been subjected to this treatment."[33]

Coinciding with these attempts to facilitate identification were immigration officials' redoubled efforts to verify Chinese claims of exempt status.[34] They thoroughly searched the luggage and belongings of a newly arriving Chinese for any evidence that might cast doubt on the veracity of his case. Moreover, because official Chinese records of births, marriages, and divorces were not available, intensive, complex, and detailed interrogations of Chinese applicants and cross-examinations of their witnesses were considered the best means to determine exempt status and thus became standard practice.[35] Inspectors first questioned applicants in great detail and then turned to the witnesses in separate hearings. All statements were checked against each other to substantiate the applicant's claim of exempt status. If any discrepancies arose during the testimony, the inspectors assumed that the parties did not know each other or that one or all of the subjects were lying and that the applicant's claim was false.[36] These procedures exposed the government's belief that Chinese were inherently cunning and devious.[37]

The exhaustive interviews, background checks, identification procedures, and invasive physical examinations set Chinese apart from other immigrants.

U.S. immigrant inspector examining an immigrant's personal belongings, c. 1916. In an attempt to find evidence that might disprove an applicant's claim for admission, luggage and personal effects were routinely searched and even confiscated. Courtesy of the California Department of Parks and Recreation.

Government statistics detailing the cost of handling all arriving and departing Chinese provide evidence of the disproportionate amount of time, energy, and cost associated with examining Chinese immigrants. The Bureau of Immigration estimated that from 1903 to 1906, processing Chinese immigrants cost fifty to sixty times more than the processing of non-Chinese.[38]

Over time, Chinese immigrants were able to end some of the discriminatory treatment they faced. In 1906, in addition to the Bertillon system of identification,[39] some of the medical exclusions related to filariasis and clonorchiasis that pertained to Chinese only were eliminated.[40] Nonetheless, racial bias continued to shape exclusion enforcement. By the early 1900s, the immigrant interrogations had grown longer and more complex. Because they placed Chinese at such a disadvantage, they were generally considered the most important part of the immigrant inspection process and remained in place throughout the exclusion era.

Coolie or Merchant: Exclusion and Class

Built into the exclusion laws was a class hierarchy that prohibited Chinese laborers but allowed some of the most privileged Chinese to enter the United States. This class bias also affected exclusion enforcement. It was common knowledge among immigrants, for example, that immigration officials treated Chinese traveling in first-class cabins with much less suspicion than those traveling in steerage. Immigrant inspectors apparently reasoned that passengers who were wealthy enough to pay for the finer accommodations were less likely to fraudulently claim exempt-class status. This "unwritten local regulation" had very real consequences. Passengers who traveled in first or second class tended to be released on the day of their arrival, whereas third-class passengers, regardless of their immigrant status, were brought to the detention station.[41]

Nevertheless, Chinese merchants, students, officials, and travelers were never automatically admitted or given special treatment solely on the basis of their class. Immigration officials feared (sometimes with justification) that Chinese claiming exempt-class status were either laborers in disguise or likely to become laborers after being admitted.[42] They thus judged the class status of Chinese immigrants through the lens of race, and race through the lens of class status. Chinese applying for admission were viewed as Chinese first and merchants, students, or officials second. Sometimes class provided protection from racial discrimination; often times it did not.

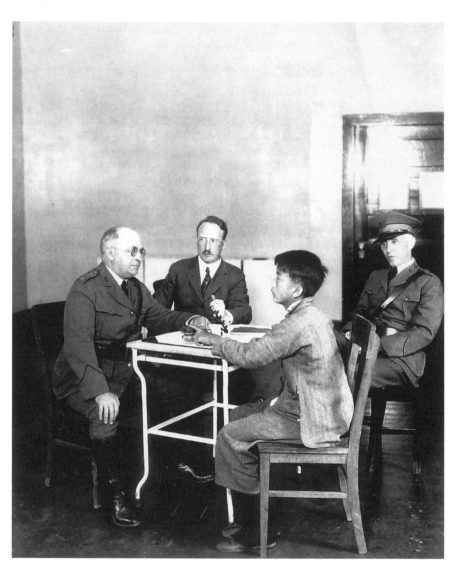

A Chinese applicant being interrogated at Angel Island. Interrogations could last anywhere from a few hours to several days. Rigid enforcement of the exclusion laws by the U.S. government and illegal immigration among the Chinese turned the interrogations into exhaustive cat-and-mouse games. In one extreme case, an applicant was asked almost nine hundred questions. Courtesy of the National Archives, Washington, D.C.

Merchants, by far the largest group of Chinese professionals who applied for admission, came to be viewed through racialized markers of class that distinguished them from Chinese laborers. If the latter were supposed to be cheap, servile workers who competed with white workingmen, then Chinese merchants, officials rationalized, should be wealthy, educated, and refined gentlemen who posed no threat either to white labor or to American society in general.[43] Chinese merchants were thus expected to be highly literate, and the government required them to take a literacy test as early as 1906, nine years before a national literacy test for all immigrants was approved by Congress.[44] The literacy standards were sometimes extremely high. Ko Piu, who applied for admission as a merchant in 1911, passed the standard test by writing a sample business letter and bill in Chinese that was then translated and read by immigrant inspectors. He was denied entry, however, on the grounds that the letter, though accurate, indicated that he lacked "an extensive knowledge in business" and thus placed doubt on Ko's merchant status.[45]

Chinese merchants were also expected to look like merchants. What this look actually entailed, of course, was extremely subjective, but it is clear that officials believed that bona fide merchants' wealth would be apparent in their dress and appearance. Thus, one Chinese immigrant applying as a merchant in 1912 was denied entry in part because officials judged his appearance to be "exceedingly poor." His handwriting, which they characterized as also "particularly poor," only confirmed their suspicions, and when the applicant's trunk was searched for additional evidence to be used in the case, his "poor quality" clothes were used as the final evidence to deny him entry.[46] In contrast, in another case, an immigration official reported that he was inclined to admit returning merchant Lee Kan because he had "the appearance of an exempt."[47]

Lastly, immigration officials measured the merchant status of Chinese by whether or not they had performed physical labor. Returning merchants were required to testify that they had not engaged in manual labor for one year.[48] And Chinese warned each other to deny having skills that might be associated with common laborers. Soo Hoo Fong, an interpreter and immigration agent in the United States, thus advised Chinese applying as tailors that government officials were likely to deny them entry on the grounds that a tailor was a laborer. In the official interrogations, Fong warned, inspectors would try to pressure these applicants into admitting that they performed manual labor. To help applicants avoid being tripped up by inspectors' questions, Fong instructed his partner in China to advise new applicants to answer carefully. "Should they be asked: Do you know how to sew button holes? Are you an old hand in threading needles? And in sewing garments? Tell them to say 'No, I don't know anything about manual labor.' To answer carelessly 'I am not a laborer' will make trouble. The most important thing is that they be taught to hold firmly to the contention that they are business people, having all the time been merchants."[49]

Immigration officials also used physical examinations to uncover evidence that applicants had performed manual labor. As Hart Hyatt North, commissioner of immigration in San Francisco, explained to his superiors, "I have been making a physical examination of the faces, hands, shoulders, feet and legs of these people before passing upon their cases." North denied entry to one Chinese merchant applicant not only because of a slight discrepancy in his Section 6 certificate but also because the "applicant had calloused hands and the general appearance of a laborer."[50] Another inspector used skin color to determine whether applicant Lee Kwock Chow, a merchant's son, had performed labor outside. "Didn't you ever engage in farm labor? You look like you have been exposed in the open field to farm work all your life," he asked. Lee quickly retorted that he "was born dark."[51]

Commissioner North justified such examinations because he believed that "coolie importers" were bringing in "large numbers of coolie laborers under the guise of merchants." If it were not for his desire to vigilantly enforce the exclusion laws, North explained, he would happily cease the "exceedingly disagreeable and nauseating" examinations of "a lot of dirty Chinese."[52] Demonstrating the subjectivity in such procedures, North's judgment that one particular applicant was a "coolie" was not shared by Commissioner-General Frank Sargent. The Bureau of Immigration in Washington reversed North's decision to deny the applicant entry, stating that the contradictions in the case were immaterial and that, moreover, the applicant's photograph attached to the file "was not that of a coolie."[53]

While immigration officials continued to rely on overt class markers in the processing of Chinese merchants, over the course of the exclusion era, the admission and exclusion of this class became increasingly defined through the context of race. Merchants—along with other Chinese—came to face more stringent restrictions on their immigration, especially as the U.S. government narrowed the parameters under which merchants could be admitted. The original Chinese Exclusion Act did not provide a definition of "Chinese merchant," but by 1893, U.S. immigration regulations had defined him as a "person engaged in buying and selling merchandise at a fixed place of business and performing no manual labor."[54] The next year, the Treasury Department instructed local immigration offices to keep records on all Chinese businesses. Chinese were required to provide for these files exact descriptions of business activities, the volume of merchandise, photographs of the establishments, and lists of all partners and the amounts of each person's share in the establishment. Businesses were then required to file updated lists every year, and immigrant inspectors would confirm the accuracy of this information by making site visits.[55] In 1901, new government rules narrowed the definition of merchant to exclude Chinese salesmen, buyers, book keepers, accountants, managers, store keepers, apprentices, agents, and cashiers. Managers and proprietors of restaurants and laundries were also excluded.[56] The Immigration Act of 1924 further narrowed the definition of Chinese merchant so that it only applied to those who were engaged in international trade. In 1932, an amendment to the act declared that only Chinese merchants who conducted trade between the United States and the "foreign country of which he is a national" would be considered bona fide. Merchants were also required to operate their mercantile establishment for the duration of their residence in the United States.[57]

The government's restrictive redefinition of the term "merchant" served two purposes. As later chapters will illustrate, immigration officials suspected (often correctly) that Chinese took advantage of the elastic interpretation of the term in order to gain admission. The government's new restrictions and detailed requirements purportedly targeted immigrants who falsely claimed merchant status. But they also clearly served the goals of exclusionists by further limiting all Chinese immigration to the United States. The objective was no longer to exclude certain classes of Chinese who might threaten white workers, as the original Chinese Exclusion Act had been designed to do, but Chinese immigrants in general. Amendments to the laws, as well as new bureau regulations, thus affected professional Chinese who presumably served primarily the Chinese community, such as restaurant owners, interpreters, lawyers, and dentists.[58]

Race took precedence over class in the processing of Chinese merchants in other ways as well. Reflecting the belief that all Chinese, regardless of class, were prone to lying, bureau regulations explicitly stated that claims for exempt status could not rest on Chinese testimony alone. Chinese merchants reentering the United States were required to have "two credible witnesses, other than Chinese, to testify on behalf of the applicant's status and mercantile business." Although the regulations did not specify that these witnesses were to be white, in practice, only white witnesses were used. For many years, these witnesses were required to board the ship and identify the applicant in the presence of one of the inspectors.[59] Later, they were required to properly identify a photograph of the applicant and give sworn testimony of their association with him to the immigration service. The rationale behind this requirement reveals the ways in which immigration officials tied markers of Chinese class to whiteness. Bona fide Chinese merchants, the rule suggested, would conduct business with white businessmen. Such policies not only served to exclude Chinese based on their class and race but also functioned as additional barriers to Chinese immigration in general.

"Bad Women"/Dependent Women: Exclusion, Gender, and Sexuality

Because relatively few Chinese women immigrated to the United States during the exclusion era, much of the literature on Chinese immigrant women has understandably focused on their absence. Some scholars argue that from the 1870s on, the exclusion laws were the "most significant" of a multiplicity of factors contributing to lower migration rates for Chinese women. Laws targeting Chinese women preceded the general exclusion of Chinese laborers, and Chinese women were ignored in the list of so-called exempt classes in the original Exclusion Act. Those who did immigrate were forced to take their cases to court to secure the right to enter the country. Upholding the class hierarchy established in the laws, these court decisions allowed merchant wives and children to immigrate but excluded the wives of laborers. Wives of U.S. citizens also won the right to immigrate. These courtroom struggles and additional immigration restrictions, historian Sucheng Chan has argued, symbolized the "ever-tightening noose . . . [of exclusion] constrict[ing] the volume of Chinese female immigration."[60] Historian Adam McKeown, on the other hand, claims that the exclusion laws "played little role" in creating a gender imbalance among Chinese immigrants in the United States. While it was apparently more difficult for Chinese women to enter after 1882, he contends that the restrictive effects of the exclusion laws were "equal for both men and women." Other factors, he argues, especially transnational migration patterns and family structures, were more important in shaping Chinese female immigration to the United States.[61] While the exclusion laws alone cannot explain the low number of Chinese women in the United States, their impact on Chinese female immigration should not be overlooked. Gendered interpretations of the exclusion laws by both immigration officials and Chinese families made it more difficult for women to come to the United States. To claim that the exclusion laws eventually "opened more doors than [they] closed," as McKeown has, is to ignore the fact that few women were actually eligible to apply for entry through those doors on their own.[62]

As with other Chinese applying for admission into the country, Chinese women were judged by intersecting notions of race, class, gender, and sexuality. As Chinese, they were assumed to be excludable, rather than admissible. As Chinese women, they were subjected to additional scrutiny based on immigration officials' fears that most female applicants were either practicing or potential prostitutes. Chinese merchant wives might deflect suspicions by emphasizing their class status, but all Chinese women were subject to the gendered provisions in the exclusion laws that classified and judged them primarily as dependents of males.

The belief that most Chinese women in the United States were prostitutes had fueled much of the anti-Chinese sentiment in the 1870s and continued to have a detrimental effect on Chinese women's admission cases during the exclusion era. Viewed as symbols of social decay, exploitation, and even slavery, Chinese prostitutes — and by extension all Chinese women — were considered to be one of the most dangerous threats of Chinese immigration. A series of sensationalized investigations of prostitution in San Francisco during the 1890s magnified the perceived danger and kept the issue alive in public discourse.[63]

Exclusionists became especially concerned in 1890 when the federal district court in Oregon and the secretary of the treasury in Washington, D.C., ruled in favor of permitting the wives and minor children of Chinese merchants to enter the United States.[64] Correspondence to and from the immigration bureau in San Francisco following the two decisions indicates that many Chinese men desired to bring their wives and children to the United States. The service's correspondence logs record a multitude of inquires from Chinese men and their lawyers from across the country, including the cities of Santa Rosa, Merced, Watsonville, Bakersfield, and Los Angeles, California; Omaha, Nebraska; Menominee, Mississippi; and Tampa, Florida. Most inquirers sought information about the admission regulations for merchant families.[65] Alarmed immigration officials were reluctant to accept the new rulings and responded by instituting additional measures to control or stop Chinese female migration. In 1895, John H. Wise, the collector of customs and chief of the Chinese Bureau in San Francisco, most likely spoke for many immigration officials when he warned inquirers that he would "do as much as I can to discourage Chinese from sending for their alleged wives and children. I am satisfied that . . . many women and young girls [would be] brought for immoral purposes.

It is well known that the cunning of Chinese often circumvents the vigilance of the officers."[66] In responses to letter after letter from Chinese themselves or their lawyers and acquaintances, Wise repeated this warning and explicitly discouraged the immigration of Chinese women.[67] When pressed to explain what documents Chinese women would need to land, Wise made it clear that *all* Chinese women would be considered prostitutes until they could prove they were not.[68]

Chinese marriage customs and gender relations also provided the immigration service with ammunition to bar Chinese women. While Victorian American unions were believed to be based upon attraction, affection, and companionship between prospective spouses, traditional Chinese customs of arranged marriages and multiple wives were associated with subservience, concubinage, and prostitution. In the words of one American observer, all Chinese wives were "worse than slaves."[69] Immigration officials argued that such relationships among Chinese men and women hardly qualified as marriages at all and thus immigrants claiming to be married should be dealt with accordingly. As Collector Wise made it clear to one correspondent, "The Chinaman would have to demonstrate to me that woman is his wife according to our ideas of marriage."[70] To another Wise warned, "I shall demand, upon arrival of the alleged wives the most convincing proof that they are the wives of the Chinese residents." Exclusion policies dictated that "convincing proof" of the marriage did not include the unsupported testimony of the Chinese themselves. Only the testimony of white witnesses or documentation of the marriage—both of which were difficult to produce—would be accepted.[71] Although this last regulation proved to be short-lived, immigration officials throughout the exclusion era continued to give preference to Chinese who were married according to American rather than Chinese customs.[72]

The sensationalist furor over Chinese prostitution reached its peak at the turn of the century, but it continued to color the ways in which Chinese women were screened by immigration officials well into the twentieth century. Immigrant case files reveal that Chinese women who exhibited obvious class markers such as wealth and status faced less scrutiny and were less likely to be suspected of prostitution. Those who conformed to Victorian gender ideals of "respectability" and "decency" were also at an advantage.[73] Following the rationale used in merchants' cases, immigration officials expected bona fide merchant wives to possess fine clothing, a respectable manner, and, especially, bound feet, which were considered a mark of wealth and status in China. In 1885, for example, when Jow Ah Yeong and Chun Ah Ngon, a merchant's wife and their daughter, respectively, arrived in San Francisco, their applications emphasized that both mother and daughter had "compressed feet," which, the affidavit explained, "is a mark of respectability." On the women's ticket jacket, the immigrant inspector made a special note of "small feet," and the two were admitted into the country.[74] Thereafter, immigration officials generally viewed bound feet as overwhelming evidence of a women's exempt-class status. In fact, bound feet became a marker not only of class but also of Chinese female virtue, a quality a prostitute would allegedly never possess. In 1899, Collector of Customs John P. Jackson went so far as to write that a "decent Chinese woman" was "known to be such by the proofs she presents, and having the badge of respectability of bandaged and small feet." Ironically, the U.S. government's reliance on bound feet to determine a woman's class membership occurred at the same time that Chinese reformers in China launched campaigns to ban foot binding as part of a larger movement for reform, modernization, and women's equality.[75]

While markers of wealth, status, and respectability helped to distinguish elite Chinese women from Chinese prostitutes, many women—especially those who were not members of the merchant class—continued to be routinely suspected of being potential prostitutes and were often unfairly detained and/or denied entry.[76] One such case involved Lau Dai Moy, who applied for admission into the country as the wife of a U.S. citizen on June 12, 1917. Her papers were in order, but as part of the regular process at the immigration station on Angel Island in San Francisco, she and her husband Fong Dai Sing were brought in for extensive questioning. To immigration officials, the case appeared to be suspicious. Lau was much younger than her husband, and immigrant inspectors assumed that the two were not legally husband and wife (and that Lau was possibly a prostitute). Fong's own status as a citizen and his sponsorship of his wife were also scrutinized because immigration officials routinely assumed that Chinese claiming citizenship secured their own admissions through fraud. The inspectors grilled the couple about various aspects of their wedding ceremony, their home, and their family. The questions were exacting in their detail, and both Lau and Fong were expected to give specific answers that agreed with one another. Some of the questions put to Lau included the following:

Q: What presents or ornaments has your husband given you?
Q: When did your husband give you the hair ornament?
Q: Did he buy that hair ornament in his home village?

Q: Did you really wear the gay head-dress and the bead[ed] veil at your wedding?

Q: Just when did you wear the head-dress?

Q: How long did you wear the head-dress?

Q: Did you wear it while you served tea?

Q: Who were the guests that you poured tea for?

Such detailed questions not only reflect the gendered procedures of exclusion — the questions asked Lau revolved around strictly feminine behavior — but also illustrate the ways in which the government sought to prove or disprove the validity of relationships and marriages. If there were too many discrepancies in a couple's story, the immigration officials ruled that the relationship was based on fraud and that the applicant was thus inadmissible. Discrepancies, of course, did not always mean a fraudulent case. As in the case of Lau and Fong, the interrogation revolved around very minute details of their arranged marriage and wedding ceremony that had taken place a year prior to the interrogation. Other questions involving their village, their house, and their shared life were even more difficult to answer because the couple had spent only a few months together before living apart for a year with little or no contact. Yet they were still expected to provide consistent answers or risk a denial. Because of discrepancies between her answers and her husband's, Lau was detained at the station for six weeks.[77]

Lau's case was not an anomaly. Local Chinese leaders charged that reputable Chinese women were consistently asked "improper" questions that suggested that they were prostitutes, though the questions were seldom included in the official records.[78] Editor Ng Poon Chew consistently complained that the insinuations made by immigration officials would never be made "in the hearing of American ladies."[79] As late as 1940, sociologist Wen-hsien Chen found that "over-suspicion on the part of immigration officers [continued to cause] great embarrassment to respectable young Chinese women." Several women in the Chinese community in San Francisco told Chen that immigration officials suspected all Chinese women, save those who were able to travel in first class, of being prostitutes. Others claimed that any Chinese woman under sixty years of age who took third-class passage would be suspected of being a "bad woman."[80]

Decisions related to a Chinese woman's admission to the country were also based on her dependent status, that is, her relationship to a male relative and sponsor and his ability to support her.[81] Chinese women could — and increasingly did—apply for admission independently as teachers or students. Nevertheless, all of the exempt categories listed in the exclusion laws—merchant, student, teacher, diplomat, and traveler—were those that, in most cases, only men could take advantage of in nineteenth- and early-twentieth-century China. Most women were thus not eligible to enter independently. From 1910 to 1924, of the total number of women who entered the country, 2,107 women (27 percent) entered as independent immigrants and 5,702 women (73 percent) entered as dependents. Most Chinese immigrant women, then, were dependent on men and their continuing relationships with them to gain entry to and to remain in the country. This dependent status both mirrored and strengthened American gender roles and ideology in U.S. immigration law. Women of all backgrounds immigrating independently not only were subject to the "likely to become a public charge" clause in immigration law, they were also considered morally suspect.[82] But the ways in which the gendered face of immigration law intersected with Chinese exclusion made Chinese women especially vulnerable to the unequal environment and opportunities that resulted.

Since most Chinese women derived their right to enter the country from their male relatives' immigration status, they were dependent upon their husbands and fathers even before they arrived in the United States. With the decision to migrate placed largely in the hands of male relatives, some Chinese women did not have the option to come to the United States at all. Moy Sau Bik, for example, was eligible to enter the country as a merchant's daughter, but her father sold or gave her immigration slot to a male cousin, and the sponsorship papers he filed with the immigration service list a son instead of a daughter. Acting on the prevailing patriarchal Chinese attitudes that privileged sons over daughters, Moy's father apparently believed that his nephew was more worthy of immigration than his own daughter. Ineligible to enter as an independent immigrant herself and without the sponsorship of her father, Moy Sau Bik was effectively excluded from the country until she entered as a merchant's wife in 1931.[83]

It is difficult to determine how many other families chose males to immigrate in the place of their female family members, but it is clear that there were simply more opportunities for males to come to the United States. This was especially true if the immigration involved fraudulent papers, which by the mid-1900s was increasingly the norm.[84] A 1925 investigation by the San Francisco immigration office, for example, revealed that most of the immigration slots claimed by exempt-class immigrants were for male children. During

TABLE 2. CHINESE WOMEN ADMITTED, BY CLASS, 1910–1924

Year	Merchant Wife No. (%)	Merchant Daughter No. (%)	Wife of U.S. Citizen No. (%)	New or Returning Merchant No.	Returning Laborer No. (%)	U.S. Citizen No. (%)	Student No. (%)	Teacher No.	Total Chinese Women Admitted (Including Other Classes)
1910	120 (35)	27 (8)	110 (32)	0	0	49 (14)	3	0	344
1911	136 (41)	19 (6)	80 (24)	0	0	69 (21)	5 (2)	0	329
1912	118 (32)	28 (8)	88 (24)	0	0	67 (18)	9 (2)	2	367
1913	155 (35)	28 (6)	126 (29)	0	1	95 (21)	19 (4)	0	442
1914	133 (33)	27 (7)	122 (30)	0	6 (2)	75 (19)	11 (3)	0	401
1915	107 (27)	15 (4)	106 (27)	2	7 (2)	55 (14)	29 (7)	0	394
1916	108 (29)	28 (7)	108 (29)	0	1	61 (16)	16 (4)	0	378
1917	111 (27)	23 (6)	110 (27)	2	8 (2)	102 (25)	2	0	409
1918	88 (20)	28 (7)	132 (31)	1	4	78 (18)	28 (7)	3	429
1919	91 (24)	24 (6)	91 (24)	2	7 (2)	50 (13)	33 (9)	0	377
1920	166 (30)	35 (6)	141 (25)	3	7 (1)	68 (12)	47 (8)	5	562
1921	271 (30)	59 (7)	290 (32)	3	15 (2)	119 (13)	59 (7)	4	896
1922	301 (26)	47 (4)	396 (34)	9	44 (4)	221 (19)	75 (6)	3	1,166
1923	319 (26)	56 (5)	387 (32)	4	43 (1)	238 (20)	52 (4)	4	1,208
1924	273 (21)	78 (6)	396 (31)	3	42 (3)	233 (18)	81 (6)	8	1,284
Total	2,756 (28)	522 (6)	2,848 (30)	29	185 (2)	1,580 (18)	469 (5)	29	9,565

Sources: See Table 1.

a three-month period, 256 Chinese men who were American citizens and held the proper return documents reentered the port. The group claimed a total of 719 children, 670 of whom were males and only 49 females. The commissioner of immigration pointed to the skewed sex ratio of the group's foreign-born children and suspected fraud. "While individual families may have boys and no girls," he wrote, "it is, of course, absurd to suppose that such a proportion of boys to girls could exist among the children of men of any race." The surplus number of sons claimed as dependents, the San Francisco office concluded, probably filled immigration slots intended for others.[85] Given such statistics, it is not difficult to conclude that many other women, like Moy Sau Bik, were deprived of their opportunities to immigrate in favor of their male relatives or other males who purchased their family's immigration papers.

The immigration procedures designed to process Chinese dependents during the exclusion era also served as barriers to entry. Chinese family members applying as dependents were held responsible for meeting two sets of requirements, while independent immigrants only had to satisfy one. Wives and children of merchants and citizens first had to reconfirm the exempt-class standing of the sponsor himself. They then had to prove that the relationship to their sponsor did indeed exist. Dependent immigrants were, in effect, tested twice. In most cases, both exempt status and relationship were eventually established without too much difficulty, and the wife, son, or daughter was admitted. It was not uncommon, however, for problems to arise.

Even if the exempt-class sponsor of a potential immigrant was a longtime resident of the United States, the investigations pertaining to his or her immigration status could be lengthy. Yong Shee, for example, was detained for two months in 1915 while immigration officials investigated the status of her husband, Lee Kan, a merchant in San Francisco and partner in Chong, Kee, and Company. Because she was unable to apply for admission independently, Yong Shee had to rely on her husband. Thus, when immigration officials began to scrutinize her husband's company's holdings in order to determine that it was a bona fide mercantile establishment, at stake was not only Yong Shee's right to enter and reenter the country but also the status of the business. The couple hired an attorney, rallied friends and acquaintances to their cause, and eventually gained admittance to the country.[86] In another case, Jung Shee was almost denied entry because a recent injury had prevented her husband from working and supporting her. Fearful that the lack of a male provider would make Jung Shee a public charge, immigration officials released her only with assurances from relatives and social workers that Jung would be able to support herself.[87] Dependent status had severe consequences even for Chinese American women who were citizens by virtue of their birth in the United States. Under the 1922 Cable Act, Chinese American women who married "aliens ineligible to citizenship" lost their citizenship and could face problems reentering the country.[88]

Defining Citizens: Exclusion and Chinese American Citizens

Some of the most significant issues raised by the Chinese exclusion laws involved Chinese Americans and their citizenship rights. Although the laws themselves were designed to regulate immigrants, the government's enforcement procedures extended to all Chinese, including those born in the United States who traveled abroad and sought reentry into the country. From 1894 to 1940, 97,143 Chinese claiming to be native-born citizens of the United States were readmitted into the country. They made up 48 percent of the total number of Chinese admitted.

Ideologies of race and citizenship acted in concert to extend the exclusion laws to include Americans of Chinese descent. Targeting Chinese Americans in this way was largely a result of the widespread support for Chinese exclusion in general, as well as the government's concern over illegal immigration, especially that involving Chinese who fraudulently claimed U.S. birth and citizenship. However, the idea that Chinese as a race were "unfit" for American citizenship, an argument resurrected from the 1870s, was also a motivating factor. All three of these factors combined to affect the ways in which Chinese American citizens were perceived and processed as they traveled to and from the United States. The conflation of the Chinese American citizen with the allegedly dangerous Chinese immigrant alien had an especially damaging effect on the Chinese community in America.

The argument that Chinese would not make good citizens had been a centerpiece of the anti-Chinese movement prior to 1882. In 1875, Representative Horace Page of California argued in Congress that Chinese were "a class of people wholly unworthy to be entrusted with the right of American citizenship." Citizenship among the Chinese, he continued, would only be used "for corrupt purposes by corrupt individuals."[89] Other politicians claimed that unlike "Aryan or European races," the Chinese lacked "sufficient brain capacity . . . to furnish motive power for self-government," having "no comprehension of any form of government but despotism."[90] In 1877, a congressional committee investigating Chinese immigration concluded that Chinese were "an

TABLE 3. CHINESE ADMITTED, BY CLASS, 1894–1940

Year	Total	Exempt Class		Returning Residents		U.S. Citizens	
		No.	%	No.	%	No.	%
1894	5,599	5,599	100	N/A	N/A	N/A	N/A
1895	2,075	2,075	100	N/A	N/A	N/A	N/A
1896	3,616	3,510	97	106	3	N/A	N/A
1897	6,517	5,478	84	1,039	16	N/A	N/A
1898	7,195	5,698	79	1,497	21	N/A	N/A
1899	5,718	3,925	69	1,793	31	N/A	N/A
1900	5,799	3,802	66	1,997	34	N/A	N/A
1901	4,064	1,784	44	2,280	56	N/A	N/A
1902	3,768	1,273	34	2,495	66	N/A	N/A
1903	2,982	1,523	51	1,459	49	N/A	N/A
1904	2,676	1,284	48	1,392	52	N/A	N/A
1905	3,153	1,348	43	1,171	37	634	20
1906	2,720	714	26	1,091	40	915	34
1907	3,215	788	25	1,498	47	929	29
1908	4,563	1,298	28	1,656	36	1,609	35
1909	6,245	1,818	29	1,897	30	2,530	41
1910	5,792	1,777	31	1,906	33	2,109	36
1911	4,986	1,142	23	2,205	44	1,639	33
1912	5,253	1,301	25	2,196	42	1,756	33
1913	5,496	1,303	24	2,022	37	2,171	40
1914	5,563	1,481	27	1,881	34	2,201	40
1915	5,467	1,628	30	1,849	34	1,990	36
1916	4,984	1,503	30	1,549	31	1,932	39
1917	4,567	1,240	27	1,309	29	2,018	44
1918	2,887	930	32	1,011	35	946	33
1919	2,969	1,084	37	930	31	955	32
1920	4,172	1,566	38	845	20	1,761	42
1921	7,315	2,806	38	1,270	17	3,239	44
1922	9,391	3,116	33	2,231	24	4,044	43

TABLE 3. CONTINUED

		Exempt Class		Returning Residents		U.S. Citizens	
Year	Total	No.	%	No.	%	No.	%
1923	9,889	2,766	28	2,433	25	4,690	47
1924	9,806	2,483	25	2,569	26	4,754	48
1925	5,909	911	15	1,975	33	3,023	51
1926	5,435	1,282	24	1,757	32	2,396	44
1927	6,339	1,349	21	1,814	29	3,176	50
1928	6,618	1,423	22	1,919	29	3,276	50
1929	7,045	1,716	24	1,795	25	3,534	50
1930	6,564	1,636	25	1,708	26	3,220	49
1931	6,456	1,175	18	1,697	26	3,584	56
1932	5,625	823	15	1,550	28	3,252	58
1933	4,593	653	14	1,155	25	2,785	61
1934	4,335	420	10	1,018	23	2,897	67
1935	4,687	497	11	896	19	3,294	70
1936	3,972	353	9	308	8	3,311	83
1937	5,112	905	18	709	14	3,498	68
1938	7,199	967	13	836	12	5,396	75
1939	5,495	984	18	183	3	4,328	79
1940	4,472	979	22	142	3	3,351	75
Total	248,298	84,116	35	67,039	29	97,143	48

Sources: U.S. Treasury Department, *Annual Reports of the Commissioner-General of Immigration* (Washington, D.C.: 1898–1902); U.S. Department of Commerce and Labor, *Annual Reports of the Commissioner-General of Immigration* (Washington: GPO, 1903–11); U.S. Department of Labor, *Annual Reports of the Commissioner-General of Immigration* (Washington: GPO, 1912–24); Helen Chen, "Chinese Immigration into the United States: An Analysis of Changes in Immigration Policies" (Ph.D. diss., Brandeis University, 1980), 181.

Note: These figures do not include Chinese allowed to pass in transit through the United States. N/A = figures not available. Due to inconsistencies in the sources, total percentages may not equal 100.

indigestible mass in the community." Prohibiting them from citizenship was not only desirable, the committee concluded, it was also a "necessary measure" for the good of the public.[91] The Chinese Exclusion Act legitimized this belief by barring all Chinese immigrants from naturalized citizenship, but the question of birthright citizenship for Chinese born in the United States remained unresolved until 1898.

Following the passage of the Chinese Exclusion Act, various politicians and anti-Chinese spokespersons attempted to extend the logic used to bar Chinese immigrants from naturalization to those born in the United States. Because Chinese were incapable of assimilation, they charged, even the second generation born in the United States would inherit the deficient characteristics that made their parents so objectionable to Americans. The first court case to rule on the question of birthright citizenship involved Look Tin Sing, a fourteen-year-old boy born in Mendocino, California, who attempted to re-enter the United States in 1884 after studying in China. As U.S.-born Chinese were not explicitly listed as an exempt class in the original Exclusion Act, and because Look Tin Sing had no other documentation proving his membership in another exempt class, he was denied entry by immigration officials in San Francisco. Look appealed, and the U.S. District Court for the Northern District of California reversed the decision and ruled in his favor. Declaring that the Fourteenth Amendment provided that "all persons born or naturalized in the United States" were citizens, the court ruled that Look Tin Sing was indeed a citizen and that the Exclusion Act did not apply to him.[92]

Dissatisfied with the court's decision, anti-Chinese exclusionists attempted to reverse it and the birthright citizenship it granted to Chinese. The forum they chose was the case of Wong Kim Ark, a San Francisco native returning from a visit to China in 1895. Born in 1873 to parents who ran a mercantile establishment in San Francisco's Chinatown, Wong traveled to China with his parents in 1890 and returned to the United States later that year. Collector Timothy Phelps promptly readmitted Wong into the country as a citizen. In 1895, Wong made a second visit to China. Upon his return, the notoriously anti-Chinese collector John H. Wise denied Wong readmission, basing his decision on his belief that Wong was not a citizen of the United States and, as such, excludable under the exclusion laws. Wong was placed under custody of the U.S. marshall and detained on board the steamship.[93] Wong hired Thomas Riordan, a prominent attorney in San Francisco, and filed a writ of habeas corpus in the federal district court alleging that he was being "unlawfully confined and restrained of his liberty on board the steamship 'Coptic.'" He also claimed the

Wong Kim Ark, c. 1898. A native-born Chinese American citizen, Wong Kim Ark was denied reentry into the United States in 1895 after a trip to visit his parents in China. He appealed, and his case eventually went to the U.S. Supreme Court, which affirmed that all persons born in the United States, including Chinese whose parents themselves were ineligible for citizenship, were indeed birthright citizens under the Fourteenth Amendment. Courtesy of the National Archives, Pacific Region, San Bruno, California.

right to reenter as a native-born citizen under the Fourteenth Amendment, stating that he had "always subjected himself to the jurisdiction and dominion of the United States, and had been taxed, recognized and treated as a citizen of the United States."[94]

Henry S. Foote, the U.S. district attorney, argued the case on behalf of the U.S. government. In his opinion, the question at hand was whether or not native-born Chinese could be considered citizens if their parents were not and could never become naturalized citizens. Foote argued that birth within the United States did not necessarily confer the right of citizenship, especially in the case of Chinese, who were unassimilable and unfit for citizenship. Foote claimed that Wong had been made a citizen only "by accident of birth" on American soil, but his "education and political affiliations" remained "entirely alien" to the United States.[95] Since both of Wong Kim Ark's parents were "subjects of the Emperor of China," Foote continued, Wong himself inherited this nationality and was also a "Chinese person and a subject of the Emperor of China." A child born in the United States may "nominally be a citizen" but if he is raised by alien Chinese parents, the district attorney reasoned, the child remained "an alien loyal to the country of his father and indifferent to the country of his birth."[96] Conflating "Chineseness" with "alienness" and implying that being "Chinese" and being "American" were incompatible, Foote declared that Wong could not possibly be considered an American citizen, for he had "been at all times, by reason of his race, language, color, and dress, a Chinese person."[97] Allowing Chinese such as Wong Kim Ark to be recognized as citizens, Foote warned, would be extremely dangerous. Foote asked, "Is it possible that any Court in the United States will deliberately force upon us as natural born citizens, persons who must necessarily be a constant menace to the welfare of our Country?" He answered, "We submit that such things cannot be without imperilling [sic] the very existence of our Country."[98] The district attorney concluded his brief for the court with the extreme position that even if Wong Kim Ark was found to be a citizen by birth, he should still be excluded by the Exclusion Act, because he was a laborer excludable by law.[99]

Judge William Morrow of the U.S. District Court for the Northern District of California soundly refuted Foote's arguments. "It is enough that he is born here whatever the status of his parents," he wrote. "No citizen can be excluded from this country except in punishment for crime. The petitioner must be allowed to land, and it is so ordered."[100] U.S. District Attorney Foote appealed the decision but lost again in the U.S. Supreme Court in 1898. *United States v. Wong Kim Ark* affirmed that regardless of race, all persons born in the United States were, in fact, native-born citizens of the United States and entitled to all of the rights that citizenship offered.[101]

The rulings in the *Look Tin Sing* and *Wong Kim Ark* cases established the legal parameters in citizenship cases. Immigration officials, however, continued to wield enormous influence in the processing of returning U.S. citizens' applications. Left without any court-defined standards of *how* citizenship would be determined in such cases, immigrant inspectors established their own means of measuring citizenship status and "American-ness." In cases of returning citizens, the ways in which officials interpreted and defined these categories were inextricably tied to racialized assumptions that positioned Chinese Americans as fraudulent or inferior citizens and perpetuated the construction of all Chinese as "perpetual foreigners."[102]

Chinese claiming citizenship thus had to undergo the same lengthy investigative and interrogation processes to which aliens were subjected in order to prove their nativity and their right to reenter the country. Proof of birth in the United States was not easily verified. Because Chinese women often delivered their children at home, many citizens did not have birth certificates. After the 1906 earthquake and fire in San Francisco destroyed all birth records in the city, even if Chinese had such records they were nearly impossible to find. The immigration service was thus forced to accept applicant and witness testimony to prove birthplace.

Much like the ways in which relationships to white Americans were seen as favorable markers of class status in merchant cases, they were similarly interpreted to illustrate "American-ness" in citizenship cases. Beginning in 1892, a Department of Treasury mandate required Chinese to have two non-Chinese, that is, white, witnesses to verify their claims of nativity.[103] In 1895, as a means of determining his nativity, Wong Kim Ark was asked whether any white men in San Francisco knew he had been born there. Wong readily produced two white witnesses who remembered him as a young boy on Sacramento Street.[104] Yee Kim, returning to the United States in 1900, was asked the same question and was landed without any delay, largely because of the seven affidavits of well-known white citizens of Los Angeles in his file.[105] However, most Chinese Americans did not have these kinds of connections, for in the segregated Chinese communities in the United States, white witnesses to the birth of Chinese children were extremely rare. As one incredulous immigration official who disagreed with this ruling requiring white witnesses asked his superiors, "Who else [but the Chinese relatives of the applicant] would be likely to have the knowledge required as a witness in a case of native birth, if not those closely related to the party born?"[106] By 1902, the bureau had amended its regulations to allow the admission of citizens based solely on Chinese testimony.[107] Nevertheless, in practice, the presence of white witnesses continued to be viewed as favorable to a case, and Chinese American organizations continued to complain about it. In 1910, the Native Sons of the Golden State, a civil rights organization founded by Chinese American citizens, wrote to the secretary of labor that white witnesses were increasingly difficult to find. They were "departing from the country, dying, or removing to parts unknown," thus making it almost impossible for citizens to prove their birth in the United States.[108]

Returning U.S. citizens of Chinese descent were also judged according to how well they could speak English, how much they conformed to American customs and dress, and how well they could identify local landmarks and recite basic facts about U.S. history. It was not uncommon for immigration officials to note favorably that an applicant claiming citizenship dressed in American-style clothing and could speak English fluently. In recommending that applicant Moy Goon be landed in 1905, for example, immigrant inspector Alfred W. Parker noted that Moy was "an extraordinarily bright, intelligent Chinaman, dresses in American clothes, and speaks good English. By appearances and conduct, I should say that his claim to American birth is quite reasonable." Another reported that Moy used the American name "Charlie" and was "thoroughly Americanized" and "highly respected."[109]

Chinese applicants claiming citizenship were also commonly required to pass a test in spoken English. Fon Toy, a native applying for reentry in 1905, responded in English to nearly half of the questions put to him during his examination, including those asked by inspector H. C. Kennah:

Q: How much can you speak?
A: I can ask a person's name and how much money will you give me.
Q: Well, let us hear you.
A: How much money you give me?
Q: You understand "wash clothes?"
A: Yes, wash clothes, iron collars, cuffs, shirts, and drawers.[110]

Largely because of Fon's ability to speak and understand some English, Kennah concluded that he was indeed a native-born citizen. In another instance, Lim Tong, who claimed to have voted for Benjamin Harrison in the 1888 presidential election, gave his 1905 testimony in English and was also landed easily.[111] On the other hand, when Lee Toy Mock, a citizen who was arrested on suspicion of being in the country illegally, failed to respond when he was examined in English and when "asked to do things in the English language," Inspector P. J. Farrelly concluded that Lee was not a citizen but an "alien [who] has not the slightest knowledge of the English language."[112]

Chinese American citizens were also tested on their geographical knowledge, history, and familiarity with San Francisco or their claimed hometown. In 1905, Woo Wee Nuen, who was born in San Francisco, was grilled about specific dates and locations of events in San Francisco Chinatown: "Did you go to the Mid-Winter Fair? When was it held? Do you remember any fire at the Hong Far Lao restaurant? Do you remember any procession in honor of the opening of any Joss House in San Francisco? Can you name any streets in Chinatown here? Any theatres? What streets are the principal Joss houses on?"[113] Lee Toy Mock was also asked equally detailed questions about the 1906 earthquake and fire in San Francisco and what Lee had been doing at the time of the quake. Inspector P. J. Farrelly peppered Lee with questions supposedly designed to determine if Lee was really in San Francisco in 1906: "Did it happen while you were asleep or were you awake when it occurred?" "Was it after dinner or before dinner?" "Was it after or before breakfast?" "What time did you have your breakfast?"[114]

Although some of these tests certainly helped immigration officials to expose fraud, the standards they set for Chinese American citizens were high, and sometimes unrealistic. The language test was especially challenging for many Chinese Americans. Well into the mid-twentieth century, most Chinese immigrants and their American-born children still resided in segregated urban enclaves and had little contact with non-Chinese. Although many American-born children did attend public school and learned English, not all of them learned to speak the language fluently.

As late as 1934, Lee You Fong struggled in vain against the government's institutionalized conflation of citizenship with the ability to speak English. The twenty-five-year-old Lee had never learned to speak English formally and instead spoke a very limited form of pidgin English common in Chinese communities. He had never attended an American school, and because he worked and lived in the segregated community of Chinatown, he had also never learned the language on his own. At his deportation hearing, Inspector F. O. Seidle framed the case against Lee on this lack of training in English. Seidle asked one of Lee's witnesses, "Can you offer any explanation why it is that he is unable to speak the English language with any degree of fluency whatsoever?" The relative answered, "He cannot speak English because he has not attended any American school. . . . There are some native born men [in Chinatown] who cannot speak English." Seidle, however, was not convinced. Lee's inability to speak English, as well as other inconsistencies in his case, led to his deportation.[115]

Even demonstrated fluency in English, proper documentation, "Americanized" appearance, and well-respected white witnesses did not insure that an American-born citizen would be granted prompt reentry or would not be harassed. In 1924 and 1926, Chinese American citizens living in Hawaii and traveling to the mainland for temporary visits complained bitterly and loudly to the commissioner-general of immigration. These citizens, some of whom were territorial government officials, charged that while they carried the necessary documents establishing their native status and their right to enter the mainland United States, immigration officials in San Francisco needlessly detained them and gruffly grilled them about their native status.[116] Edna and Sarah Hing, born in Springfield, Massachusetts, also complained of mistreatment during their return to the United States through San Francisco. Their immigration files note that they were fluent in English and that the immigration service had copies of their birth certificates, as well as affidavits from white family friends in Massachusetts. Nevertheless, the two experienced "a great deal of red-tape" upon their return. When they planned to go abroad for a second trip in 1923, Edna wrote to the commissioner of immigration, "We don't wish to leave the United States unless we're sure of getting back."[117] Classified as U.S. citizens under the Constitution, Chinese Americans found that this status offered them little protection from the Chinese exclusion laws. Reinforcing the belief that Chinese as a race were unassimilable, immigration officials approached citizenship cases with an institutionalized suspicion. As later chapters will discuss, after 1906 the increase in immigrants making fraudulent claims to citizenship further exacerbated the situation.

Conclusion

After immigration policies are enacted into law, they take on lives of their own when they are interpreted and enforced on a day-to-day basis. The enforcement of the Chinese exclusion laws reveals how popular stereotypes became embedded in state policy and how immigration laws are used to control immigrant populations, define American race, gender, and class relations, and mark the parameters of citizenship. As Chapter 4 illustrates, the Chinese in America felt the adverse effects of the exclusion laws immediately, but they did not stop immigrating. Instead, they protested and challenged the policies and learned how to find and exploit the few passageways to the United States still open to them.

CHAPTER FOUR

I clasped my hands in parting with my brothers and classmates.
Because of the mouth, I hastened to cross the American ocean.
How was I to know that the western barbarians had lost their hearts
and reason?
With a hundred kinds of oppressive laws, they mistreat us Chinese.
—Anonymous Poem Carved into the Barrack Walls,
Angel Island Immigration Station

ONE HUNDRED KINDS
OF OPPRESSIVE LAWS

The Chinese Response to American Exclusion

THE CHINESE EXCLUSION laws affected every aspect of the lives of Chinese immigrants and the Chinese in America. They determined who would be able to immigrate, they shaped immigration strategies, and they influenced Chinese activism during the exclusion era. Although the laws severely limited Chinese immigration, they did not prevent Chinese immigrants from entering the country. Worsening political and economic conditions in China combined with employment opportunities in the United States encouraged thousands of Chinese to immigrate in spite of U.S. attempts to exclude them. The estimated 300,955 Chinese who from 1882 to 1943 successfully gained admission into the United States for the first time or as returning residents and native-born citizens did so by constantly adapting their migration patterns to fit the shifting terrain of the exclusion laws.

Immigrant correspondence, newspapers, and government records demonstrate how Chinese formed and maintained transnational networks that helped to facilitate migration during the exclusion era.[1] That Chinese were also consistent and vocal critics of the discriminatory American immigration laws helped as well.[2] These efforts, however, ultimately failed to overturn the policy of exclusion. Consequently, by 1910, Chinese in America had shifted their strategies from diplomatic and legal attacks against the policy of exclusion itself to campaigns to reform the ways in which the laws were enforced. This tactical change was shaped by class- and citizenship-based differences within the Chinese community and reflected attempts by merchants and Chinese American citizens to distinguish themselves from other Chinese applying for admission or readmission. Seeking to protect their own limited advantage as members of the merchant class or as American citizens under the law, these two groups eventually turned away from appeals and actions based on racial solidarity. At the same time, individual Chinese employed daily acts of resistance. They astutely conformed to or evaded the regulations established to exclude them. They also relied upon well-organized networks of family and friends, immigration lawyers, and sympathetic whites. In the end, many managed to find the means to immigrate within the confines of the laws and the rigid and restrictive ways in which they were enforced.

In Search of Gold Mountain: Chinese Immigration Patterns

The Chinese who emigrated to the United States were but one segment of a much larger population of Chinese who sought new lives abroad as part of an international migration of labor that stretched from Southeast Asia to South America. Chinese bound for the United States during the late nineteenth and early twentieth centuries came almost exclusively from the southeastern coastal regions of China. More than 60 percent of the Chinese in the United States today trace their roots to the districts of Namhoi, Punyu, Shuntak, Sunwui, Sunning (renamed Toisan), Hoiping, Yanping, and Heungshan in the Pearl River delta in Guangdong province. Scholars estimate that over 70 percent of the Chinese living in California in the nineteenth century came from Toisan, Sunwui, Hoiping, and Yanping alone.[5]

The inhabitants of the Pearl River delta region, the seat of European and American trade in China, initially benefited from the infusion of international capital. Over time, however, the delta suffered from the adverse effects of imperialism in the form of increased taxes and the unequal economic relationship between China and its trading partners. Overpopulation, ethnic and civil conflicts, and a range of natural disasters created further instability. Residents of the region who could no longer make a living on the farms or as laborers first went to larger cities. Such migration often became the initial steps to sojourns abroad. Like other immigrants to America, Chinese were not all from the poorest segment of society but were members of the middling classes who migrated in order to accumulate additional wealth and to maintain their family's prosperity and status in China for future generations.[4]

In the early twentieth century, China experienced further economic, political, and social instability as attempts to restore order under the Qing Empire faltered and Japan defeated China in the Sino-Japanese War (1894–95). European imperialist powers tightened their grip on China's economy by forcibly occupying more territory and port cities. The Chinese revolution led by Sun Yat-sen in 1911 failed to bring the needed stability. Powerful warlords emerged as the power brokers in many parts of the country, and foreign imperialism continued to hinder China's economy. Internal rivalry between Sun Yat-sen's Guomindang (Nationalist) Party and the Communists beginning in the late 1920s and a full-scale war with Japan in the 1930s continued to foster economic, social, and political insecurity and provided additional incentives for Chinese to seek work and even permanent resettlement abroad.

In the United States, industrialization and the expansion of American capitalism created an incessant need for labor, and employers remained more than willing to hire Chinese laborers in spite of the exclusion laws. In 1905, labor contractors in the American West even complained to immigration officials that because of their strict enforcement procedures, there were "fewer Chinese available every year." They were eager to hire Chinese labor whenever possible, for, the contractor explained, "we would put to work every Chinaman we could get." Labor shortages were so rife that another contractor told the immigration service that he was unable to take contracts because he could not secure the necessary Chinese laborers.[5] Five years later, immigration officials in California admitted that as a result of the exclusion of Chinese and Japanese laborers, there was a "large demand for all kinds of unskilled labor in this State." Farms and railroad companies offered "all sorts of inducements" to get laborers into the country, and the California state labor commissioner admitted that the Chinese labor shortage was a severe blow to the state's agricultural economy.[6] But contractors were not the only employers eager for Chinese labor. Immigration officials who in their official capacity approved of restricting immigration from Asia were at the same time hiring Chinese servants to work in their households. In 1905, Victor H. Metcalf, one of the leading anti-Chinese politicians in California and the secretary of the Department of Commerce and Labor, which supervised the Bureau of Immigration, made inquiries in San Francisco about hiring Chinese servants for his Washington household.[7]

Chinese were no longer dominating the labor market at the turn of the century, as they had prior to exclusion, but the economic incentive for Chinese to continue immigrating remained high.[8] The low wages a laundry worker earned in the United States were still better than what he could earn in China. During a productive week in the 1920s, for example, a laundryman could earn up to fifty dollars. He could generally support his family in China on that salary if he was frugal.[9] When the Great Depression caused a dramatic wage decrease (to only twenty-five dollars a week), the laundryman was still able to support his family. Sociologist Paul Siu found that in the 1920s and 1930s, immigrants with a little bit of savings were still able to buy a laundry for the relatively low sum of $2,800–$3,000.[10] Such opportunities continued to lure Chinese immigrants to the United States, and although Chinese did not find the mountains of gold they had wished for, they did find jobs that could better provide for their families than the vocations available to them in China.

For some Chinese, the exclusion laws did act as a major deterrent. Fong Ing Bong, an applicant for admission in 1907, explained to immigration officials that he "understood it was impossible to get in before," so he did not even try.[11] Many others, however, viewed immigration as the only means available to improve their economic and social standing in an increasingly unstable and tumultuous environment. Frequently, migration to the United States was regarded as nothing less than a means of survival. As Lee Chi Yet, orphaned at a young age in Poon Lung Cheng, Toisan, put it, he was "kill[ing] himself for nothing" as a farmer in the early 1900s. With the situation in his village desperate, he emigrated to the United States in 1917.[12] Conditions were equally bad in Jeong Foo Louie's village of Kung Yick, Toisan; 40 percent of its inhabitants traveled to the United States in the early twentieth century.[13] Like the villages of Lee Chi Yet and Jeong Foo Louie, others in Guangdong province were filled with talk about going to the United States and fantastic tales of wealth in *Gam Saan*—Gold Mountain.

Despite the restrictions on laborers in the exclusion laws, Chinese from the farming and laboring classes continued to make up a bulk of the immigrants. Eighty to 90 percent of exclusion-era immigrants were young, able-bodied men who planned to work and send money home.[14] As Table 4 indicates, returning laborers and U.S. citizens (who most often took laboring positions) made up 56 percent of all admissions and readmissions into the country from 1910 to 1924, while new and returning merchants, as well as sons of merchants, made up a total of 30 percent of all admissions and readmissions during the same period. As conditions worsened in the Pearl River delta, an increasing

TABLE 4. CHINESE MEN ADMITTED, BY CLASS, 1910-1924

Year	New Merchant No. (%)	Returning Merchant No. (%)	U.S. Citizen No. (%)	Returning Laborer No. (%)	Merchant Son No. (%)	Total (Including Other Classes) No.
1910	228 (4)	869 (16)	2,060 (37)	1,037 (19)	882 (16)	5,606
1911	199 (4)	1,092 (23)	1,570 (33)	1,113 (23)	404 (9)	4,778
1912	170 (3)	1,093 (22)	1,689 (34)	1,092 (22)	412 (8)	5,029
1913	105 (2)	986 (19)	2,076 (40)	1,035 (20)	555 (11)	5,220
1914	180 (3)	881 (16)	2,126 (40)	994 (19)	647 (12)	5,372
1915	238 (5)	958 (18)	1,935 (37)	882 (17)	624 (12)	5,267
1916	242 (5)	859 (18)	1,871 (39)	689 (14)	605 (13)	4,815
1917	180 (4)	689 (16)	1,906 (44)	610 (14)	560 (13)	4,365
1918	128 (5)	520 (19)	868 (32)	487 (18)	274 (10)	2,737
1919	136 (5)	512 (17)	905 (31)	411 (14)	190 (6)	2,963
1920	102 (2)	525 (13)	1,693 (41)	313 (8)	443 (11)	4,128
1921	284 (4)	702 (10)	3,120 (42)	353 (5)	986 (13)	7,427
1922	642 (7)	762 (9)	3,823 (43)	1,423 (16)	1,012 (11)	8,859
1923	495 (5)	978 (11)	4,452 (48)	1,410 (15)	1,002 (11)	9,350
1924	452 (5)	1,226 (13)	4,521 (48)	1,298 (14)	745 (8)	9,410
Total	3,781	12,652	34,615	13,147	9,341	85,326

Sources: U.S. Department of Commerce and Labor, *Annual Reports of the Commissioner-General of Immigration* (Washington: GPO, 1910–11); U.S. Department of Labor, *Annual Reports of the Commissioner-General of Immigration* (Washington: GOP, 1912–24).

number of nonlaborer Chinese immigrated to the United States as well. By the 1920s, village storekeepers, Hong Kong merchants, office clerks, politicians, schoolteachers, students, seamen, and others were seeking fortunes in the United States.[15]

Chinese male outnumbered Chinese female immigrants throughout the exclusion era. Patriarchal cultural values that discouraged and even forbade "decent" Chinese women from traveling abroad, traditional patterns of male sojourning and transnational family structures, anti-Chinese legislation, and the expense and trouble associated with immigration all discouraged Chinese women from joining their husbands, brothers, and fathers in the United States. Over time, however, changing attitudes about gender roles in China, the easing of cultural restrictions on Chinese female emigration, an expansion of the exempt categories, and an increase in educational and employment opportunities in the United States prompted an increase in female migration.[16] Immigration authorities also began to turn their attention from controlling Chinese prostitution to stemming the problem of Chinese illegal immigration, which, as will be discussed in Chapter 6, tended to involve males. An estimated 40,000 Chinese women were admitted into the United States from 1882 to 1943. Although the numbers of male and female immigrants were never equal, immigration statistics do indicate a trend toward parity over time.[17] In 1900, women made up only 0.7 percent of the total number of Chinese immigrants entering the country. In 1910, that figure had risen to 9.7 percent. In 1920, they made up 20 percent of incoming immigrants, and by 1930, the figure had increased to 25.7 percent. These statistics do not include American citizens of Chinese descent.

Chinese female immigrants were a diverse group, but the class biases in the laws continued to structure their immigration patterns. From 1910 to 1924, the largest group of Chinese female applicants (34 percent) were either wives or daughters of Chinese merchants. Thirty percent were wives of U.S. citizens, and 18 percent were U.S. citizens. Only 5 percent of female applicants were students. The remaining women applied for admission as new or returning merchants (often taking over a business from a deceased husband), returning laborers, teachers, or under other miscellaneous categories. (See Chapter 3, Table 2.) The increase in female migration beginning in the second half of the exclusion era reflects a significant change in Chinese immigration patterns away from temporary stays in America and toward permanent settlement. This does not mean that the exclusion laws had any less of an impact on immigration patterns and admission processes. Rather, Chinese grew increasingly adept at challenging and negotiating their exclusion from the United States.

Transnational Migration and Its Limitations

Chinese immigrated to the United States for a variety of reasons, but many often came as sojourners—immigrants who worked abroad temporarily with the intention of returning home. Practiced in Asia for centuries and by European, Asian, and Mexican immigrants to the United States during the nineteenth and twentieth centuries, sojourning benefited both the immigrant and

TABLE 5. CHINESE ADMITTED, BY SEX, 1870–1960

| Year | Males | | Females | | Total |
	No.	%	No.	%	
1870	14,624	92.9	1,116	7.1	15,740
1871	6,786	95.1	349	4.9	7,135
1872	7,605	97.7	183	2.3	7,788
1873	19,403	95.6	889	4.4	20,292
1874	13,533	98.2	243	1.8	13,776
1875	16,055	97.7	382	2.3	16,437
1876	22,521	98.9	260	1.1	22,781
1877	10,518	99.3	76	0.7	10,594
1878	8,641	96.1	351	3.9	8,992
1879	9,264	96.5	340	3.5	9,604
1880	5,732	98.8	70	1.2	5,802
1881	11,815	99.4	75	0.6	11,890
1882	39,463	99.7	116	0.3	39,579
1883	7,987	99.5	44	0.5	8,031
1884	241	86.4	38	13.6	279
1885	12	54.5	10	45.5	22
1886	25	62.5	15	37.5	40
1887	8	80.0	2	20.0	10
1888	21	80.8	5	19.2	26
1889	90	76.3	28	23.7	118
1890	1,401	81.6	315	18.4	1,716
1891	2,608	92.0	228	8.0	2,836
1892–95	N/A	N/A	N/A	N/A	N/A
1896	1,382	95.9	59	4.1	1,441
1897	3,334	99.1	29	0.9	3,363
1898	2,061	99.5	10	0.5	2,071
1899	1,627	99.3	11	0.7	1,638
1900	1,241	99.3	9	0.7	1,250
1901	2,413	98.4	39	1.6	2,452
1902	1,587	91.3	44	2.7	1,631

TABLE 5. CONTINUED

Year	Males		Females		Total
	No.	%	No.	%	
1903	2,152	98.2	40	1.8	2,192
1904	4,209	97.3	118	2.7	4,327
1905	1,883	95.5	88	4.5	1,971
1906	1,397	94.1	88	5.9	1,485
1907	706	91.7	64	8.3	770
1908	1,177	93.2	86	6.8	1,263
1909	1,706	92.7	135	7.3	1,841
1910	1,598	90.3	172	9.7	1,770
1911	1,124	86.0	183	14.0	1,307
1912	1,367	85.0	241	15.0	1,608
1913	1,692	83.7	330	16.3	2,022
1914	2,052	87.2	302	12.8	2,354
1915	2,182	88.4	287	11.6	2,469
1916	1,962	87.6	277	12.4	2,239
1917	1,563	84.8	280	15.2	1,843
1918	1,276	81.0	300	19.0	1,576
1919	1,425	84.0	272	16.0	1,697
1920	1,719	80.0	429	20.0	2,148
1921	3,304	82.3	713	17.7	4,017
1922	3,622	81.1	843	18.9	4,465
1923	3,239	79.5	835	20.5	4,074
1924	3,732	79.9	938	20.1	4,670
1925	1,526	88.7	195	11.3	1,721
1926	1,182	86.0	193	14.0	1,375
1927	830	79.0	221	21.0	1,051
1928	668	71.8	263	28.2	931
1929	800	74.7	271	25.3	1,071
1930	721	74.3	249	25.7	970
1931	523	69.9	225	30.1	748
1932	317	58.2	228	41.8	534

TABLE 5. CONTINUED

Year	Males		Females		Total
	No.	%	No.	%	
1933–47	N/A	N/A	N/A	N/A	N/A
1948	257	7.2	3,317	92.8	3,574
1949	242	9.7	2,248	90.3	2,490
1950	110	8.5	1,179	91.5	1,289
1951	126	11.6	957	88.4	1,083
1952	118	10.2	1,034	89.8	1,152
1953	203	18.6	890	81.4	1,093
1954	1,511	55.0	1,236	45.0	2,747
1955	1,261	48.0	1,367	52.0	2,628
1956	2,007	46.0	2,443	54.0	4,450
1957	2,487	48.5	2,636	51.5	5,123
1958	1,396	44.0	1,799	56.0	3,195
1959	2,846	47.2	3,185	52.8	6,031
1960	1,873	51.0	1,799	49.0	3,672

Sources: Fu-ju Liu, "A Comparative Demographic Study of Native-Born and Foreign-Born Chinese Populations in the United States" (Ph.D. diss., University of Michigan, 1953), 223; Helen Chen, "Chinese Immigration into the United States: An Analysis of Changes in Immigration Policies" (Ph.D. diss., Brandeis University, 1980), 201.
Note: N/A = figures not available.

the family and community he left behind.[18] Most of the young men in the southern Chinese countryside tried to leave by the time they were of working age, and in some villages, as many as 80 percent of the men went overseas. The remaining village population relied on them for income.[19] The United States was just one of the destinations of Chinese immigrants during the early twentieth century, but it had a special appeal to the Chinese. Immigrant Wong Ngum Yin reflected most sojourners' hopes in a 1916 letter to his elder brother. "After years of planning and trading [in America]," Wong wrote, "property [in China] is regained, hundreds of *mous* of fields acquired and a mansion for the use of my maiden [wife] and myself is built. I clothe myself in the finest of fur garments and mount a fat horse. Upon bended knees I care for my parents and freely provide for my family. All these [are] my desires!"[20]

Chinese female immigrants on Angel Island, c. 1917. Although the exclusion laws themselves and the ways in which they were enforced made it extremely difficult for Chinese women to immigrate to the United States, they did so in increasing numbers by the 1910s and 1920s. Here, a Chinese interpreter and two immigrant inspectors review applicants' paperwork. Courtesy of the California Department of Parks and Recreation.

A successful sojourn involved not only the accumulation of wealth but also the maintenance of transnational economic and familial ties between the sojourner and his family and village back home. Evelyn Nakano Glenn and Madeline Hsu have demonstrated that such "split-household families" were created and perpetuated by the sojourning strategy but not destroyed by it.[21] Immigrant letters reveal that Chinese sent a constant stream of remittances home to their villages. One envelope seized by the Bureau of Immigration listed as its contents "$15.00 in three gold pieces, for my father Louie Yee Ung of Lung Tsue village, from son Louie Sere Mow." Another included "one $5.00 gold piece, for my son Louie Kim Ming of Ngoot Ming village, from Louie Yee Fon, Stockton, California."[22] Sojourners in the United States could arrange to send remittances home through *Gam Saan jong,* or, literally, "Golden Mountain firms," which were based both in the United States and in Hong Kong. Prospective immigrants in Hong Kong could also use these companies to buy tickets, arrange health exams, secure proper documentation, fill out consular forms, and purchase foodstuffs and other items for the long journey across the Pacific.[23]

Letters sojourners received from family members in China kept them abreast of the latest developments in the family and village, and the letters sojourners sent helped to preserve their patriarchal roles as fathers and heads of households. Wong Jou, for example, who worked as a store clerk in San Diego, was informed regularly of the successes and failures of family members, marriages and births, land conditions, the development of the village, and other news through letters from his wife, Lee Shee, and their son Wong Cheung. A 1926 letter Wong Jou received from son Wong Cheung contained a bevy of information: the youngest son, Wong Fai, was "entirely cured" from his addiction to opium; the price of unshelled rice was low, so the family had discontinued leasing land for rice cultivation; cousin Wong Chor's son was to be married soon; mother's health was failing and she thus needed some deer horn; and the public roads in the district were recently completed so that automobiles were now able to be used there. Wong Jou's presence was strongly felt in his home village of Kue Tou, Heungshan, through his own letters as well. In 1934, when he received a letter informing him that Wong Fai had resumed his opium smoking, Wong Jou, reinforcing his role as father and disciplinarian, replied with a severe rebuke to his youngest son to put an end to the habit.[24]

Letters and remittances bound Chinese immigrants to their families and villages, but these ties could be fragile. It was not uncommon for the *Chung Sai Yat Po*, San Francisco's main Chinese-language daily newspaper, to print advertisements of Chinese looking for lost relatives. In 1906, a relative of Lam Chang from Toisan placed a notice in the paper stating that Lam had been in the United States "for more than twenty years and has not sent any letters home." "If any relatives or friends knows his whereabouts," the notice continued, "would you please let him write to me?"[25] A worried mother inquired about her son Ng Sou from Namhoi in another notice: "He has not sent information or money home. We do not know his whereabouts and whether he is still alive."[26] Deer Cheung's two brothers placed an ad asking readers who might know his whereabouts to "persuade him to pack up quickly to embark on a return trip" in order to console their elderly father.[27] Immigration records also reveal that the number of visits to China that immigrants were actually able to make over the course of their sojourn was limited. A survey of over six hundred immigrants reveals that only 4 percent were able to make two visits home to China, and only another 9 percent made one visit.[28] For those Chinese whose legal status was uncertain, travel back and forth was especially risky—and costly. It was not uncommon to have to buy expensive immigration documents for each visit abroad.[29] Even families who had successfully maintained contact through the mail grew weary of the separation. Wong Jou's family had communicated by letter between San Diego and Kue Tou for more than twelve years. But Lee Shee's last letter to Wong Jou was full of despair. The youngest son had resumed his opium habit and refused to listen either to his older brother or to his mother. Lee Shee was on the verge of forcing her son out of the house, and she begged Wong Jou to return home. "I am getting old, so just come home and don't hesitate about it," she wrote. There is no record documenting whether or not Lee Shee's entreaties resulted in her husband's return to China.[30]

Sojourning as a strategy to preserve or increase wealth and to accumulate lands in the homeland also failed to live up to immigrant expectations. Again, immigrant letters indicate that despite remittances coming from the United States, families in China experienced difficulty getting out of debt. Lew Git, a fruit and vegetable seller in Los Angeles, made seventy-five dollars a month and sent nearly all of it back to his wife and two children in Ming Gong village, Toisan. Similarly, Wong Sheong Yin and his son, working in Hollister, California, both regularly sent the bulk of their paychecks home. Both the Lew and Wong families wanted to use the money to buy land and build houses in a new section of the village reserved for Gold Mountain families. Correspondence between members of the Wong family in 1906 reveal that the remittances were going only to the family's creditors. Wong Ngum Yin at home in China bluntly asked for more money. Each plot of land in the "new village" cost one hundred dollars, and the family was in such poor financial health that they had already borrowed two hundred dollars from "old Jock Sut" to simply cover their living expenses and their old debt. "In these days, without money, you cannot be happy in matters either large or small," wrote Wong Ngum Yin. "This is certainly a fierce way."[31] The Lew family was in no better shape. In October 1918, Lew Chew Mei, Lew Git's oldest son, reported that the family had borrowed one hundred dollars at 12 percent interest to buy land. Three months later, Lew Git had been able to send home only sixty dollars. In the meantime, the family had borrowed additional money from another lender to repay the previous debt and an additional three hundred dollars to begin construction on a house. By May 1919, Lew Git had sent back fifty dollars, but the debts continued to pile up. Lew Git concluded that he alone could not pay for the family expenses and attempted to bring Lew Chew Mei into the United States to earn money to repay the debts. Convinced that Lew Chew Mei was not the "real" son of Lew Git, however, immigration officials in San Francisco denied entry to the younger Lew and returned him to China in July of 1921. Lew Git remained in the United States, trapped by his family's burden of debt.[32]

Challenging Exclusion

Despite the hardships involved, many Chinese continued to respond to exclusion by maintaining transnational households, even for several generations.[33] Others engaged in fierce battles against the laws and the ways they were enforced, charging the U.S. government with racial discrimination and injustice. Beginning in the 1880s, Chinese immigrants began to both challenge the legality of the exclusion laws through the judicial system and protest American exclusion policies as individuals and through community organizations. They hired lawyers and used the courts to affirm the rights of merchant families, returning laborers, and American citizens of Chinese descent and their families to enter and reenter the country. Many of the early court cases were sponsored by the Chinese consulate or the Chinese Six Companies, the umbrella organization for the large kinship and mutual benefit organizations established in the United States to serve Chinese immigrants and preserve order in the community.[34] Chinese were extremely successful at using the federal courts to overturn individual denials by the immigration service.[35] At the same time, Chinese in America also used the courts to challenge the policy of exclusion itself, including a failed Supreme Court challenge to the 1892 Geary Act, which extended the ban on immigration for ten years and required all Chinese to register with the federal government.[36]

Outside of the courts, Chinese protested American exclusion policies through a variety of forums. Both Chinese diplomats and working-class immigrants were persistent and vocal critics of the discriminatory treatment Chinese immigrants received.[37] In 1892, Yung Hen, a poultry dealer in San Francisco, asked a newspaper reporter, "Why do they not legislate against Swedes, Germans, Italians, Turks and others? There are no strings on those people. . . . For some reason, you people persist in pestering the Chinamen."[38] In 1899, a Chinese woman told government immigration investigator Oscar Greenhalgh that the Chinese "had as much right to land in America as the Irish, who [are] always drunk and fighting."[39] Thirty years later, anger and a sense of injustice remained deeply ingrained among Chinese in America. As Woo Gen, a Chinese merchant in Seattle excitedly explained to interviewers in 1924, "We have exclusion law on Chinese. All other countries have what are called immigration laws."[40]

Chinese leaders sent petitions, memorials, and letters to American presidents Theodore Roosevelt, William Howard Taft, and Woodrow Wilson.[41] In 1900, Chinese minister Wu Ting-fang complained to the American secretary of state that Chinese were "entirely at the mercy of inquisitors, who . . . are generally unfriendly, if not positively hostile, to them."[42] Chinese American organizations also fielded complaints about immigration officials and the draconian conditions and procedures of exclusion enforcement.[43] In 1913, the Chinese Chamber of Commerce, an organization of Chinese merchants, and the Chinese-American League of Justice of Los Angeles complained to the Bureau of Immigration that "many immigration officers apparently interpret the exclusion laws to suit their own personal prejudices and desires. Each [one] acts as judge, jury, and executioner in every case involving the rights of Chinese to land, or live in the United States."[44] Such attitudes about immigration officials even appeared in Cantonese folk rhymes. One described the immigration officers as "wolves and tigers, all ruthless, all wanting to bite me." Another complained of the "unendurable tyranny of immigration officials."[45]

Chinese also protested their detention and the deplorable conditions in the detention shed maintained by the Pacific Mail Steamship Company at San Francisco's Pier 40, where they awaited the outcome of their cases. Established to house Chinese prior to the opening of the immigration station on Angel Island, the quarters consisted of only one room, with a total of six windows and one exit. Although it had been built to house two hundred inmates, at times it held more than twice that many. Additional bunks were added, but they were placed in the aisles, which only exacerbated the chronic overcrowding in the shed. The ventilation was poor, and the inmates often fell sick, and some even died.[46] One immigrant inspector declared the place a "veritable fire trap."[47] Another referred to the detention shed as having "inhuman" conditions.[48] Immigrants themselves referred to it generally as the *muk uk*, or "wooden barracks," but more commonly the terms "iron cage" and "Chinese jail" were used.[49] So bad were the conditions that a detainee named Huey Dow complained to the commissioner of immigration that he felt as if he were "a prisoner expiating a crime."[50] Wong Ngum Yin, another immigrant detained in the shed, charged that the American "barbarians" had "neither mercy or compassion and are like the lions and the tigers. Our countrymen hate them."[51] In 1902, Chinese detainees' anger over the miserable conditions reached the boiling point. Several immigrants who were in transit from Latin

America back to China had been detained for over seven months. Loy Yuen Wing spoke for the group in a mass meeting and threatened to "tear the shed apart" unless they were immediately returned to China on the very next boat.[52] Other Chinese grew so frustrated that they risked their lives to escape. Between September and November of 1908 alone, thirty-two Chinese succeeded in escaping the shed.[53] Although the numerous protests and complaints did result in some slight improvements to the detention shed in 1903, it remained a problem until its closing in 1909.[54]

Despite their consistent complaints, Chinese failed to change significantly either the laws or the government's enforcement procedures. The Bureau of Immigration remained largely unmoved and unresponsive. Chief Inspector James Dunn of San Francisco denounced Chinese charges that immigration officials were overly zealous and hostile as "stinging epithets" and defended the force without having investigated the validity of the charges.[55] Likewise, Commissioner-General of Immigration Frank Sargent claimed that any harshness or inconvenience involved in enforcing the Chinese exclusion laws were not the result of "the injustice or inhumanity of the officers, but of the failure of the Chinese themselves to comply with the provisions of the law."[56] Even when Harold Bolce, the Bureau of Immigration's special investigator, concluded that the Bureau of Immigration did indeed resort to "unnecessary harshness in the enforcement of the Chinese exclusion laws," Sargent dismissed the report and questioned Bolce's own motives.[57]

In 1905, Chinese were dealt another blow when the federal district courts were barred by the Supreme Court from hearing Chinese admission cases in *Ju Toy v. United States*. Following the decision, Chinese anger and frustration over the exclusion policy and continued racial discrimination reached a climax. Responding to racial injustice in the United States and reflecting the growing Chinese nationalism throughout China, Chinese merchants in China staged a boycott of American goods in May of 1905. In a demonstration of what historian Yong Chen has described as a newfound trans-Pacific Chinese nationalism, teachers, students, urban professionals, laborers, and women in China and Chinese in the United States joined them.[58] Nevertheless, American diplomats in China, as well as American immigration officials in the United States, continued to deny that Chinese immigrants attempting to enter the United States were treated harshly. Commissioner-General Sargent went so far as to charge that the boycotters were simply "interested in the importation of coolies." Any relaxation of Bureau of Immigration policies, he warned, would result in the "emasculat[ion], if not repeal of the exclusion policy."[59]

While the boycott eventually collapsed, Secretary of Commerce Victor Metcalf and President Theodore Roosevelt did respond to the protests by supporting some changes in enforcement procedures. "In the effort to carry out the policy of excluding Chinese laborers . . . grave injustices and wrongs have been done to this nation and to the people of China," Roosevelt wrote.[60] Immigration officials were reminded that the purpose of the Chinese exclusion laws was "to prevent the immigration of Chinese laborers and not to restrict the freedom of movement of Chinese persons belonging to the exempt classes. . . . The law must be enforced without harshness."[61] Many of the rules that the Chinese had found so onerous were dropped; others were modified or liberalized. One of the most important changes was the end of the Bertillon system of identification. The new rules also allowed attorneys to examine and make copies of testimony in preparation for their cases, and the time given to make an appeal was lengthened.[62] In a further concession to the Chinese, the commissioner-general of immigration ordered in 1907 that Chinese applying for admission could have their attorneys and interpreters present at their hearings, though their representatives could not participate in the proceedings.[63] Although such changes were welcomed, the Chinese boycotters in the United States and in China had fallen far short of convincing the United States to repeal the laws. Indeed, both the secretary of commerce and labor and the president of the United States had reiterated their full support of the policy of exclusion. At the height of the agitation, the secretary had confirmed his "full recognition of the fixed character of the present policy" and President Roosevelt had likewise assured the American people that there was no "serious proposal to alter the immigration law as regards to the Chinese."[64]

By 1906, the policy of Chinese exclusion was thus firmly entrenched in American immigration law. There is no better symbol of its institutionalization than the new immigration station on Angel Island. First conceived of in 1903, its establishment represented the achievement of several goals of the Bureau of Immigration. As San Francisco commissioner of immigration Hart Hyatt North explained, the new station would provide immigration officials with larger offices and Chinese immigrants with better detention quarters. Most important, its location on an island would be the most effective means of keeping a watchful eye over the resourceful Chinese. They would be separated from their Chinese friends and families who might try to coach them on how to pass the interrogations, a practice common among the "wily Chinee," North explained. They would also be segregated from the rest of the nation, thereby protecting Americans from their threatening presence. Furthermore, it was escape-proof. Angel Island, North explained, was "ideal," for "it is impossible for anyone to escape by swimming to the mainland."[65]

Congress approved the building of the station in 1905, and the facility was completed in 1908.[66] Although leaders in San Francisco's Chinatown vehemently opposed the move, the immigration station on Angel Island officially opened on January 21, 1910. The next day, over four hundred passengers, mostly Chinese, were transferred from their ships to the station without incident.[67] The editors of the *Chinese World*, a Chinese-language newspaper in San Francisco, marked the event with a special editorial on the treatment of Chinese immigrants under the exclusion laws. At the Pacific Mail Steamship Company detention shed, the editors explained, the "mistreatment of us Chinese confined there was worse than for jailed prisoners." The barren offshore island, they predicted, would be no better.[68] The editors had reason to be pessimistic. Admission through the island station proved to be much more difficult for Chinese immigrants. The number of Chinese rejected increased dramatically only one year after the facility began operating. According to the annual report of the commissioner-general of immigration, the ratio of rejections to admissions was approximately 73 percent higher in 1910 than in 1909; 92 percent higher than in 1908; 89 percent higher than in 1907; and 100 percent higher than in 1906. He credited the opening of the Angel Island station for the increased rejection rate.[69]

Chinese continued to protest their treatment by immigration officials for years after the Angel Island station opened. The Chinese Six Companies issued a circular throughout San Francisco's Chinatown calling on residents to "protest for equal rights," and it sent telegrams to Hong Kong and Canton warning new immigrants to avoid entering the United States through San Francisco's new station.[70] It also joined forces with the Chinese Chamber of Commerce to send a lengthy petition to the San Francisco Chamber of Commerce in May 1911. The petition documented numerous cases of alleged injustice. Angel Island immigration authorities responded by inviting the San Francisco Down Town Association, a local commercial organization, Robert Dollar of the Dollar Steamship Company, and Ng Poon Chew, editor of the *Chung Sai Yat Po*, for an extensive tour of the immigration station. The group was appalled at what they witnessed and concluded that the examinations were "unreasonable." An applicant, the commission reported, was "considered guilty until he proves himself entitled to land." The "high standards of proof required of Chinese in admission cases and the ways in which applicant and witness testimonies were read against one another," they charged, "were sufficient to exclude every man,

Wharf and administration building, Angel Island Immigration Station, c. 1910. Despite strident protests by the Chinese American community, the immigration station on Angel Island was opened in January 1910. The station was considered "ideal" because its island location made it escape-proof. Courtesy of the National Archives, Washington, D.C.

woman, and child from landing."[71] In addition, the observers reported that detainees were allowed to leave their quarters only once or twice a week for one-half hour. Moreover, they complained, the lavatories were "exceedingly unsanitary," and the hospital was horribly inadequate. The dormitories were so crowded and dismal, in fact, that one visitor demanded of the commissioner of immigration, "Is this a jail . . . and must all Chinese imprisoned here be treated as felons? This is not the least unlike a cattle pen!"[72] Some improvements to the facility were eventually made, but the substandard conditions in the "island cage" continued to symbolize the enduring reach of Chinese exclusion.

By 1910, Chinese had begrudgingly accepted that the exclusion policy could not be overturned and they focused instead on attacking the methods with which it was enforced. At a 1911 dinner for Chinese and American merchants in Hong Kong, the American vice consul general there reported that the group was no longer quarreling with the actual laws, only with the "regulations imposed by the officials."[73] In a 1924 letter, leaders of the Chinese Chamber of Commerce also seemed to express a bitter acceptance of exclusion: "Let the American government do as it pleases, we as a nation seem powerless to resist, witness the encroachments of this government through its Labor Department upon our vested treaty rights."[74] In 1927, sociologist R. D. McKenzie observed that the Chinese in America had "stopped fighting against the principle of exclusion" but continued to focus on the method of enforcement.[75]

The post-1910 Chinese response to exclusion reflected internal class- and citizenship-based divisions within the community, with merchants and citizens protesting on behalf of their classes only instead of all Chinese, as they had done earlier.[76] As Ng Poon Chew conceded in 1908, the exclusion of Chinese laborers had become a "fixed policy in the United States." What was now at issue was how the exempt classes would be treated.[77] Thus, much like the ways in which established, acculturated European immigrants scorned the newly arrived "greenhorns" and Mexican Americans attempted to distinguish themselves from recent Mexican immigrants, Chinese merchants and Chinese American citizens also sought to distance themselves from returning laborers and other Chinese attempting to enter the country illegally.[78]

Chinese merchants were an especially vocal group that insisted on better treatment from immigration authorities. As early as 1884, representatives and lawyers for the Chinese Merchants Exchange in San Francisco had sent a lengthy petition to President Chester A. Arthur calling attention to the alleged mistreatment of merchants and their families. They emphatically pointed out their class-based rights to enter and reenter the country.[79] In 1900, Chinese minister Wu Ting-fang complained that merchants were being imprisoned "for weeks and months, compelled to await the pleasure of the Bureau of Immigration for examination." Immigration inspectors acted as "inquisitors," and the general mistreatment resulted in "untold mental and financial suffering."[80] After the Chinese exclusion laws were renewed and the immigration station on Angel Island was built, merchants increased their calls for justice on the basis of class privilege and the future of U.S.-Chinese commercial relations. In 1910, Chinese merchants in Hong Kong wrote President William Howard Taft charging that the "rash, unjustified actions and conduct" of immigration officers were designed to intentionally "prevent a merchant or student from landing."[81] In 1911, Chinese merchants and sympathetic representatives of the Down Town Association of San Francisco sent a ten-page memorial to President Taft reminding him that China and her population of four hundred million could "make the United States her closest occidental neighbor, the marketing place for her requirements." However, the merchants passionately warned, the mistreatment of Chinese merchants on Angel Island could potentially destroy commercial relations between the United States and China. The memorial concluded with fifteen detailed recommendations for improving conditions and the handling of merchant cases.[82] A 1918 telegram from the Chinese Consolidated Benevolent Association to President Woodrow Wilson repeated how Chinese merchants were central to Chinese-U.S. trade and then demanded an end to the "ruthless insults" made by immigration officers to "unoffending merchants" and their families.[83] In the 1920s, the Chinese Chamber of Commerce charged the immigration service with harassing "honorable men and women" of the exempt classes with "absurd technicalities" and with launching a "reign of terror" on merchants and their families who were deported "on very flimsy pretext of very catchy questions after days of examination and months of detention."[84]

Chinese Americans also used their status as citizens to demand better treatment by immigration officials. In 1910, the Native Sons of the Golden State, one of the leading Chinese American citizens' organizations and the Chinese American Citizens Alliance's predecessor, issued a formal complaint to the secretary of commerce and labor. Among its many grievances, the group charged that Chinese Americans suffered from constant harassment by immigration officials both when traveling abroad and when residing in the United States. "The regulations of your department are oppressive and unjust to the native born citizen of Chinese parentage," the letter stated.[85] Another letter writer complained to President Woodrow Wilson that both reputable Chinese merchants and American citizens were "held like criminals for months . . . without opportunity to consult counsel or their friends or families." These citizens, he emphasized, were "AMERICAN CITIZENS IN THE FULL MEANING OF THE LAW."[86] Ng Ah Ben, a citizen attempting to bring his son into the country, also tried to distinguish himself from others who acquired native status through fraud. In a personal appeal to Commissioner of Immigration Hart Hyatt North in 1909, he wrote, "I was born and raised in this country, having lived here for more than thirty years and it could be said that I am a good man. I swear that I never tell a lie. This boy is really my own son. It is different from other cases."[87]

These protests involved a common strategy of explicitly setting apart Chinese merchants and citizens from other Chinese applying for admission into the country. In emphasizing how Chinese merchants (and, more important, Chinese-U.S. trade) benefited the United States, Chinese merchants and their allies made clear that they were "inoffensive" and not a detriment or threat to American society, as Chinese laborers allegedly were. Likewise, American citizens of Chinese descent demanded equal treatment as citizens under the law. The injustice of Chinese exclusion enforcement, they charged, was that no distinction was made between Chinese merchants, Chinese American citizens, and the common laborer. Despite their class and citizenship status, merchants and citizens were housed along with Chinese "coolies," said another letter writer. Chinese laborers were "justly suspected of disease and vermin" and therefore deserved the harsh treatment, but merchants, students, and citizens deserved more courtesy.[88]

In 1910, the Bureau of Immigration responded to its critics with new instructions designed to facilitate the examination of students, merchants, returning citizens, and their families on the arriving steamships. The new rules specifically provided that all officials, merchants holding Section 6 certificates, citizens with return certificates, pre-investigated returning merchants, students, and teachers, and pre-investigated wives and children of returning merchants and natives were to be examined on the boat only. All others (returning laborers, returning merchants and citizens who had not been investigated before departure, wives and children of merchants and citizens arriving for the first time) were to be examined on Angel Island. Although these new rules probably did help facilitate the immigration and reentry of some merchants and citizens, they failed to substantially improve the treatment of those who were detained. Immigration authorities were still instructed to vigilantly enforce the exclusion laws in all Chinese cases. Moreover, if any doubts were raised about an applicant's eligibility to enter the country during the investigation on the steamships, he or she was transferred to Angel Island for further review.[89] Merchants and citizens thus continued to be subjected to many of the same procedures and practices of exclusion applied to all Chinese aliens. They continued to file complaints with local and national immigration service offices for the remainder of the exclusion era, but they also learned to adapt to the government's harsh enforcement policies.[90]

Adapting to Exclusion

The first of the different strategies the Chinese used to negotiate their way around exclusion was to educate themselves about the details, loopholes, and enforcement procedures of the exclusion laws. Beginning in the 1880s, Chinese and their friends turned to federal immigration officials for information about admission and readmission standards and regulations. Hundreds of letters of inquiry written by Chinese residents and their attorneys, ministers, neighbors, politicians, and friends poured into the San Francisco Chinese Bureau from Norfolk, Virginia; Rochester, New York; Peoria, Illinois; Denver, Colorado; Springfield, Massachusetts; East Las Vegas, New Mexico; Baltimore, Maryland; Jersey City, New Jersey; Boise City, Idaho; Fairmont, Nebraska; New Brunswick, New Jersey; Memphis, Tennessee; Augusta, Georgia; as well as San Francisco, Los Angeles, New York, and Boston.[91] Networks of kin also proved to be essential in facilitating an immigrant's journey to the United States and his navigations through the bureaucratic maze established by the Bureau of Immigration. New immigrants first relied upon a steady stream of information and advice from their relatives already in America. While Wong Quong Ken sailed to San Francisco in 1917, for example, news of his impending arrival was sent by Wong Gong Kim, whose two brothers were already settled there. "If he should write you for assistance," instructed Wong Gong Kim, "be sure to go to the immigration office and give him whatever assistance needed. If you have to spend a little money for him, it will be all right; he will give it back to you when he is landed."[92] Likewise, Lee Young Sing in Hong Kong wrote to his brother in San Francisco asking him to look after a clansman about to arrive in the city and to give advice to their young nephew who was also sailing soon and "knew very little about things in the world."[93] Other letters and interviews chronicle how Chinese emigration was often financed by relatives. Arthur Lem, who immigrated to the United States in 1925, explained that "the cost was usually assembled by the applicant's close friends and family members. Everyone was very willing to help another family member to come to the Gold Mountain."[94] In 1906, Wong Ngum Yin relied upon his uncles and cousins in San Francisco to gain his release from the detention shed and to provide clothes to protect him from the cold. "I will surely repay you [and not] bring shame unto our Tribe," he promised.[95]

At that exciting but oftentimes terrifying moment when a steamer finally docked in San Francisco, new immigrants could count on their relatives to greet them, and there were always huge crowds of friends and relatives of newcomers waiting for them on the steamship docks. In December of 1899, Wong Hong and Chew Dong Ngin were part of one such crowd in San Francisco. They had made a special trip to the Pacific Mail Company dock to welcome young Fong Tim, the son of one of their Chinatown friends and probably a fellow villager from Ting Ching village in the Ying Ping district. Fong Tim, recognizing the two faces in the crowd, nodded his head and waved.[96] The two family friends would later spend much time in the interrogation room filing affidavits and answering questions on behalf of Fong Tim. They were expected to know every minute detail about the Fong family and were subjected to an intensive examination.[97] Witnesses had to be prepared to answer questions not only about their friend or relative but also about themselves and their right to be in the United States. They thus put themselves at risk of government scrutiny every time they testified on behalf of a new applicant. In 1903, when merchants Lee Jung and Ching Bow provided affidavits and testified in front of the Bureau of Immigration on behalf of Lee Jung's nephew Lee Kwock Chow, for example, they had to answer just as many questions about themselves and their exempt status as they had to answer about Lee Kwock Chow. The bureau investigated the two witnesses' claims of exempt status, recorded details about their joint business, checked their names against the firm's partnership list, and demanded their registration certificates.[98]

The immigration interrogations were often not only hostile but also lengthy. When Fong Dai Sing, a native, returned to the United States in February of 1899, he was denied entry. He took his case to court. His uncle Fong See and a family friend Lee Yow Son had to testify twice, once at the Bureau of Immigration's office and then again in the courthouse. The entire process spanned several months, during which time both witnesses needed to be available for questioning.[99] That Chinese willingly traveled great distances, invested many hours, and allowed themselves to be scrutinized by the government in order to help relatives and friends is evidence of the importance of family networks in the immigration process. Sociologist Wen-hsien Chen wrote in 1940 that Chinese aliens without relatives or friends in America were at an inherent disadvantage. If denied entry, these immigrants "seldom made an effort to force entry." Those who had relatives and friends in the United States had the financial and moral support to fight the decision and "make every effort to secure entry" to the United States.[100]

Chinese responses to the exclusion laws also had important class-, gender-, and citizenship-based dimensions. Fully aware of the markers by which immigration officials judged Chinese cases, applicants learned to conform to these government standards. Chinese merchants, for example, emphasized their class status. When Lee Fook's attorney appealed his client's case to the secretary of the treasury in 1899, he referred to Lee as a "capitalist," a "gentlemen of means, of elegant leisure." "Certainly a Capitalist is not one of the class against

Male immigrants before U.S. immigration officials and a Chinese interpreter on Angel Island, c. 1916. In an effort to impress immigration officials, Chinese often wore their best clothes during their interviews. Western-style suits in particular were considered signs of economic success and acculturation and were interpreted favorably by immigration officials. Courtesy of the California Department of Parks and Recreation.

which the exclusion laws are to act," the lawyer chided.[101] Likewise, knowing that immigration officials generally treated first-class passengers better than those in steerage, Lee Chi Yet saved his wages as a laundry worker for an extra year in order bring his wife over in first class. When Wong Lan Fong did arrive at Angel Island in 1927, she was processed and admitted within one day.[102]

Chinese women also defied exclusion through daily acts of resistance, what Lisa Lowe has called "immigrant acts."[103] Although they often held unequal positions within their own families and communities, Chinese women proved to be quite resourceful, developing strategies to overcome the barriers erected by the Chinese exclusion laws. Exempt-class Chinese women, for example, learned how to avoid being branded as prostitutes or women of questionable morals. One way was through evidence of "proper character," including credible testimony, documentation, or clear markers of class. One of the first women to apply for admission through the port of San Francisco after the Chinese Exclusion Act was passed was Leong Cum, a U.S. citizen born in Lewiston, Idaho. Applying for readmission in May of 1884, Leong made sure to distinguish herself from less desirable female applicants. A garment maker by profession, Leong supplied immigration officials with three affidavits, each of which emphasized that she was "a woman of excellent reputation and irreproachable character." One of the affidavits was from Jerome Millian, a Chinese interpreter who likely worked for the immigration service. Both the affidavits and Millian's endorsement worked in Leong's favor. She was landed two days after her initial arrival.[104]

Chinese women applying for admission as wives of merchants had to go one step further. They had to prove not only their status as respectable women but also their membership in the merchant class. Because early immigration officials expected merchant women to possess fine clothing, a respectable manner, and especially, bound feet—a symbol of wealth and status in traditional China—Chinese women and their attorneys learned to highlight these traits. In 1901, Gee See, a merchant's wife residing in Los Angeles, submitted an application for return admission complete with a full-length photograph and an X ray of her feet. Her affidavit explained that she was "a small-footed woman or bound-footed woman." The photograph showed Gee See sitting down and holding a small child. Her small feet were clearly displayed. The X ray was described as showing "conclusively that the feet of this woman are what is known as 'small' or 'bound,' the position of the bones and their abnormally small size distinctly appearing."[105] In 1915, the attorneys for Lam Yin Shee, another wife of a merchant, convinced immigration officials that because their client had bound feet, she was "undoubtedly a woman of the better class; that there can be no question to her respectability in any way."[106]

Chinese merchants and U.S. citizens also quickly learned how to emphasize their class and citizenship status and their relationships with whites in order to better negotiate immigration service regulations. They relied upon sympathetic neighbors, friends, politicians, employers, attorneys, and ministers from across the country to file affidavits, write letters, and even travel to the immigration office to testify on behalf of a returning Chinese resident.[107] As the Bureau of Immigration valued (and at times required) testimony from whites over Chinese in order to substantiate claims of entry and reentry into the United States, this assistance and support was very valuable. In 1889, A. S. Schell, a longtime resident of Knights Ferry, California, wrote to a lawyer to assist his two neighbors, American-born citizens Jin Young and Charley Foo,

Gee See and child, 1901. Because U.S. immigration officials during the exclusion era routinely suspected Chinese women of being prostitutes, Chinese women presented their bound feet as proof of their respectability. This photograph, attached to Gee See's application for admission, clearly showcases her bound feet and western-style furnishings, symbols of wealth and position. Gee See and her lawyer also included an X ray of her feet as further proof of her status as a merchant's wife. Courtesy of the National Archives, Washington, D.C.

in their attempts to reenter the United States. The letter was full of compliments, and Schell used his influence to sway immigration authorities in favor of his friends. "I trust that with your assistance, backed up with this and perhaps other testimonials, he will have no difficulty in landing. Both are excellent and good men," Schell wrote. Schell also sent around a petition to a dozen more non-Chinese residents of Knights Ferry who signed it, corroborated the two Chinese residents' good characters, and called for the prompt admission of their two neighbors. Jin Young and Charley Foo were landed.[108] Likewise, in 1890, McConnell Jenkins, of Logansport, Indiana, wrote to Collector of Customs James Blaine on behalf of a longtime Chinese neighbor who desired to go to China to visit his mother and then return to the United States. "He is a laundryman, a good citizen, industrious, temperate, and highly esteemed by all who have business relations with him," McConnell wrote.[109]

The social and class standing of witnesses in Chinese immigrant cases could have a profound impact on their outcomes. In Leung Fook On's case, immigration officials discredited his claim to reenter the United States based on the character of his witnesses. William D. Schultz, F. Rothman, and W. D. Hobro were plumbers, "Hebrews," and suspected to be "professional witnesses" who were paid for their services. While all three men vehemently protested the charges, their involvement cast doubt on Leung's claims.[110] On the other hand, Wong Let, a merchant in Riverside, California, astutely recognizing that credible white witnesses from the middle and upper classes increased his chances of reentering the country, secured affidavits from a number of merchants, lawyers, and even the city marshal, postmaster, and ex-postmaster, confirming his long-term residence in the city and the status of his business. A later affidavit was filed by J. S. Noyes, a superior court judge for the state who supported the character of both Wong and the witnesses attached to the case.[111]

Chinese also turned to Christian organizations like the Young Men's Christian Association and the Presbyterian Mission Home in San Francisco to substantiate their claims. Both organizations were active in the Chinese American community and were well respected by the immigration service. In 1915, the YMCA even had a full-time immigration secretary in San Francisco, and the YMCA and the Mission Home frequently intervened on behalf of Chinese immigrants and returning residents. In 1915, for example, Lee Sue Ben, a returning student and former teacher at the YMCA in Canton, China, sought the organization's assistance while he was being detained on Angel Island. Frank B. Lenz, the YMCA's immigration secretary, wrote a letter to the immigration inspector in charge and pointed out Lee's right to enter the United States. He also urged a "speedy settlement of the case."[112] Lee also wrote to influential Chinese newspaperman Ng Poon Chew to ask for his assistance. Ng wrote directly to Samuel Backus, commissioner of immigration in San Francisco, to "find out what the trouble is" with the student's landing. He also urged a prompt admission.[113] After several days of detention, Lee was finally landed the day after Commissioner Backus received the letters.

Donaldina Cameron, director of the Presbyterian Mission Home, a "rescue" home for Chinese prostitutes, was a particularly important ally to Chinese immigrants attempting to enter the United States.[114] Historian Judy Yung notes that "it was generally known that a supporting letter from Donaldina Cameron . . . often helped get cases landed."[115] In 1916, Cameron came to the assistance of Lee Kan, a Chinese merchant whose wife and two sons were being detained on Angel Island. In her letter to the commissioner of immigration, Cameron stated that she had known Lee Kan for some years and that he was indeed a bona fide merchant. At Lee's request, Cameron had even traveled to Angel Island to meet the family, and in her letter, she asked that parole be granted for the wife and youngest child if the family could not be landed immediately. She also made an investigation herself into Lee's status and reported to the immigration service, "I have made special inquiry and investigation to further assure myself that Mr. Lee Kan's interests [are] centered in the store. . . . I have been assured from reliable sources that he has been at all times engaged in the mercantile business. . . . In view of these and other facts, I trust that in due course of time it will be deemed advisable to land the family of Mr. Lee Kan."[116] With Cameron's help, Lee Kan's family was finally landed.

Such assistance from non-Chinese acquaintances, friends, and allies enabled Chinese to continue immigrating to the United States while the exclusion laws were in effect. Indeed, Chinese immigrants learned to depend on non-Chinese acquaintances and allies in some of the same ways that they depended on their own families. The fact that so many Chinese immigrants and Chinese American citizens were successful in enlisting non-Chinese to speak on their behalf reflected their astute adaptation to the rigid regulations established by the immigration service. It also highlights a high level of interracial cooperation that is often overlooked in existing analyses of Chinese immigration and exclusion.

Immigration Attorneys

By far, Chinese immigrants' most valuable resource during the exclusion era was an organized network of immigration lawyers who facilitated Chinese entry and reentry by keeping track of the necessary paperwork and lobbying on behalf of clients, tasks that would have been extremely difficult for Chinese to accomplish on their own. The number of immigration lawyers performing Chinese immigration work grew in direct proportion to the increasing complexity of the exclusion laws and their ever more severe enforcement. Chinese had a long history of hiring the best American lawyers to challenge anti-Chinese legislation even before 1882.[117] This practice continued into the exclusion era, especially as Chinese appealed to the courts to overturn immigration officials' decisions to deny them entry. Collector John Wise noted in 1895 that "the interests of the Chinese are looked out by a Chinese Consul and also by shrewd lawyers."[118] In 1899, the Treasury Department found that the

Chinese, as a rule, were represented by the "very best attorneys in the city."[119] One might suspect that only those Chinese with the most financial resources could afford to hire lawyers, but Chinese from all class backgrounds routinely sought legal counsel despite the cost. Sociologist Wen-hsien Chen observed that by the 1930s, "without exception," all Chinese aliens arriving at the port for the first time with an application for permanent residence were looked after by lawyers and that even returning Chinese residents secured the services of an attorney "as a safeguard" because of the precarious nature of immigration investigations.[120] A survey of over six hundred Chinese who entered the United States during the exclusion era revealed that 90 percent had hired immigration attorneys to process papers and to represent them before immigration authorities.[121]

Immigration attorneys were not allowed to participate in or be present at the initial hearings and interrogations conducted by the immigration service, but if Chinese applicants were denied entry, their attorneys could examine their files in order to rebut the decision. Attorneys lacked access to the entire files, but, despite this handicap, they continued to be invaluable assets to new and returning immigrants.[122] They effectively and consistently pointed out flaws in immigration officials' judgments, oftentimes forcing a reversal in the decision. They were also known to marshal outside experts, previous rulings and court decisions, witnesses, and evidence to challenge the government's findings.[123] As Commissioner of Immigration John D. Nagle commented in 1927, attorneys remained "indispensable" allies to the Chinese.[124]

Most of the lawyers who represented Chinese clients in the first decades of exclusion were San Francisco's prominent attorneys who worked not only on behalf of individual Chinese clients but also for the Chinese Six Companies and the Chinese consulate. Thomas Riordan, for example, was the principal attorney representing the Chinese in the 1880s and 1890s and was retained by the Chinese consulate to represent all high-profile cases. His successor, Oliver P. Stidger, also became a vocal critic of the exclusion laws and built a formidable practice based on Chinese immigration business.[125] In 1915, Stidger was listed as the official attorney for the Chinese Chamber of Commerce as well, and the firm of Stidger, Stidger, and Kennah became one of the leading law firms representing Chinese immigrants.[126] In 1924, Oliver Stidger published a pamphlet regarding the 1924 Immigration Act and its negative effects on Chinese immigrants and Chinese Americans.[127] George A. McGowan, along with his partner, Alfred L. Worley, also represented a great majority of Chinese immigrants from the early 1900s to the 1920s. According to their professional letterhead, the licensed attorneys and counselors at law practiced in both the federal and state courts and retained an office in the prestigious Bank of Italy building in downtown San Francisco.[128]

Other individuals representing the Chinese before the Bureau of Immigration acted more like brokers, arranging for witnesses to testify before the immigration service, filing witness affidavits, and arranging for more experienced counsel if necessary. Some had deep-rooted connections with the Chinese community; a few had even been former members of the Bureau of Immigration and found that their inside knowledge of the agency translated into lucrative employment opportunities outside of the service. Clarkson Dye, an immigration broker who was regularly used by Chinese immigrants beginning in 1909, for example, was also an insurance agent in Chinatown.[129] Henry C. Kennah, a member of the Stidger, Stidger, and Kennah law firm, had been an immigrant inspector in San Francisco for several years in the early 1900s and apparently joined Oliver Stidger and his son, Jason, in their practice around 1912.[130] While the vast majority of lawyers and brokers representing Chinese before the immigration service were white, there is evidence that beginning in the 1920s, a few Chinese American attorneys were practicing and representing immigrants as well. In 1920, for example, an attorney by the name of Chan Chung Wing, of the law firm of Wing, O'Malley, and McGrath, represented Quan Shee, a merchant's wife applying for admission into the country at San Francisco.[131]

That the business of immigration lawyers was a lucrative one cannot be doubted. In 1885, Treasury Department officials estimated that an attorney's fee for habeas corpus cases was no less than $100.[132] Moreover, as long as the exclusion laws remained in effect, the demand for skillful lawyers remained high. Advertisements placed by lawyers and others claiming expertise in Chinese immigration matters appeared throughout the pages of the *Chung Sai Yat Po*. In 1906, Alfred Worley claimed that "most Chinese in this city" depended on him and that "the charge was fair." Alongside his photograph, Worley claimed that "if you entrust me with a case, I will handle it with heart and soul."[133] Charlie D. O'Connor claimed in his advertisement to have worked at the Bureau of Immigration for over ten years, and he promised "fast, convenient, and cheap" service.[134] R. H. Jones promised readers that he would come to their assistance in person should they "have obstacles with the immigration service" when they came back to the United States. Likewise, the firm of Ball, Straus, and Atwood boasted that lawyer Straus "had a very good mastery of Chinese."[135]

Attorneys proved their worth in a variety of ways. When Chin Sing, a native returning from China to the United States, was denied reentry after a two-year absence in 1911, for example, he counted upon his attorneys to file the necessary documents and arrange for witnesses to travel to Angel Island. Immigration authorities had denied him admission on the suspicion that he was not the real Chin Sing but an impostor. Although Chin could speak English and demonstrated a "good knowledge" of his hometown of Dutch Flat, California, he had neither the necessary certificate of identity that proved his status as a returning native (it had been burnt in a fire) nor any witnesses (preferably white) who could identify him and confirm his birth in the United States. Chin hired attorneys George McGowan and Alfred Worley to appeal the decision and launch a search in Dutch Flat for any old acquaintances who could come and testify on his behalf. After a two-month search, the lawyers located two witnesses and brought them to Angel Island, where they and Chin immediately recognized each other. Chin was finally landed in July 1911, five months after he had first arrived back in the United States.[136]

The various strategies adopted by Chinese immigrants and returning residents and citizens to adapt to and negotiate their way through the exclusion laws proved to be highly successful. As Table 6 indicates, most Chinese men and women who applied for admission were allowed to enter the country. From 1910 to 1924, the average admission rate for both men and women under the exclusion laws was 93 percent. This figure does not, however, take into account the number of Chinese excluded under the general immigration laws.[137] Moreover, the gap between the number of Chinese rejected and the number of non-Chinese rejected is quite large. As Table 7 indicates, from 1908 to 1932, an average of 28 percent of all Chinese applicants were denied entry under both sets of laws. In comparison, Table 8 demonstrates that during this same period, only 3 percent of all non-Chinese immigrants and immigrant aliens were denied entry under the general immigration laws. Chinese were clearly being excluded from the country at a greater rate than other immigrant groups. In the end, both the discriminatory exclusion laws and the unfair application of the general immigration laws placed very real limits on Chinese immigrants.

Conclusion

In spite of the exclusion laws, Chinese immigrants did not abandon their dreams of coming to Gold Mountain, and they remained consistent and vocal critics of the exclusion policy during the sixty-one years that it was in effect.

TABLE 6. ADMISSION RATES OF CHINESE WOMEN AND MEN,
1910–1924

Year	Women		Men		Total Applications	Total Admissions	
	No.	Rate	No.	Rate		No.	Rate
1910	344	92%	5,606	86%	6,919	5,950	86%
1911	329	95	4,778	88	5,862	5,170	88
1912	345	94	5,029	93	5,886	5,374	91
1913	442	94	5,220	94	6,046	5,662	94
1914	401	94	5,372	93	6,183	5,773	93
1915	394	98	5,267	95	5,929	5,661	95
1916	378	97	4,815	92	5,630	5,143	92
1917	409	95	4,365	94	5,095	4,774	94
1918	429	96	2,737	90	3,474	3,166	91
1919	377	96	2,963	96	3,491	3,340	96
1920	562	99	4,128	97	4,815	4,690	97
1921	896	99	7,427	96	8,619	8,323	97
1922	1,166	99	8,859	95	10,540	10,025	95
1923	1,208	97	9,350	93	11,264	10,558	94
1924	1,284	95	9,410	93	11,445	10,694	93

Sources: U.S. Department of Commerce and Labor, *Annual Reports of the Commissioner-General of Immigration* (Washington: GPO, 1910–11); U.S. Department of Labor, *Annual Reports of the Commissioner-General of Immigration* (Washington: GPO, 1912–24).

Believing that exclusion targeted them unfairly, the Chinese in America mobilized in an attempt to overturn the laws altogether and, failing that, at least to change the ways in which they were enforced. Their efforts garnered some significant victories, and Chinese immigrants demonstrated an adept understanding of the American judicial system and the protections it was supposed to extend.

Chinese learned to adapt to exclusion utilizing a wide range of strategies. Merchants and Chinese American citizens used their class and citizenship status to lobby for preferential treatment. Many other Chinese relied upon extensive and well-organized networks of family, white allies, and lawyers.

TABLE 7. CHINESE DEBARRED UNDER EXCLUSION LAWS AND
GENERAL IMMIGRATION LAWS, 1908-1932

Year	No. Debarred under Exclusion Laws	No. Debarred under General Immigration Laws	Total Applicants	Total Debarred
1908	190	177	1,263	367 (29%)
1909	413	133	1,841	546 (30)
1910	819	90	1,770	909 (51)
1911	605	164	1,307	769 (59)
1912	350	83	1,608	433 (27)
1913	333	69	2,022	402 (20)
1914	322	88	2,354	410 (17)
1915	228	40	2,469	268 (11)
1916	377	60	2,239	437 (20)
1917	279	42	1,843	321 (17)
1918	261	47	1,576	308 (20)
1919	101	71	1,697	172 (10)
1920	60	108	2,148	168 (08)
1921	80	324	4,017	404 (10)
1922	225	379	4,465	604 (14)
1923	321	449	4,074	770 (19)
1924	509	542	4,670	1,051 (23)
1925	255	433	1,721	688 (40)
1926	256	221	1,375	477 (35)
1927	451	147	1,051	598 (57)
1928	400	62	931	462 (50)
1929	376	8	1,071	384 (36)
1930	287	4	970	291 (30)
1931	260	7	748	267 (36)
1932	168	23	534	191 (36)

Sources: Wen-hsien Chen, "Chinese under Both Exclusion and Immigration Laws" (Ph.D. diss., University of Chicago, 1940), 122, based on U.S. Department of Commerce and Labor, *Annual Reports of the Commissioner-General of Immigration* (Washington: GPO, 1908–11), and U.S. Department of Labor, *Annual Reports of the Commissioner-General of Immigration* (Washington: GPO, 1912–32).

TABLE 8. NON-CHINESE IMMIGRANTS AND NON-IMMIGRANT ALIENS
DEBARRED UNDER GENERAL IMMIGRATION LAWS, 1908–1932

Year	Total Applicants	Total Debarred
1908	935,597	10,902 (1.2%)
1909	954,646	10,411 (1.1)
1910	1,222,307	24,270 (2.0)
1911	1,052,649	22,349 (2.1)
1912	1,035,935	16,057 (1.6)
1913	1,447,165	19,938 (1.4)
1914	1,436,122	33,041 (2.3)
1915	458,355	24,111 (5.3)
1916	385,615	18,867 (4.9)
1917	378,905	16,028 (4.2)
1918	219,150	7,297 (3.3)
1919	245,647	8,626 (3.5)
1920	633,371	11,795 (1.9)
1921	991,942	13,779 (1.4)
1922	446,236	13,731 (3.1)
1923	694,025	20,619 (3.0)
1924	909,586	30,284 (3.3)
1925	483,825	25,390 (5.3)
1926	516,656	20,550 (4.0)
1927	557,756	19,755 (3.5)
1928	519,470	18,839 (3.6)
1929	497,454	18,127 (3.6)
1930	454,447	8,233 (1.8)
1931	290,423	9,744 (3.4)
1932	181,935	7,064 (3.9)

Sources: U.S. Department of Commerce and Labor, *Annual Reports of the Commissioner-General of Immigration* (Washington: GPO, 1908–11); U.S. Department of Labor, *Annual Reports of the Commissioner-General of Immigration* (Washington: GPO, 1912–32).

Note: Non-immigrant aliens refer to either permanent residents of the United States returning from temporary visits abroad or permanent residents of other countries making temporary visits. The figures do not include immigrants or non-immigrant aliens from the Philippines, who were classified separately. See U.S. Department of Labor, *Annual Reports of the Commissioner-General of Immigration* (Washington: GPO, 1920), 10.

As the laws and their enforcement increased in severity, Chinese grew more and more resourceful. Instead of accepting the exclusion laws, some Chinese turned to circumventing them, and as Chapters 5 and 6 make clear, illegal entries increasingly characterized Chinese immigration and had a profound effect on America's approach to gatekeeping.

PART III
CRACKS IN THE GATE

Illegal immigration was a logical, if highly unintentional, outcome of the Chinese exclusion laws. The efforts to exclude Chinese from the United States contrasted too sharply with Chinese immigrants' intense desire to seek entry at almost any cost. Consequently, Chinese took advantage of the loopholes in the laws and the cracks in the government's enforcement practices. They became, in effect, the first "illegal immigrants," both in technical, legal terms and in popular and political representations. Other immigrants also came into the country illegally, but because of the exclusion laws, more Chinese did so than other groups. They were also the main targets of government efforts to crack down on illegal immigration. Their persistence in immigrating forced the United States to deal with two interrelated problems: stopping illegal immigration at the nation's ports and borders and expelling illegal immigrants already residing in the country.

Most contemporary observers and scholarly accounts of Chinese illegal immigration have focused on the resourcefulness of the Chinese themselves. In these analyses, the highly organized and ingenious Chinese are placed in direct opposition to vigilant immigration officials charged with enforcing the exclusion laws. The two groups, as Lucy Salyer has pointed out, were "natural enemies with diametrically opposite goals."[1] While this characterization of their relationship was oftentimes correct, it nevertheless ignores the role that the law and state institutions and officers played in shaping and perpetuating Chinese illegal immigration. It also overlooks the complex ways in which illegal immigration corrupted both immigrants and immigration officials and blurred the lines of opposition. As Peter Andreas, a scholar of contemporary illegal immigration, has recently observed, the relationship between the state and illegal immigration is a "paradoxical one, defined by irony and contradiction." He notes that illegal immigrants are pursued by the state but are also created by the state. Government laws restrict immigration, but the gaps in enforcement also provide the opportunities for (and high profitability of) illegal immigration. State crackdowns regulate illegal immigration but do not end it. Rather, they merely change its location, form, size, cost, and structure. Indeed, the persistent "threat" of illegal immigration sustains the immigration service itself.[2]

This section demonstrates how Chinese immigrants and U.S. immigration officials became locked in an interdependent and self-perpetuating cycle that created and maintained illegal immigration. The discriminatory nature of the exclusion laws coupled with the government's zealous enforcement practices greatly limited the immigration opportunities for a wide range of Chinese, just as the government had intended. However, Chinese found ready allies in corrupt immigration officials, lawyers, and other individuals in China, the United States, and across the Americas who were willing and able to assist them in the profitable business of illegal immigration. The government's efforts to stem this new migration only forced Chinese immigration further underground. Such consequences of Chinese exclusion not only point to the complicated origins of illegal immigration and immigration law enforcement in the United States; they also highlight the futility of unsound immigration policies.

Chinese often circumvented exclusion by entering the country via the "back doors" of Canada and Mexico. Chapter 5 considers Chinese exclusion in America within this larger, transnational context and explores the ways in which Chinese illegal immigration transformed the northern and southern border regions into experiments in American border diplomacy and border enforcement. Assisted by Chinese, Canadian, Mexican, and American guides, Chinese border crossers turned illegal immigration into a thriving international and interracial business. At the same time, Chinese illegal immigration prompted a new imperialist assertion of American sovereignty in the form of border controls and the imposition of American nativism, immigration laws, and enforcement practices on both Canada and Mexico. Chapter 6 examines illegal immigration at the nation's ports, focusing on the transnational business of false immigration papers, on corrupt immigration officials, and on the ways in which lies, evasion, and bribes became primary modes of entry for many Chinese during the exclusion era.

In any discussion of illegal immigration, it is necessary to explain one's choice of terminology. As historian David Gutiérrez points out, the terms used to describe illegal immigrants have always been readily manipulated to serve different purposes in the political debates over U.S. immigration policy. Almost all of the common terms regularly used to describe illegal immigration raise questions and problems. Undocumented Mexican immigrants, for example, have been derogatorily labeled "wetbacks" or "fence jumpers."[3] During the exclusion era, Chinese immigrants were referred to as being "smuggled" or "imported" into the country. Both terms invoked earlier charges that Chinese did not voluntarily come to the United States but were rather pawns under the control of powerful corporations or clandestine organizations. The connections made between smuggled goods such as liquor and drugs and Chinese migrants also portrayed the Chinese as contraband commodities that did not belong in the United States. Significantly, such terms have endured and have only increased in popularity. Indeed, contemporary news reports and scholarly accounts often refer to "smuggled Chinese" in Europe, South America, and the United States.[4] In discussions of contemporary migration, "illegal immigrant" and "illegal immigration" are by far the most common terms. Placing the burden of illegality on the shoulders of the immigrants only, these terms ignore the large role that the U.S. government, U.S. immigration law, and business interests played and continue to play in promoting illegal immigration. They also fail to acknowledge the complexity of illegal status. Immigration laws — as constructions of American society and politics — often change and are unevenly applied. Certain immigrant groups — most often marked by race — are often recognized as being more "illegal" or potentially "illegal" than others. As David Haines and Karen Rosenblum cogently argue, "Many of the illegals shouldn't be illegal, wouldn't be if they had happened to come from a different country at a different time, and often won't be as their legal cases are resolved or additional legislation brings them within the borders of legality."[5] The term "undocumented" has been favored because of its more neutral description of immigrants who enter the country "outside officially established and sanctioned procedures."[6] However, this label does not apply to all illegal immigrants. As Haines and Rosenblum point out, while those who enter the country without inspection might lack documents, many others have documents, just not the right ones.[7]

I have tried to avoid using such loaded and coded terms. Despite my misgivings, however, I do continue to use the terms "illegal immigration" and "illegal immigrants" to describe Chinese immigrants who either evaded the exclusion laws by entering the country uninspected from Canada or Mexico or who circumvented the laws utilizing fraudulent papers and identities. They remain the most conventional terms and point to a larger set of political and legal issues and relationships important to this study. In this book, I emphasize immigrant agency, and the terms "illegal immigration" and "illegal immigrants" are meant to invoke not only the more common understanding of immigration outside the proper channels but also the role that the law and the state have played in creating and maintaining this type of migration.

CHAPTER FIVE

*There is no part [of the northern border] over which a Chinaman may
not pass into our country without fear of hindrance; there are scarcely
any parts of it where he may not walk boldly across it at high noon.*
—*Journalist Julian Ralph, 1891*

*There is a broad expanse of land with an imaginary line, all passable,
all being used, all leading to the United States. The vigilance of your
officers stationed along the border is always keen, but what can a handful of people do? It is a deplorable condition of affairs; we seem to be
compelled to bear it; the Chinese do come in from Mexico.*
—*U.S. immigrant inspector Marcus Braun
to Commissioner-General of Immigration Frank Sargent, 1907*

ENFORCING THE BORDERS

Chinese Exclusion along the U.S.-Canadian and U.S.-Mexican Borders

IN SEPTEMBER 1924, a Chinese male immigrant named Lim Wah entered
the United States illegally from Mexico. His goal was to find work and join his
father, a farm laborer in northern California. Legally barred from the United
States by the Chinese exclusion laws, Lim paid two hundred dollars to be
taken from Mexicali, Mexico, to Calexico, California. He and his guide waited
until nightfall and then crossed the border, ending up in San Francisco three
days later.[1] The Chinese exclusion laws greatly hindered Chinese immigration into the United States, but as Lim Wah's case demonstrates, they did not
serve as the total barriers that exclusionists hoped they would. An estimated
17,300 Chinese immigrants entered the United States through the back doors
of Canada and Mexico from 1882 to 1920.[2] U.S. Bureau of Immigration reports and newspaper accounts indicate that they entered the country through
Seattle, Washington; Buffalo, New York; San Diego, California; San Antonio
and El Paso, Texas; and numerous other points along the northern and southern borders of the United States.[3]

Chinese illegal immigration across the U.S.-Canadian and U.S.-Mexican
borders had considerable transnational consequences for both Chinese immi-

grants and America's immigration and border policies, as this chapter shows. The scale of Chinese immigration via Canada and Mexico during the exclusion era pales in comparison to that of late-twentieth-century Mexican migration across the southern border, and recent scholarship has all but ignored this chapter of Chinese exclusion history.[4] Nevertheless, Chinese immigration and exclusion in the United States transformed both its northern and southern borders into sites where illegal immigration, race, citizenship, immigration policy, and international relations were contested and reshaped. Considering Chinese immigration and exclusion from the vantage point of the borders illustrates both the racialization of U.S. immigration policy and the diasporic nature of Chinese immigration throughout the Americas. It also demonstrates how a seemingly national issue can only be understood in a wider, transnational context. Race, borders, and immigration policy in the United States, Canada, and Mexico became intertwined at the turn of the twentieth century over the issue of Chinese immigration and exclusion.[5]

The United States responded to Chinese illegal immigration by asserting its national sovereignty over its borders and by imposing American nativism, immigration laws, and enforcement practices on both Canada and Mexico. The ways in which these responses played out in the north and the south, however, were considerably different. In the north, U.S. efforts centered on border diplomacy based on a historically amicable diplomatic relationship and a shared antipathy for Chinese immigration. In contrast, U.S. control over the southern border relied less upon cooperation with Mexico and more upon border policing, a system of surveillance, patrols, apprehension, and deportation. Both methods connected American immigration policy with American imperialism and eventually closed the northern and southern borders to Chinese immigration altogether. In doing so, they laid the foundations for racialized conceptions of the "illegal immigrant problem" and of American border enforcement and nation-building at the beginning of the twentieth century.

Crossings along the U.S.-Canadian Border

The most numerous and earliest border crossings occurred along the Canadian border. Some of the first illegal border crossers were likely Chinese residents of the United States who had immigrated to Canada to work on the Canadian Pacific Railroad in the 1870s and then found themselves unable to reenter the United States after the 1882 Chinese Exclusion Act was passed.[6] Others went straight to Canada from China, with the intent of eventually entering the United States, or they chose entry from Canada as a backup plan after they were first denied entry at an American port.[7] The largely unguarded boundary between the United States and Canada made such border entries possible. Moreover, although Chinese immigrants in Canada were targets of racial hostility, Canada's Chinese immigration laws contrasted sharply with American ones. Instead of replicating America's direct exclusion of Chinese laborers, Canada's first efforts at restricting Chinese immigration were indirect. In 1885, Canada's Chinese Immigration Act imposed a fifty-dollar head tax on all Chinese laborers, to be collected by each ship captain at the point of departure. Thus, while the United States explicitly singled out all Chinese laborers, Canada's early measures allowed all Chinese to enter provided that they paid the landing fee.[8]

Despite its intent to restrict Chinese immigration, Canada's head-tax system was not completely effective. The tax was not a sufficient enough deterrent because Canada was such a convenient back door into the United States. While the tax might reduce the appeal of Chinese immigration to Canada, it did not prevent Chinese from entering the United States through Canada. Chinese immigrants destined for America were also permitted to remain in the dominion for ninety days without paying the head tax and could presumably later cross the border at will. Those who did pay the head tax could also easily leave Canada.[9]

The comparatively lenient Canadian laws combined with the increasingly stringent U.S. Chinese exclusion laws led directly to an increase in illegal border entries. After the United States passed the Scott Act in 1888, which nullified the U.S. return permits of an estimated 20,000 Chinese laborers, 773 Chinese immigrated to Canada. In 1890, the number had increased to 1,069, and during the next year, 2,108 Chinese entered Canada. In 1892, 3,264 more Chinese immigrated to Canada following the passage of the Geary Act.[10] Many of these Chinese found their way into the United States. One American journalist estimated that ninety-nine out of one hundred Chinese arriving in Canada intended to "smuggle themselves over our border."[11] U.S. immigration authorities estimated that at least a few thousand Chinese entered the country undetected from the northern border every year from the 1880s to the early 1900s.[12]

Even after Canada raised its head tax to one hundred dollars in 1900 and then to five hundred dollars in 1903, Chinese border entries continued, and American officials complained that the Canadian laws "practically nullified . . . the effective work done by the border officers."[13] In 1907, a U.S. immigrant inspector pointed out with alarm that the Canadian border had become the "most prolific field for the introduction into the United States of Chinese of the coolie class."[14] Thus, until 1923, when Canada passed a more complete exclusion bill, the country remained a convenient alternative route into the United States to anyone willing and able to pay the head taxes. This migration across the border prompted one Oregon magazine editor to complain that "Canada gets the money and we get the Chinamen," and reporters began to write about the growing "Chinese leak" coming in from Canada.[15]

Chinese wanting to enter the United States took advantage of established smuggling networks used for opium and other contraband substances along the Canadian-U.S. border. The Vancouver–Puget Sound area was widely known as a "smugglers' paradise" in the opium trade, and Chinese and their American or Canadian guides used the same boats and routes to make the journey to the United States.[16] The cost of a border crossing along this route ranged from twenty-three to sixty dollars in the 1890s. One decade later, entry through Washington State could cost up to three hundred dollars.[17] Other popular entry points were along the northeastern border. The completion of the Canadian Pacific Railway, which stretched several thousand miles from Vancouver, British Columbia, to Montreal, Quebec, allowed immigrants to enter at a western sea port in Canada and then travel across the country to the East, where the border with the United States was even less guarded.[18] Conducted by Chinese already in the United States and white Americans looking for a ready profit, the business of guiding Chinese into the country through Buffalo, New York, for example, was especially well organized and profitable. In 1909, one newspaper reporter found that two to four Chinese were brought into Buffalo weekly, at a price of two hundred to six hundred dollars per person.[19] Chinese were also commonly taken to Boston and New York City from the Canadian border in groups ranging in size from two to seventy-five.[20]

Border crossings were risky endeavors that not only involved the danger of being detected but sometimes also resulted in death and injury. In 1906, the Bureau of Immigration reported on one entry attempt gone awry. The plan involved placing a Chinese immigrant in a railcar at a point on the Canadian railway north of Windsor, Ontario, directly across from Detroit, Michigan. In order to conceal his presence, the immigrant was to be put in the railcar that supplied ice to the rest of the train. He was supposed to be removed as soon as the train reached the American side. Unfortunately a snowstorm delayed the train, and the immigrant froze to death.[21] In Buffalo, another attempt was made to bring ten Chinese across Lake Erie in an open boat. When a severe

THE CHINESE PILOT: "THAT IS THE UNITED STATES."

"The Chinese Pilot: That Is the United States." Chinese illegal immigration across the U.S.-Canadian and U.S.-Mexican borders was part of a transnational and interracial business in illicit trade. This illustration depicts an "American" pilot guiding a Chinese male toward the border. Reprinted from *Harper's New Monthly Magazine*, March 1891.

storm arose, the boat was dashed against the sea wall, drowning six of the immigrants. The remaining four and their two white guides were rescued with great difficulty.[22]

Most Chinese border crossers were probably entering the United States for the first time, but many were also returning residents who believed that re-entry via Canada would be easier than risking denial at the regular seaports. Wong Yuen King, Wong Yin Hing, and Wong Sang, for example, were all residents of Baltimore, Maryland, in 1898 when they were caught entering the country through Malone, New York. All worked in Chinese businesses in Baltimore but perhaps did not have the correct papers or no longer worked in occupations defined as "exempt" under the exclusion laws.[23] In 1915, Inspector Richard Taylor in Buffalo, New York, reported to his superiors that many "well-known residents" chose to enter via Canada as well.[24]

Over time, Chinese entering the country from Canada took advantage of changes in the laws. Following the 1898 Supreme Court ruling that affirmed birthright citizenship for American-born Chinese, Chinese seeking entry from Canada began to claim that they were born in the United States.[25] Many were likely false claims. By 1903, the Bureau of Immigration reported that falsely claiming citizenship constituted "the chief means" of violating the Exclusion Act.[26] As Chinese interpreter and inspector John Endicott Gardner reported,

Chinese first entered the country in the districts located along the Canadian border with the goal of proving their citizenship claims in the U.S. federal district courts. Similar to the situation at American seaports, Chinese preferred judicial hearings over immigration service interrogations because the former were known for their more lenient interpretation of the Chinese exclusion laws.[27] In court, the Chinese and their attorneys were often well prepared, prompting Gardner to report scornfully: "At the time set for the case, Ah Sing, or some other 'Ah' would be called . . . and one other Chinese would be put upon the stand to testify to the defendant's having been born in the United States—most likely in the Chinatown of San Francisco, the alleged birthplace of tens of thousands of others that have made the claim at various times and at various places before him. Upon the uncorroborated testimony of this one Chinaman, the other Chinaman . . . would be declared a native of the United States. This goes on week after week and month after month and has been going on for years."[28]

In Inspector Gardner's analysis, the border was like a revolving door through which entered interchangeable "Chinamen" who all looked alike, had the same names, and recited the same practiced stories about native birth. While Gardner pointed to the inherent, duplicitous nature of the Chinese race to explain their strategic use of the courts, the government's own system of enforcing the laws and governmental corruption were more likely factors encouraging this approach. As Lucy Salyer has demonstrated, habeas corpus cases involving Chinese immigration were usually tried in courts under U.S. commissioners. Because these courts and their officers were beholden to principles and procedures of due process, Chinese litigants were often successful in proving their claims.[29] Moreover, some commissioners were also known to be more lenient, careless, easily bribed, or all of the above. The figures compiled for the northern border regions alone show that at least 5,714 Chinese were admitted as American-born citizens between 1895 and 1905.[30] U.S. commissioner and judge Felix W. McGettrick of St. Albans, Vermont, for example, testified that he tried and probably falsely discharged 1,100 Chinese as being citizens of the United States from March 1894 to July 1897.[31] Corruption was common in the immigration service as well. In 1898, immigration officials along the northern border were accused of admitting Chinese without papers in exchange for money.[32] In 1911, immigrant inspector Adam Hoffman was dismissed for "aiding and abetting the unlawful entry into the United States" of a Chinese immigrant.[33]

Corrupt officials, persistent migrants, organized networks of Canadian, American, and Chinese guides, an ineffective Canadian immigration policy, and the porous, unguarded northern border thus combined to facilitate Chinese border migration. As U.S. immigration officials began to understand the magnitude of the problem facing them along the U.S.-Canadian border, they also looked warily to the south and correctly predicted that the Mexican boundary would "undoubtedly be the next point of attack."[34]

Crossings along the U.S.-Mexican Border

As in Canada, Mexican policies on Chinese immigration contrasted sharply with American laws, leaving open another back door into the United States. At the same time that the United States passed its exclusion laws, both Chinese and Mexican authorities were encouraging Chinese migration to Mexico. The Chinese government believed that Mexico and other South American countries could be convenient alternatives to the United States, and Mexican officials believed that foreign immigration was an essential ingredient in the development and modernization of the country's infrastructure under President Porfirio Díaz. Attempts to attract Europeans—considered to be the most desirable immigrant group—failed, but Chinese came in significant numbers and increasingly moved into local trade and commerce, meeting demands for goods and services in the newly expanding society. After China and Mexico signed the Treaty of Amity and Commerce in 1899, Chinese immigration into Mexico increased.[35]

Like their fellow migrants in the north, however, the Chinese in Mexico also faced racial hostility, and an organized anti-Chinese movement developed in the northern state of Sonora in 1916. Stereotypes of Chinese as vice-ridden, diseased, and unassimilable surfaced in local newspapers, and charges of economic competition merged with the larger antiforeign, especially anti-American, sentiments that were an integral part of Mexico's revolutionary nationalism.[36] Nevertheless, the anti-Chinese movement in Mexico did not result in the legal restriction of Chinese immigration until 1926.[37] Moreover, it did not seem to hinder border migration into the United States. One reason was that while Mexican officials found Chinese immigrants "undesirable," they also admitted that Chinese labor was beneficial and necessary. One amendment to the country's immigration laws in 1907 did attempt to restrict the entry of diseased immigrants, and foreign observers reported that the law was aimed at Asians, but the law was inconsistently enforced. In 1909, British consular officials noted that "the Chinese still arrive in large quantities and undoubtedly considerable numbers of them still succeed in making their way across the frontier into the United States."[38]

The border between the United States and Mexico was largely unguarded and functioned more like an arbitrary line between the two nations. As Law Ngim, a Chinese immigrant who was caught on the U.S. side of the border across from Tijuana, explained, "I knew that I didn't have the privilege of entering the United States, but I didn't know I was *in* the United States."[39] More often than not, one did not know where Mexico ended and the United States began. As a result, the Chinese exclusion laws were ostensibly nullified. While it is impossible to determine exactly how many Chinese entered the United States across the Mexican border, reports from U.S. immigration officials indicate that several hundred entered per year in the early 1900s. One Arizona immigration official reported that some 6,000 Chinese crossed the border between 1882 and 1910 (an average of 214 persons per year), about half of whom were caught and deported. In 1910, an additional 713 Chinese were arrested for unlawful entry.[40] Mexico's statistics on Chinese immigration suggest a much larger number of Chinese border crossers; they indicate that as many as 1,000 to 2,000 Chinese entered the United States per year during the *Porfiriato*, the rule of President Díaz, from 1876 to 1911.[41]

As in the north, border crossers were most likely first-time immigrants to the United States, but many longtime residents chose the Mexican route as well to avoid being subjected to the harsh reentry requirements at the regular ports of entry. Chinese American laborers, who were allowed to be absent from the United States for a period of only one year, fell into this latter category. On the rare occasion that Chinese were able to save enough money for passage back to China for a visit, most wanted to stay longer than the allowable time. Reentering the country through Mexico allowed them to do that. In 1909, immigration officials reported that Chinese laborers often left for China, stayed as long as they liked, and returned through Mexico without the immigration service knowing that they had ever left the country.[42]

Chinese border crossings were facilitated by an organized group of experienced smugglers who began to move their business southward following the U.S. government's crackdown on the northern border in the early 1900s. Curley Roberts, well known for having made a fortune bringing Chinese across the Canadian border, planned to bring Chinese across the Mexican border and take them into Los Angeles in 1912. As he explained to a potential business partner, the profit along the southern border was just as high as it had been previously along the northern. "I have just brought seven yellow boys over and got $225 for that so you can see I am doing very well here," he reported.[43] By 1906, the Mexican border was considered the greatest trouble spot for Chinese illegal immigration. One immigrant inspector went so far as to say that legitimate immigration via Mexico was "a joke, a hollow mockery." It was estimated that 80 percent of the Chinese arriving in Mexican seaports would eventually cross the border.[44] Those headed to the eastern states might take a sea route to Florida, Louisiana, Mississippi, or other Gulf Coast states. Entry west of El Paso, Texas, was especially popular for those wishing to go to the West. In fact, the town was known as a "hot-bed for the smuggling of Chinese."[45] As an El Paso official reported in 1906, 516 Chinese laborers had arrived in Ciudad Juárez, Mexico (right across the Rio Grande from El Paso), but only five appeared to be Mexican residents. The others were presumably awaiting an opportunity to cross the border into Texas. The next year, a special government investigator reported that while Mexican trains brought twenty to fifty "Chinamen" into Juárez every day, the Chinese population there never increased. On the contrary, the investigator explained, it "very often decreases, and the most diligent research has failed to show that any Chinamen ever leave that town for the interior or the western part of the Mexican republic." Thus, he concluded wryly, "Chinamen coming to Ciudad Juárez either vanish in thin air or cross the border line."[46]

Because direct steamship travel between China and Mexico did not commence until 1902, early Chinese immigrants choosing the circuitous route through Mexico usually traveled to San Francisco first and then transferred to a Mexican boat into Mexico. They disembarked in Ensenada, Manzanillo, Mazatlan, or Guaymas and then took either another steamer going back north or the railroad, making sure to disembark well before the trains had reached the United States, where immigration officials were tracking passengers. From there, they either hired a guide to help them get to the border or took their chances alone. Some simply walked across the line by themselves or hitch-hiked northward.[47] Others engaged in highly organized plans. Those attempting entry along the coast posed as crew members on fishing vessels. They then rendezvoused with a waiting schooner in the Gulf of Mexico and, under the cover of night, made their way to a designated place along the coastline.[48] In 1903, a "band of fifteen to twenty Chinamen" was found camped out in a "safe house" about seventy-five miles southeast of San Diego. While the Chinese hid inside the building, their Mexican guides went into town to buy provisions and make further preparations.[49] The average cost for a guide ranged from twenty-five to seventy-five dollars in the 1890s, depending on where the crossing took place. By the 1930s, it had increased to two hundred dollars.[50] One could also arrange for an "all-inclusive package" directly from Hong Kong. In 1932, for example, Jew Yick sought to enter the United States via Mexico to find work. He traveled from Hong Kong to Mexico, with assurances from a Japanese immigration broker that he would be admitted into the country. From Mexico, a "black man" drove him into the United States. The total cost of his journey, including the steamship fare, was nine hundred dollars, which he had paid to the Japanese guide in Hong Kong. Unfortunately for Jew, he was arrested in a raid in a Chinese restaurant in San Francisco just six weeks after he had crossed the border.[51]

Migrants also entered the United States hidden in railcars, often under trying and dangerous conditions. According to Clifford Perkins, a Chinese inspector in the Southwest, Chinese "hid in every conceivable place on trains: in box cars loaded with freight, under staterooms rented for them by accomplices, and even in the four-foot-wide ice vents across each end of the insulated Pacific Fruit Express refrigerated cars, iced or not."[52] In the wake of such reports, the commissioner-general of immigration concluded that "a Chinaman apparently will undergo any hardship or torture, take any risk or pay any sum of money . . . to enjoy the forbidden, but much coveted privilege of living and working in the United States."[53]

As in Canada, Chinese border migration in the south was built upon an established foundation of trade and smuggling networks that thrived in the border towns close to California and the American Southwest. There, Chinese border crossings were an "open secret," and American immigration officials along the southern boundary complained that illegal immigration was "carried on with the cognizance if not with the concealed cooperation of the local [Mexican] authorities."[54] Illegal immigration along the southern border depended on these networks, and Chinese on both sides of the border could be counted on to provide assistance. Newly arrived Chinese immigrants in Mexico were provided with American money, Chinese-English dictionaries, Chinese American newspapers, and U.S. railroad maps.[55] Immigrant guidebooks to Mexico were also shared among immigrants, and fraudulent immigration documents manufactured in Mexico arrived at the El Paso post office "almost daily."[56] One Bureau of Immigration report complained that both working-class Chinese and Chinese merchants in El Paso were "banded together as one man for the purpose of concealing . . . those Chinese coolies who have crossed the line." Rumors of hidden chambers built between the ceilings and roofs of Chinatown businesses also circulated among El Paso residents and immigration officials alike.[57]

Crossings and Contact Zones in the Borderlands

That the Chinese of El Paso, Texas, "banded together" with the Chinese coming in from Juárez, Mexico, illustrates not only the transnational connections between Chinese communities in the United States and those in Mexico but also the permeability of the border region for Chinese immigrants. Indeed, Chinese communities along both sides of the southern border inhabited "a world in motion"—much like the U.S.-Mexican borderlands in the late twentieth century—made up of shifting and multiple identities and relationships constructed for the purpose of illegal migration.[58] One of the best examples of how Chinese shifted their identities was their attempts to "pass" as members of another race in order to cross the border undetected. Even though Chinese migration to both Canada and Mexico dated as far back as the middle of the nineteenth century, Chinese were not viewed as "natural" inhabitants of the northern and southern borderlands, as were Native Americans or Mexicans. Some Chinese immigrants and their guides thus learned early on to try to "pass" as members of these two groups as they crossed the border. In 1904, for example, the *Buffalo Times* reported that it was not uncommon for white "smugglers" to disguise Chinese as Native Americans crossing from Canada to the United States in pursuit of trade. They would be dressed in "Indian garb," given a basket of sassafras, and rowed across the border in a boat.[59]

In 1907, special government inspectors reported on a highly organized, Chinese- and Mexican-run illegal immigration business headed by Chinese-Mexican Josè Chang in Guaymas, Mexico. Chinese immigrants bound for the United States were landed in Mexico on the pretense that they had been hired to work in the cotton fields there. Chang then brought them to his headquarters in Guaymas, where letters from the immigrants' U.S. relatives were distributed and further preparations for the border journey were made. One of the most important aspects of Chang's operation involved disguising the newly arrived Chinese as Mexican residents. The Chinese cut their queues and exchanged their "blue jeans and felt slippers" for "the most picturesque Mexican dress." They received fraudulent Mexican citizenship papers, and they also learned to say a few words of Spanish, in particular "Yo soy Mexicano" ("I am Mexican"). This disguise was supposed to protect Chinese in case they should be "held up by some American citizen" while attempting to cross the border.[60] The disguise was apparently quite successful. In 1907, immigrant inspector Marcus Braun traveled to Mexico City, where he discovered Chinese immigrants using fake Mexican citizenship certificates to get into the United States. Upon examining the photographs attached to the documents, Braun expressed with some amazement that it was "exceedingly difficult to distinguish these Chinamen from Mexicans." He included in his report to the commissioner-general of immigration several photographs of the Chinese in question, demonstrating how they could easily "pass" as Mexican.[61]

The use of racial disguises was not confined to the northern and southern borders. One government report on the illicit entry of Asian and European immigrants via Cuba into the United States included a particularly successful strategy of "painting the Chinese black" to disguise them as part of the steamship's crew. They apparently "walked off the steamer in New Orleans without trouble."[62] In Mobile, Alabama, an immigrant inspector reported on a project to bring in newly arrived Chinese from Mexico and then "disguise the Chinamen as negroes." Mobile was apparently a popular destination point because it was home to a man whom his fellow Chinese referred to as "Crooked Face," whose specialty was disguising Chinese immigrants as African Americans.[63] Chinese immigrants in effect traded their own racial uniforms — which elicited suspicion in the borderlands — for others that would allow them to blend into particular regional and racial landscapes. In the north, the most dominant racial others were American and Canadian Indians. In the Southwest, it was Mexicans and American Indians, and in the South, it was African Americans. Chinese illegal immigrants learned to use the ways in which race marked each regional landscape to their advantage, entering the country undetected.

The multiracial character of Chinese illegal immigration transformed the borders into "contact zones" where people — mostly men — of different races, classes, and nationalities met and sometimes formed fragile alliances.[64] Most smugglers were white American or European immigrant men working with Chinese accomplices and organizers. Many were often already involved in illegal activities. In 1911, for example, Walter Bradley, who was under investigation for bringing Chinese into the country along the Windsor-Detroit border, was described as a "refugee from justice . . . having committed some crime in Windsor, to which place he dare not return."[65] Others apparently participated in the business on the side. Either their regular occupations or their geographical locations facilitated covert activities. In Seattle, for example, a locomotive

"'Exhibit J,' Chinese Posing as Mexicans," 1907. Disguising themselves to "pass" as Mexicans was a common strategy used by Chinese entering the United States from the U.S.-Mexican border. In 1907, a U.S. government investigation discovered these photographs attached to fraudulent Mexican citizenship papers. Immigrant inspector Marcus Braun reported that it was "exceedingly difficult to distinguish these Chinamen from Mexicans." Courtesy of the National Archives, Washington, D.C.

engineer named Billie Low and a fireman named Bat Nelson reportedly took advantage of Low's railroad connections to bring both Chinese immigrants and opium into the United States from Vancouver.[66] In Mississippi, a government informant reported that a "certain ring of Greeks" who owned and ran a store and factory headquartered in Bay St. Louis, Mississippi, were "running Chinese" through Mexico. The two buildings provided a cover for the operation as well as substantial housing for the newly arrived immigrants.[67] Another man joined the immigration business using his expertise as a map surveyor. He had assisted the U.S. Army in preparing maps of Lower California and Mexico and later turned his skills to providing similar maps to Chinese immigrants and their guides.[68] Even individuals working in the highest levels of law enforcement were involved in the business of Chinese illegal immigration. In 1908, several witnesses and government informants came forward with evidence that the former chief of police of El Paso, Edward M. Fink, was "the leader of one of the gangs of smugglers" in El Paso.[69]

American Indians were also known to guide Chinese into the country, especially along the northern border. In the south, however, the Papago Indians "seemed to have a natural antipathy for Chinese," according to immigrant inspector Clifford Perkins, and thus were routinely employed as government informants.[70] Mexicans were the primary guides along the southern border, and they made a handsome profit from both boarding the Chinese while they waited to cross into the United States and guiding them across the border.[71] Often, Mexican guides collaborated with Chinese and/or Americans. In 1912, Luis Fernandez, Jordan Felize, and Wong Gong Huey of Mexicali joined Ethel Hall, Muy Fat, Lin Fat, and Chin Man of San Francisco in a transnational "notorious smuggling ring" that came under government scrutiny.[72] Another large operation along the southern border was discovered by undercover agent Frank Stone. This collaboration involved Ming Wah (alias Frank Chin) as well as Mexicans and Americans who brought not only Chinese immigrants across the border but opium as well. They were also known to rob freight cars on railroads leading out of El Paso.[73] Mar Been, another Chinese merchant in El Paso, employed two Mexican women to transport opium and assist in the Chinese immigration operation from Juárez. He also had an agreement with a "negro" brakeman on the Santa Fe railroad who, in exchange for money, stopped the train at Montoya, Mexico, and "put the Chinese boys in the Pullman car."[74] Mexicans were not always working on the same side as the Chinese. Some Mexicans were well-known informants, employees of the immigration service, and even witnesses in courts, while many others who were in the position to assist Chinese refused to do so for fear that their actions would call unwanted attention to themselves.[75]

"John Chinaman and His Smugglers":
Constructing the Chinese Illegal Immigrant

Although those engaged in the business of illegal immigration relied upon their ability to function beyond the reach and sight of government authorities, illegal Chinese immigration itself became the very public symbol of the continuing "Chinese problem" that had inspired the passage of the Chinese Exclusion Act in 1882. As a result, Chinese border crossers came to represent a new type of immigrant—the "illegal." The American public learned about Chinese border crossings through sensationalist regional and national newspaper reports, magazine articles, and government investigations. The reportage borrowed extensively from existing racial stereotypes of Chinese, often merging the illegal aspect of their migration with the older view that Chinese were cunning criminals who would endanger American society with their alien presence, and servile "coolies" who would threaten the white working class. As Robert Lee has illustrated, beginning in the 1850s, the racialized character of "John Chinaman" in American plays, songs, minstrel shows, and fictional stories created and reinforced these popular representations of Chinese immigrants. By the 1880s, "John Chinaman" also came to be the primary image used to describe Chinese illegal immigration in both popular magazines and political discourse.[76]

The San Francisco–based weekly illustrated journal *The Wasp* was one of the first periodicals to articulate fears of the Chinese illegal immigration problem from Canada and Mexico. The two-page cartoon titled "And Still They Come!" was printed in 1880, while anti-Chinese politicians were still laying the groundwork for the eventual passage of the Chinese Exclusion Act. Having just failed to enact into law the 1879 Fifteen Passenger Bill that would have limited to fifteen the number of Chinese passengers on any ship coming to the United States, the supporters of Chinese exclusion worked tirelessly to keep the specter of an alien invasion alive and well.[77] "And Still They Come," picturing two endless streams of slant-eyed "Johns" or Chinese "coolies" disembarking from over-crowded steamships and flowing into the United States, expressed the Chinese exclusion message perfectly. Racial difference is clearly communicated through the exaggerated features and the alien dress and hairstyles of the Chinese figures. The dark slits that are supposed to be eyes are the physical manifestations of what was believed to be the surreptitious, sneaky nature of the Chinese. Their loose-fitting garments, broad "coolie" hats, and distinctive baskets and shoes emphasize the strange customs that will pollute America. Finally, the long, rat-tail-like braided plaits of hair worn by the Chinese men represent a cultural anomaly that is both sexually and racially ambiguous and threatening. Entering surreptitiously through two back doors, "British Columbia" and "Mexico," the Chinese gleefully flout U.S. attempts to bar them. They easily evade an eaglelike Uncle Sam, who is trying in vain to shut America's main gates to a third wave of Chinese "coolies" entering by sea. With his back turned away from the Chinese entering from the north and south, Uncle Sam is oblivious to the larger threats posed by the open borders and fails to notice the Chinese thumbing their noses at him, U.S. law, and the sovereignty of the American nation. As a symbol of the imminent invasion of Chinese to come, the two steamships docked in British Columbia and Mexico sag with the weight of countless Chinese hanging from the mastheads and streaming down the gangplanks into the United States. On the distant horizon, dozens of Chinese vessels and even air balloons filled with Chinese leave China and make their way to the shores of the United States. Each ship and balloon is marked by the number fifteen, alluding to the unsuccessful Fifteen Passenger Bill and demonstrating how the cunning Chinese would undoubtedly evade and take advantage of America's ineffectual immigration and border policies through an outright invasion.[78]

Beginning in the 1890s, after Chinese border entries had indeed become a reality, the specter of the Chinese illegal immigrant received more national press coverage. Speakers before the U.S. Congress likened the influx of Chinese from Canada to the "swarming of the Huns" in early European history.[79] In 1891, *Harper's New Monthly Magazine* published an exposé written by journalist Julian Ralph titled the "Chinese Leak," in which Ralph explained in detail the strategies used by Chinese to enter the United States from Canada and Mexico. Lax Canadian laws, "wily" Chinese, and profit-hungry Canadian and American smugglers and "pilots" all figured prominently in Ralph's investigation. Four illustrations accompanied the article. One, simply titled "John," portrays a young, disheveled Chinese male walking, presumably across the border. His queue trails in the wind behind him. His dress and shoes are distinctly Chinese, and the slant of his eyes is overemphasized. The image of "John Chinaman" connects the standard racialized caricature of Chinese immigrants as alien "coolies" to the new phenomenon of illegal immigration. Ralph's text running alongside the image elaborates on this connection.

"And Still They Come," from *The Wasp*, Dec. 4, 1880. Cartoons and illustrations dramatically portrayed the threat of Chinese illegal immigration via the "back doors" of Canada and Mexico. In this illustration, Uncle Sam is kept busy guarding the main "gateway" to the United States while floods of Chinese enter undetected and thumb their noses at ineffective U.S. immigration policies. Courtesy of the San Francisco History Center, San Francisco Public Library.

Readers are told that this "John" and other "Chinamen" who crossed the border were especially "impenetrable," "shrewd," and "intelligent tricksters." Ralph also interpreted the fact that the Chinese subjected themselves to inhuman conditions in order to enter the United States as signs of Chinese racial inferiority. In 1891, Ralph happened to witness the interdiction of the *North Star*, a "tiny" smuggling boat in "desperately bad condition" that frequently carried as many as thirty Chinese males in her hold from Victoria, Canada, to the United States. Noting the small stature of the Chinese and their "raisin-like adaptability . . . to compressed conditions," Ralph observed that it would have been difficult, if not unthinkable, to transport "men of any other nationality" in the same fashion. Another more graphic image titled "Dying of Thirst in the Desert" accompanies Ralph's exploration of Chinese border crossings along the southern border and portrays an abandoned, parched, and dying Chinese male in the desolate southwestern desert. His canteen empty, his hat and walking stick abandoned on the desert floor beside him, this "John" crawls on his

DYING OF THIRST IN THE DESERT.

"Dying of Thirst." Chinese border crossings at the turn of the twentieth century were risky endeavors, often resulting in death. Reprinted from *Harper's New Monthly Magazine*, March 1891.

bony, clawlike hands and knees toward the U.S. border. *Harper's* comfortable, middle-class readers no doubt were shocked by the illustration, which served to sensationalize the phenomenon of Chinese illegal immigration. Although it could be perceived as a somewhat sympathetic image because it points to the desperate measures Chinese were willing to take in order to enter the United States, "Dying of Thirst" nonetheless also reinforced racialized notions of Chinese criminality, alienness, racial inferiority and difference, and the threat of invasion in that very same depiction of desperation and tragedy.[80]

This way of depicting the Chinese illegal immigrant was especially prevalent in the American West and in the northern and southern border regions, where most of the illicit migration took place. Both American and Canadian newspapers from the border regions regularly covered the "smuggling" of Chinese from the north into the south. All of the major newspapers in Buffalo, New York, for example, covered Chinese illegal immigration in minute detail. One *Buffalo Express* article prominently displayed a stereotypical image of a disheveled, menacing, and subhuman Chinese male under the headline "Wily Tricks Played by John Chinaman and His Smugglers." Contending that the

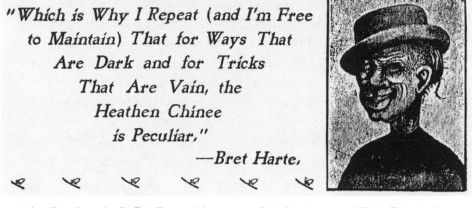

WILY TRICKS PLAYED BY JOHN CHINAMAN AND HIS SMUGGLERS.

"Which is Why I Repeat (and I'm Free to Maintain) That for Ways That Are Dark and for Tricks That Are Vain, the Heathen Chinee is Peculiar."

—Bret Harte.

A headline from the *Buffalo Express*, Mar. 4, 1904. Racialized images of "John Chinaman" as an illegal immigrant built on existing stereotypes of Chinese as racially inferior, wily tricksters who could easily evade the Chinese exclusion laws and endanger the nation. Such portrayals were especially popular in border cities, where illegal immigration was relatively common. Reprinted from the *Buffalo Express*.

evasion of exclusion laws was common among the "wily" and "heathen" Chinese, the newspaper warned that the "smuggling business" would continue to "flourish and defy authorities." Explicitly connecting the new threat of illegal Chinese immigration with the standard anti-Chinese rhetoric from the 1870s, the headline was accompanied by a few lines from Bret Harte's popular anti-Chinese poem first published in 1871: "Which is why I repeat (and I'm free to maintain) that for ways that are dark and for tricks that are vain, the Heathen Chinee is peculiar." In another article in the *Buffalo Morning Express*, a Chinese immigrant who was caught trying to illegally enter the country was described as a "Chink" who used his "long, talon-like nails" in a struggle with law-enforcement officials.[81]

Chinese immigrants may have been the first immigrants to enter the United States illegally, but by the early 1900s, they were joined by a much larger number of immigrants from other countries who also chose the border as an alternative to the rigorous immigration inspections at American seaports. Syrians, Greeks, Hungarians, Russian Jews, Italians, and some "maidens" from France, Belgium, and Spain were the main groups entering through Canada and Mexico. All were suspected of having been denied entry at the Atlantic ports of entry, but the back door of Canada offered them a second chance. Canadian immigrant inspection in the late nineteenth and early twentieth centuries was considerably less rigorous than U.S. procedures and primarily consisted of a limited health screening. Both European and Asian immigrants quickly learned that they could buy steamship tickets for Canada and then attempt a border crossing into the United States. It is not known exactly how many individuals entered the United States illegally through Canada in the early twentieth century. One sensationalist congressional report claimed that as many as 50,000 European immigrants entered via this route in 1890 alone. Bureau of Immigration estimates, which are probably more accurate, placed the figure at "several thousand" each year in the early 1900s.[82] American officials were consistently frustrated by what they deemed to be overly lax immigration laws in Canada. As U.S. immigrant inspector Robert Watchorn explained in a 1902 report, "Much that appears menacing to us is regarded with comparative indifference by the Canadian government." Consequently, Watchorn claimed, "those which Canada receives but fails to hold . . . come unhindered into the United States." By 1909, general immigration via the Canadian and Mexican borders was so great that the U.S. Bureau of Immigration identified them as second in importance only to New York as gateways to the United States.[83]

Despite the fact that Europeans and Asians both were illegally crossing the borders into the United States, the discourse surrounding each of these immigrant groups differed sharply, reflecting an existing American racial hierarchy that viewed European immigrants—even illegal ones—as more desirable than Asian immigrants. That the image of the illegal immigrant was, from its inception, a highly racialized one is clear in the contrast in the ways in which the U.S. government discussed the challenges of illegal European immigration and those of illegal Chinese immigration. Immigration authorities were certainly concerned about the large numbers of European immigrants evading inspection at the regular ports of entry by crossing the borders, suspecting that these immigrants were diseased or likely to become public charges. Nevertheless, Europeans' unlawful entries were not defined as threats to the American nation, as were those of the Chinese. In 1890, the secretary of the treasury, whose agency administered U.S. immigration laws until 1903, articulated this distinction most clearly. Illegal European entries from Canada were considered a potential problem, but the attitudes toward European immigration in general remained welcoming and supportive and reflected the view that Europeans — even illegal immigrants — were still future American citizens. "Our country owes too much in greatness and prosperity to its naturalized citizens to wish to impede the natural movement of such valuable members of society to our shores," Secretary William Windom noted. The next year, Windom merely noted an increase in the number of European aliens crossing the northern border illegally and made a general suggestion for increased border inspection. In later years, European immigrants crossing the border illegally were commonly portrayed in government reports as "forlorn," "unfortunate victims of unscrupulous agents in Europe" who were misled and overcharged in the border migration scheme.[84] In other words, the illegal European immigrants were merely exceptions to the generally acceptable population of European immigrants as a whole. They were not a reflection of *all* European immigrants.

The same year that Treasury Secretary William Windom praised the country's "naturalized citizens" of European heritage, he warned in alarmist terms of the "organized attempts . . . by Chinese laborers to force their way into the United States by way of Mexico, British Columbia, and Canada." The next year, he warned that the department was "unable . . . to withstand the great influx of Chinese laborers along our Canadian border. . . . They are at liberty to invade our territory." Similarly, the commissioner-general of immigration blamed the border enforcement problem on the "difficulties inherent in the character of the Mongolian race," and Chinese immigration through Mexico was characterized as an "evil, constant and systematic evasion of our laws."[85]

The racialization of Chinese immigrants as illegal also contrasted sharply with the government's treatment of Mexican immigrants crossing the U.S.-Mexican border. Compared to the estimated 17,000 Chinese who entered the country illegally from 1882 to 1920, approximately 1.4 million Mexicans migrated largely unrestricted into the United States from 1900 to 1930. While some nativists argued that the large numbers of "Mexican peons" entering the country in the 1920s were just as dangerous as the Chinese that "invaded" in earlier years, anti-Mexican nativism worked differently in practice from the anti-immigrant sentiment targeting Asians in the pre-1924 period. Instead of excludable aliens, Mexicans were more often characterized as long-term residents of the Southwest or as "birds of passage" who returned to Mexico after the agricultural seasons ended.[86] Mexican immigration was not wholly unregulated, but it did exist in a state of "benign neglect," and "little attention" was paid to Mexicans who crossed the border into the United States. Indeed, while the immigration service began to record entries and inspect aliens at the southern border in 1903, these procedures did not apply to Mexicans.[87]

This disparate treatment is directly related to the expansion of the southwestern economy from the 1890s through the 1920s and the related need for a steady pool of labor. The curtailment of Asian and southern and eastern European immigrant labor beginning in 1882 and continuing through 1924 made Mexico a logical source of new labor. Immigration laws like the Immigration Act of 1917, which required Mexican immigrants to pass a literacy test and pay an eight-dollar head tax, were aimed at restricting Mexican immigration, but until the late 1920s, companies and agriculturalists often waived these requirements. U.S. officials at the border also consistently allowed Mexican migrants to bypass the head tax and literacy test.[88] In 1905, Commissioner of Immigration Hart Hyatt North reported matter-of-factly that Mexicans and Indians were "crossing at will" at Mexicale and other points along the line without either immigration or medical inspection. However, the Chinese, he warned, warranted the government's full and "most vigilant attention." In the eyes of the government and the public, Chinese were the illegals, and they became the targets of concerted federal efforts to control illegal immigration. American newspapers in the Southwest during the early 1900s reported on "Chinese wetbacks" rather than Mexican ones.[89] In effect, the border was controlled in order to facilitate Mexican immigration and restrict Chinese immigration.

Identifying Chinese and not Europeans or Mexicans as dangerous and illegal had direct consequences on the ways in which immigration officials dealt with Chinese immigrants in general. One result was the government's blanket association of Chinese immigration with illegality. The mere presence of Chinese along the border was enough to raise suspicions among government officials. Chinese residents of El Paso, Texas, for example, complained to the government that they were routinely suspected of being illegal immigrants and were treated with "undue harshness and strictness." The dehumanization of all Chinese immigrants was another consequence. Government officials described Chinese immigrants as "contraband," as if they were the same as a banned drug or product being smuggled into the country. Investigators of smuggling activities routinely referred to the subjects of their inquiry as "chinks." The reward system offered by the government to those who gave information leading to the arrest of Chinese in the country unlawfully also reinforced this dehumanizing attitude. One 1908 agreement between the government and G. W. Edgar, a Seattle farmer, established a fee of "five dollars per Chinese head" or two hundred and fifty dollars for "fifty or more Chinamen" in exchange for information that would lead to the arrest of illegal Chinese immigrants.[90] The classification of Chinese as illegals also gave anti-Chinese exclusionists' arguments even more power and legitimacy. Moreover, it greatly influenced the way in which the borders were policed and closed to Chinese immigrants. That the conflation of "Chinese" with "illegal" was embedded in border policy was made explicitly clear when the immigration service established a special department whose primary responsibility was to deal with illegal aliens. Its name was the Chinese Division.[91]

American Empire/American Border Enforcement

Chinese illegal immigration highlighted grave weaknesses in American immigration law. Because it concentrated on immigrant entry through the seaports, America's restrictive immigration legislation was perceived as largely ignoring the country's lack of control over its own borders. As one border patrol inspector commented in 1924, the nation's immigration laws provided "locked doors," but there was no "connecting wall between them" because of the open borders.[92] The United States responded by devising a border enforcement policy designed to assert its sovereignty and control over the northern and southern borders and to protect the American nation within. This policy was part of a larger extension of American laws, ideologies, and systems of control that characterized American imperialism in the late nineteenth and early twentieth centuries.[93] Indeed, the subject of Chinese exclusion, traditionally defined within the confines of domestic or U.S.-China relations, spilled over many national boundaries. Border anxiety and U.S. immigration policy were directly linked to, and products of, U.S. expansionism.

If we understand "imperialism," as Matthew Frye Jacobson has recently suggested, to encompass both a "projection of vested interest in foreign climes . . . and overt practices of political domination," it becomes clear that U.S. border enforcement in relation to Chinese immigration was inextricably tied to the expansion of U.S. imperialism.[94] At its very foundation, Chinese exclusion had always been articulated and justified through the language of American national sovereignty and self-preservation, American nation-building and empire-building. U.S. immigration law, for example, explicitly equated threats posed by Chinese immigration with threats to national sovereignty. Two Supreme Court cases, *Chae Chan-ping v. United States* (1889) and *Fong Yue Ting v. United States* (1893), asserted that the state held the same rights and duties to curb the foreign menace of immigration as it did to protect its citizens in time of war. As the American empire advanced across the Pacific, colonizing Hawaii and the Philippines in 1898, both anti-Chinese nativism and assertions of American sovereignty followed the flag. Following the annexation of Hawaii in 1898, Congress prohibited all immigration of Chinese into the islands despite strenuous Chinese protests from the islands. In 1902, the final Chinese Exclusion Act included a section prohibiting Chinese immigration to the Philippines as well.[95] In both cases, the United States also took the unusual step of prohibiting Chinese immigrants already in Hawaii and the Philippines from entering the mainland United States. Like the export of capital, politics, religion, and culture, immigration laws and immigration control thus became a central aspect of American imperialism. The "white man's burden," the term used by American imperialists to describe the United States' responsibility to uplift and civilize savage peoples abroad, also involved the protection of Americans from the foreign menaces plaguing the mainland United States.

As the cases of Canada and Mexico illustrate, the projection of American interests—in the form of anti-Chinese nativism and legislation—extended beyond the United States and its territories. Through an increasingly rigid set of Chinese exclusion laws, the United States had protected itself from the menace of Chinese immigration, yet it still remained vulnerable, because of the lax enforcement of immigration restrictions in Canada and Mexico. Increasingly, the United States began to define as its prerogative the right to extend its immigration agenda to neighboring sovereign countries. One immigration official justified tough measures at the border by citing the "law of self-preservation." If Chinese illegal immigration through Canada was indeed "a threat against our very civilization," as the U.S. commissioner-general of immigration believed, then extending American legal and state jurisdiction over a foreign country to control this threat was a logical outcome of this philosophy.[96] However, the United States could not force its immigration agenda onto Canada and Mexico as it had over its newly annexed territories. Instead, U.S. officials employed a variety of other measures to induce both countries to cooperate with the United States and to adopt compatible immigration laws. The United States achieved this through two new arms of imperialism in modern America: border diplomacy and border policing.

Northern borderland scholars write that, historically, the international boundary at the forty-ninth parallel was largely ignored as both people and goods (legal and illegal) crossed it without interference. After border disputes between the United States and Canada were resolved in the eighteenth century, the lack of significant geographical, racial, linguistic (except in the case of Quebec), or religious barriers between the American and Canadian populations helped to construct and reinforce the image of the Canadian-American border as "the world's longest undefended border." The success of Chinese border crossings through Canada does partially support the notion that the boundary line was nothing more than an arbitrary mark in the landscape.[97] Nevertheless, recent scholarship has suggested that the Canadian border was not a racially neutral site and that it had undergone a major transformation by the 1890s.[98] Indeed, Chinese exclusion was a primary means through which the border was demarcated and racialized. Because Canada's immigration policies clashed with American goals of Chinese exclusion and facilitated illegal entry, the U.S. increasingly viewed the northern border as a site to be policed. Initially frustrated and derisive of Canada's immigration policies, U.S. immigration officials eventually turned to border diplomacy. Canada's and the United States' shared antipathy for Chinese immigrants and the historically amicable relations between the two countries fostered cooperation and, finally, control of the northern border.

Early on, border enforcement was an inherently difficult task in both the north and the south. There were too few inspectors for the large expanse of land that required monitoring. As a result, one of the government's first imperatives was to increase the number of inspectors along the borders. In 1902, the total force numbered only sixty-six inspectors, and most were stationed along the northern border. The next year, the number had increased to one hundred and sixteen, again with most inspectors located along the U.S.-Canadian border. By 1909, three hundred officers and other employees of the immigration service were committed to work along the northern and southern borders.[99] Even the increased staff faced challenges. The lucrative illegal immigration business between Canada and the United States was both well organized and extensive. The operations running out of Buffalo, New York, for example, were reported to be in the hands of six men, with thirty or so "understrappers of various kinds" also employed. They paid their accomplices well and used the latest technology, such as motor boats and automobiles. The government had only three men along that part of the border with too few resources to match those of the operators of the illegal immigration business.[100] Another source of difficulty was the fact that there were simply too many people benefiting from illegal immigration. The Canadian steamship companies that brought Chinese from Hong Kong to Vancouver profited from the steady number of passengers, as did Canadian and Chinese operators and guides. Lastly, Canada itself profited from the revenue of the head tax imposed on Chinese, but it did not have to suffer the repercussions of increased Chinese immigration to its shores. From 1887 to 1891, revenues from the Chinese head tax amounted to $95,500, or about $3,000 per month. Canadian officials publicly acknowledged that the Chinese came to Canada "mainly to smuggle themselves across the border." As one prominent official explained to an American journalist in 1891, "They come here to enter *your* country. You can't stop it, and we don't care."[101]

In 1901, the Bureau of Immigration tried to push a bill through Congress that would have allowed Chinese to enter the United States only through certain seaports. Those who were arrested in the land border areas would have been deported without trial or appeal. The bill was defeated.[102] The U.S. government thus turned to three main strategies: pressuring Canada to assist the United States in enforcing the Chinese exclusion laws; moving the enforcement of immigration law beyond the border and into the Canadian ports of entry where Chinese first entered; and encouraging Canada to adopt Chinese immigration laws that were more compatible with American objectives. All measures reflected a new imperialist American assertion of national sovereignty over its borders and marked the extension of American immigration control beyond its own territory. The goal, as Terence Powderly, commissioner-general of immigration, put it, was to make the border so "airtight" that no one would be able to "crawl through."[103]

U.S. authorities first suggested that all ports of entry along the Canadian border be closed to Chinese immigration, but they reluctantly conceded that this drastic measure would interfere with free trade between the two countries. Instead, beginning in 1894, the U.S. Bureau of Immigration began to extend U.S. immigration law and control into Canadian seaports through the so-called Canadian Agreement. The agreement, made between all Canadian steamship and rail companies and the commissioner-general of immigration, allowed U.S. immigration inspectors to enforce U.S. immigration laws on steamships arriving in Canada and on Canadian soil at specifically designated border points. Inspectors were instructed to examine all U.S.-bound Asian and European immigrants arriving in Canada in exactly the "same manner" and with the "same objectives" as they would arrivals at American seaports. Those who passed inspection were issued a certificate of admission and were required to present that document to border officers when entering the United States. Those who failed to do so were returned to Canadian railway companies, who were then required to return the individuals back over the border into Canada.[104]

Despite these measures, the problem of Chinese illegal immigration in particular continued to vex U.S. immigration officials. Even with the Canadian Agreement, the U.S. government was unable to establish the same level of control over Chinese immigration through Canada as it had over Chinese sailing directly into the United States. Chinese passengers on Canadian steamship lines, for example, were not required to undergo the same rigorous predeparture physical examinations to which those bound for the United States were subjected. Nor were they automatically placed in detention and prevented from receiving mail and visitors while awaiting inspection as their counterparts in the United States were. U.S. officials believed that such "gaps" in enforcement made it easier for newly arriving Chinese in Canada to be "coached" for their U.S. immigration inspections. With study and practice, they could more easily survive the exhaustive interrogations designed to ferret out those making fraudulent claims of admission.[105] Thus, the U.S. government began to consider more specific and drastic remedies.

In 1903, Commissioner-General Powderly began by negotiating a new agreement with officials of the Canadian Pacific Railway Company (CPR), which operated both the transcontinental Canadian railway and the main line of passenger and cargo ships between China and Canada. Unlike the earlier 1894 agreement, the new initiative applied more border controls on Chinese immigrants exclusively. The agreement first required the Canadian Pacific Railway Company to examine all Chinese persons traveling on its steamships to determine "as reasonably as it can" that U.S.-bound passengers claiming to be admissible were in fact entitled to enter. Canadian Pacific Railway officials in effect agreed to interpret and enforce U.S. immigration law. Second, the company agreed to deliver under guard all Chinese passengers seeking admission into the United States directly to U.S. inspectors stationed at four designated ports along the Canadian border (Richford, Vermont; Malone, New York; Portal, North Dakota; and Sumas, Washington). With these agreements, the Bureau of Immigration was able to fully control the movements of Chinese immigrants and to replicate the rigid procedures to which Chinese immigrants were subject at American seaports.[106]

Believing that compliance with such an agreement would be detrimental to its profitable trans-Pacific steamship business, the Canadian Pacific Railway Company was at first reluctant to agree to the U.S. government's demands. When the United States threatened to close the entire border unless the CPR agreed to the proposed terms, however, the company eventually signed the agreement. The Canadian government itself was not a formal party to the agreement, but it certainly consented to its terms and means of enforcement. Relations had been strained between the two countries over the issue of border enforcement, but the agreement, American officials noted, was mutually satisfactory. The United States gained protection "from the evils of unrestricted immigration," and Canada realized "the extensive benefits" of being on friendly terms with its southern neighbor. The 1903 agreement was quite successful. Just one year after it had been signed, the bureau could report that "no Chinese person from China can enter the United States through Canada without submitting to an examination by Bureau officers. At present there are but a few Chinese coming to this country by way of Canada." The U.S. Bureau of Immigration applauded their counterparts for their cooperation and their "cordial spirit of friendship for us and for our exclusion policy." By 1908, inland border inspection points had been established across the boundary to regulate all cross-border migration.[107]

Another explicit goal of American border policy in the north was to "induce" Canada to adopt immigration laws similar to those of the United States. Agreements with Canadian transportation companies were effective, but they could only extend U.S. control to immigrants who were destined for the United States. They could not control the increasing number of Chinese claiming Canada as their final destination and then crossing the border surreptitiously. American officials grumbled that Canada's relaxed attitudes about immigration were detrimental to the United States and that complete control of the borders required transnational efforts. As the secretary of the treasury pointed out in 1891, "Any legislation looking to exclude will fail of its full purpose so long as the Canadian government admits Chinese laborers to Canada."[108] In 1903, both homegrown anti-Chinese sentiment and "patient and persistent" pressure from U.S. Bureau of Immigration and Department of Justice officers motivated Canada to increase its head tax on Chinese immigrants from one hundred to five hundred dollars. The increased head tax proved to be a strong deterrent for potential Chinese border crossers. In 1912, Canada agreed to end the practice of admitting Chinese immigrants who had already been denied entry into the United States. Finally, in 1923, under increasing pressure from the U.S. government as well as anti-Chinese activists within the dominion, Canada overhauled its Chinese immigration policies altogether to more closely mirror U.S. law. The 1923 Exclusion Act completely abolished the head-tax system and instead prohibited all people of Chinese origin or descent from entering the country. Consular officials, children born in Canada, merchants, and students were exempted.[109]

The 1923 bill was the effective barrier to Chinese immigration that American immigration officials had sought. During the next twenty-four years, only fifteen Chinese persons were admitted into Canada. The bill was not repealed until 1947.[110] That Canada's 1923 exclusion law closely resembled U.S. regulations regarding Chinese immigration was no coincidence. Border diplomacy — in the form of converging U.S. and Canadian policies — proved to be effective and finally closed the border to Chinese immigration.

Border Policing and Border Enforcement in the South

Chinese illegal entries via Mexico were a direct consequence of successful border enforcement in the north. Much to the U.S. government's chagrin, it found that Chinese immigrants, "having been practically defeated at every turn along the Canadian frontier," were increasingly turning their attention to entry via the southern border of the United States.[111] Unlike the northern border, the southern border had always been marked by conquest and contestation between the United States and Mexico. No "'undefended' border," the U.S.-Mexican border has been described by border studies scholar Gloria Anzaldúa as an "herida abierta," or an open wound. Boundary disputes lasted well into the early twentieth century, and the border was routinely the site of conflicts that tested the relationship between Mexico and the United States: Indian raids, banditry, smuggling, revolutionary activities.[112] Chinese immigration and exclusion introduced further discord as the border region became the site of U.S. immigration control and immigration law enforcement.

Unlike Canada, Mexico did not have extensive or consistently enforced immigration laws aimed at Chinese or other immigrants. Mexico did not require any examination of aliens entering the country, and in general, its immigration policies were designed to recruit, not restrict, labor. Although Chinese were targets of periodic racial hostility, they played a vital role in the economy from which both Mexican and American businesses operating in Mexico benefited.[113] The United States could not simply "piggy-back" or extend its own immigration policies onto an already existing framework in Mexico as it had in Canada. Moreover, Mexican officials were much more reluctant to cooperate with the United States than were Canadian officials. In 1907, the U.S. government initiated talks with President Porfirio Díaz to discuss American control over Chinese immigrants entering through Mexico. American government investigator Marcus Braun reported that it was the United States' intention to institute an agreement similar to that made with Canadian transportation companies. Under this agreement, both immigrant inspectors and public health officials would have the right to enforce all provisions of U.S. immigration law at various Mexican seaports, including Vera Cruz, Tampico, Matamoras, Acapulco, Manzanillo, Mazatlan, and Guaymas. Mexican transportation companies would also be required to screen immigrants in accordance with American immigration law. All Chinese persons, including residents and citizens of Mexico, would have to be examined under the Chinese exclusion laws of the United States.[114] President Díaz was reported to have expressed concern that American control over Chinese immigration would result in a loss of valuable labor needed in the country. Nevertheless, he did offer some limited cooperation. As investigator Braun reported, Díaz was amenable to allowing the immigration service to place officials in Mexico "wherever the Bureau thinks it necessary" and to take down a description of "every Chinaman and other alien who lands there" so that they could be identified when they tried to enter the United States.[115]

In practice, there seemed to be little cooperation between Mexican and American officials over the issue of Chinese immigration. In fact, Mexican officials were openly resistant and hostile to U.S. immigration authorities attempting to track Chinese immigrants entering from Mexico. For example, U.S. officers in El Paso in 1907 tried to send a number of inspectors to Ciudad Juárez every day to meet the incoming trains. They were instructed to "take a good look at every Chinaman who arrived" so that they might be able to identify them in case they should later be caught in the United States. As one official reported, however, the surveillance had to be abandoned because the authorities in Ciudad Juárez "threatened our officers with arrest if they should take pictures or descriptions of any Chinamen to come through."[116] Mexican transportation officials also showed little inclination to assist American immigration officials. A meeting between U.S. authorities and an agent for the Mexico-Canadian Steamship Company demonstrated this clearly. When asked to cooperate, the agent reportedly remarked that his next ship would carry about three hundred Chinese as far north as Guaymas. "For all I know they may smuggle into the United States and if they do I do not give a d—n, for I am doing a legitimate business."[117] After 1910, U.S. immigration officials seem to have been more successful, although they were not granted any official jurisdiction in Mexico, as they had been in Canada.[118]

American goals of Chinese exclusion were thus viewed as threats to Mexico's labor needs, and it was simply unclear to both the Mexican government and the transportation companies what benefit was to be gained by allowing American immigration officials to exercise so much power within their country.[119] Moreover, Mexican reluctance to cooperate may have been tied to larger anxieties about the increased American presence in the country in general. The end of the nineteenth century and the beginning of the twentieth was a period of increasing American economic penetration into the country, especially in the northern state of Sonora. Mexican state-building activities also played up anti-American themes. Although the transnational economy benefited both regions, border relations—of which Chinese immigration and exclusion soon became a part—embodied this ambivalence.[120] Consequently, the U.S. government's numerous attempts to forge an agreement with Mexico and Mexican transportation companies consistently failed.

Southern border enforcement thus presented very different challenges to the U.S. Bureau of Immigration from those in the north and led to an alternate approach. Chinese immigration at the southern border was regulated not by border diplomacy and cooperation but through policing and deterrence. Immigration officials at the border were charged with preventing illegal entries in the first place and apprehending those caught in the act of crossing the border.[121] To accomplish this, they imposed a three-pronged system of transnational surveillance within Mexico and the United States, began patrols at the border, and conducted immigration raids, made arrests, and deported Chinese already in the United States.

Surveillance of Chinese immigrants in Mexico involved a large, informal and formal network of immigration officers, train conductors, consular officials, and Mexican, Native American, and American informants.[122] American diplomatic officers stationed in Mexico routinely warned U.S. immigration officials on the other side of the border of new Chinese arrivals in that country. A typical telegram came from Clarence A. Miller, stationed at Matamoros, warning of an upcoming "flood on the Mexican side" in November of 1909 and urging immigration officers to "keep up their vigilance to a high point."[123] Government surveillance of Chinese immigrants in Mexico also involved elaborate undercover investigations by special agents of the immigration service. Immigrant inspector Marcus Braun, who surveyed the Mexican border situation in 1907, first suggested that a "Secret Service Squad" watch the Chinese in Mexico.[124] In 1910, Inspector Frank Stone, praised as "one of the best criminal investigators" in the immigration service, went undercover as a smuggler to investigate the Chinese immigration operations in El Paso, Texas. Stone unearthed a wealth of evidence: fraudulent U.S. certificates of residence (that is, green cards), which Chinese in the United States were required to hold, and counterfeit seals of two immigration officials and a judge for the U.S. District Court for the Northern District of California. Stone's investigation resulted in twelve indictments for conspiracy: the four Chinese principals and masterminds in the operation, three Mexican "river-men" who were known for their ability to ford the Rio Grande, one Mexican driver, and four Chinese immigrants holding fraudulent U.S. documents. Stone was also able to take photographs of the four Chinese leaders (one in which Stone himself posed), the exact locations at which the immigrants usually crossed the border, the fraudulent immigration documents, and the adobe huts that served as "safe houses."[125] The immigration service also sent one of its own officers, Inspector G. G. Gonzales, undercover. Perhaps not Mexican himself, he could reportedly "pass as a Mexican" and spoke Spanish fluently. Gonzales was ordered to "mingle" with the mostly Mexican population along the border in order to obtain information on Chinese border crossings.[126]

Mexican informants and government witnesses also tracked the movements of Chinese immigrants within Mexico by taking photographs of potential border crossers. These photographs were then sent to the immigration offices at Tucson, Arizona, to be used to identify newly arrived Chinese who had recently passed through Mexico. Likewise, photographs of suspected illegal immigrants already in the United States were taken and then sent back to the Mexican border region so that inspectors could obtain further information from Mexican residents and officials there.[127] Mexican informants on the American side of the border were used as well. Mrs. Blaza Avilez, of El Paso, Texas, for example, was hired by the U.S. government to spy on Chinese illegal immigration operations in that city. She rented the room adjoining that of Theodore Villescas, "a well-known Mexican smuggler," from which she could see and hear practically everything that transpired between the occupant and his guests. Moreover, she was a close confidant of the woman who lived with Villescas. For two dollars a day for thirty-two days, Mrs. Avilez noted suspicious activity and plans made in the next room. Her work paid off hand-

U.S. immigrant inspector Frank Stone posing with Chinese "smugglers" who were arrested, 1910. As part of the government's efforts to control the U.S.-Mexican border, Stone went undercover in El Paso, Texas, to investigate Chinese "smuggling" activities. Courtesy of the National Archives, Washington, D.C.

somely for the government, for she tipped it off to a new arrival of Chinese immigrants coming from Juárez in October 1908. She also confirmed suspicions that El Paso deputy constable Duran was connected with this "gang."[128] Americans living and working in the U.S.-Mexican border region volunteered information and assistance to the Bureau of Immigration as well. Train conductors reported sightings of Chinese immigrants boarding trains in Mexico and in the border area. One Pullman porter reported in 1914 that two Chinese men were to enter Los Angeles from Calexico disguised as Mexican women.[129] Local ranchers also loaned horses and offered meals to inspectors.[130]

The burden of enforcement work along the Mexican border lay in the detection and arrest of "contraband Chinese" and the prosecution of those who assisted in their unlawful entry. The U.S. government's attempts to control the southern border thus centered on "maintaining a much closer patrol, night and day," which involved an increased number of officers and a "very vigorous policy with regard to the arrest of Chinese found in this country in violation of the law."[131] Patrolling the border was inherently difficult because of the expanse of land to be covered, as well as the paucity of officers to patrol it. As Inspector Marcus Braun complained to the commissioner-general of immigration in 1907, all of the rivers, carriage roads, pathways, highways, and mountain trails needed to be patrolled. "There is a broad expanse of land with an imaginary line, all passable, all being used, all leading into the United States. The vigilance of your officers stationed along the border is always keen; but what can a handful of people do?"[132]

In response, the Bureau of Immigration increased the number of immigrant inspectors every year. The first patrol officer in the south was Jeff Milton, who in 1887 resigned from the Texas Rangers and became a mounted customs inspector with the U.S. Customs Service at El Paso, Texas. By 1891, three men in the customs service patrolled the Mexico-California border, so Chinese immigrants turned away from the heavily trafficked areas toward more remote, interior entry points through Texas, New Mexico, Arizona, and California.[133] By the early 1900s, the governor of Arizona, and even President Theodore Roosevelt, agreed that the Chinese entering along the Mexican border should be treated as "contraband," and Milton was hired by the immigration service as a border guard in the El Paso district to "prevent the smuggling of Chinese from Mexico into the United States." With jurisdiction over the border from El Paso to the Colorado River, he was known as the "one-man Border Patrol."[134] By 1904, an estimated eighty mounted inspectors were patrolling the border.[135] The so-called line riders of the Customs Service continued to "pick up any suspects they ran into," and Milton expanded the scope of his job to "pick up Hindus and Japanese" as well.[136] From 1907 to 1909, 2,492 Chinese were arrested by U.S. officials for illegal entry along the Mexican border.[137] In 1908, patrol officers were placed under the jurisdiction of the Chinese Division of the immigration service, which took over the responsibility for dealing with illegal aliens.

Patrolling the border involved not only "walking the line" but inspecting the railroads as well. Every car in every train was inspected in an effort to find Chinese attempting to enter clandestinely. In 1908, inspectors arrested twelve different groups of Chinese on boxcars and six different groups of Chinese on the passenger trains. A total of 150 Chinese were arrested that year in the trains alone.[138] In El Paso, any Chinese who entered the city by train was required to show his papers to the officer stationed there. If he did not have valid documents, he was arrested. The same procedure was required of any Chinese wishing to leave El Paso by train.[139] The Bureau of Immigration

A Texas and Pacific Railroad freight car in which eighteen Chinese were apprehended, Oct. 20, 1908. Chinese illegal immigration across the northern and southern borders set in motion new U.S. border enforcement policies and procedures, including the systematic search of all railcars traveling from Mexico to the United States. Courtesy of the National Archives, Washington, D.C.

was constantly trying to keep up with the persistence and ingenuity of the Chinese border crossers. Soon after immigrants began to use high-powered boats to enter the United States by sea, the immigration service reported that it had purchased a similar craft to pursue them. When Chinese began to use automobiles to cross the border, the immigration service warned that it would need to follow suit and requested the appropriate funds.[140]

Indeed, it was the government's inability to keep up with Chinese illegal entries that led to the formulation and practice of the third feature of the government's border policy: expanding its border enforcement into the interior cities and regions and instituting a "vigorous policy" of immigration raids, arrests, and deportations of immigrants suspected of being in the country illegally. "Let it be known," Commissioner-General Frank Sargent declared in 1906, "that even thickly settled city districts will not afford, as in the past, a safe harbor for those who clandestinely enter."[141] By 1909, a system of interior enforcement was in place, and the service was concentrating on "ridding the country of undesirable aliens."[142] The Bureau of Immigration divided the country into separate districts and assigned special agents, commonly known as "Chinese catchers," to find and arrest Chinese in the country unlawfully.[143] Catchers with high records of arrests and deportations were "celebrated" and transferred throughout the country so they could share their expertise. Chinese inspector Charles Mehan, for example, began his career in San Francisco, which was widely known as the most difficult port of entry for Chinese. He was praised by the service and by supporters of Chinese exclusion for his rigid interrogations and energetic enforcement of the Chinese exclusion laws. Mehan, "one of the most celebrated Chinese catchers," was transferred first to El Paso, Texas, to deal with the problem of Chinese border crossings from Mexico. He was then transferred to Canada in 1899.[144] Inspector J. D. Putnam, another celebrated "Chinese catcher," bragged to the *El Paso Herald* of his ability to tell one Chinaman from another. "People who know a little about the Chinese often say that one Chinaman looks just like another," Putman explained. "Whenever I meet a Chinaman I can tell whether or not I have ever seen him before, and if so, where. I never forget any Chinaman's face. It is very easy to detect a newcomer — a Chinaman who has come unlawfully into the country. . . . His walk, his gestures, his manner, all make it as easy to find him out as it is to tell a white man from a negro."[145]

Border surveillance, policing, and deportation proved to be successful in stemming illegal Chinese border entries from Mexico. In 1905, immigration officials reported that the Chinese were "becoming desperate," waiting in Ensenada and Tijuana for an opportunity to cross the line. The numbers of Chinese arrested and deported also increased.[146] In 1898, the ratio of Chinese admitted to Chinese deported was 100:4. By 1904, the ratio was 100:61.[147] Border enforcement also became more centralized. In 1907, the policing of the border states — Arizona, New Mexico, and most of Texas — was placed under the jurisdiction of the newly created Mexican Border District. Demonstrating the great influence Chinese immigration had on southern border enforcement, the first commissioner hired to manage the new Mexican district was Frank W. Berkshire, who had overseen the Chinese service along the New York–Canadian border and in New York City.[148] At the same time, events in Mexico, including a revolution, and increasing anti-Chinese sentiment placed additional barriers to Chinese immigration.[149] By 1911, the border division reported in its annual report that it was "no longer acting upon the defensive." Immigration had decreased to such a degree by World War I that the immigration service transferred its Chinese inspectors away from the region.[150] In 1917, Congress passed an act that provided that aliens who entered the country by land from places other than those designated as ports of entry or entered without inspection (as many Chinese crossing over the borders had done) could be taken into custody and summarily deported.[151] By 1926, the commissioner-general of immigration declared that "the smuggling of Chinese over the land boundaries, which was a vexatious problem in the past, has been greatly reduced."[152]

Conclusion

Divergent Chinese immigration policies in the United States, Canada, and Mexico, as well as different relationships between the United States and its neighbors, led to the evolution of distinct border policies. While the northern border was eventually closed through U.S.-Canadian border diplomacy and a mutual antipathy for Chinese immigration, southern border enforcement was the product of conflicting Chinese immigration policies in the United States and Mexico, as well as inconsistent cooperation between the two countries. Border diplomacy thus gave way to border policing designed to deter and apprehend illegal Chinese immigrants already at the border and within the United States.

By the 1920s, both the northern and southern borders were effectively closed to Chinese immigration. In 1925, the U.S. Border Patrol was established, further limiting illegal immigration across the border in general.[153] While Chinese border entries did not completely end, they ceased to warrant the same level of attention from the immigration service as they had at the turn of the century. Nevertheless, Chinese immigration and exclusion along the U.S.-Canadian and U.S.-Mexican borders had transformed immigration policy, international relations, the border region, and border enforcement. Chinese immigrants—racialized as perpetual foreigners—became the country's first illegal immigrants. With the establishment of the Chinese Division, "Chinese" became synonymous with "illegal" in the same way that "Mexican" is racialized today. Indeed, Chinese exclusion along the northern and southern borders appears to have been an important trial run for the federal government's much larger efforts to control Mexican immigration in later years.

We didn't want to come in illegally, but we were forced to because of the immigration laws. They particularly picked on the Chinese. If we told the truth, it didn't work. So we had to take the crooked path.
—*from an interview with Mr. Chan, former detainee on Angel Island*

There are doubtless now in this country at least as many Chinese not entitled to residence here as of the lawfully resident class, and they have entered in every way that can be imagined. . . . A Chinaman apparently will undergo any hardship or torture, take any risk or pay any sum of money . . . to enjoy the forbidden, but much coveted privilege of living and working in the United States.
—*Commissioner-general of immigration, 1909*

THE CROOKED PATH

Chinese Illegal Immigration and Its Consequences

FOR MANY CHINESE, taking "the crooked path" offered the only means of entering the United States while the Chinese exclusion laws were in effect. The high-profile legal, political, and economic attempts to repeal the exclusion laws were extremely important but largely ineffective. As a result, most working-class Chinese spent their energy devising strategies to circumvent the laws altogether. In 1928, sociologist Ching Chao Wu observed that Chinese in the Pearl River delta simply wished "to get into the United States." They did not wait for the American courts or the U.S. Congress to end exclusion. Instead, they merely "disguised themselves as members of the exempt classes or smuggle[d] themselves into the United States."[1] Illegal immigration became yet another survival strategy, another means of adapting to the exclusion laws. Indeed, one of the greatest ironies of the Chinese exclusion era was that because of the restrictive laws, the stringent government enforcement procedures, the persistence of the immigrants, and the corruptibility of immigration officials, Chinese illegal immigration was a thriving, transnational business that had long-term repercussions for both Chinese immigrants and American immigration policy.

This chapter examines how Chinese immigrants and immigration officials created and maintained a system of illegal immigration during the exclusion era. It first focuses on the immigrants who created the demand for false documents and unlawful entry into the United States. It then turns to the immigration brokers, immigration officials, and others based in the United States, China, and throughout the Americas who facilitated this migration and turned it into a profitable business. Illegal immigration involved a complex set of variables and relationships. The class and citizenship status and gender of Chinese shaped both their strategies to enter the country and how they were evaluated by immigration officials. Illegal immigration also perpetuated a cycle of increasingly risky migration strategies and ever more powerful state actions. When it became harder to enter through regular channels, Chinese took advantage of loopholes in the laws and the government's enforcement procedures or turned to methods of entry in which they avoided the immigration service altogether. Ironically, Chinese learned how to use the state's documentary requirements to institute a chain migration, in which one immigrant sponsored other immigrants for admission, who later themselves sponsored additional immigrants. These sponsorships were often based on fraudulent identities and relationships. Illegal immigration was successful, but this success came with harsh consequences. In the end, illegal immigration was the clearest symbol of the folly and futility of the exclusion policy. The exclusion of Chinese did not end Chinese immigration; it merely forced it underground and supported a transnational business of illegal immigration that corrupted both the Chinese community in America and the American government itself.

Becoming Illegal

Illegal immigration, by its very definition, is difficult to quantify, and the statistics available for the exclusion era either are suspect or fail to cover the entire sixty-one-year period. In 1909, San Francisco commissioner of immigration Hart Hyatt North asserted that of the thousands of Chinese who had successfully gained admission into the country, "nearly 90 percent" did so fraudulently.[2] It is highly likely that this estimate was greatly exaggerated. Given the government's institutional and racialized suspicion of Chinese, officials might have easily read Chinese fraud and deception where there was none.[3] Commissioner North, for example, was somewhat obsessed with the subject of Chinese criminal behavior, and when he retired from the immigration service, he published two articles on Chinese criminal gangs.[4] Despite his professed expertise, many of his decisions to exclude Chinese based on his belief that their cases were fraudulent were overturned by his superiors in Washington, D.C. Interviews of Chinese immigrants who were detained on Angel Island during the 1920s and 1930s also indicate that a very high percentage of entries were based on fraud. A few interviewees claimed that 90 to 95 percent of all Chinese used false papers during those two decades. Arthur Lem explained that using false papers was so common that "when one announced that he was leaving for the United States, the first remark would be 'Whose papers are you using?'"[5] These estimates, however, refer only to the 1920s and 1930s. One last estimate of the magnitude of Chinese illegal immigration comes from the so-called anti-Communist Confession Program of 1959–65, a project in which the U.S. government encouraged (and in many cases coerced) Chinese into "confessing" to illegal entry. The figures gathered from these confessions implicated 30,530 Chinese.[6] This statistic, which is less than 10 percent of the total number of Chinese admitted into the country during the exclusion era, is almost certainly far below the number of actual illegal entries. Many Chinese refused to "confess" to illegal entry, and a good number of suspected illegal immigrants were never located by the government. While it is nearly impossible to know how many immigrants entered the country illegally during the exclusion era, what we do know is that Chinese illegal immigration thrived, and it left a mixed legacy.

Several factors contributed to Chinese illegal immigration. First were poor economic conditions in South China and the availability of jobs in the United States. Sociologists, politicians, and immigration officials alike recognized the paradox in cutting off the supply of Chinese labor while the demand for immigrant labor in general remained high. Indeed, European and Mexican immigrants continued to enter freely or under limited restrictions for most of the exclusion era. In 1892, one U.S. senator was forced to concede that because "the rewards of labor are so great [in the United States] . . . there are thousands of Chinese eager to circumvent this law and eager to come [to this country]."[7] Labor contractors told immigration officials that they "would put to work every Chinaman [they] could get."[8] And even the commissioner-general of immigration admitted that the exclusion laws "damm[ed] up a more or less placidly flowing stream." Instead of drying up, as lawmakers had expected, Chinese immigration "simply flowed around the dam," keeping immigration officers "busy day and night stopping the leaks."[9]

Likewise, the Chinese desire to join family already in the United States provided a major incentive. Family reunification in the United States not only lessened the pain of separation but also meant that additional wages could be sent back to China.[10] Between 1884 and 1941, one-quarter of a random sample of Chinese who applied for admission at the port of San Francisco traveled with a family member and over three-quarters claimed they had family already in the United States.[11]

The state's zeal in enforcing the exclusion laws was equally important in encouraging illegal immigration. As Chapter 5 explains, the harsh legal restrictions placed on the departure and return of Chinese already residing in the United States inspired many returning residents to cross the border illicitly rather than risk rejection at a regular port of entry. The decreasing number of exempt-class categories such as that of the Chinese merchant also forced previously exempt-class Chinese to resort to illegal immigration. Simply put, as one steamship company official observed in 1909, "the more restrictions . . . put around the Chinese . . . the more energetic they become in trying to find means of escape."[12]

Another factor encouraging illegal entry was simply the ease with which the law could be evaded. When the Chinese Exclusion Act was passed in 1882, the government lacked an efficient and centralized bureaucracy to handle the steady flow of Chinese and to expose the strategies they used to get around the exclusion laws. The thousands of miles of unguarded borders in Canada and Mexico provided the first opportunity for Chinese to enter and to work in the United States undetected. Corrupt immigration officials and judges also facilitated illegal immigration.

Lastly, the Chinese in America simply believed that the exclusion laws were unjust and highly discriminatory, and it thus became culturally acceptable to work around the laws or ignore them altogether.[13] Consequently, many otherwise law-abiding Chinese assisted others to enter the United States by illegal or fraudulent means. In 1899, Oscar Greenhalgh, a special investigator for the Treasury Department, found that the sentiment in San Francisco's Chinatown was so intensely against the exclusion laws that many immigrants, from the common laborer to the most respected leaders, were willing to assist their fellow Chinese in illegally entering the United States. One Chinese woman pointedly told Greenhalgh that she was "against the Chinese exclusion laws . . . [and that] anything she could do to assist the Chinese to land would be done."[14] A well-known Chinese merchant in Seattle also reportedly told the assistant commissioner of immigration there that while he was a scrupulously law-abiding resident, he "did not hesitate to help . . . and protect . . . a fellow countryman" attempting to enter the country fraudulently. "It is not wrong, under the Chinese moral law," he explained, "for a Chinaman to swear falsely in support of an application made by a fellow clansman to gain admission into the United States." When asked why not, the merchant reportedly said, "Because God never said that the Chinaman shouldn't come to this country."[15] Likewise, immigrants interviewed by sociologist Wen-hsien Chen in 1940 felt that since the exclusion laws were unjust, discriminated against Chinese, and were "inhuman in separating families," they therefore did not deserve to be "dealt with in an honest manner." One interviewee went so far as to declare that since Chinese residents in America did not enjoy "the same protection and privileges as other races or nationalities," illegal immigration was nothing less than a form of self-protection and survival, a way "to keep life going" in the United States.[16]

The Transnational Business of Illegal Immigration

Chinese immigrants' desire to enter the country fed a highly organized and profitable transnational underground business that involved prospective immigrants, immigration agents, professional smugglers, corrupt immigration officials, and other government employees in China, the United States, and throughout the Americas. The business strategies evolved in response to loopholes in the laws and cracks in the government's enforcement practices. For example, as Chinese immigrant inspection grew more dependent on government-issued exempt-class documents, certificates of identity, and passports, a steady trade in fake or stolen documents sprang up to meet the demand. American consular officials in China readily sold merchant and student certificates for a handsome profit for several years.[17] In 1904 and 1905, the government confiscated dozens of fraudulent immigration service certificates and stamps produced and sold by two former American convicts based in Sonora, Mexico, and a clerk in the office of the collector of internal revenue at San Francisco.[18]

As inspection at the regular ports of entry grew more intense, illicit entry from Canada and Mexico increased, and when those land borders became subject to tighter government scrutiny, Chinese immigrants and the illegal immigration business turned toward routes via the Pacific, Gulf, and Atlantic seaports. In 1909, the commissioner-general of immigration observed that as the government "drew the lines tight on the land borders . . . [officials] soon found that the base of operations has been changed from Canada and Mexico to Jamaica and Cuba."[19] American diplomats based in Jamaica reported that commercial vessels started Chinese on a three-legged journey from Mexico to Jamaica and then to Florida, Louisiana, and Mississippi, where they disembarked for northern cities like Baltimore, New York, Philadelphia, and Boston. Another route was even more complex. Chinese arrived first in Vancouver, British Columbia, then traveled south to Jamaica, where they waited for yet another trip to the United States. The cost of the inter-American transport only (excluding transportation costs from Hong Kong to Vancouver) ran as high as $600 in 1909.[20] Other reports indicate that Chinese were disguised as seamen or hidden aboard fishing, fruit, or lumber vessels from the West Indies. Like the border-crossing business, Chinese illegal immigration via sea routes involved a range of multiracial, international networks that included Chinese immigrants and agents, Jamaican sailors, Greek American lumber boat operators, and British and American sea captains.[21]

Immigrants entering the United States illicitly via the borders or seaports did avoid the immigration service and its lengthy interrogations, medical examinations, and detentions, but in doing so, they became undocumented immigrants who lacked the necessary government documentation proving their status as legal residents. Vulnerable to immigration raids, arrest, and deportation, they were forced to hide in the shadows.[22] Consequently, Chinese increasingly chose to deceive, rather than sidestep, immigration authorities. They did so by exploiting the loopholes related to exempt-class immigration. It was common, for example, for Chinese to falsely claim membership in one of the exempt classes and obtain the necessary documentation or witness testimony to verify that claim. Identification papers for children or spouses of exempt-class immigrants were especially useful because the U.S. government often lacked reliable documentary evidence verifying births and marriages that had taken place either in the United States or in China. As a result, a brisk business in the production and sale of immigration documents grew to dominate illegal immigration by the 1920s.

Immigration papers and identities were regularly traded among prospective immigrants and Chinese already residing in the United States. Transnational networks of family were especially fruitful sources of information and papers. "When I saw you last," wrote Lum Bun Chong in Toisan to Lau Ding Sing in San Francisco in 1917, "you said you were expecting to return to China soon and that you had saved a 'paper' for my cousin to come to the United States. If the paper fits him, please let me know."[23] Wong Bing Foon also relied on a contact in the United States, in this case, his father in San Francisco, for assistance in immigration arrangements for other interested Chinese. "If you have any 'son-of-native' papers that fit Wong Him Yuen's age," he wrote, "[contact me so that] we can get him over to the United States so that he can make his living there."[24] Immigrant families also often claimed more children than they had in order to sponsor relatives or sell the remaining slots to interested parties. Hui Chung Man, a merchant who arrived in San Francisco in 1920, for example, claimed his two nieces and one nephew as his children in addition to his own two sons, Hui Bing Gee and Hui Bing Yon.[25] Likewise, Lee Yut Sing claimed his four nephews and his son-in-law as his own sons over a twenty-five-year period.[26]

If close ties of kinship could not be used, prospective immigrants could rely upon family friends, fellow villagers, or acquaintances. Chin Hing Kee, Chin Yee, and Chin Suey Hin, all fellow villagers in Koo Chung village in the Chungshan district, became "paper brothers" when they applied for entry as the "sons" of U.S. native Gin Yow.[27] Similarly, when Lee Fong You emigrated to the United States in 1922, his father called upon family friend Fong Norm, who was a U.S. citizen. After memorizing the Fong family history, Lee entered the United States under the name of Fong Toy, the son of Fong Norm. Lee was not the only paper son brought over by Fong Norm. "My paper father had three sons including myself," Lee confessed to immigration investigators decades after his arrival. Although no blood relationship existed between Fong Norm and Lee Fong You, the bonds of paper kinship obligated Fong Norm to take care of Lee after his arrival in San Francisco. In fact, Lee lived with Fong for one year in Stockton after landing in 1922. Likewise, Lee was obligated to Fong to corroborate Fong's claim as a native and as a father of three sons. When another paper son arrived a few years later, Lee served as a witness to the brother—and the new addition was admitted as well.[28]

Professional immigration agents provided expertise and connections— often with corrupt immigration officials—that further fueled the business in illegal immigration. Some brokers arranged everything from booking passage on the steamship and purchasing papers, to securing witnesses and attorneys. As Immigration Inspector S. J. Ruddell explained to a congressional committee in 1890, "A Chinaman who desires to come to this country can go to an agency in Hong Kong and there, by depositing $170, he will receive a guaranty to be landed in San Francisco."[29] Twenty years later, the cost of these services ranged from several hundred dollars to three thousand dollars, depending on the age of the applicant and the ease with which the deception might be pulled off. Brokerage houses like the *Gam Saan jong,* or Gold Mountain firms, also sold immigration papers in addition to handling remittances and correspondence of overseas Chinese.[30]

Chinese interpreters for the steamship companies were among the earliest immigration agents to seize upon the lucrative business opportunities that the exclusion laws created. Soo Hoo Fong, an interpreter for the Pacific Mail Steamship Company in San Francisco in the 1890s, bluntly wrote to a partner that the illegal immigration business was so profitable, it was like "the catching of fish or shrimps in a pond." By all accounts, he ran a highly efficient and profitable business. He first determined when his clients would be arriving at the port. Working with corrupt immigration officials, he then found out what questions would be asked during the interrogation. "I then know what to say and what warning to give," he explained. He then rushed into San Francisco Chinatown to warn the applicant's witnesses about what they should expect and what answers they should give. "If they answer positively and their testimony agrees with those on board, escaping discrepancies, etc., then the fellows would go ashore without any anxiety," Fong explained.[31]

Immigration agents such as Lo Yu Ting, an interpreter for the Occidental and Oriental Steamship Company, also sent crucial information about any changes in the exclusion laws and Bureau of Immigration regulations back to China so that prospective immigrants could be prepared. In one letter written in October 1898, Ting sent instructions through his nephew that the immigration officials were beginning to keep "partnership files" listing all the merchants of each Chinese firm. If a newly arrived immigrant claimed an interest in a firm, his name had to appear on the official list kept at the customhouse. "Tell those who shall be newcomers that when asked by the customs people upon arrival, they may answer according to these lists and it will be all right," he instructed.[32]

Although false papers granted immigrants the right to apply for admission into the United States, the mere possession of these papers did not guarantee the right to land. Chinese had to first prove to the immigration officials that they were indeed the same individuals as their papers claimed them to be. This requirement sustained another sector of the transnational illegal immigration economy, professional "coaching book" writers, who recorded all the details of the applicant's new paper family's history, village life and geography, occupations, and relationships.[33] Coaching papers acquired and translated by the Bureau of Immigration in San Francisco reveal how those involved in the illegal immigration business mastered the art of the government interrogation by securing and preparing exact answers to a range of questions regularly asked by immigration officials. One book clearly warned its readers, "You will be asked whether there are any bricks, chickens, dog, or photograph in your house."[34] Another contained over four hundred questions applicants could expect in a typical interrogation and the answers the immigrants would have to provide:

Q: Has your house an ancestral loft, shrine shelf, and tablets? What [are they] made of?

A: Yes. We have an ancestral loft, a shrine shelf and five ancestral tablets. The shrine shelf has two sections, the upper section contains the tablet for the goddess of mercy; the lower section holds the tablet for the entire ancestry of the family in the center, those for the great grandparents on the left and those for the grandparents on the right. The shrine shelf has carved figures painted in gold.

Q: When you left for the U.S., what kind and color clothes did your mother wear?

A: She wore plain black Chinese clothes for women, made from cloths woven in China.

The author of this coaching book also cautioned the immigrant to "give answer only to the questions asked; do not say more than the question requires. If an inspector or interpreter talks loudly to show anger, do not be afraid, but be composed and answer the question in easy manner."[35]

Another set of coaching papers acquired and translated by the bureau included a detailed map of what interpreter H. K. Tang believed to be Sar Hong village, in the Sun Wui district of China. In addition to providing the specific arrangement of houses in the village, the papers also included detailed notes about the inhabitants of each house. According to the map, "Moy Park, forty years old, wife Chin Shee, bound feet, one son Ah Wee, twenty odd years, not married," lived in the last house in the eleventh alley of the village. "Mow Sing, age forty, wife Chin Shee, bound feet, two sons, attending school somewhere else," lived in the thirteenth alley, according to the papers. The Ngee Ging Ancestral Hall, where "Yip Teung taught," was noted as being near the left-hand side of the village, near the fifteenth alley. The author of the note also called the immigrant's attention to the houses around the hall, "because it is feared they will ask who live next or back of Ngee Ging Ancestral Hall. These few people or houses are added. Be sure that all agree in their testimony."[36]

While arrangements between buyer and seller, immigration broker and coaching book writer were often made in South China, a team of paid witnesses, agile attorneys, and corrupt officials and other employees of the immigration service were available to facilitate the admission of immigrants once they arrived in the United States. In 1899, the Treasury Department sent an investigator into San Francisco's Chinatown to confirm reports of suspicious activity. He concluded that "San Francisco is full of old men, that will for five dollars identify ANY Chinaman as his son. . . . Both stories always agree, for months are given in each case for these parties to see each other, and be drilled." There were also elderly Chinese women and many others, the investigator continued, "who will come forward and testify that they were present at the wedding [of the applicant's parents] and at the birth of the 'HOPEFUL.'" Chinese witnesses were easily found, for as the investigator bluntly explained, "Chinamen are ready to sware [sic] to ANYTHING for twenty dollars." White witnesses were also easily bribed and were so well coached that "there is no possible chance [they would make] a mistake."[37] These kinds of witnesses and immigration brokers in the United States, in addition to coaching book writers and family and friends in China, made the transnational business of illegal immigration highly organized and extremely profitable, and it attracted additional accomplices every year.

Government Corruption

Some of these accomplices invariably came from within the U.S. government, and one of the single most important factors sustaining the business in illegal immigration was the corruptibility of U.S. immigration officials and other government employees. In fact, many of them were heavily invested in the business of illegal immigration, helping to sustain it even while they worked in their official capacities as gatekeepers. Even before the Chinese Exclusion Act was passed in 1882, Chinese merchants had discovered that U.S. customs officials could be regularly bribed, and in 1877, the collector of customs in San Francisco complained of the extensive corruption in the service. Rather than blaming the officers, however, he accused the Chinese, who "were cunning and prolific in [their] desire to deceive the Customs officers."[38] After 1882, more and more government officials were willing to be "deceived." An investigation in 1899 concluded that the American consul in Hong Kong would "indorse [sic] ANYTHING for a five dollar bill." Over time, such small bribes added up to a nice sum, or as the government's investigator calculated, it would take only

800 immigrants paying five dollars to net the consul $4,000.[39] The corruption in the American consul's office in China had become so extensive that it took a directive from President Theodore Roosevelt in 1906 to reform the office.[40]

Corruption among immigration officials was pervasive across the United States, and it proved to be an enduring problem for the immigration service. Three years after the passage of the Exclusion Act, the chief clerk in the San Francisco Chinese Bureau's registration office was charged with selling over 200 certificates of residence to immigration brokers in Hong Kong, charging $80 each for men and $300 for women. His scheme was uncovered in 1885 when his fellow officers became suspicious of his "extravagance and irregular habits [that] indicate[d] an income much beyond his salary."[41] In the early 1900s, a Chinese letter confiscated and translated by immigration authorities in San Francisco uncovered a collaboration between Chinese agents and an immigration inspector stationed in El Paso, Texas. In the letter, it was noted that "everybody knows [the inspector] accepts bribes right along."[42]

Chinese interpreters were also known to demand bribes from immigrants in order to facilitate their illegal entry. In 1899, Carlton Rickards was dismissed after Treasury Department investigators accused him of involvement in the landing of hundreds of illegal Chinese in Port Townsend, Washington, three years earlier.[43] Chief Chinese inspector B. E. Meredith was removed that same year after an investigation disclosed that he was one of the primary brokers involved in admitting Chinese with fraudulent certificates. Investigators found that Meredith, working together with the Chinese interpreter of the Southern Pacific Steamship Company, was so successful in this operation that the steamship company had placed advertisements throughout South China guaranteeing the landing of patrons of their line.[44] In 1900, after ten years of service, Albert H. Geffeney, another inspector and interpreter in the San Francisco office, resigned after admitting his guilt of bribery.[45]

Even federal employees not directly involved in the inspection of immigrants profited from the illegal immigration business. In September 1903, San Francisco immigration officers found that U.S. marshals in charge of Chinese deportation cases routinely substituted Chinese who had been ordered deported back to China with other Chinese who wanted to make visits or to return permanently to China. They were paid handsomely for these services.[46] In 1909, a bureau investigation also revealed that the guards employed to watch the Chinese held in the detention shed (located at that time on a dock on the bay) could also be bought off to carry in contraband messages to the Chinese detainees. As Mason S. Blackburn, a Chinese watchman in San Francisco, told an investigator, "Well, I do know they [other watchmen] would not be adverse to earning a dollar or two for carrying of a coaching letter. One dollar to them would mean twenty steam beers."[47]

Although reforms in the immigration service attempted to curb the corruption in the bureau, the problem persisted for years. San Francisco was especially plagued with corruption scandals. In 1899, a Treasury Department official observed that the government's investigations were mainly for political purposes and that once the new men were appointed or promoted, they "soon became worse than those removed."[48] Almost twenty years later, in 1917, investigator J. B. Densmore reported that the city was the center of an international smuggling ring that netted hundreds of thousands of dollars each year.[49] Immigration inspectors commonly substituted the photographs in Chinese files or changed immigrant testimony to suit a particular case. They were also caught selling immigration papers belonging to Chinese who had returned to China permanently.[50] Employees were also willing to steal records from the Angel Island immigration station for immigrants who had forgotten the details of their past interviews. Duplicate copies of the records cost Chinese from $100 to $150 around 1917, and inspectors could expect to receive $200 for substituting a photograph.[51] The extent of corruption in the service was so great that when Densmore's investigation concluded, twenty-five employees of the immigration service were dismissed, including seven out of the eleven inspectors hearing Chinese cases. Altogether, thirty people were indicted by a federal grand jury, including government employees, lawyers, and a few Chinese immigration brokers.[52]

Paper Identities and Paper Lives

The paper identities and lives of illegal immigrants were shaped by the ability of immigrants and agents to exploit the weaknesses in the laws. They were also structured by the ideologies of race, class, gender, and citizenship embedded in the exclusion laws and in the environment that exclusion created. The class and citizenship exemptions in the exclusion laws, for example, created loopholes that were easily exploited to create additional paper immigration slots. Chinese companies regularly sold partnerships (and the merchant status that accompanied them) to Chinese who would otherwise be prohibited from entering the country, and the business was both lucrative and widespread. In 1917, the average cost of a partnership was $1,000.[53] An immigrant inspector in Washington State reported that "a number of stores in the cities are organized just for the purpose . . . [of giving] the Chinese a chance to be a merchant."[54]

Moreover, Chinese posing as members of the exempt classes also learned how to exploit the U.S. government's assumptions about class membership and citizenship status. Chinese masquerading as merchants and students took special pains to insure that they appeared to be bona fide members of the middle and upper classes. In 1911, an attorney in Seattle, Washington, helped one hundred school-age Chinese males enter as immigrants on fraudulent students' certificates. They all had supporting letters (also fraudulent) from prestigious private high schools in Seattle and San Francisco affirming their status as students, and all traveled in second-class accommodations (rather than steerage) aboard the steamship. Both the prestigious school names and the second-class steamship accommodations were strategically employed to deflect suspicion.[55] Chinese posing as merchants also took advantage of the government's tendency to connect merchant status to the applicant's relationships with prominent white Americans. In 1899, a Chinese informant told Treasury Department investigator Oscar Greenhalgh that many Chinese regularly forged their fake merchant's papers with signatures of prominent whites, such as the postmasters or mayors of their towns. These papers were generally accepted by the collector of customs, especially in cases in which government investigations were impractical due to the remote location of the town or city. This scheme was apparently so successful that one set of papers could be duplicated several times and sold to numerous other Chinese immigrants who affixed their own photographs and added their own names to the papers.[56]

The exempt status of Chinese American citizens was another loophole in the laws that was relatively easy to exploit.[57] Immigration officials suspected fraud in citizens' cases as early as the 1890s, but the problem was confirmed after 1906, when the great earthquake and fire that destroyed all of San Francisco's birth records corresponded with a dramatic increase in the number of Chinese applying as returning citizens. The Bureau of Immigration's annual reports show that the number of Chinese claiming U.S. citizenship or claiming to be relations of U.S. citizens rose from 634 in 1905 to 4,754 in 1924. By the 1920s and 1930s, Chinese entered more often as U.S. citizens than as members of any other class, a fact most likely explained by the success of illegal immigration. (See Chapter 3, Table 3.) In one investigation, the commissioner-general of immigration estimated that 10,000 to 12,000 Chinese claiming citizenship by birth in the United States had applied for admission beginning in 1894. What made these cases suspicious was the fact that virtually all of them were males, around twenty years old, claiming birth in the Pacific states of California, Oregon, and Washington. Given that the census had recorded only 1,746 Chinese women in those states in 1900, the commissioner concluded that to assert that Chinese male citizens were born in the United States at the rate of 1,000 per annum was "making a draft on [the country's] credulity." It was even harder to believe, the commissioner continued, that all of those thousands had traveled back to China and that all survived to return to this country.[58] Another official concluded that the number of Chinese claiming citizenship was so great in comparison to the number of Chinese women in the country at the time of the applicants' births that there would have had to have been "at least ten times as many Chinese women in this country . . . as actually ever have been in this country since the first Chinaman landed on its shore."[59]

Despite the increased government scrutiny, being admitted as a citizen was a preferred way to enter, because as an immigration category, it generally offered more rights than the other classes. Whereas merchants were forced to maintain their professional status and their businesses or risk being deported, citizens were free to labor in any occupation. Like merchants, they could sponsor their foreign-born children and, for most years, their wives. Although Chinese American citizens also enjoyed the right of enfranchisement, which was denied to their immigrant brethren, this benefit was probably not a primary reason that immigrants chose to enter posing as a citizen over another category. Confessions of Chinese immigrants indicate that a few Chinese who entered fraudulently as citizens did in fact vote in political elections, but the vast majority of them probably did not.[60]

Moreover, native status was especially difficult for immigration officials to verify. While merchants needed two non-Chinese (that is, white) witnesses to corroborate their claims every time they exited and reentered the country, immigration officials did not consistently require the same of natives. The destruction of all of the city's birth records in 1906 was a great stroke of fortune for the Chinese. As one Seattle immigration official explained, "There is not much way of checking on the Chinese when they get in here. A number will have papers, a number will not have papers, and when asked why, they say that they were born in San Francisco. Cannot show birth, for fire destroyed all."[61] Finally, the citizenship claim was an especially successful strategy because, until 1905, Chinese claiming U.S. citizenship could be admitted by the courts, which were known to be more liberal in their interpretations of the laws than immigration officials. False claims of citizenship proved to be so advantageous to the Chinese that a 1906 Bureau of Immigration report found that the Chinese were now using the nativity strategy "to the exclusion of [any] other."[62]

As did Chinese posing as merchants, those who attempted to enter as citizens were careful to craft biographies and statements that measured up to the Bureau of Immigration's standards for determining residence and "Americanness." In an effort to strengthen the credibility of their claims, many applicants pinpointed their exact places of birth in San Francisco, oftentimes citing the same buildings, including the Spanish building in Chinatown, 778 and 805 Commercial Street, 750 Dupont Street, and 786 Johnson Street. In New York City, several thousand Chinese entering through Ellis Island who falsely claimed to have been born in the United States cited 32 Mott Street as their place of birth.[63] Chinese applying as natives also studied their San Francisco geography and history, and a brisk business supplying detailed maps developed in China among immigration agencies and brokers. Usually, the maps included the location of public buildings and the dates of important events in Chinatown. In 1906, the San Francisco Chinese Bureau reported that 10,000 copies of one such map had been published and distributed.[64] Although the information on the maps was elaborate and complicated, Chinese were quite adept at memorizing and reciting the geography and history of San Francisco Chinatown. Chinese effectively deceived officers, or, at the very least, did not provide them with adequate grounds for dismissing their cases.

Chinese immigrants' successful strategies to secure exempt status not only allowed them to enter the country, they also paved the way for later generations of Chinese to apply for admission as paper sons. Paper son migration illustrates well how exclusion-era illegal immigration was created and maintained by both immigrants and the state. The government's early attempts to track Chinese immigrants and returning citizens through partnership files, entry and departure records, and applicant and witness testimonies were part of its efforts to prevent illegal immigration. Ironically, they had the opposite effect, creating many additional opportunities for fraud and evasion. Once a Chinese applicant secured admission into the United States and received the proper documentation, he could use that same paper record to create as many sponsored immigration slots as he desired. Because documentary evidence of family births, marriages, and deaths in China remained difficult to obtain, the immigration service continued to rely upon Chinese testimony. As one immigration official observed, once a Chinese immigrant was admitted into the country, "the groundwork is provided for the subsequent coming of another generation . . . and so the process grows by accretion and is never ending."[65]

"The trick is this," explained Mr. Yuen, a former detainee on Angel Island and a paper son. "You tell the immigration office, 'I have been in China three years, I have three sons, these are their birthdays, the names and so forth.' Few years later, if you do have your own [sons,] then you bring them over here, if not, then you could sell these papers, you know. There's always a lot of buyers ready to buy. You try to sell to your own village, or a similar last name."[66] Wong Tim was especially successful at this business. Declared a U.S. native in 1899, he claimed to have a total of eight children. His two real sons, Wong Kwong Ning and Wong Yuey Ning, joined him in the United States when they were old enough to work. He sold four of the other slots to paper sons Wong Kan Ship, Wong Kam Sum, and Wong Ngen Kee, who all arrived in the 1920s, and to "paper daughter" Wong Jim Ping, who arrived in 1934. Two of the slots Wong Tim had set aside for two more male immigrants were never used.[67] As Wong Tim's case shows, by the 1920s, members of a second generation of Chinese were applying for admission into the country as the foreign-born children of U.S. citizens or merchants.[68] Beginning in 1912, Chinese admitted as the foreign-born children of citizens (258) began to outnumber those claiming to be native-born citizens returning to the United States (188). By 1924, the figures were 2,136 and 476, respectively.[69]

The paper son system thus instituted a chain migration pattern that allowed multiple generations of Chinese to enter the country using fraudulent papers, and it facilitated the reunification of family members (mostly male) within the United States. Ironically, the system enabled the Chinese immigrant community to grow, thus thwarting the efforts of anti-Chinese exclusionists to rid the country of Chinese immigrants altogether. The family of Ho Foo Ning clearly illustrates the effective use of the paper son system. Ho, a twenty-two-year-old native of China, accompanied by his wife, Lee Fung, first sailed into San Francisco in 1889 claiming to have been born in the United States.[70] With the assistance of a skilled attorney, Ho was admitted by the federal district court as a U.S. native. His wife, now considered a wife of a U.S. citizen, was also admitted. During his interviews with immigration authorities, Ho Foo Ning claimed five sons still in China, thus opening the door for members of his family or others who might purchase those slots.

The first "son" Ho Foo Ning brought to the United States was his nephew Ho Yin, who arrived in San Francisco in 1909.[71] Ho Yin, admitted as a son of a citizen, was later able to bring his own son, Ho Gan Lit, into the country in 1938. He also helped bring three immigrants who posed as his sons into the country.[72] One of these paper sons eventually brought his own son into the

In re:
YEE SHEW NING,
17279/7-7
ex ss "Korea Maru"
June 30th, 1918.

State of California)
City and County of) ss
San Francisco.....)

Photograph of
YEE SHEW NING.

Photograph of
YEE YOOK HOW.

YEE YOOK HOW, being first duly sworn upon oath according to law deposes and says:-

That your affiant is a resident Chinese merchant, lawfully domiciled within the United States, and his status as such was the subject of executive examination and determination when your affiant was incoming passenger manifest No. 17279/7-14 ex ss "Korea Maru", June 30th, 1918, when your affiant presented as evidence of his right to admission into the United States a Section 6 Canton merchant's certificate. That your affiant was thereafter and on the 5th day of July, 1918, permitted to enter the United States as such merchant.

That your affiant was accompanied on his said trip by his son YEE SHEW NING, the applicant above described, and this affidavit is made to facilitate in establishing the identity of the said YEE SHEW NING as the minor son of your affiant.

That the photographs which are hereunto annexed are of your affiant and of your affiant's said son, YEE SHEW NING.

Subscribed and sworn to before me
this ___ day of July, 1918.

Harry Horn
Notary Public in and for the City
and County of San Francisco, State
of California.

余延荒何

(Yee Yook How)

Affidavit of Yee Shew Ning, the author's grandfather using his paper name, and Yee Yook Haw, 1918. As a laborer, Lee Chi Yet was barred from the United States by the Chinese exclusion laws. As did many Chinese, he bought papers that allowed him to apply as the son of a merchant. This affidavit spells out Lee's (fictional) relationship to Yee Hook Haw. Courtesy of the National Archives, Pacific Region, San Bruno, California.

country. The buyer of Ho Foo Ning's second paper slot entered the country in 1909 as "son" Ho Quon. Ho Quon later claimed two sons of his own, and he sold these slots to two immigrants not related to him. Another unrelated paper son, who used the name Ho Woon, entered using Ho Foo Ning's third paper slot. He first arrived in the United States in 1912, and in 1923 he was able to bring his own son into the country under the assumed name of Ho Hing.[73] Ho Foo Ning's fourth paper slot was used by an unrelated paper son who assumed the identity of Ho Nuey in 1912. In 1932, this paper son was also able to bring in his own son into the country. The fifth slot was never used. Altogether, a total of sixteen immigrants over four generations were able to enter the United States based on Ho Foo Ning's initial fraudulent claim of citizenship in 1889.

Ho Foo Ning's case demonstrates how the paper trail created by the government to track Chinese immigrants became the most successful means of circumventing the exclusion laws. Ho's paper family also demonstrates the highly gendered character of the paper son system. As Chapter 3 illustrates, the business of selling and securing false immigration documents involved a mostly male clientele. With so many more immigration slots available to males, the paper son system reflects the unequal immigration opportunities available to Chinese women in general. Surprisingly, however, the overwhelming male character of Chinese illegal immigration could benefit Chinese women by deflecting government scrutiny away their cases. Since the vast majority of the immigrants applying for admission from the suspected classes—as U.S. citizens or children of U.S. citizens—were male, immigration officials began to view cases involving female applicants as more credible and less likely to be fraudulent. By the time the immigration station on Angel Island in the San Francisco Bay opened its doors in 1910, government officials' concern about controlling Chinese prostitution or discouraging Chinese female immigration had decreased. One immigration official employed at the Angel Island station admitted that by the 1930s, he and his colleagues were not scrutinizing Chinese women as closely as they did Chinese men. Because women rarely used false papers to enter the country, he explained to an interviewer, "it was the general feeling among the immigration officers and personnel that if a man were bringing a female child into the country, that child was probably his" (that is, not a paper daughter).[74] Such attitudes among governmental officials worked to the advantage of many female applicants. From 1910 to 1924, Chinese women enjoyed somewhat higher admission rates than their male counterparts, reflecting their position among the most "favored" groups of Chinese immigrants.[75] An average of 98 percent of all merchant wives applying for admission were allowed into the country. Ninety-seven percent of all female U.S. citizens or wives of citizens were admitted. Ninety-six percent of all women applying as merchant daughters were admitted. In comparison, 94 percent of new male merchant applicants, 93 percent of male U.S. citizens, and 82 percent of merchant sons were admitted into the country during the same period. (See Chapter 4, Table 6.)

The Cycle of Exclusion

The public spectacle of Chinese jumping the borders, entering from the Gulf of Mexico, and lying their way into the country raised grave doubts about the government's ability to control its borders and seaports. Viewing the evasion of the exclusion laws as a major threat to its credibility and to the welfare of the nation, the Bureau of Immigration responded with strong words and even stronger actions. By the 1920s, however, the enforcement of the exclusion laws had evolved into a self-perpetuating cycle in which each government action was met by an equally forceful reaction by Chinese. Illegal immigration solidified the government's suspicion of all Chinese applicants and justified the continuation of harsh interrogations, extensive medical examinations, and lengthy detentions. These measures in turn made the immigration process even more difficult and arbitrary for all Chinese. Some were unfairly excluded from the United States, while others gained admission through fraud and evasion. Illegal immigrants' success only fueled more illegal entries, and the cycle continued.

Chinese illegal immigration first perpetuated the exclusion cycle by reaffirming immigration officials' beliefs that Chinese as a race were an especially dangerous immigrant group, constantly at odds with Americans and American laws. The government had obvious reason to be suspicious, but the immigration service's views perpetuated existing racialized images of Chinese. As the commissioner-general of immigration explained in 1900, Chinese had "totally different standards of morality," and their seemingly "natural" and inherent "mental acuteness and ingenuity" were by far the most serious obstacles in the enforcement of the exclusion laws.[76] Twenty-five years later, immigration inspectors were still complaining that "these Chinese testify against the law of nature itself."[77] False claims of citizenship were considered to be particularly heinous examples of Chinese cunning and its grave threat to the republic. Officials in San Francisco and Washington, D.C., predicted that with the power to vote, the Chinese could wreak incalculable harm on the nation.

Officials also suspected that most of these fraudulent citizens were common Chinese laborers, thus representing a double threat. "No one will contend for an instant," Commissioner-General of Immigration Frank Sargent wrote in 1905, "that a Chinese coolie is a desirable addition to our citizenship." Chinese immigrants were, Sargent continued, a "threat against our very civilization."[78]

Such sentiments sustained an institutional suspicion of every Chinese applicant, as well as Chinese already living in the United States. On Angel Island, Chinese bore the burden of proof to establish their right to enter the country, and, in fact, the government required that immigration officials weigh any doubtful points in the case "in favor of the *exclusion* of the alien."[79] The agency automatically considered the Chinese, and other Asians excluded by law, ineligible for entry as a group first and foremost. For example, immigration officials were instructed to treat arriving Chinese as aliens "seeking to enter contrary to the law," and officials readily admitted that they were "on guard from the time the Chinese arrives at the station until he is either admitted or deported."[80] Consequently, Chinese spokespersons regularly complained that the immigration service regarded "every Chinese applicant . . . as a cheat, a liar, a rogue and a criminal." Ng Poon Chew, editor of the Chinese daily newspaper the *Chung Sai Yat Po*, charged immigration officials with examining Chinese "with the aim in mind of seeing how [they] may be excluded, rather than of finding out whether [they are] legally entitled to land."[81]

In practice, this suspicion and the government's desire to weed out fraudulent cases translated into a very complicated process in which applicants, their family members, their business partners, and other supporting witnesses were subject to extensive interviews that could last days, weeks, and even months. Testimony was carefully checked and cross-referenced with earlier statements made by all parties. On-site investigations of Chinese businesses, schools, and residences in San Francisco or in other cities across the nation became commonplace.[82] After 1919, Chinese cases might also be heard by an additional panel of inspectors in a board of special inquiry. These hearings, to which non-Chinese immigrants were also subjected, were established to pass judgment on questionable cases.[83]

By far, the most crucial part of the inspection process lay in the interrogations. It was here that immigration officials could uncover and exploit inconsistencies in the various statements in the case, but it was also the most time-consuming process, and the inspection of Chinese immigrants became longer and more complex than for any other immigrant group. As Chinese learned to match the government's efforts, both parties found themselves trapped in a "battle of wits." The resulting process resembled what Ching Chao Wu observed in 1928 as a protracted trial during which a multitude of material and immaterial evidence was collected in an effort to prove or disprove the applicant's immigration status or claimed relationship to a sponsor.[84]

Some of the most heavily scrutinized cases were those involving families. Applicants and their parents were required to demonstrate that the parent-child relationship did indeed exist and that the father continued to maintain legal residence in the United States. The child also had to be under twenty-one years old, and if the father was a sojourner who lived apart from his wife and children, the family had to confirm that the father had made a return trip to China that coincided with the approximate time that the child was conceived. In extreme cases, Chinese couples were even asked how many times they had had intercourse during a visit.[85] To prove the claimed relationship, the entire family was questioned about a wealth of minute details concerning everyday life in the family's home village. Immigrant inspectors believed that family history or facts about relationships and village life should be "common knowledge" to all parties. If any discrepancies were discovered in the testimonies, they concluded that the claimed relationship did not exist and the entire case was discredited.[86]

The first questions officials routinely asked at the beginning of an interrogation were standardized and fair. Among the most common were: How many brothers/sisters do you have? What are the marriage and birth dates of your family members? When was the last time that you saw your father? Where are your grandparents buried? How often do you go to the grave sites? Further into the interrogation, however, the officials pressed applicants for ever more trivial details. In one case, almost nine hundred questions were asked of an applicant.[87] Inspectors regularly asked, for example: How many steps lead up to your house? How many chickens do your neighbors own? In one case, Inspector B. E. Barnes asked Lee Wai Bong: "How many rows of houses in your village?" "Who lives in the third row?" "Who is the oldest man in your village?" The same questions were asked of Lee's brother and father during their interrogations.[88] Fong Tim, testifying on behalf of his son and daughter who were detained on Angel Island, was the subject of even more detailed questions: "Are there any entrances to your village [Lin Jong village]?" "How are the gates [to the village] constructed?" "How far is it from your village to the nearest hill?" "How many windows in the outer walls of [your wife's] house?" "How many clocks are kept in that house?" "Was there ever a stationary stove in that house?" "When were the windows put in that house?"[89]

Some inspectors went further and used intimidation and even threats to test applicants. An immigration inspector on Angel Island bluntly admitted to visitors in 1911 that many of the questions in the interrogations were "not material to the point at issue" but were necessary "to draw [the Chinese] out." The intention was "to make them aware that we have some indirect means of finding out [the truth]."[90] Likewise, the San Francisco Chamber of Commerce complained that government inspectors "often intentionally lead the witnesses into error and leave them there."[91] In 1927, San Francisco commissioner of immigration John D. Nagle conceded that his officers were "reluctant to accept defeat" and would reexamine applicants and witnesses on "every conceivable point" until they had found a discrepancy.[92] The following exchange between Fong Hoy Kun, who was applying for admission as a son of a native in 1918, and immigration officials illustrates just how far some inspectors would go:

Q: Which direction does the front of your house face?

A: Face west.

Q: Your alleged father has indicated that his house in How Chong Village faces east. How do you explain that?

A: I know the sun rises in the front of our house and sets in the back of our house. My mother told me that our house and also the How Chong Village faces west.

Q: Cannot you figure this matter out for yourself?

A: I really don't know directions . . .

Q: How many rooms in all are there on the ground floor of your house?

A: Three; (changes) I mean there is a parlor, two bedrooms and a kitchen. There are five rooms in all downstairs. The two bedrooms are together, side by side, and are between the parlor and kitchen.

Q: Do you wish us to understand you would forget how many bedrooms are in a house where you claim to have lived seventeen years?

A: Yes, I forgot about it.

Q: Did you visit the Sar Kai Market with your father when he was last in China?

A: No.

Q: Why not, if you really are his son?[93]

Although the Bureau of Immigration tried to curb its overzealous officials in 1928 by issuing an order calling for an "expedition of Chinese cases" and an end to examinations on "collateral and extraneous matters," such practices generally did not cease.[94]

Additional tests required applicants to create maps of their villages by tracing wooden blocks on paper.[95] After marking the exact locations of family residences, cultivated land, schools, wells, ancestral halls, etc., they were then asked to name the inhabitants of each dwelling. Yee Sing, a merchant's son applying for admission in 1910, drew up such a map of Sing Hong village in the Toisan district. His notations included such details as: "Yee Lim Jung, second row, first house, is married and has one boy; Yee Jit, not married, lives alone, second row, fifth house; school house is in sixth row, south side; ancestral hall and school where Yee Jung Nam teaches is in the fifth row, south side."[96] Family members of applicants and witnesses related to their cases were often required to perform the same activity so that officials could search for further discrepancies.

Because immigration officials believed that Chinese routinely lied about their ages in order to conform to the life histories documented in bought papers, they ordered immigrants to be examined by doctors to verify them. The bureau had officially stopped using the humiliating Bertillon system to identify nonexempt classes of Chinese in 1906. Still, the extensive medical examinations and measurements of body parts in these examinations mirrored some of the agency's earlier tactics. In 1918, Yee Shew Ning, applying to enter the country as a son of a merchant, was told to strip himself of all clothing before he was examined by J. P. Hickely, a medical examiner on Angel Island. Hickely carefully scrutinized, measured, and made notations regarding Yee's "hair, (caputal, axillary, facial, and pubic), condition of skin, eruption and development of teeth, development of sexual organs, facial expression, and general attitude."[97] Although physicians on Angel Island conceded that "there was a large opportunity for error" in these examinations and that in fact they were an unreliable method to determine the age of applicants, they were nevertheless allowed and even recommended by immigration officials.[98]

Medical examiners were charged to make informed, "scientific" judgments proving or disproving an applicant's paternity and age, but immigration inspectors often took it upon themselves to judge whether or not the applicant resembled his or her claimed relatives. Entry was denied if an inspector happened to believe that the immigrant in question bore no resemblance to his or her claimed parents and siblings. Immigration officials would routinely study the shapes of the heads, mouths, eyes, noses, and ears of applicants and compare them with those of the claimed fathers or siblings who were already in the country. Inspectors Smith, Lawrence, and Avery, for instance, all agreed to land Lee Shuk Wah in 1924 because there was "quite a marked resemblance between the applicant and his alleged father."[99] In 1909, Commissioner Hart Hyatt North denied entry to Moy Luk because he could "note no family resemblance at all" between the applicant and his alleged brother. The applicant's head, he explained, was "bulging, whereas the older brother's seems to be rather rounding." Moreover, Moy Luk had "typically almond shaped" eyes, whereas the brother's seemed "to be rather open for a Chinese person." Moy and his attorney objected to the judgment and appealed the decision to the Department of Commerce and Labor. Secretary Victor H. Metcalf reversed the ruling nine days later.[100]

The interrogations, medical examinations, and even the highly subjective judgments made by immigration officials often did turn up glaring discrepancies and helped prevent many illegal entries. In one instance, Lew Wah was denied admission because he claimed that his paternal grandparents were alive and well, living in the last house, in the third row of his native village, while his alleged father and brother both testified that the grandparents had died twenty years earlier.[101]

Nevertheless, in multiple cases, the questions asked by immigration inspectors were too challenging for even close relatives. Young children were especially prone to shyness, nervousness, and confusion in front of the immigration officials, who were often the first non-Chinese they had ever met. Still, the children were held responsible for their testimony, and any discrepancies between the child's responses and those of the other family members were used against the case. In one situation, a twelve-year-old applicant was subjected to eighty-seven pages of questioning. When discrepancies between his answers and his family members' were detected, he was denied admission by the immigration service. A federal court later admitted him on appeal, ruling that the burden of proof in this case was too high and that any applicant could make a mistake in so many pages of testimony.[102]

Correspondingly, Chinese complained bitterly about such procedures. The seemingly endless cross-examinations would result in discrepancies "no matter how real a case or how honest a man is," Chinese merchants charged in 1910.[103] Representatives from the Chinese Chamber of Commerce and Chinese-American League of Justice of Los Angeles objected to "the grossest third degree sweating [of] countless impertinent questions calculated to confuse the Chinese."[104] A joint commission of white and Chinese merchants from San

Francisco also concluded that the examinations were "unreasonable." The applicant is "considered guilty until he proves himself entitled to land," and the high standards of proof were "sufficient to exclude every man, woman, and child from landing."[105]

Some immigration officials acknowledged that the rigorous inspection process occasionally resulted in the wrongful exclusion of a bona fide exempt-class immigrant. In 1909, the commissioner-general of immigration wrote that on the one hand, the present laws were "illy adapted to either exclude or expel the Chinese laborer," and on the other, the laws were "unduly and worse than uselessly rigid" in relation to exempt-class and resident Chinese already living in the United States.[106] One Angel Island immigration inspector confessed that his own two children probably could not have passed the rigorous and detailed examinations that he had administered to Chinese immigrants.[107]

From its extensive interrogations to its lengthy investigations, the government's responses to Chinese illegal immigration were imperfect and perpetuated the cycle of exclusion. Without any other foreseeable alternative available, however, illegal entries continued, and they had enduring repercussions for both Chinese immigrants and U.S. immigration officials.

The Consequences of Illegal Immigration

The immigration service's efforts to stem illegal immigration certainly impacted Chinese immigration, but not in the ways in which officials had planned. Rather than putting an end to illegal entries altogether, the tougher inspection procedures merely motivated Chinese to take greater risks and invest more money and time in their attempts to get around the exclusion laws. They also encouraged more illegal immigration, which, in turn, became normalized within the Chinese community, leaving very few Chinese untouched. They prompted a new arm of the illegal immigration business to spring up in the form of coaching book production and distribution. And, finally, one of their most enduring effects was longer detentions for all Chinese on Angel Island.

As immigration authorities increased the difficulty of immigrant interrogations, Chinese were forced to delve even deeper into the fabricated histories and relationships. Sometimes inspectors asked questions that were not covered by the coaching book. Other times, immigrants forgot important details in their fictitious identities and lives. To address these problems, detainees found ways to acquire the right information by relying on outsiders to send them

Coaching notes found inside peanut shells and banana peels, no date. Interrogations of Chinese immigrants were so detailed and exhaustive that both legal and illegal Chinese immigrants learned to rely on coaching notes, such as these hidden inside a handful of peanuts and a banana, to remember correct answers and pass their examinations. These notes had been carefully concealed inside a care package to a detainee on Angel Island, but they were found and confiscated by immigration officials to be used in an exhibit to the commissioner-general of immigration. The note hidden inside the peanut coached the would-be recipient on the details of his apparently fictional identity. The note inside the banana included questions and answers of a relative's interrogation as well as a diagram of the family village. Courtesy of the National Archives, Washington, D.C.

notes. Until 1909, while Chinese immigrants were still being held in the detention shed on the Pacific Mail Steamship Company's dock, coaching notes, food, and even tools used to escape the shed were passed in through the windows by friends and relatives or by corrupt watchmen. As one investigator found, "The Chinese are permitted to converce [*sic*] with their friends at all times [while in the detention shed]. I am told that strings are lowered down, and letters received in this way. There is a 1½ inch wire mash [*sic*] screen, over the windows, but this does not stop the letter delivery nor conversation."[108]

Immigration officials thought that moving the immigration station to the isolated location on Angel Island in the San Francisco Bay would prevent the

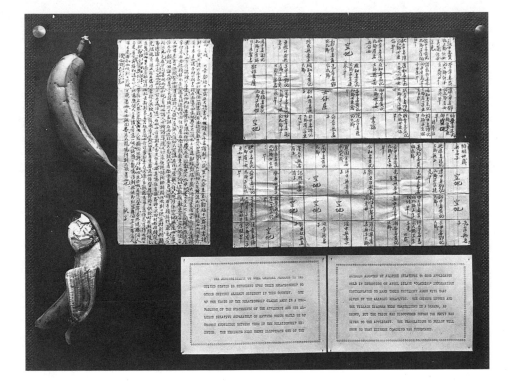

friends of Chinese detainees from coaching them, but they were proven wrong. As both government records and interviews with Chinese detainees illustrate, immigrants were still able to acquire information that they needed in their interrogations. The methods used for passing these notes were nothing less than ingenious. In one case, government officials confiscated a handful of U.S. quarters and nickels on which Chinese characters had been carefully written. Together the characters read: "When Immigration officials ask you if your maternal grandmother is living, be sure that you say that she has been dead for more than ten years." In another case, several peanuts, whose shells had been carefully pried apart and glued back together again, contained tiny scraps of paper with dates and names written on them. Similarly, an orange peel was carefully wrapped around crumpled up coaching notes and glued back together to resemble a whole, uneaten orange.[109] *Char siu bows* (pork buns) were also hollowed out and filled with coaching notes.[110] These items were commonly passed to immigrants by visitors and by the Chinese kitchen staff. According to Mr. Tom, a former detainee on Angel Island, cooks "would shop in San Francisco for groceries and food [and] would put the coaching notes in an envelope in the groceries and sneak it in. Sometimes they hid it secretly on their bodies."[111] Visitors were not allowed to see the detainees, but they could still sneak notes into care packages bound for the island. For a fee, corrupt immigration guards would also smuggle in notes during meal times or in packages.[112]

Such communication was invaluable to both detainees and their relatives and friends off the island. Detainee Yee You Tai sent the following message to his uncle through a Japanese fellow passenger on board his ship: "To my uncle Chuen Tat: This evening the Immigration officials questioned me. I therefore send up my testimony for your information. He asked me why I returned [to China via Boston]; I said because father was at Boston. If you should be asked with reference to anything that happened to me after I went to Boston from the time I was 5 or 6 years old, you just simply say, 'I cannot state positively about that.'"[113] Another coaching note sent to a detainee berated him for his poor performance during his interrogation. "When you came to the United States, you had been in the village and seen the place for over one year, and you, so big, ought to know the things that have passed!" the author chided. "You carelessly told the inspector that I came to U.S. in 1892 and that I returned to China in 1905 and that your sister was born in 1906. All these are wrong! In truth, I came to U.S. in 1902, returned (to China) 1902, your sister Ah Yung was born in 1905."[114] Still another coaching note discovered by immigration officials on Angel Island contained a photograph and a description of the applicant's "paper brother" so that the detainee would be able to identify him if necessary. As the author of the note explained, "He will have on a dark woolen coat; the American buttons on it are inside. His pants are of slightly yellow color. He will have his cap in his right hand. The cap will have the color of hemp. The hair on the top of his head is parted in the middle. Should the immigration officer ask you to identify a man be sure to identify him aright."[115] Coaching notes revealed just how dependent Chinese immigration had become on lies, false documents, and corruption.

As illegal immigration increased, it also became normalized, affecting entire families and communities regardless of class background and immigration status.[116] The lines between legal and illegal immigrants became blurred. Family members, witnesses, friends, and acquaintances easily became involved in illegal immigration simply by testifying on behalf of an applicant committing fraud. Moreover, because all Chinese immigrants were placed under suspicion, the government's crackdown ironically resulted in forcing many legal immigrants to turn to illegal immigration. Exempt-class Chinese, for instance, sometimes bought fraudulent papers if they believed that route would be the safest means of entering the country. In 1910, Chew Wey and Chew Dung purchased citizens' papers even though they were both the legal sons of Chew Choon, a San Francisco merchant and the president of a vegetable and grocery company in Chinatown. As their brother explained to government investigators decades after their arrival, "At that time it was considered better to come as sons of citizens rather than as merchants' sons and that is why my father had us come in that way."[117]

The intense questioning by immigration officials also prompted many Chinese—regardless of their immigration status—to go to the same professional coaching book writers used by illegal immigrants. In fact, coaching books became a necessity for all immigrants because of the number, nature, and scope of the questions asked in the interrogations. Many simply believed it was humanly impossible to answer them without preparation.[118] In 1913, immigrant inspector W. H. Wilkinson admitted that it was "a well known fact that even in genuine cases the testimony to be offered by the principals has frequently been prepared, or coached in advance."[119]

The lengthy inspection processes also increased the detention time for Chinese. Indeed, most immigrants who were selected for further investigation had to endure incarceration on Angel Island for several days, months, and even years while awaiting the final decisions in their cases. When the station first opened, immigrants waited for their first appearance before immigration officials for months.[120] By the mid-1920s, the delay averaged two to three weeks.[121] Japanese and European immigrants were often released on the day of arrival, while Chinese were detained for indefinite periods of time. No other immigrant group was detained at ports of entry as long as the Chinese.[122] Both the long detentions and the harsh treatment by immigration officials took its toll. Chinese felt that they were treated like criminals. Some even referred to Angel Island as "Devil Island."[123]

The conditions under which Chinese were detained on Angel Island only deepened their despair. Although the immigration station on the island was a vast improvement from the detention shed on the wharf in San Francisco, the barracks windows were enclosed with iron bars, and the only time that detainees were allowed outside of their dormitory was during mealtimes, when they were escorted by armed guards to the dining hall. Lights were turned off promptly at a certain hour, and guards would then count the immigrants. All Chinese male applicants were housed in one large room, where bunk beds were arranged in double or triple rows. A small recreation yard was adjacent to the barracks, but no educational or recreational programs were provided. Sociolo-

Angel Island immigration station barracks, c. 1910. Chinese were separated from immigrants from other countries in the detention barracks, and there were separate quarters for men and women. Immigrants were closely guarded and monitored at all times. Frustrated detainees wrote or carved poems of despair and protest onto the building's walls. Courtesy of the National Archives, Washington, D.C.

gist Wen-hsien Chen reported in 1940 that "the Chinese aliens under custody in detention quarters are much neglected; little consideration is given to their physical comfort, personal needs, and emotional satisfaction."[124] Many of the detainees on Angel Island simply awaited their fates. Others vented their frustration by carving or writing Chinese poems on the barracks walls while they waited for the outcome of their cases. Some poems revealed anger and frustration over their circumstances, the discriminatory exclusion laws, and China's weakened status as a world power unable to protect its citizens. Other authors complained of uncertainty, despair, and homesickness. More than 135 poems have been recorded from the walls of the barracks to date. They document not only protest but also the futility and folly of the exclusion laws themselves.[125]

Conclusion

The exclusion of Chinese immigrants from the United States did not stop them from coming. It merely shifted their migration underground and fueled a transnational business in illegal immigration. Spawned and sustained by the very efforts designed to thwart its growth, Chinese illegal immigration proved difficult to prevent. Stringent enforcement practices designed to crack down on illegal immigration generally only resulted in the creation of riskier, more expensive illegal operations that placed even greater burdens on Chinese, Chinese communities, and the U.S. government. The immigration service's methods to deter illegal immigration became the impetus for new immigration strategies.

Both historical and contemporary narratives of illegal immigration tend to focus solely on immigrants and immigrant criminality alone, but immigration officials, immigration agents, and a wide transnational, multiracial network of middlemen who guided, hid, and transported Chinese into the country by land and sea clearly took part in and sustained the cycle of Chinese exclusion. Chinese were indeed resourceful, and they readily adapted to changes in the laws, mobilizing family, business partners, and other accomplices throughout China and the Americas. But, at the same time, the American government's weak, corrupt, and still-formative system of immigration enforcement created additional opportunities for a wide range of people that sustained the business of illegal immigration.

The cost of illegal immigration was high. Admission became more and more difficult, and some legal immigrants were unfairly excluded. Chinese immigrants were forced to await the outcome of their cases in crowded and dismal conditions under armed guard and barbed wire. Immigration officials suffered from overwork. As sociologist Ching Chao Wu observed in 1928, there were complaints on both sides: "The immigration officers charge that many Chinese come in through crooked methods, and the Chinese charge that the immigration officials are unjust in dealing with the Chinese." Yet, he could not predict any change in the system in the near future. "So long as the wage scale in the United States is high, exclusion law cannot prevent the Chinese fortune-seekers from knocking at the Golden Gate in disguise," he explained. "And so long as the Chinese continue to come in violation of the exclusion laws, the immigration officials will continue to be harsh toward the Chinese."[126] Wu was correct. It took fifteen more years and a world war before the Chinese exclusion laws were repealed. Chinese immigrants were then subjected to the same regulatory procedures as other immigrants. The entire process improved for Chinese immigrants in 1950 when the United States incorporated advance immigration inspection into immigration law. Thereafter, immigrants could be inspected prior to emigration instead of after the long voyage to the United States.[127]

PART IV

THE CONSEQUENCES
AND LEGACIES
OF EXCLUSION

By the early twentieth century, the Chinese exclusion laws had evolved from a system of admission and exclusion of newly arriving Chinese immigrants to one that also controlled Chinese immigrant and Chinese American communities already in the United States. The two systems were inextricably related. The goal of the Chinese Exclusion Act had been to close the gates to Chinese immigrants, but it failed to completely prevent them from entering the country and forming families and communities. Most Asian immigrants and Asian Americans remained confined to specific ethnic ghettos, but "persistent questions [arose] as to the solidity of those borders." The government responded to the exclusion policies' failure with what David Palumbo-Liu has described as "crisis management."[1] Consequently, American gatekeeping extended to the nation's interiors, leading to an increase in the state's role in "disciplining" Chinese immigrants and Chinese Americans and the establishment of a system of arrest and deportation.[2]

This section shifts our attention to the ways in which racist and anti-immigrant policies came to be enforced in Chinese homes, places of business, and communities. That the Chinese living in America were targeted this way further illustrates the gap that separated them from other immigrants groups in the United States. Chapter 7 emphasizes how the "shadow of exclusion," in the form of surveillance, arrest, and deportation policies had far-reaching and long-term consequences. The threat of deportation and the conflation of legal and illegal immigrants also rendered all Chinese vulnerable to exploitation and extortion and produced a psychology of fear that resulted in their segregation, marginalization, and return migration.

The Epilogue turns to the legacies of Chinese exclusion for American immigration policy in the post-exclusion era and in the late twentieth and early twenty-first centuries. The exclusion laws set important precedents for subsequent restrictionist immigration laws in the early twentieth century. The repeal of Chinese exclusion during World War II set in motion a new wave of reform in immigration law, but the legacies of Chinese exclusion remain embedded in American gatekeeping, especially in the government's recent efforts to control both the U.S.-Mexican border and Mexican immigrants. Chinese exclusion ended more than fifty years ago, but the United States is still contending with its legacy today.

CHAPTER SEVEN

Instead of welcoming them like other aliens, we have denied American
citizenship to the Chinese, discriminated against them as against no other
race, degraded, oppressed, and insulted them, and established this
monstrous deportation and exclusion system against them, which is
based upon the assumption that they have none of the "rights of man."
How could we possibly expect them to be assimilated as other people are?
—Max Kohler, assistant U.S. district attorney, New York, 1901

IN THE SHADOW
OF EXCLUSION

The Impact of Exclusion on the Chinese in America

WHILE DETAINED IN the barracks of the immigration station on Angel Island, Chinese immigrants dreamed of the day when they might finally be
admitted into the United States. Passing through America's gates, however,
did not mean freedom from the exclusion laws. The government's failure to
prevent or deter illegal immigration resulted in an expansion of the exclusion
laws into the nation's interiors and a vigorous policy of surveillance, arrest,
and, finally, deportation. As part of the 1882 Chinese Exclusion Act, deportation became a primary means of controlling and disciplining the Chinese community in America. This shadow of exclusion extended not only to legal and
illegal Chinese immigrants but also to native-born Chinese American citizens,
whose plight was inextricably connected to that of their immigrant brethren.
Consequently, members of the Chinese community in America began to re-
evaluate both their place in the United States and their status as Americans.

Deportation was the government's last chance to protect its citizens from allegedly dangerous aliens. Viewed as an essential feature of exclusion enforcement, American deportation policy further racialized Chinese immigration as a serious threat to national peace and security. As Commissioner-General of Immigration Frank Sargent remarked in 1903, "Any reasonable amount of success in the continuance of the exclusion policy [depends upon] the success of the expulsion [policies] as well."[1] In other words, if one failed, the other might succeed.

The Chinese Exclusion Act provided the legal means for deporting Chinese. The act gave local and state police officers (listed as "peace officers") and U.S. marshals the authority to arrest any Chinese person suspected of being in the country unlawfully. After being brought before a justice, judge, or commissioner of a federal court in a deportation hearing, the person was either released if found innocent, or, if found guilty, returned to the "country from whence he came," at the expense of the U.S. government.[2] The establishment of the deportation clause in the Chinese Exclusion Act was immensely significant. Before 1882, the first and only time that the U.S. government had allowed for the deportation of immigrants already in the country was from 1798 to 1800, under the Alien and Sedition Acts of 1798. Although never enforced, these acts required oaths of allegiance from aliens residing in the United States and gave the president the power to deport aliens who were natives, citizens, or subjects of any country with which the United States was at war.[3] In 1882, politicians tried to legalize the deportation of paupers and convicts who became public charges upon their arrival. This effort failed. The deportation provisions of the Chinese Exclusion Act of that same year were, however, approved, largely because Chinese immigrants were considered much greater threats than the (mostly European) paupers and convicts whom the other bill targeted. Just as they were the first to be excluded on the basis of their race and class, Chinese immigrants also became the first group to be classified as deportable. By the time the Chinese exclusion laws were repealed in 1943, Chinese were no longer an anomaly, and the U.S. government had added many other classes of immigrants to the deportable list.[4]

Amendments to the exclusion laws passed after 1882 refined the deportation policies relating to Chinese immigrants and established the system by which deportation would be accomplished. In 1888, the Scott Act reaffirmed the nation's legal right to deport Chinese found to be in the country unlawfully, but it did allow them to appeal the decision.[5] The 1892 Geary Act expanded and centralized the system by which the government could identify and track Chinese immigrants. All laborers found without the certificate of residence that the Geary Act required were arrested and taken before a deportation hearing.[6] Although exempt-class Chinese did not have to register, they were subject to harassment by immigration officials just the same. Moreover, since the Bureau of Immigration required them to leave their exempt-class (Section 6) certificates with the agency, Chinese merchants, students, teachers, and diplomats were often left without proof of lawful residence and, in the event of a raid, were vulnerable to arrest.[7]

The Chinese community challenged both the registration and the deportation provisions of the 1892 Geary Act through the courts, and one case made it all the way to the U.S. Supreme Court in *Fong Yue Ting v. United States*. Some justices argued that the power to expel should not apply to lawful and long-term resident aliens. They contended that the Tenth Amendment to the Constitution offered constitutional protection to citizens and aliens alike. Thus, any expulsion of lawful residents would be in violation of constitutional guarantees of liberty and due process of the law. However, the majority of justices ruled that the power to exclude aliens and the power to expel them were within the rights of a sovereign government.[8] After the 1893 Supreme Court ruling, the power of Congress to enact legislation expelling aliens, even long-term residents, from the United States remained unchallenged, and the government began to exercise this new power of the state vigorously and forcefully.[9]

The initial intent of the country's deportation activities had been to catch, arrest, and deport those who failed to produce the necessary documentation proving their status as legal residents in the United States. By the 1900s, however, the deportation system expanded to include additional classes of Chinese not originally covered in the 1882 act, such as border crossers. Beginning in 1908, the immigration service also began to deport Chinese under the general immigration laws whenever possible, thereby bypassing the judicial hearings required under the exclusion laws. Chinese who failed to maintain the professional or exempt status under which they were admitted also became targets for deportation.[10] Prior to the 1924 Immigration Act, the courts uniformly held that treaties between the United States and China exempted from deportation those Chinese whose status changed from exempt to laborer (that is, former merchants who had suffered business losses and were now laborers) unless their original entries were fraudulent.[11] In practice, immigration officials ignored these judicial decisions and increased their efforts to find and deport Chinese who had lost their exempt status. In 1905, for example, the Bureau of Immigration authorized its agents to arrest a number of students who were found to be working in Chinese laundries and restaurants.[12] Moreover, beginning in 1909, all persons of Chinese descent, including U.S. citizens, were required to carry a certificate that identified them as having been legally admitted to the country. Chinese American citizens could work as laborers, but if exempt-class Chinese were caught performing manual labor, their certificates of identity were confiscated and they were liable for arrest and deportation.[13]

By the early 1900s, deportation became an essential tool of control and security in the nation's interiors. In 1902, the number of Chinese arrested (1,128) was more than double the number in 1900 (539), and in 1904, a record 1,793 Chinese were arrested based on their suspected illegal residence. Court cases also supported the government's deportation policies. In *Li Sing v. U.S.* (1901), for example, the court ruled that aliens were not protected against unreasonable search or seizures, nor could they claim the right of trial by jury. Moreover, only white witnesses could testify on behalf of potential deportees.[14] With the Chinese boycott of American goods in 1905 and 1906 total arrests and deportations decreased.

In 1915, however, Bureau of Immigration guidelines expanded the parameters of what constituted an "illegal immigrant" as part of the government's efforts to crack down on Chinese who entered the country illegally from Mexico or Canada. Agency regulations of that year gave inspectors the right to examine "all Chinese persons in the United States not personally known to them" to determine if they were legally entitled to be and remain in the country. In essence, that meant that any Chinese immigrant whom an officer did not personally know could be suspected of having entered the country illegally. The regulations also allowed for the deportation of any wives and children of exempt-class Chinese who were found to be in the country illegally, even if this meant disrupting families.[15]

The strictest deportation provisions were established in the 1924 Immigration Act, which further codified the requirement that Chinese immigrants maintain their exempt-class status in order to remain in the country. Although the number of arrests and deportations remained far lower after 1924 than during the government's intense crackdown in the early 1900s, the harsh new provisions served to punish not only Chinese who had entered illegally but also long-term residents and those who were ignorant of the changes in the law or innocently overstayed their visas. In 1940, sociologist Wen-hsien Chen

TABLE 9. CHINESE ARRESTS AND DEPORTATIONS
UNDER EXCLUSION LAWS AND GENERAL IMMIGRATION
LAWS, 1898–1930

Year	Arrests under Exclusion Laws	Arrests under General Immigration Laws	Total Deported
1898	756	N/A	220
1899	566	N/A	192
1900	539	N/A	288
1901	897	N/A	440
1902	1,128	N/A	519
1903	1,420	N/A	704
1904	1,793	N/A	783
1905	1,088	N/A	647
1906	503	N/A	319
1907	503	N/A	336
1908	912	N/A	477
1909	836	N/A	665
1910	977	N/A	825
1911	669	N/A	522
1912	616	N/A	397
1913	191	N/A	165
1914	225	N/A	131
1915	296	N/A	119
1916	212	N/A	104
1917	115	N/A	69
1918	104	N/A	51
1919	96	N/A	35
1920	31	N/A	15
1921	59	282	341
1922	83	307	390
1923	135	89	224
1924	172	129	301

TABLE 9. CONTINUED

Year	Arrests under Exclusion Laws	Arrests under General Immigration Laws	Total Deported
1925	93	168	261
1926	178	133	311
1927	141	73	214
1928	139	92	231
1929	33	88	121
1930	166	90	256
Total	15,672	1,451	10,673

Sources: U.S. Treasury Department, *Annual Reports of the Commissioner-General of Immigration* (Washington: GPO, 1898–1902); U.S. Department of Commerce and Labor, *Annual Reports of the Commissioner-General of Immigration* (Washington: GPO, 1903–11); U.S. Department of Labor, *Annual Reports of the Commissioner-General of Immigration* (Washington: GPO, 1912–30); Wen-hsien Chen, "Chinese under Both Exclusion and Immigration Laws" (Ph.D. diss., University of Chicago, 1940), 180.
Note: N/A = figures not available.

pointed to the explicitly racist component of the country's deportation policies. Such expulsions, she charged, were "peculiar only to the Chinese. . . . Some with an established good reputation were held deportable, not because of undesirability but because they were Chinese and ineligible for citizenship."[16]

Shadowed Lives

As were all other aliens residing in the United States, Chinese were entitled to the safeguards of the Constitution and to the protection of the laws regarding their rights of person and property. But the deportation policies established by the exclusion laws, affirmed by the Supreme Court, and expedited by the Bureau of Immigration made the Chinese in America more vulnerable to infringements on their rights than other immigrant groups. Wen-hsien Chen observed, "Those who are eligible to citizenship secure protection. But the Chinese, to whom citizenship is not available, [are] subject to deportation more frequently than other aliens."[17] Moreover, because the Chinese community

Chinese deportees, 1932–34. By the 1920s, arriving and departing Chinese were being photographed with their case file numbers for easier identification by government officials. This dehumanizing practice is evident in these "mug shots" of individuals ordered deported from the United States. Courtesy of the National Archives, Pacific Region, San Bruno, California.

had little political power, American politicians did little to ameliorate abuses against them, and there was little public outcry on their behalf.

Chinese immigrants and residents thus often lived a shadowed existence, constantly anxious about their immigration status, about harassment by immigration officials and others, and about their personal safety in general. All Chinese were required to produce on demand the documentation verifying their right to remain in the United States. If the officers were not satisfied with the proof or if the individual under question could not immediately produce the documentation, he or she could be arrested. Albert King, a Chinese merchant in Seattle, told an interviewer in 1924 that while only some Chinese "told lies," government inspectors "think [all] Chinese underground; take them all to be fraud, or kick them out and tell them they will send them to jail. Chinese are afraid of them. Americans shouldn't take it to represent all

Chinese."[18] Likewise, in 1928, sociologist Ching Chao Wu asserted that "just as many innocent Chinese suffer at the Immigration Office because of some Chinese coming behind masks, [and] so many resident Chinese suffer in the United States because of the smugglers and contraband Chinese."[19]

One of the most effective tools of the immigration service was the immigration raid. Instituted in the early twentieth century under Commissioner-General Frank Sargent, raids proved to be particularly useful means of catching and arresting a large number of suspected illegal immigrants at one time. No neighborhood, place of business, school, or church was beyond the government's reach. As the Chinese Chamber of Commerce complained, vegetable gardens, stores and other places of business, as well as private residences and homes, were "raided repeatedly, sometimes as often as once a month, even though the Immigration Inspectors generally fail[ed] to find contraband Chinese employed or concealed there." Moreover, the Chinese-American League of Justice in Los Angeles charged that immigration officials routinely acted with "the grossest insolence and most brutal conduct." Inspectors forcibly broke locks and crashed through doors, unlawfully searched through trunks and baggage, and physically abused and insulted the Chinese under their control.[20]

Immigration officials were required to get the commissioner-general's approval before they conducted an immigration raid on suspected illegal Chinese, but apparently they did not need to provide much evidence to support their suspicions. For example, in 1903, the immigrant inspector in charge at New Orleans sought and received permission from Sargent to conduct a raid on the Chinese community in that city based on his belief that it was "not unreasonable to suppose that some Chinamen may have affected an unlawful entrance . . . and are now hiding here."[21] In another raid in New York, zealous immigration officials fabricated statements and misleading reports in order to apprehend twenty-seven Chinese suspected of being in the country illegally. Five years later, the actions of the inspectors involved were discovered, and they were forced to resign. The disclosure, however, came too late for the Chinese already arrested and deported.[22]

One of the best-known raids occurred in Boston on October 11, 1903. Prior to the raid, local police officers had informed the U.S. district attorney that they suspected that many Chinese residing in Boston were illegal immigrants. It was also rumored that members of a Chinese secret society were blackmailing Chinese residents into paying large sums of money in exchange for not reporting their illegal status to immigration authorities. Together with the police department and the district attorney, the Bureau of Immigration consented to rectify the "evil conditions" in Boston not by going after the blackmailers, but by deporting all Chinese who were in the country in violation of the law.[23] Accordingly, on the evening of Sunday, October 11, 1903, a number of immigration agents from Boston, New York, and other cities, assisted by the local police, made a sudden and unexpected descent upon the Chinese quarter of Boston. As one witness reported, the police and immigration officials "fell upon their victims without giving a word of warning" and surrounded all of the area's private homes and clubs, as well as restaurants and other public places. No warrants for arrest were produced, and all Chinese residents who failed to show their identification papers were detained.[24] The raid resulted in the arrest of 234 Chinese. After they spent twelve hours in jail, 122 of them were found to be legal residents. In the end, only 45 Chinese were deported back to China.[25]

The raid in Boston was not an isolated event. Smaller, less-publicized raids occurred on a regular basis over the next several years, causing sociologist Mary Coolidge to write that "all Chinese are treated as suspects, if not as criminals."[26] The *Nation* reported that in the early 1900s, police and immigration officials swept into the Chinatowns of Cleveland, Chicago, Boston, Philadelphia, New York, and other cities, smashing down doors and arresting "thousands of peaceful Chinese waiters, laundrymen, merchants, and laborers." They jailed the offenders without warrant and left the broken homes and businesses unguarded and vulnerable to looting. "When this epidemic of lawlessness was over," the reporter dryly explained, the police and federal agents announced "that they had been acting in the name of the law."[27]

By the 1910s, vocal Chinese complaints made the rounds in Washington, D.C. In 1918, the Chinese Six Companies grew so infuriated by the mistreatment of Chinese residents that they sent a telegram to President Woodrow Wilson. "No matter how long their residence or how firm their right to remain, Chinese are being arrested, hunted, and terrorized," they charged. As a result, they continued, the Chinese population of the Pacific Coast was "fast decreasing."[28] Despite such complaints, the government raids and harassment continued. In 1923, San Francisco's Chinese community complained that the Bureau of Immigration had instituted nothing less than a "veritable Reign of Terror" against them.[29]

Immigration raids on Chinese communities became the public face of the government's efforts to control Chinese immigration within the nation's interiors. They also served to sanction the harassment of Chinese throughout the country by other law-enforcement officials and the general populace as well. Thus, Chinese residents found themselves constantly at risk of being questioned, detained, or physically or verbally assaulted. Aggressive government deportation policies had effectively brought Chinese exclusion into every corner of the country, making every place potentially dangerous for Chinese. Longtime Chicago resident and merchant Hong Sling experienced this harassment first hand in 1901. While on a train en route to Decatur, Illinois, Hong was pounced upon by a U.S. marshal. After the marshal declared that it was his intention to "arrest every Chinaman in this district," he demanded that Hong show proof of his right to be in the country. Hong complied, giving his name, place of residence, and a description of his business. He also provided other evidence of his status as a merchant, including a letter signed by Secretary of the Treasury Lyman Gage, who certified that he personally knew Hong to be a merchant. The marshal was not satisfied and searched Hong's baggage. Upon finding Hong's registration certificate, the officer let him go, but only after kicking and hitting Hong in front of a large crowd gathered around him.[30]

Such abuses were apparently widespread. In 1905, Reverend Leighton Parks of New York City complained to the Department of Commerce and Labor that the Chinese residents of that city lived in "continual dread" of the Chinese inspectors, because they were blackmailed and subjected to other unjust treatment by them.[31] By 1914, the Chinese Consulate felt it necessary to file a formal protest with the immigration service in Los Angeles against its unnecessary force in apprehending Chinese. The immigration officials, the consul-general complained, "make a big show of force where absolutely none is necessary, and that in many cases, exceptionally high bonds have been asked in cases where the ordinary amount would have answered all purposes. In other words, they are making the matter one of *persecution* as well as prosecution."[32] Those who were most vulnerable to persecution were, of course, Chinese who had entered the country under fraudulent purposes, lost their legal immigration status, or possessed no documentation whatsoever. San Francisco immigration agents, for instance, chased down Wong Bew in 1908 after learning that although he had been granted admission into the country as a Chinese merchant, he was actually working as a cook in a local hospital. When inspectors unexpectedly showed up at the hospital, Wong immediately fled the kitchen through a back alley but was eventually caught and brought in for questioning.[33]

Similarly, a merchant, Wu Wah, and his wife, Ngoon Shee, found themselves hunted by immigration officials for five years beginning in 1932, because Wu had been forced to sell his Oakland, California, business in the wake of the economic depression. Although they had six children, all born in the United States as citizens, immigration officials issued a warrant for the arrest of both parents in 1932, charging the couple with violating the Immigration Act of 1924 and failing to maintain their exempt-class status. The two were apparently aware of the government's intentions and hurriedly left their home in Oakland just a few days before immigrant inspector E. C. Benson arrived with the arrest warrant. Benson attempted to track them down through the U.S. postal system and the California Department of Motor Vehicles. Meanwhile, Ngoon Shee and Wu Wah were forced into a life of hiding and secrecy, moving from place to place, but never staying in one location for very long. When immigrant inspectors finally caught the family in 1937, the couple hired attorney W. H. Wilkinson, a former law officer in the Bureau of Immigration, who argued that both legal precedent and the service's own regulations nulli fied the government's charges against the couple. Immigration officials in San Francisco had no choice but to cancel the arrest warrants for Ngoon Shee and Wu Wah. In October of 1937, their deportation cases were finally closed, five years after they had first been filed.[34]

For illegal and undocumented immigrants, exploitation and extortion came from many quarters. Oppressive employers, corrupt government bureaucrats, other Chinese, suspicious Americans, and lawyers and con artists all preyed upon Chinese whose vulnerable legal status made them unable or unwilling to press charges. In 1895, Chinese immigrants in San Francisco complained through their attorney, Thomas D. Riordan, that two men, representing themselves as customs inspectors, were extorting money from Chinese immigrants. The two suspects continually entered Chinese stores without warrants and searched the premises for illegal immigrants and opium for the purpose of blackmailing the residents.[35] The following year, other Chinese also complained of harassment by another officer who visited homes in Chinatown and charged the Chinese with being in the country illegally. If the family paid him enough money, he would leave them alone. If not, he threatened to take the case to the immigration service.[36]

Similar methods of extortion were common outside of San Francisco. In February 1905, Ah Quan and Ah Fong, two Chinese laundrymen in Brooklyn, New York, were victims of an extortion attempt. A person claiming to be a Chinese inspector entered their Brooklyn laundry, displayed a badge, and demanded their certificates of residence. After the two men complied, the officer claimed that the certificates were not correct and that they were under arrest.

When the two men balked, the officer told them that if they were to pay him thirty dollars apiece, he would release them and say nothing further about it. Ah Quan and Ah Fong refused and reported the incident to the Bureau of Immigration, which launched an extensive investigation, but no suspect was ever found.[37] In Mississippi, a well-known extortionist named John Ashon terrorized local Chinese by sending false letters to the immigration service in 1922 revealing their allegedly illegal status.[38]

Members of the general public who were concerned that Chinese laborers were taking away jobs from white workers aided the government in its deportation campaign by providing tips to immigration authorities about places of business they suspected of hiring illegal Chinese workers. In 1896, for example, a resident of Antioch, California, wrote to the San Francisco collector of customs of his suspicion that a Chinese working in a laundry there had been "smuggled" into the country.[39] In 1928, William Billing of Alpaugh, California, reported to the commissioner of immigration in San Francisco that a local "Chinaman peddling vegetables" appeared to be illegal because he was unable to "talk English." Billing also claimed to have "very little against foreigners as a class," but he did take offense that if the "Chinaman were not doing this work, we would have a place for a white man to work." On the basis of this complaint, inspectors traveled to Hanford, California, and arrested Go Seu, the "Chinaman" in question. Although Go produced his certificate of residence, he was interrogated and the government concluded that he was in the country unlawfully. The case was brought before the federal district court, which found in Go Seu's favor and released him.[40]

Similarly, in 1935, H. William Nelle, managing director of the Laundry-owners Association of Alameda County in California, wrote to his congressman to inform him of a "heavy influx of Chinese into Alameda County within the last two years." Nelle believed that most of these Chinese were in the United States illegally. The news made it into the *Congressional Record*, and the local press and radio in California picked up the story. Immigration inspectors then launched an investigation of all sixty-six laundries operated by Chinese in Oakland. A total of 125 Chinese were questioned, the majority of whom were able to establish that they had lawfully entered the United States. Two Chinese suspected of being illegal immigrants were forced to flee to another location.[41] Other complaints filed with the immigration service maintained that Chinese were endangering the health of citizens. In 1936, the "league of laboring council" in Berkeley, California, wrote to officials in San Francisco to warn them of Loo Fat, an alleged illegal immigrant employed at the Columbia

Meat Market who had "a bad disease in the back of his hand." The council provided an exact description of Loo, down to his horned-rimmed glasses and his wrinkled hands. "He is endangering the health of lots of people," the writers explained. "Therefore, we wish the deportation of this undesirable alien."[42]

Some of the most active government informants came from an unlikely quarter: the Chinese community itself. Both immigrants and residents regularly informed immigrant inspectors about Chinese men and women they suspected were engaged in illegal activity. Much of the correspondence was in Chinese; some of it was in English. Many letters were signed. Some letters were clearly a manifestation of individual grievances or rivalries, evidence that the exclusion laws created and exacerbated divisions among the Chinese in America. Others were directed at exerting control over illegal immigration, prostitution, and other vices by calling upon the power of the state to regulate the Chinese community and settle internal differences. In an environment in which the illegal activities of some had adverse effects on the entire community, these letter writers perhaps believed that their actions were justified, and even necessary.

In 1919 an anonymous letter informed the Bureau of Immigration of an allegedly dishonest man who cheated immigrants with promises of guaranteed admission into the country. According to the writer, the individual was an immigration broker named Chan George who had promised "a fast and easy landing of a son" for $400. "But when my son arrived at San Francisco," the author continued, "his application was denied." The boy was finally deported, but only after the writer had spent his entire life savings in legal fees. "I am writing you this information," explained the author, "to expose his low character, so that in the future he does not dare to come around to us to make fish out of us again."[43]

The Bureau of Immigration readily acted upon such reports.[44] In fact, letters from Chinese informants were among the most damaging, for they could provide very detailed information to the government and in some cases suggested ways officials could apprehend the suspect in question. One letter delivered to immigration inspector Charles Mehan at his San Francisco home in 1910, for example, provided information regarding a Chinese barber named Lee Jeung and suggested specific strategies designed to expose Lee's illegal activities. "There is a tricky merchant, Lee Jeung by name, who . . . was landed to this country as a native by deceiving the Bureau," the letter began. "He claims that he has seven sons, he has really but one son, a few years old." The author then instructed the authorities to study Lee's papers carefully. Lee's real surname, the writer declared, was Chin. "When you examine Lee Jeung, go down to the steamer when it arrives and investigate his luggage, you will find a Chin seal in it as evidence. Please investigate this case in Chinatown . . . please arrest Lee Jeung."[45] A letter from "Sing," dated December 1930, also gave specific instructions relating to two Chinese who were "smuggled" into the United States and who worked at the Quong Lee laundry in Oakland, California. "If you go there, you must send two officers," Sing instructed. One was supposed to watch the back door, while the other asked for their residence certificates. "In this way they cannot escape through the back door by pretending not to understand English and to go in to call for the boss," Sing explained. Immigration authorities visited the laundry two weeks later, found incriminating letters in the possession of one of the individuals, and called for his deportation by the end of that month.[46]

Other informants sought the immigration inspectors' help in controlling prostitution, polygamy, and corruption within the community. One series of letters sent by an anonymous group and translated by interpreter John Endicott Gardner in 1905 called attention to a Chinese male named Lee Wah. He not only allegedly brought prostitutes into the country but was also married to three of them at the same time and was attempting to bribe officers of the immigration service. "Last month arriving as European steerage passenger on the *s.s. Siberia* was Ng Shee. [She] is brought over for immoral purposes. She is not a family woman at all," explained the first letter. A second letter explained that the applicant's witness would be posing as the applicant's mother. "All the witnesses are false, and no part of the case is true," advised the author. Finally, the writers implored the officials to "make a careful examination . . . in order that the woman may be sent back to China. We will be thankful and so will all the members of the woman's family."[47]

Most Chinese depended upon and cooperated with one another to get into the country and then to make a living. Chinese immigrants' extensive use of the immigration service against other Chinese in California, however, indicates that serious divisions did exist. A proliferation of anonymous tips to the immigration service in 1923 caused so much friction that the Chinese Six Companies made a public call for peace in the Chinese-language newspaper the *Chinese World*. Calling upon all "brother immigrants" to end the attacks on one another, the organization implored readers to "firmly join ourselves . . . [to] let peace and goodwill obtain for all."[48] Despite this call for peace, damaging Chinese correspondence to immigration officials continued. In 1940, sociologist Wen-hsien Chen observed that "numerous arrests" of Chinese by the immigration service still resulted from "anonymous letters or telephone messages" from rivals, including other Chinese.[49]

A "Psychology of Fear" and Unequal Citizenship

In the 1930s, sociologist Paul Siu found that Chinese immigrants and Chinese American citizens suffered from a deep-rooted sense of insecurity, a "psychology of fear" brought on by the fact that the Chinese "did not feel at home under the conditions of exclusion and race prejudice."[50] This fear reinforced the process of social, political, and economic segregation of Chinese communities, resulting in a high rate of return migration and perpetuating the sojourning pattern.[51] Unwelcome in the United States, plagued by a tenuous legal status, and prevented from becoming full-fledged citizens, many Chinese immigrants continued to view the United States as a sojourner would: a place in which to make money and then leave. As one Chicago laundryman interviewed by Paul Siu explained: "I have no other hope but to get my money and get back to China. What is the use of staying here; you can't be an American here. We Chinese are not even allowed to become citizens. If we were allowed, that might be a different story. In that case, I think many of us Chinese would not think so much of going back to China. Many would get a woman and settle down here."[52]

Many immigrants shared these views about the United States and their intentions to return to China. Indeed, in 1928, sociologist R. D. McKenzie identified return migration as the most significant effect of exclusion upon the Chinese immigrant community. He observed that "exclusion tends to expel the resident population of the race in question in addition to preventing newcomers from entering."[53] While other immigrant groups came in large numbers at the end of the nineteenth and beginning of the early twentieth centuries, more Chinese left the United States than came. From 1908 to 1923, 36,693 Chinese came to the United States, but 47,607 departed, or, for every 100 hundred Chinese who came in during that period, 130 departed. During the same period, the ratio of immigration to emigration was 100:5 for Jewish immigrants, 100:11 for Irish immigrants, and 100:33 for Japanese immigrants.[54] The high rate of departures over arrivals suggests many Chinese chose to give up their immigrant status in the United States and return to China instead of staying and being subjected to harassment and discrimination.[55] In addition, the number of new immigrants remained small during the same period. As a result, the census reports also indicate a rapid decrease in

TABLE 10. CHINESE POPULATION IN
THE UNITED STATES, 1880–1920

Year	No.	Increase/Decrease
1880	105,465	
1890	107,488	+2,023
1900	89,863	−17,625
1910	71,531	−18,332
1920	61,659	−9,872

Source: Abstract of the Fourteenth Census of the United States, 1920, p. 94.

the Chinese resident population. While the exclusion laws may not have succeeded in closing all of the gates to Chinese immigration, the atmosphere they created drastically reduced the size of the Chinese community in America.

Another significant consequence of Chinese exclusion was its impact on native-born Chinese American citizens who were also the targets of discriminatory legislation and policies affecting their rights of travel and citizenship. They found that their status offered little protection from government harassment. Although the 1898 Supreme Court case *Wong Kim Ark* protected their birthright citizenship, this status was constantly attacked well into the twentieth century. In 1913 and 1923, politicians introduced bills in Congress designed to disfranchise citizens of Chinese ancestry.[56] In addition, the 1922 Cable Act revoked the citizenship of women who married "aliens ineligible for citizenship," a code phrase that applied to Asians only. The main victims of this law were Asian American women who married Asian male immigrants. Once a woman lost her citizenship, her rights to own property, vote, and travel freely were also revoked. When Lon Thom, one of the first American-born Chinese in New York City's Chinatown, met and married Chinese student Wing Ark Chin in 1922, she was stripped of her citizenship. She remained in the country of her birth as a noncitizen for eighteen years. Only in 1940, when Congress amended some of the provisions of the Cable Act, did Lon Thom regain her American citizenship.[57] Though American-born, she had to face a naturalization hearing and swear her allegiance to the United States just like an immigrant alien.[58] The Immigration Act of 1924 also explicitly excluded "aliens ineligible to citizenship," which barred alien wives of citizens.[59]

The impact of these immigration laws on Chinese American citizens was great. They were subjected to inconvenience and even harassment every time they reentered the country, tried to sponsor a relative, or even happened to be in Chinatown during an immigration raid. For example, when Lee Quock Chow, admitted by the bureau as a native citizen in 1903, notified immigration officials that he was intending to go back to China for a brief visit in 1920 and wanted to facilitate his reentry into the United States upon his return, he was asked to complete a standardized form, "Application of Alleged American Citizen of the Chinese Race for Pre-investigation Status." All native-born Chinese American citizens intending to depart the country were required to fill out this document. Clearly, even though Lee had been recognized as a native by immigration officials themselves when he entered the United States, he was still suspected of fraud.[60]

Unequal treatment motivated Chinese American citizens to renew their activism. In 1910, the Native Sons of the Golden State issued a formal complaint to the secretary of commerce and labor.[61] Among their many grievances, the group charged that the Chinese American citizen was "liable to arrest at any time and place by zealous immigration officials upon the charge of being unlawfully in the country. . . . He moves from place to place at his peril."[62] During the 1920s, the organization complained to California congressman Julius Kahn that citizens were routinely "stopped on the streets, in stores, dwellings, and apartments by inspectors; [they] are searched and ordered to deliver their papers and are subjected to numberless insults and intimidations. Our unoffending people are being treated with little more respect than animals and every guaranty of the Constitution against unlawful searches is being defied in this ruthless campaign just launched against our people."[63]

Chinese American citizens were unable to escape the shadow of exclusion. Citizens interviewed in 1931 expressed a marked loss of admiration for the United States, as well as a frustrated sense of alienation. One explained, "I speak fluent English, and have the American mind. I feel that I am more American than Chinese. I am an American citizen by birth, having the title for all rights, but they treat me as if I were a foreigner. They have so many restrictions against us." Another observed, "I thought I was American, but America would not have me. In many respects she would not recognize me as American. Moreover, I find racial prejudice against us everywhere. We are American citizens in name but not in fact."[64] Like these two individuals, many other Chinese Americans believed they were citizens in name only, with few of the benefits accorded to citizens of other ethnic and racial backgrounds.

This disillusionment combined with the general hostility the Chinese faced in America discouraged citizens from sending for their foreign-born wives and children to join them and settle in the United States. One citizen directly cited the restrictive immigration laws and the harassment by immigration officials as the main reasons why he would not sponsor his wife into the country. As he told an interviewer in 1924, "My wife is still in China. I have not seen her for ten years. You wonder why I don't bring my wife here? Well, that is the question. Because my wife come over and you Americans cause her lots of trouble. You pen us up in Immigration Office and then they have doctors come and say we have heart disease, liver trouble, hook worm. . . . How would you like to be treated that way? Now, when my little boy come to this country he was kept at the immigration office for over two months. . . . I am an American citizen, and yet they kept my boy in immigration office so long. Isn't right."[65] The experiences of these citizens are indicative of the high personal costs of exclusion for Chinese Americans in the first half of the twentieth century. Born in the United States, they were nevertheless lumped together with other Chinese as "Orientals" or foreigners.[66] The tendency of government officials and many other Americans to ignore the distinction between Chinese American citizens and noncitizens devalued their American citizenship.[67]

False Identities and the Confession Program

Although the Chinese exclusion laws were eventually repealed in 1943, the Chinese in America continued to feel the impact of exclusion for many years thereafter. Those who came in under fraudulent identities were forced to live with their false names out of fear of detection by immigration authorities. Family members joining Chinese living in the United States under false identities were forced to continue the ruse. Moreover, once a paper son reached adulthood and wanted to sponsor his own wife and children into the country, he had no choice but to pass on his fictional family history and relationships to the next generation. "There are cases," Paul Siu reported in the 1930s, "where a Mr. Chan came to the United States as 'Mr. Wong.' Later, he had a family here, but his wife became Mrs. Wong instead of Mrs. Chan to the Americans and all their children went to school and registered as Wongs. But they remain Chan in the Chinese community." In China, changing one's surname may have been considered a disgraceful act, but in the United States, using an "immigration name" was a necessity.[68]

The secrecy involved in maintaining double identities could be damaging. Charles Choy Wong, whose father had entered as a paper son during the exclusion era, found that the need for secret names created a "split personality of fractured identity" in himself that he never quite reconciled.[69] False identities also exacerbated the alienation felt by most Chinese in the United States. Outside of the Chinese community, Chinese were forced to maintain the tangled web of fictional family relationships. Many found it was easier to avoid contact with non-Chinese altogether. As Kaimon Chin recounted, "most of the Chinese were afraid because most of them had something to hide. They turn the other way. It's fear."[70]

Even after the repeal of the Chinese exclusion laws in 1943, Chinese continued to be held accountable for their initial illegal entry into the United States despite their long-term residence. During the 1950s, anticommunism and the continuing concern over illegal entries led the federal government to begin large-scale investigations in Chinese communities across the country. The goal was to end the admission of paper sons, which had continued after 1943. In an effort to protect Chinese immigrants, the Chinese Six Companies opened negotiations with the immigration service. The result was the "Confession Program," established in 1956 to allow Chinese who had entered the country by fraudulent means to make voluntary confessions of their status. Confessors who were longtime residents would be granted amnesty. Aliens who had served in the U.S. armed forces for at least ninety days could also become naturalized citizens.[71]

By singling out the Chinese for government scrutiny again, the Confession Program sent shock waves of alarm throughout the Chinese community. The government's goal was to stem the inflow of illegal immigrants to this country, but authorities did not fully explain how it was to be done. As Arthur Lem, an immigrant brought before the service during the program, explained, "They left it to the INS agents who bull-dozed their way around, threatening anyone who they thought were here under an assumed name. They had a field day."[72] Moreover, while the program ostensibly offered some protections to those who confessed, each individual who entered the program did so at great risk and expense. By confessing to fraudulent status, Chinese automatically became aliens once again, dependent upon the immigration service to allow them to become legal residents. Many hired attorneys to represent them in the hearings and to provide protection, a service that cost around $250 per person. Since entire families often had entered the country illegally, the total cost of legal fees could run as high as a few thousand dollars. Additionally, because confessors were encouraged, if not forced, to implicate all of their family members, the confessions created a domino effect that caused havoc in the community. Immigrants who were in a position to legalize their status could adversely affect the status of their paper relatives or even real relatives who were reluctant to confess or who were in the process of sponsoring in family on the basis of their fraudulent admissions. Arthur Lem described the Confession Program as a "no win situation."[73]

Altogether, some 30,530 Chinese immigrants confessed.[74] The legalized status was a welcome benefit for many. For others, the secrets revealed during the Confession Program caused a great deal of personal anguish. Charles Choy Wong had grown up believing he was Charles Choy Leong, a bona fide U.S. citizen whose status was derived from his father, Leong Gun Chown, who had been admitted into the United States as a returning American-born citizen. During the Confession Program, it was revealed that Leong Gun Chown had secured entry through fraudulent papers. He was neither a citizen nor from the Leong family. Instead, he was a paper son born to the Wong clan. Consequently, Charles Choy Wong experienced a major identity crisis. "I was no longer Charles Choy Leong, but Charles Choy Wong, a tainted person with an illegal family history and a fractured identity," he wrote. "I was not who I thought I was: The fragile wholeness of my desired 'all American' identity was now cracked into pieces, like Humpty Dumpty."[75]

Many other Chinese immigrants opted not to confess and retained their false names. After so many years in the United States, Chinese American families had established all of their business and personal accounts in their immigration names. Confessing would mean not only implicating other family members but also exposing themselves to personal and professional contacts. Over the years, their false identities created for the purpose of immigration to the United States superseded their true names, and it became less important to revert back to their original surnames. Many never forgot their true identities, however, and the false names served as a potent reminder of the actions they had taken in order to come to America.

Conclusion

Like many immigration policies, the Chinese exclusion laws affected not only newly arriving immigrants but also the Chinese community in America. Exclusion sanctioned the harassment of all Chinese, making them vulnerable to extortion, arrest, and deportation. Deportation policies extended exclusion far beyond the nation's ports of entry into Chinese American homes and businesses. The conflation of all Chinese — whether they were legal, illegal, or native-born citizens — as alien threats was reflected both in government policy and in the actions of officials, employers, and the general American public. Even Chinese themselves learned to use the power of the state for personal gain or to control the illicit activity within the community, often with severe consequences. Long after the exclusion laws were enacted, Chinese lived in a state of anxiety, suffering from a psychology of fear and becoming further segregated and marginalized from mainstream society. Even American-born citizens found themselves to be unequal before the law and their fellow Americans. The Chinese exclusion laws were repealed in 1943, but their impact was felt for generations afterward.

EPILOGUE

Echoes of Exclusion in the Late Twentieth Century

ON DECEMBER 17, 1943, President Franklin D. Roosevelt signed the Magnuson Bill repealing the Chinese exclusion laws. Chinese immigration was placed under the same quota system regulating European immigration under the 1924 Immigration Act.[1] While the president cited the need to "correct a historic mistake," the repeal of the exclusion laws was mostly a symbolic gesture of friendship to China (a wartime ally against Japan). Because the U.S. immigration quota for China allowed only 105 Chinese to enter the country per year, it hardly meant that America's gates were fully open to Chinese immigration.[2] The Magnuson Bill did, however, allow Chinese immigrants to become eligible for naturalization. Several war-related measures also expedited naturalization for Chinese American members of the armed forces, and the War Brides Acts of 1945 and 1947 permitted citizen members of the military to bring their foreign-born spouses and minor children into the United States outside of the quota.[3] These new opportunities for Chinese immigrants and the Chinese in America were enormously significant. In the immediate postwar period, more Chinese women entered the United States than ever before. From 1948 to 1952, an estimated 90 percent of new Chinese immigrants were women joining their husbands after years of separation.[4] Chinese sojourners were able to bring their families to the United States, and transnational families were reunited. The 1965 Immigration and Nationality Act, which abolished the national origins quota system, instituted a family reunification program, placed immigrants from all countries on equal footing, and ushered in a surge in immigration from Asia and Latin America, which continues today.[5] Chinese American communities across the country immediately felt the changes in the immigration laws. When sociologist Paul Siu completed his study of Chinese laundrymen in Chicago in 1953, he observed that the repeal of the exclusion laws and the passage of the War Brides Act marked "the dawn of a new era of Chinese immigration."[6]

While repeal may have marked a new beginning for Chinese Americans, the Chinese exclusion laws had lasting consequences for American immigration in general. Exclusion had helped to establish and normalize American gatekeeping and had transformed both immigration policy and the ways in which Americans thought about race and immigrants. Chinese exclusion, which had begun as an aberration in America's immigrant tradition, became instead a model for subsequent immigration regulation. Following the passage of the Chinese Exclusion Act in 1882, Congress increasingly used the law to restrict the number of immigrants entering the country, and with each new immigration act, the list of excludable classes grew longer. The Immigration Act of 1882 barred criminals, prostitutes, paupers, lunatics, idiots, and those likely to become public charges.[7] The Alien Contract Labor Law of 1885 prohibited the immigration of laborers already under contract for employment with American companies.[8] In 1891, Congress forbade the entry of polygamists and any person convicted of a crime involving "moral turpitude."[9] In 1903, another immigration law excluded anarchists. Four years later, in 1907, Congress broadened the moral exclusion clauses of the general immigration laws, and a diplomatic agreement known as the Gentlemen's Agreement between the United States and Japan effectively ended the immigration of Japanese and Korean laborers.[10] By the 1920s, the campaign to restrict immigration even further had succeeded. With the passage of the Quota Act of 1921 and the Immigration Act of 1924, quotas were set for every nation in the Eastern hemisphere, severe restrictions were placed on the admission of southern and eastern European immigrants, and the exclusion of Asians was perfected.[11] Moreover, the economic depression of the 1930s renewed calls for the restriction and deportation of other immigrants, most notably Filipinos and Mexicans.[12]

America's emergence as a superpower following World War II, Cold War politics, and civil rights activism exposed the hypocrisy in American regulation of immigration. In an effort to portray itself as the egalitarian leader of the free world, the United States was forced to reconsider its discriminatory immigration policies. The 1965 Immigration Act was the result of these reform efforts, and like the Chinese Exclusion Act, it ushered in a new era of immigration and immigration law. The new law abolished the national origins quotas established in 1924 and created a new set of preference categories based on family reunification and professional skills.

Cloaked in the rhetoric of liberal and civil rights reform, the 1965 act has been portrayed as representing a "high-water mark in a national consensus of egalitarianism."[13] A closer examination, however, demonstrates that the bill was designed to give preference to European immigrants and that the new waves of immigration from Asia and Latin America after 1965 were in fact its great "unintended consequences." Moreover, most of the barriers first established in the nineteenth century (for example, the clause regarding immigrants likely to become a public charges and the physical and mental health requirements) remained firmly in place. The 1965 act did end the explicitly discriminatory structure of previous immigration laws, but there was continuity, as well as change, in the new system of regulation.[14]

The Chinese exclusion laws themselves remained the legal and ideological touchstones that critics of late-twentieth-century U.S. immigration policy cited to highlight injustices in the system. In 1982, when U.S. senator Alan Simpson and representative Romano Mazzoli proposed abolishing the preference given to adult brothers and sisters of U.S. citizens to immigrate under the 1965 Immigration Act—provisions that would have severely curbed new Asian immigration—Asian American activists named the proposal the "Exclusion Act of 1982" and lobbied hard against it.[15] In a 1993 case involving the rights of Haitian refugees in exclusion proceedings, lawyer Robert Rubin compared refugee policy to the Chinese Exclusion Act, which he argued "has long stood for the (legal) principle that immigrants don't enjoy any rights under our laws."[16] Similarly, critics of the Illegal Immigration and Responsibility Act of 1996 charge that the new border control campaign violates civil and human rights, and they have dubbed it the "Mexican Exclusion Act."[17]

Chinese exclusion's legacy has also manifested itself in a resurgence of racialized nativism, tremendous growth in the state's control of immigration, and an increase in illegal immigration during the late twentieth and early twenty-first centuries. The immigration from Asia and Latin America beginning in the 1970s and continuing through today inspired what George Sánchez describes as a new racialized hostility toward immigrants and a "new American racism . . . that has no political boundaries or ethnic categorizations."[18] Illegal immigration in particular became a central political issue again in the 1970s in the midst of a deep recession and an overall loss of confidence within the nation. Both the U.S. government's reaction to it and the effects of illegal immigration on Americans' perceptions of all immigrants echoed earlier responses and sentiments from the Chinese exclusion era. Alarmists' rhetoric about the "loss of control" over the country's borders was similar to that in which anti-Chinese politicians urged the passage and then the strengthening of the Chinese exclusion laws for the "peace and security" of the country in the 1870s and 1890s. Like the immigration officials who participated in the anti-Chinese campaigns of the late nineteenth and early twentieth centuries, officials of the Immigration and Naturalization Service were some of the most strident anti-immigrant voices in the 1980s and 1990s.[19]

Present-day political discourse and government policies related to illegal immigration are highly racialized, tainting entire communities. Despite some observers' claims that contemporary nativism is not as racially based as that of the pre-1924 period, the persistence of racialized understandings of immigration, especially illegal immigration, and the U.S. government's immigration and border enforcement policies demonstrate otherwise. As Neil Gotanda argues, "Nativist movements have *never* been indiscriminately directed against all foreigners—they have been directed against those immigrants that can be racialized. . . . Popular understandings of 'foreignness' suggest that the concept is now infused with a racial character."[20] Debates about immigration during the 1990s became a way of expressing anxiety and fear about the unprecedented demographic changes brought on by the "new" post-1965 immigration. Metaphors of war became increasingly common, as they were in the 1880s. Words and phrases like "invasion," "conquest," and "save our state" were commonly employed by xenophobes.[21] Undocumented migrants have come from all over the world. A large percentage of the Irish immigrants who arrived in the 1980s had no proper documentation or overstayed their visas.[22] The high-profile cases of Chinese "smuggled" into the country by boat along the West and East Coasts in the 1990s also point to a dramatic return of Chinese illegal immigration.[23] Yet just as "John Chinaman and his smugglers" were the dominant public image of the illegal immigrant during the Chinese exclusion era, undocumented immigrants from Mexico became the nearly exclusive targets of government and public concern at the end of the twentieth century.[24] In 1994, Californians attacked the Mexican immigration "problem" with Proposition 187, which barred California state agencies from providing benefits to illegal aliens. The anti-immigrant mood and the government crackdown on illegal immigration that followed placed the entire Mexican American community at risk, and the treatment of Mexican Americans as perpetual "foreigners" harks back to the plight of Chinese during the exclusion era.[25] Echoing attempts by politicians and immigration officials to deny birthright citizenship to American-born Chinese during the exclusion era, contemporary anti-immigrant lawmakers have sought to do the same for more recent immigrants. In 1998, a bill submitted to Congress (by a California politician) proposed to deny U.S. citizenship to children born in the United States to undocumented immigrants and to those born to immigrants who were in the country without permanent resident status.[26]

The Chinese exclusion laws may have transformed the United States into a gatekeeping nation and launched massive changes in the state's regulation of immigration, but these early state efforts pale in comparison to recent campaigns to control immigration. With initiatives like "Operation Gatekeeper" in San Diego, California; "Operation Rio Grande" in Brownsville, Texas; "Operation Safeguard" in Nogales, Arizona; and "Operation Hold the Line" in El Paso, Texas, in particular, the government's efforts to control the U.S.-Mexican border have increased exponentially since the Chinese exclusion era, turning it into a militarized zone designed to deter illegal immigration at any cost. Instead of "Chinese catchers" and "line riders," the government relies upon surveillance in the form of night scopes, motion sensors, and communications equipment, as well as jeeps and three parallel, fourteen-mile-long fences on the U.S.-Mexican border south of San Diego. In the late 1990s, the Border Patrol became one of the government's largest police agencies in the country. And the United States currently spends $2 billion a year to build walls and manage a twenty-four-hour patrol over the border. During the Chinese exclusion era, the number of "mounted inspectors" patrolling the line was around 80. In 2001, the Border Patrol had 9,400 agents.[27] Such efforts at border enforcement have proven to be successful, but at a very high cost. Despite a 22 percent drop in apprehensions along the 1,952-mile Mexican-U.S. border in the first four months of the 2001 fiscal year, most contemporary observers agree that illegal entry has not been reduced, and there is little evidence to suggest that large numbers of migrants are giving up and returning home. Instead, the tightening of border controls has only forced migrants into more difficult and dangerous situations.[28] Instead of hiding in boxcars or risking their lives as stowaways across choppy seas like the Chinese did, today's illegal immigrants subject themselves to the heat and drought of the desert. Since 1998, 1,113 migrants are known to have died from exposure to heat and cold while attempting to enter the United States from Mexico.[29] In addition, contemporary immigrants — as did their exclusion-era counterparts — have turned to other strategies of entering the country, and the government has reported an increase in smuggling and the use of counterfeit green cards and other documents.[30] Illegal immigration continues to be a highly profitable business, and immigrants continue to be its victims.

The government also still uses immigration raids in ethnic neighborhoods, most notably those of the Latino community, to catch immigrants suspected of residing in the country illegally. Critics complain that zealous immigration raids threaten the rights of citizens and noncitizens, violating constitutional protections, destabilizing families, and undermining workers' rights.[31] Immigration lawyers, therefore, have become even more essential to contemporary immigrants than ever before. Much as the Chinese and their lawyers had to wade through the complexities of the exclusion laws and regulations of the immigration service, today's immigrants need to keep abreast of an enormous number of laws affecting not only their admission into the country but also their eligibility for certain occupations and benefits, their permitted length of residence, and their ability to sponsor family members into the United States. Scholars note that even the detailed and exacting interrogations first instituted by the immigrant inspectors of San Francisco's Chinese Bureau in the 1890s survive in the form of separate interviews of couples to test the validity of marriages between aliens and American citizens. Examples abound of married couples being asked overly detailed and seemingly irrelevant questions, prompting one British immigrant to charge that the immigration service interrogations are "un-American."[32] Indeed, as Lucy Salyer observes, contemporary critics of the INS have many of the same complaints that Chinese had during the exclusion era: the unchecked power of the agency, the vulnerability of aliens to frequent immigration raids and official intimidation, the influence of nativist politics on enforcement procedures, and the long waiting periods for visas, green cards, and citizenship status.[33] The kinds of difficulties the Chinese experienced under the exclusion laws have become mainstream phenomena, shared by all immigrant groups and integrated into the very fabric of American life.

Chinese Americans themselves have come nearly full circle with the act of remembering and preserving the stories of Chinese exclusion. Paul Chow, founder of the Angel Island Immigration Station Foundation in 1983, often told visitors to the island that whenever he asked his parents about how they came to America, they would answer, "Angel Island. Shhhhh," an admonition to keep a painful past buried. Instead of following his parents' advice and keeping silent, Chow spent twenty-five years preserving the history of Chinese immigration at the immigration station. "This is our [Chinese Americans'] Plymouth Rock," he often declared.[34] No longer relegated to the historical margins, Angel Island has been embraced as a different type of Ellis Island in the West. In 1991, the San Francisco office of the Immigration and Naturalization Service celebrated its 150th anniversary on Angel Island with a naturalization ceremony for 125 new citizens. In 1993, another naturalization ceremony sponsored by the INS and the Angel Island Immigration Station Foundation commemorated the fiftieth anniversary of the repeal of the Chinese Exclusion Act. In 1997, the immigration station was named a National Historic Landmark, and in 1999, it was put on the National Trust for Historic Preservation's 1999 list of America's Most Endangered Historic Places.[35]

Angel Island has come to represent the indomitable immigrant spirit that is routinely celebrated as part of America's immigrant heritage. But what makes it unique is that it also commemorates the very worst American tradition of racial discrimination. In fact, it is Angel Island—and not Ellis Island—that best personifies America's true relationship with immigration. We are indeed a "nation of immigrants," but we are also a "gatekeeping nation," and it is the tension between these two identities that continues to shape not only America's ambivalent immigration policy but also Americans' ambivalence toward immigrants.[36]

AFTERWORD

Following September 11, 2001

In the wake of the terrorist attacks on America on September 11, 2001, the core components of American gatekeeping that originated in Chinese exclusion—racialization, containment, and protection—have been pushed to the forefront of U.S. and international policy, with important national and transnational consequences. In the search for the perpetrators and their accomplices, blanket racialized associations of Arabs and Muslims in America with "terrorists" or "potential terrorists" proliferated. Within days of the attacks, law enforcement officials had arrested more than 1,200 people, only a handful of whom were proven to have any links to terrorism. At the end of November 2001, approximately 600 people were still in custody, held on unrelated immigration violations.[1] Despite U.S. government appeals to prevent racial scapegoating, hate crimes directed against Middle Eastern Americans and those who appeared Middle Eastern were committed throughout the nation, resulting in at least one murder, that of a South Asian Sikh gas station owner in Mesa, Arizona. Racialized as the latest immigrant menace, entire ethnic communities found themselves under suspicion once again.[2] During November and December of 2001, U.S. government agents targeted 200 college campuses nationwide to collect information on Middle Eastern students.[3]

In an effort to manage the new terrorist threat, drastic changes in immigration policy took effect in the few short months immediately following the attacks. There has been no formal legislation restricting the immigration from countries suspected of being breeding grounds for terrorists, but other important controls on immigration, and especially immigrants already in the United States, have been instituted as part of other laws. As part of the Patriot Act passed in the House of Representatives in October of 2001, Congress allowed the long-term detention of noncitizens whom the attorney general "certified" as terrorist threats.[4] Similar to earlier gatekeeping efforts, internal administrative decisions of the INS have also been significantly altered to track, control, and detain immigrants suspected of terrorist activity or those deemed potential threats to national security. The Immigration and Naturalization Service quietly amended its own administrative rules and procedures to grant the agency greater control over all foreigners. In November 2001, the Justice Department expanded the power of its officers to detain foreigners even in cases where a federal immigration judge had ordered their release for lack of evidence. The judicial order can be set aside if the immigration service believes that a foreigner is a "danger to the community or a flight risk." Immigration lawyers argue that the new law deprives detainees of the fundamental right of bond hearings, but supporters of the law claim that the change is necessary in the new war against terrorism. Still other political observers charge that the agency is using the new political climate to address long-standing concerns about the power of immigration courts.[5] Despite critics' claims that such sweeping legal changes in immigration control have institutionalized racial profiling and have suspended liberties for immigrants, the proposals coming from President George W. Bush's administration command strong public support.[6]

Policy makers also renewed their focus on increased border security, especially along the northern border. Several of the suspected hijackers who took control of the commercial flights that crashed into the World Trade Center in New York City and the Pentagon in Washington, D.C., had allegedly spent time in Canada and entered the United States from the north. As did critics of Canada's supposedly lax immigration policies during the nineteenth century that facilitated illegal Asian and European immigration into the United States, contemporary American politicians have called for renewed efforts to close the "back doors" of illegal entry across the borders. They blame Canada for allowing foreigners to enter with false or no passports, apply for asylum, travel freely, and raise funds for political activities while their asylum applications are pending. Canada's open doors, it is argued, jeopardize U.S. national security.[7]

Recent suggestions for increased border security echo earlier efforts first articulated during the pre-1924 period. In the early twentieth century, U.S. government officials sought to "induce" Canada to adopt Chinese immigration policies that more closely mirrored U.S. laws. In late September of 2001, Paul Celluci, the U.S. ambassador to Canada, publicly called for Canada to "harmonize its [refugee] policies with those of the United States." President George W. Bush sketched out a vision of a "North American security perimeter," of which transnational immigration controls would be central. The United States has also secured Mexico's cooperation in improving security over the U.S.-Mexican border.[8] As of this writing, there is little agreement on what such a "harmonization" would mean. And it is not clear how other U.S. immigration and North American border policies might change. What is certain is that in America's "new war" against terrorism, American gatekeeping and immigration policy will undoubtedly remain central issues facing not only the United States but the world in the twenty-first century.

NOTES

Abbreviations

AIHF   Angel Island Historical Files, 1894–1941, Records of the U.S. Immigration and Naturalization Service, San Francisco, California, RG 85, National Archives, Pacific Region, San Bruno, Calif.

AIOHP   Angel Island Oral History Project, Asian American Studies Library, University of California, Berkeley

AR-CGI   *Annual Reports of the Commissioner-General of Immigration* (Washington: GPO, 1894–1932)

AR-ST   U.S. Treasury Department, *Annual Reports of the Secretary of the Treasury* (Washington: GPO, 1890–91)

BL   Bancroft Library, University of California, Berkeley

CAF, H   Chinese Arrival Files, Honolulu, Records of the U.S. Immigration and Naturalization Service, RG 85, National Archives, Pacific Region, San Bruno, Calif.

CAF, SF   Chinese Arrival Files, San Francisco, Records of the U.S. Immigration and Naturalization Service, RG 85, National Archives, Pacific Region, San Bruno, Calif.

CCF   Customs Case File No. 3358d Related to Chinese Immigration, 1877–91, Records of the U.S. Immigration and Naturalization Service, RG 85, National Archives, Washington, D.C.

CCTR   Correspondence, Circulars, Telegrams, Reports, Port of Ogdensburg, New York, 1866–1919, Records of the U.S. Bureau of Customs, RG 36, National Archives, Northeast Region, New York, N.Y.

CECF, NY   Chinese Exclusion Case Files, New York, Records of the U.S. Immigration and

	Naturalization Service, RG 85, National Archives, Northeast Region, New York, N.Y.
CGC	Chinese General Correspondence, 1898–1908, Records of the U.S. Immigration and Naturalization Service, RG 85, National Archives, Washington, D.C.
CGI	Commissioner-General of Immigration
CR	*Congressional Record*
DIF, SF	Densmore Investigation Files (1917), San Francisco, Records of the U.S. Immigration and Naturalization Service, RG 85, National Archives, Pacific Region, San Bruno, Calif.
GCC	General Correspondence to the Office of the Collector, Port of San Francisco, 1894–1928, Records of the U.S. Bureau of Customs, RG 36, National Archives, Pacific Region, San Bruno, Calif.
GCOCC	General Correspondence from the Office of the Collector of Customs, San Francisco, 1869–1931, Records of the U.S. Bureau of Customs, RG 36, National Archives, Pacific Region, San Bruno, Calif.
IF, SF	Case Files of Investigations Resulting in Warrant Proceedings (12020), 1912–50, San Francisco, Records of the U.S. Immigration and Naturalization Service, RG 85, National Archives, Pacific Region, San Bruno, Calif.
INS	U.S. Immigration and Naturalization Service
INSSC	Subject Correspondence, 1906–32, Records of the U.S. Immigration and Naturalization Service, RG 85, National Archives, Washington, D.C.
IRLS	Immigration Restriction League Scrapbooks, 1894–1912, Boston Public Library, Boston, Mass.
NPCC	Ng Poon Chew Collection, Asian American Studies Library, University of California, Berkeley
RCCF	Return Certificate Application Case Files of Chinese Departing, 1913–44, San Francisco, Records of the U.S. Immigration and Naturalization Service, RG 85, Pacific Region, San Bruno, Calif.
SCCAOHP	Southern California Chinese American Oral History Project, Asian American Studies Center, University of California, Los Angeles
SRR	Survey of Race Relations: A Canadian-American Study of the Oriental on the Pacific Coast, Hoover Institution on War, Revolution, and Peace, Stanford University

Introduction

1. Following Chinese custom, when referring to individual Chinese, I use the surname first and then the given name. For example, in the name Moy Dong Kee, Moy is the surname and Dong Kee is the given name. Because of inconsistencies and errors in U.S. government records and translations, Chinese names may not have been recorded correctly, but without any identification for individuals, I have had to rely on the government's renderings.

2. File 14-643, File 13-322, CECF, NY; interview with Gladys Huie.

3. Interview with Wallace Lee.

4. Act of May 6, 1882 (22 Stat. 58).

5. File 26002/1-8, CAF, SF.

6. Steiner, *On the Trail of the Immigrant,* 72.

7. I refer to members of the first generation to come to the United States as "immigrants" and use the term "Chinese Americans" to refer to the members of the second and later generations

of Chinese born in the United States. Due to the prohibitions on naturalized citizenship during the exclusion era, Chinese immigrants could be residents in the United States without being U.S. citizens. When referring to "Chinese American citizens," I mean those born in the United States. When referring to both immigrants and Chinese Americans, I use the phrase "Chinese in America."

8. On "racial nationalism," see Gerstle, *American Crucible.*

9. Chan, ed., *Entry Denied,* x; Chan, "Writing of Asian American History," 8–17.

10. See, for example, Coolidge, *Chinese Immigration;* Sandmeyer, *Anti-Chinese Movement in California;* Barth, *Bitter Strength;* Miller, *Unwelcome Immigrant;* Saxton, *Indispensable Enemy;* Mink, *Old Labor and New Immigrants;* Daniels, "No Lamps Were Lit for Them"; Gyory, *Closing the Gate;* K. Scott Wong, "Immigration and Race."

11. Roger Daniels first called for scholars to study both groups in 1966. See Daniels, "Westerners from the East," 373.

12. Salyer, *Laws Harsh as Tigers.*

13. Ibid.; McClain, *In Search of Equality.*

14. See Salyer, *Laws Harsh as Tigers;* Hing, *Making and Remaking Asian America;* and Gotanda, "Exclusion and Inclusion," 129–51.

15. Yung, *Unbound Feet;* Chan, *This Bittersweet Soil;* Siu, *Chinese Laundryman;* Renqiu Yu, *To Save China, to Save Ourselves;* Friday, *Organizing Asian American Labor;* Tsai, *Chinese Experience;* Nee and Nee, *Longtime Californ'.*

16. Nina Glick Schiller, Linda Basch, and Cristina Blanc-Szanton (*Towards a Transnational Perspective on Migration,* ix) define transnationalism as a "social process in which migrants establish social fields that cross geographic, cultural, and political borders." Schiller elaborates: "Even as migrants invest socially, economically, and politically in their new society, they continue to participate in the daily life of the society from which they emigrated but which they did not abandon" ("Transmigrants and Nation-States," 94). See also Hsu, *Dreaming of Gold,* 7.

17. For example, see McKeown, *Chinese Migrant Networks,* 4–7, 19–23, 25–32, and "Transnational Chinese Families," 73–110; Y. Chen, *Chinese San Francisco,* 3, 7, 57, 145–47; and Hsu, *Dreaming of Gold,* 3–11.

18. Marcel van der Linden ("Transnationalizing American Labor History," 1092) and Donna Gabaccia ("Nomads, Nations, and the Immigrant Paradigm," 1117) have both warned against purely transnational histories.

19. On the anti-Chinese movement being "tangential," see Higham, *Strangers in the Land,* preface and afterword. For the significance of the 1920s, see Ngai, "Architecture of Race," 69–71, and King, *Making Americans,* 4–5.

20. Omi and Winant (*Racial Formation,* 55) specifically define "racial formation" as the "sociohistorical process by which racial categories are created, inhabited, transformed, and destroyed."

21. See, for example, Skowronek, *Building a New American State.* Critical race scholars, on the other hand, argue that the state is an explicitly racial entity. See Omi and Winant, *Racial Formation,* 83. For recent historical scholarship that does emphasize the racialized foundations of modern state-building, see Torpey, *Invention of the Passport,* 1; Palumbo-Liu, *Asian/American,* 31; Fitzgerald, *Face the Nation,* 96–144; Zolberg, "Matters of State," 71–93; and Masur, "Reconstructing the Nation's Capital," 12, 14.

22. I use Michael Omi and Howard Winant's definition of the "state" as being composed of government institutions, the policies they carry out, the conditions and rules which support and justify them, and the social relations in which they are embedded (*Racial Formation,* 83). I also draw upon Michel Foucault's conceptualization of "governmentality," which studies how state regula-

tion of individuals and populations serves to protect and promote the needs of the nation-state ("Governmentality," 99–102). See also Skocpol, "Bringing the State Back In," 7, vii; Skowronek, *Building a New American State*, ix; and Shah, *Contagious Divides*, 3–4.

23. On the importance of exploring key moments in nation-building, see Thelen, "Nation and Beyond," 966–69.

24. William Deverell ("Fighting Words," 39, n. 24, 51) writes that the West "is both the place and the process of national fulfillment." Historians generally agree upon the West's significance in the anti-Chinese movement. For an alternative argument that discounts both the importance of California politicians and the pressure from workers, see Gyory, *Closing the Gate*, 1, 16.

25. On the intersections of law, state authorities, and ordinary lives, see Reagan, *When Abortion Was a Crime*, 1, 3.

26. The broader significance of law's relationship to society is explained in Merry, *Colonizing Hawaii*, 8, and Zolberg, "Matters of State," 71, 73. For traditional studies of immigration law, see, for example, Marion T. Bennett, *American Immigration Policies;* Divine, *American Immigration Policy;* LeMay, *From Open Door to Dutch Door;* Bernard, ed., *American Immigration Policy;* and Hutchinson, *Legislative History.* On nativism, see Higham, *Strangers in the Land;* Higham, "Instead of a Sequel"; David Bennett, *Party of Fear;* Knobel, *"America for the Americans";* Perea, *Immigrants Out!;* and Reimers, *Unwelcome Strangers.*

27. Salyer, *Laws Harsh as Tigers*, 94–110.

28. Daniels, *Coming to America*, 265–84.

29. Pre-exclusion era statistics taken from Yung, *Unbound Feet*, 22. Because the government did not record Chinese arrivals in a consistent manner over the entire exclusion era, the above figure includes immigrants only from 1882 to 1891 and immigrants and returning citizens from 1894 to 1940. Statistics for the years 1892–93 and 1941–43 are not available (*AR-CGI* [1898–1924]; H. Chen, "Chinese Immigration," 181; Liu, "Comparative Demographic Study," 223).

30. These goals have been outlined in Henry Yu, "On a Stage Built by Others," 152. I have also tried to capture what Lisa Lowe (*Immigrant Acts*, 7–9) has called "immigrant acts," which refer to both the history of immigration exclusion acts and the acts of resistance in which Asian immigrants and Asian Americans engaged. See also Okihiro, *Margins and Mainstreams*, 148–76.

31. Here, I rely upon critical race theory to illustrate how laws, legal doctrine, and institutions reflect and reproduce the existing racial power, hierarchies, and categories in society writ large (Omi and Winant, *Racial Formation*, 55). On critical race theory, see Crenshaw et al., eds., *Critical Race Theory*, xxv; Delgado and Stefancic, eds., *Critical Race Theory*, xv–xix; Johnson, "Race Matters," 544; Chang, *Disoriented;* Gotanda, "Exclusion and Inclusion"; and Haney-López, *White by Law.* See also Lowe, *Immigrant Acts;* Robert Lee, *Orientals;* and Palumbo-Liu, *Asian/American.*

32. McKeown, "Transnational Chinese Families," 74. For early American-centric studies, see Rose Hum Lee, *Chinese in the United States of America;* Barth, *Bitter Strength;* Sung, *Mountain of Gold;* Nee and Nee, *Longtime Californ'.* On transnationalism in general, see Schiller, "Transmigrants and Nation-States," 94, 96, 99, and Gjerde, "New Growth on Old Vines," 42. Important recent scholarship on transnational Chinese immigrant communities includes McKeown, *Chinese Migrant Networks;* Hsu, *Dreaming of Gold;* and Y. Chen, *Chinese San Francisco.*

33. McKeown, "Transnational Chinese Families," 74, 78, 83, 87; Hsu, *Dreaming of Gold*, 3; Y. Chen, *Chinese San Francisco*, 3, 7, 57, 145–47.

34. Recent studies on early-twentieth-century illegal immigration in general pay little or no attention to Chinese illegal immigration, and studies that do focus on exclusion-era Chinese illegal immigration concentrate mostly on the so-called paper son practice. On the latter, see, for example, Ngai, "Illegal Aliens and Alien Citizens," 116–72, and Hsu, *Dreaming of Gold*, 55–89.

35. *AR-CGI* (1901), 46; *AR-CGI* (1909), 127.

36. Anonymous, Poem Number 31, in Lai, Lim, and Yung, *Island*, 66.

Part One

1. See, for example, LeMay, *Gatekeepers* and *From Open Door to Dutch Door;* Glazer, *Clamor at the Gates;* Zucker and Zucker, *Guarded Gate;* and Gyory, *Closing the Gate.*

2. *New York Times*, Jan. 7, 1996.

3. For an argument related to the importance of national partisan politics in the passage of the Chinese Exclusion Act, see Gyory, *Closing the Gate*, 1–2.

4. Erika Lee, "Immigrants and Immigration Law"; Barkan and LeMay, *U.S. Immigration*, xxii.

5. Gabaccia, *From the Other Side*, 26.

6. Kraut, *Silent Travelers*, 3.

7. Immigration Act of 1917 (39 Stat. 874). My thanks to Margot Canaday for this citation.

8. Omi and Winant, *Racial Formation*, 55; Ngai, "Architecture of Race" and "Illegal Aliens and Alien Citizens." See also Sánchez, "Race, Nation, and Culture"; Jacobson, *Whiteness of a Different Color* and *Barbarian Virtues;* and Barrett and Roediger, "Inbetween Peoples."

9. Sánchez, "Race, Nation, and Culture," 66–84; Gabaccia, "Is Everywhere Nowhere?," 1132–33; Lowe, *Immigrant Acts*, ix.

10. Hing, *Making and Remaking Asian America*, 1–6. See also Saldívar, *Border Matters*, 96–97, and Behdad, "INS and Outs," 103–13.

11. Ngai, "Architecture of Race," 67–92.

12. Some exceptions are Torpey, *Invention of the Passport*, 1; Palumbo-Liu, *Asian/American*, 31; Fitzgerald, *Face the Nation*, 96–144; and Zolberg, "Matters of State," 71–93.

13. On the connections between immigration and U.S. imperialism, see Jacobson, *Barbarian Virtues*, 26–38.

14. Lowe, *Immigrant Acts*, ix; Thelen, "Nation and Beyond," 966.

Chapter One

1. California State Senate, *Chinese Immigration*, 275.

2. Gyory, *Closing the Gate*, 78; Mink, *Old Labor and New Immigrants*, 73.

3. California State Senate, *Chinese Immigration*, 4.

4. Act of Mar. 3, 1875 (18 Stat. 477); Peffer, *If They Don't Bring Their Women Here*, 28; Hutchinson, *Legislative History*, 65–66; Salyer, *Laws Harsh as Tigers*, 5.

5. Daniels, "No Lamps Were Lit for Them," 4. See also Gyory, *Closing the Gate*, 1, 258–59, on the significance of the Chinese Exclusion Act.

6. Recent exceptions are Salyer, *Laws Harsh as Tigers;* Chan, ed., *Entry Denied;* Chan and Wong, eds., *Claiming America;* Ngai, "Legacies of Exclusion"; Hsu, *Dreaming of Gold;* and McKeown, *Chinese Migrant Networks.*

7. Lucy Salyer (*Laws Harsh as Tigers*, xvi–xvii) has demonstrated how Chinese exclusion shaped the doctrine and administration of modern immigration law.

8. *AR-CGI* (1906), 43; Liu, "Comparative Demographic Study," 223; H. Chen, "Chinese Immigration," 201.

9. Said, *Orientalism*, 55; Gotanda, "Exclusion and Inclusion," 129–32; Tchen, *New York before Chinatown*, xx; Miller, *Unwelcome Immigrant*, 36, 83–94; Robert Lee, *Orientals*, 28.

10. Mink, *Old Labor and New Immigrants*, 74–75; Chan, *This Bittersweet Soil*, 51–78; Salyer, *Laws Harsh as Tigers*, 10.

11. As Sucheng Chan notes, the coolie trade in Asian Indian and Chinese laborers sprung up

in response to the end of slavery in the Americas in the early nineteenth century. These individuals often traveled and labored under extremely coercive and exploitative conditions. The Chinese who migrated to the United States did not come as coolies. Instead, they usually came using their own resources or under a credit-ticket system that financed their passage. Opponents of Chinese immigration often made no distinction between the free and semifree migration of Chinese to the United States and coerced coolies to other parts of the Americas. Labeling all Chinese immigration as a coolie migration helped to galvanize the anti-Chinese movement (*This Bittersweet Soil*, 21, 26, 31).

12. On anti-Chinese arguments in general, see Gyory, *Closing the Gate;* Saxton, *Indispensable Enemy;* Mink, *Old Labor and New Immigrants;* and Leong, "'Distant and Antagonistic Race.'"

13. Gompers, "Some Reasons for Chinese Exclusion."

14. Mink, *Old Labor and New Immigrants,* 72, 96. On labor's role in California, see Saxton, *Indispensable Enemy,* 261–65.

15. Mazumdar, "Through Western Eyes," 158–59.

16. Scholars differ on the exact number of prostitutes in California in 1870. See Chan, "Exclusion of Chinese Women," 141 n. 44; Cheng, "Free, Indentured, Enslaved," 23–29; Robert Lee, *Orientals,* 88–89; and Peffer, *If They Don't Bring Their Women Here,* 28–42.

17. Miller, *Unwelcome Immigrant,* 163, 171; Robert Lee, *Orientals,* 90; Leong, "'Distant and Antagonistic Race,'" 141.

18. Leong, "'Distant and Antagonistic Race,'" 133.

19. Ibid., 142; Robert Lee, *Orientals,* 104.

20. *Pacific Rural Press,* Nov. 9, 1901, 292. My thanks to Linda Ivey for this citation.

21. Robert Lee, *Orientals,* 47.

22. Saxton, *Indispensable Enemy,* 94–96; Almaguer, *Racial Fault Lines,* 153–82.

23. Daniels, *Asian America,* 3–4.

24. Mazumdar, "Through Western Eyes," 164; Takaki, *Iron Cages,* 216–17.

25. U.S. Congress, Joint Special Committee, *Chinese Immigration,* 289–92; K. Scott Wong, "Cultural Defenders and Brokers," 6.

26. California State Senate, *Chinese Immigration,* 260, 10.

27. Ibid., 276–77 (emphasis original).

28. White, "Race Relations in the American West," 396–416; Friday, "'In Due Time,'" 308.

29. California State Senate, *Chinese Immigration,* 280, 288.

30. Gyory, *Closing the Gate,* 238 (emphasis original).

31. Mink, *Old Labor and New Immigrants,* 109. Act of Feb. 26, 1885 (23 Stat. 332).

32. Act of Mar. 3, 1903 (32 Stat. 1222).

33. The 1882 Regulation of Immigration Act (Act of Aug. 3, 1882 [22 Stat. 214]) also excluded lunatics, convicts, and idiots. The 1891 Immigration Act added polygamists and "persons suffering from a loathsome or dangerous contagious disease" (Act of Mar. 3, 1891 [26 Stat. 1084]).

34. Gabaccia, *From the Other Side,* 37.

35. Barrett and Roediger, "Inbetween Peoples," 8–9.

36. Recent studies on racial formation in the West illustrate the importance of moving beyond the white and black binary. See Foley, *White Scourge;* Almaguer, *Racial Fault Lines;* and Friday, "'In Due Time.'"

37. Higham, *Strangers in the Land,* preface and afterword; Abbot, *Historical Aspects of the Immigration Problem,* ix; Wittke, *We Who Built America,* 458. Many of these oversights were first pointed out by Roger Daniels in "Westerners from the East," and "No Lamps Were Lit for Them," 3–18.

38. Sánchez, "Race, Nation, and Culture," 66–84; Gabaccia, "Is Everywhere Nowhere?," 1115–35.

39. *San Francisco Examiner*, June 16, 1910; *San Francisco Post*, May 24, 1910.

40. *San Francisco Bulletin*, May 4, 1891, as cited in Daniels, *Asian America*, 111; Asiatic Exclusion League, "Proceedings," July 1911.

41. Daniels, *Politics of Prejudice*, 20.

42. Chan, *Asian Americans*, 44.

43. *San Francisco Examiner*, Aug. 7, 1910, as cited in Salyer, *Laws Harsh as Tigers*, 127.

44. *San Francisco Daily News*, Sept. 20, 1910.

45. Sánchez, *Becoming Mexican American*, 19.

46. Ngai, "Architecture of Race," 91.

47. Hoffman, *Unwanted Mexican Americans*, 10.

48. Foley, *White Scourge*, 54.

49. Burnham, "Howl for Cheap Mexican Labor," 48.

50. McClatchy, "Oriental Immigration," 197.

51. Foley, *White Scourge*, 55.

52. Rowell, "Why Make Mexico an Exception?" and "Chinese and Japanese Immigrants," 4, as cited in Foley, *White Scourge*, 53.

53. Burnham, "Howl for Cheap Mexican Labor," 45.

54. Ibid., 48.

55. Higham, *Strangers in the Land*, 132–33.

56. Gabaccia, "'Yellow Peril,'" 177–79.

57. Massachusetts Bureau of Statistics of Labor, *Twelfth Annual Report*, 469–70. My thanks to FlorenceMae Waldron for this citation.

58. Lodge was quoting the U.S. Consul in Budapest (Lodge, "Restriction of Immigration," 30–32, 35, as cited in Jacobson, *Barbarian Virtues*, 76–77).

59. Stoddard, "Permanent Menace from Europe," 227–78.

60. J. H. Patten, Asst. Secretary, Immigration Restriction League, Letter to Unions, Oct. 15, 1908, IRLS.

61. J. H. Patten, Asst. Secretary, Immigration Restriction League, to Congressmen and Senators, n.d., ibid.

62. Asiatic Exclusion League, "Proceedings," Feb. 1908, 19, 71, and Dec. 1908, 17, 19.

63. Lea, *Valor of Ignorance*, 124–28; Higham, *Strangers in the Land*, 166, 172.

64. *CR*, 61st Cong., 1st sess., 9174; Asiatic Exclusion League, "Proceedings," Feb. 1908, 55, 57; Higham, *Strangers in the Land*, 174.

65. As David Roediger, Matthew Frye Jacobson, and Noel Ignatiev have shown, Irish and southern and eastern European immigrants commonly constructed and asserted their "whiteness" by allying themselves (and sometimes leading) other racist campaigns against African Americans, Native Americans, and Asian and Mexican immigrants (Roediger, *Wages of Whiteness;* Jacobson, *Whiteness of a Different Color;* Ignatiev, *How the Irish Became White*).

66. *San Francisco Call*, Nov. 22, 1901.

67. Ngai, "Architecture of Race," 70.

68. Cardoso, *Mexican Emigration*, 22; Sánchez, *Becoming Mexican American*, 20; Hoffman, *Unwanted Mexican Americans*, 30–32.

69. Ngai, "Architecture of Race," 91.

70. Solomon, *Ancestors and Immigrants*, 82–88; Jacobson, *Barbarian Virtues*, 181.

71. Grant and Davison, eds., *Alien in Our Midst*, 23.

72. Warne, *Immigrant Invasion*, 295.

73. Immigration Act of 1917 (39 Stat. 874).

74. The Quota Act of 1921 (42 Stat. 5, sec. 2); Immigration Act of 1924 (43 Stat. 153). On the 1924 act, see generally Higham, *Strangers in the Land*, 308–24.

75. Divine, *American Immigration Policy*, 60; Melendy, "Filipinos in the United States," 115–16, 119–25.

76. One estimate places the number of Mexicans, including their American-born children, deported to Mexico at one million. See Balderrama and Rodriguez, *Decade of Betrayal*, 122.

77. The Immigration Act of 1891 established the Superintendent of Immigration (26 Stat. 1084). In 1894, the Bureau of Immigration was established (28 Stat. 390). The immigration service dates its inception to 1891.

78. Peffer, *If They Don't Bring Their Women Here*, 58–59; W. Chen, "Chinese under Both Exclusion and Immigration Laws," 91. The Page Law was also enforced by U.S. Consuls in Hong Kong (Act of Mar. 3, 1875 [18 Stat. 477]).

79. Act of May 6, 1882 (22 Stat. 58), secs. 4, 8.

80. See, for example, the CAF, SF.

81. Act of May 6, 1882 (22 Stat. 58), sec. 4; Act of May 26, 1924: the Immigration Act of 1924 (43 Stat. 153); e-mail communication with Marian Smith, historian, INS, Oct. 24, 2000. See also Torpey, *Invention of the Passport*, 97–99.

82. Act of May 6, 1882 (22 Stat. 58), sec. 4; Act of July 5, 1884 (23 Stat. 115); Coolidge, *Chinese Immigration*, 183–85; Peffer, *If They Don't Bring Their Women Here*. I borrow the description of "an early . . . system of 'remote control' involving passports and visas" from Torpey, *Invention of the Passport*, 97–99.

83. Act of May 5, 1892, "Geary Act" (27 Stat. 25), sec. 7, and Act of Nov. 3, 1893, "McCreary Amendment" (28 Stat. 7), sec. 2.

84. *AR-CGI* (1903), 156; *AR-CGI* (1909), 131.

85. The use of "immigrant identification cards" was first begun under U.S. consular regulations on July 1, 1928. Green cards were the product of the Alien Registration Act of 1940 and the corresponding INS Alien Registration Program (Act of June 28, 1940 [54 Stat. 670]; e-mail communication with Marian Smith, historian, INS, Oct. 26, 2000; Smith, "Why Isn't the Green Card Green?").

86. Coolidge, *Chinese Immigration*, 209–33; Torpey, *Invention of the Passport*, 100.

87. Act of May 6, 1882 (22 Stat. 58), secs. 7 and 11.

88. Ibid., sec. 12.

89. Act of Mar. 3, 1891 (26 Stat. 1084), and Act of Aug. 18, 1894 (28 Stat. 390).

90. *AR-CGI* (1903), 32.

91. Collector of Customs to Secretary of the Treasury, Dec. 3, 1883, CCF.

92. U.S. Congress, House, Select Committee, *Investigation of Chinese Immigration*, 270–71.

93. Ibid.

94. Ibid., 279.

95. Salyer, *Laws Harsh as Tigers*, 69–93.

96. Resolution No. 17,673, Office of the Clerk of the Board of Supervisors, San Francisco, Dec. 10, 1884, CCF.

97. 23 Stat. 115. See Tsai, *Chinese Experience*, 66.

98. Act of Sept. 13, 1888 (25 Stat. 476, sec. 6, at 477).

99. Act of Oct. 1, 1888 (25 Stat. 504, sec. 2). The United States acted in retaliation in response to a rumor that China would not sign the new U.S.-China treaty.

100. Sandmeyer, *Anti-Chinese Movement in California,* 102.

101. Act of May 5, 1892 (27 Stat. 25).

102. Act of July 7, 1898 (30 Stat. 750); Act of Apr. 30, 1900 (31 Stat. 141); *San Francisco Call,* Nov. 22, 1901.

103. *San Francisco Call,* Nov. 22, 1901.

104. Act of Apr. 29, 1902, "Chinese Immigration Prohibited" (32 Stat. 176).

105. Act of Apr. 27, 1904 (33 Stat. 428).

Chapter Two

1. From 1882 to 1890, over 7,000 cases were heard in the U.S. District Court for the Northern District of California. From 1891 to 1905, 2,600 cases were heard in both the federal district and circuit courts of California (Fritz, "Nineteenth Century 'Habeas Corpus Mill,'" 348; Salyer, *Laws Harsh as Tigers,* 34, 75, 80–83).

2. Adapted from H. Chen, "Chinese Immigration," 181.

3. Previous studies have focused on immigration officials in the context of legal battles and legal doctrine. See Salyer, *Laws Harsh as Tigers,* 37–68. On the usage of "keepers of the gate," see Edward W. Cahill to George Fitch, Nov. 9, 1934, File 12030/1, AIHF. The federal agency charged with enforcing U.S. immigration laws has undergone numerous changes in name since its formal inception in 1891. Currently, it is known as the U.S. Immigration and Naturalization Service. During the exclusion era, the immigration officials who enforced the Chinese exclusion laws worked under the auspices of the U.S. Customs Service and then the Bureau of Immigration, housed first under the Treasury Department, then the Department of Commerce and Labor, and finally, the Department of Labor. I use the specific agency name (that is, Bureau of Immigration), but I also use the generic term "immigration service" throughout the book to refer to the agency that handled immigration issues during the exclusion era.

4. Lipsky, *Street-Level Bureaucracy,* xii, 3–4, 13, 24.

5. Prince and Keller, *U.S. Customs Service,* 173; Smith and Herring, *Bureau of Immigration,* 3, 7.

6. The act also vested the collectors of customs in each district where Chinese laborers entered and departed with the authority to issue return certificates, register all departing Chinese laborers, and record all facts about them necessary for identification (W. Chen, "Chinese under Both Exclusion and Immigration Laws," 95, 88–89).

7. Ibid., 86; McClain, *In Search of Equality,* 150.

8. W. Chen, "Chinese under Both Exclusion and Immigration Laws," 40; Salyer, *Laws Harsh as Tigers,* 38–40.

9. W. S. Rosencrans to Charles Folger, Aug. 22, 1882, CCF.

10. See, for example, Hart Hyatt North to Frank P. Sargent, Sept. 10, 1905, Folder 1, Box 1, H. H. North Papers, BL.

11. See, for example, *San Francisco Bulletin,* Nov. 21, 1883. Salyer, *Laws Harsh as Tigers,* 39.

12. George C. Perkins to H. H. North, Feb. 5, 1907, Folder 13, Box 1, H. H. North Papers, BL; George C. Perkins, to Frank P. Sargent, Oct. 23, 1903, File 10070, CGC.

13. H. H. North to Julius Kahn, Mar. 6, 1906, Folder 1, Box 1, and George C. Perkins to H. H. North, Dec. 18, 1905, Folder 13, Box 2, H. H. North Papers, BL.

14. James R. Dunn to Collector of Customs, Apr. 20, 1901, File 6346, CGC.

15. John Hager to Treasury Secretary, Dec. 16, 1885, CCF.

16. R. P. Schwerin to John W. Linck and Converse J. Smith, Feb. 9, 1898, File 224, CGC; R. P. Schwerin to John Wise, Dec. 14, 1896, GCC.

17. Meyer, Taylor, and Johnson, *Municipal Blue Book*, 159; McClain, *In Search of Equality*, 52, 63–67.

18. *Alta California*, Sept. 23, 1885, cited in Janisch, "Chinese, the Courts, and the Constitution," 671.

19. John Wise to Special Agents Johnson and Bean, Apr. 3, 1895, GCOCC.

20. Salyer, *Laws Harsh as Tigers*, 65; Act of May 6, 1882 (22 Stat. 58).

21. John Wise to Js. E. Hannon, Aug. 21, 1893, GCOCC.

22. John Wise to H. A. Ling, Aug. 21, 1895, ibid.

23. John Wise to Mr. Nelso, Esq., Dec. 8, 1893, ibid.

24. Coolidge, *Chinese Immigration*, 328.

25. Burdette, *American Biography and Genealogy*, 1029.

26. F. S. Stratton to the CGI, June 12, 1902, File 5125, CGC.

27. Ira E. Bennett to Senator George C. Perkins, Oct. 29, 1902, Stratton Papers, BL.

28. Coolidge, *Chinese Immigration*, 319.

29. Ibid., 319; McKee, *Chinese Exclusion*, 30.

30. James Dunn to Richard K. Campbell, Apr. 11, 1901, File 2580, and James Dunn to CGI, Dec. 8, 1900, File 2345, CGC.

31. Coolidge, *Chinese Immigration*, 320.

32. James Dunn to J. D. Powers, Nov. 28, 1899, File 532, CGC.

33. *AR-CGI* (1901), 49.

34. Walter S. Chance to Treasury Secretary, July 26, 1900, File 1617, CGC.

35. Condit, *Chinaman as We See Him*, 87.

36. The certificate allegedly did not state the exact time during which Ho had been engaged as a merchant (James Dunn to Treasury Secretary, Feb. 16, 1900, File 1094, CGC; Coolidge, *Chinese Immigration*, 321).

37. James Dunn to Treasury Secretary, Feb. 16, 1900, File 1094, CGC; Coolidge, *Chinese Immigration*, 321–22.

38. Oliver P. Stidger to George C. Perkins, Sept. 16, 1901, Files 3758, 3692, 3227, 3545, CGC.

39. "Resolution in Favor of James Dunn," Nov. 15, 1901, File 4200, CGC.

40. File 6661, CGC; Coolidge, *Chinese Immigration*, 319.

41. George C. Perkins to Frank Sargent, Oct. 23, 1903, File 10070, CGC.

42. See, for example, file entries referring to "American Citizens of Chink Descent" and "Telegram Complaining of Photographing Chinks," File 55,144-156 and 54,261-129, Subject Index to Correspondence and Case Files of the INS, 1903–52, National Archives Microfilm No. T-458, National Archives, Washington, D.C.

43. Report to Walter S. Chance, Mar. 21, 1899, File 52730/84, INSSC.

44. Some historians have noted that Coolidge may have been overly biased against the immigration service. I have found that Coolidge's claims were substantiated more often than not. See Chan, "Writing of Asian American History," 8, and Coolidge, *Chinese Immigration*, 313, 328.

45. Special Agents Linck and Smith to the Treasury Secretary, Feb. 6, 1899, File 53108/9-A, INSSC.

46. J. P. Jackson to Treasury Secretary, Mar. 16, 1899, File 215, CGC.

47. J. P. Jackson to David G. Browne, June 15, 1900, GCOCC.

48. John H. Wise to Special Agent Moore, Dec. 8, 1896, GCC.

49. *AR-CGI* (1899), 29.

50. Special Deputy of Customs to J. R. Mason, Esq., Aug. 10, 1900, Correspondence, 1872–1928,

Port of Odgensburg, New York, Records of the U.S. Bureau of Customs, RG 36, National Archives, Northeast Region, New York.

51. Frank P. Sargent to Commissioner of Immigration, Nov. 19, 1904, File 52231/1, INSSC; Jones, *Surnames of the Chinese.*

52. Special Agent Moore to John H. Wise, Dec. 10, 1896, GCC.

53. U.S. Congress, House, Select Committee, *Investigation of Chinese Immigration,* 296.

54. T. H. Gubbins to Terence V. Powderly, Jan. 30, 1902, File 4557, CGC.

55. Collector of Customs to CGI, May 28, 1901, CCTR.

56. U.S. Congress, House, Select Committee, *Investigation of Chinese Immigration,* 296.

57. Oscar Greenhalgh to Walter S. Chance, Mar. 3, 1899, File 52730/84, INSSC; *San Francisco Call,* Mar. 9, 1899.

58. The exact date when this occurred is unclear, but by 1899, interpreters who were Chinese were appearing in official correspondence (U.S. Congress, House, Select Committee, *Investigation of Chinese Immigration,* 296).

59. H. A. Moore to John G. Carlisle, Nov. 13 and 26, 1896, and Assistant Treasury Secretary to H. A. Moore, Nov. 21, 1896, cited in Prince and Keller, *U.S. Customs Service,* 176.

60. Acting Secretary of Treasury to Collector of Customs, Apr. 7, 1899, CCTR.

61. Collector of Customs to CGI, May 28, 1901, CCTR.

62. Acting Secretary of Treasury to Collector of Customs, Apr. 7, 1899, CCTR.

63. Special Agent Moore to John Wise, Dec. 10, 1896, GCC.

64. Con and Wickberg, *From China to Canada,* 58.

65. The Treasury Department apparently consulted the U.S. Attorney on the matter of Gardner's citizenship as well (ibid.).

66. See the case of Lawrence Kentwell in Chapter 3.

67. J. P. Jackson to Treasury Secretary, Mar. 30, 1899, File 53108/9-B, INSSC.

68. E. Percivale Baker to CGI, Aug. 29, 1901, File 3648, CGC. For Baker's discharge from the service, see *San Francisco Examiner,* Nov. 29, 1899.

69. Lyman J. Mowry, Esq., to J. P. Jackson, May 18, 1899, and John Endicott Gardner to W. S. Chance, May 20, 1899, File 392, CGC.

70. Coolidge, *Chinese Immigration,* 320.

71. John Martin to John H. Wise, Dec. 3, 1896, GCOCC.

72. On Dunn's work publicizing San Francisco as a model, see James Dunn to CGI, Dec. 10, 1900, Files 2477 and 2478, CGC. For Dunn's Port Townsend trip, see James R. Dunn to CGI, May 7, 1901, no file number, Box 20, ibid. For Dunn's Santa Barbara and San Diego trips, see James Dunn to CGI, Aug. 16, 1901, File 3684, Box 23, ibid. For Dunn's trips to Illinois and Ohio, see U.S. Congress, Senate, Committee on Immigration, *Chinese Exclusion,* 310, and James Dunn to CGI, May 4 and Aug. 16, 1901, and May 4, 1902, File 3684, CGC. For Dunn's report to Washington, D.C., and visit with President Roosevelt, see James R. Dunn, "Report," Oct. 21, 1901, File 4794; James R. Dunn to CGI, Feb. 10, 1903, File 6553; and James Dunn to Treasury Secretary, Mar. 26, 1902, File 4794, ibid.

73. J. P. Jackson to Treasury Secretary, Sept. 5, 1899, File 736, ibid.

74. Special Agents Link and Smith to the Treasury Secretary, Feb. 6, 1899, File 53108/9-B, INSSC.

75. Lombardi, *Labor's Voice in the Cabinet,* 125.

76. *Washington Times,* Jan. 1, 1902.

77. Terence Powderly to David Healy, July 12, 1899, cited in Falzone, *Terence Powderly,* 180.

78. Terence Powderly to John H. Mulligan, Aug. 17, 1897, cited in ibid., 181.

79. Smith and Herring, *Bureau of Immigration*, 5; Falzone, *Terence Powderly*, 177–78.

80. McKee, *Chinese Exclusion*, 29–30.

81. Ibid., 28.

82. Scanland, "Will the Chinese Migrate?," 21, cited in McKee, *Chinese Exclusion*, 29.

83. McKee, *Chinese Exclusion*, 32.

84. *AR-CGI* (1899), 34.

85. Terence Powderly to J. C. Scottron, Jan. 24, 1902, as cited in Falzone, *Terence Powderly*, 181.

86. McKee, *Chinese Exclusion*, 33.

87. Falzone, *Terence Powderly*, 188.

88. F. P. Sargent, "Memorandum," c. 1905, File 52704/12, INSSC.

89. *Peoria Journal*, Aug. 21, 1902, Scrapbooks, 1902–5, RG 85, Records of the INS, National Archives, Washington, D.C.

90. *San Francisco Examiner*, May 15, 1905.

91. *AR-CGI* (1902), 71.

92. "Disposition of Chinese Arrived at U.S. Ports and Chinese Arrested within the U.S.," *AR-CGI* (1904), 160.

93. F. P. Sargent, "Memorandum," c. 1905, File 52704/12, p. 137, INSSC.

94. *San Francisco Chronicle*, July 20, 1904.

95. V. H. Metcalf, "Memorandum," July 15, 1904, File 12592, CGC.

96. The Sundry Civil Act of June 6, 1900 (31 Stat. L., 588, 611).

97. "An Act to Establish the Department of Commerce and Labor" (32 Stat. L., 825).

98. *Ju Toy v. United States*, 109 U.S. 253 (1905); Salyer, *Laws Harsh as Tigers*, 94–116.

99. Skowronek, *Building a New American State*, 47.

100. Van Vleck, *Administrative Control of Aliens*, 25–26.

101. Howe, *Confessions of a Reformer*, 255. For coursework required of immigration officials, see Rak, *Border Patrol*, 10–11.

102. Salyer, *Laws Harsh as Tigers*, 66.

103. Straus, "Spirit and Letter of Exclusion," 481–85, cited in Salyer, *Laws Harsh as Tigers*, 166.

104. Salyer, *Laws Harsh as Tigers*, 219; Higham, *Strangers in the Land*, 127–28; McKee, *Chinese Exclusion*, 206–9; Lombardi, *Labor's Voice in the Cabinet*, 59–60.

105. *Chicago Record-Herald*, Nov. 4, 1904, in William E. Curtis to Hart Hyatt North, Nov. 4, 1908, Folder 9, Box 1, H. H. North Papers, BL.

106. H. H. North to J. S. Rodgers, June 9, 1909, Folder 3, Box 1, H. H. North Papers, BL.

107. North was a native Californian, born in Marysville and raised in Oakland. He graduated from the University of California at Berkeley, became a lawyer, and served as a Republican state representative from Alameda County in 1894. He was also the brother-in-law to architect Julia Morgan (*San Francisco Examiner*, Jan. 28, 1898, 2:1).

108. Ng Poon Chew to President William H. Taft, Sept. 19, 1910, File 53108/24, vol. 4, INSSC.

109. Acting Commissioner Luther Steward, "Visit Paid the Angel Island Immigration Station," June 6, 1911, File 52961/24-D, pp. 80–81, INSSC.

110. Diaries of John Birge Sawyer, Jan. 1907, vol. 1, pp. 41, 46, 55, BL.

111. Ibid., 65.

112. Ibid., Nov. 17, 1917, vol. 2, p. 166; see also Salyer, *Laws Harsh as Tigers*, 39. Interestingly, Mehan was previously a renowned "catcher" of Chinese immigrants suspected of crossing the U.S.-Mexican border illegally. See Chapter 5.

113. Daniel Keefe to Secretary of Commerce and Labor, Feb. 7, 1910, File 52961/26-C, INSSC; *AR-CGI* (1915), 41–42; Selig, "Lapses from Virtue," 15–19.

114. Salyer, *Laws Harsh as Tigers,* 224–25.

115. Ibid., 225–26, 244.

116. Interview with Edwar Lee, Angel Island Interviews, BL.

117. *San Francisco Call,* Sept. 16, 1910.

118. "Summary Report upon the Administration of Immigration Commissioner H. H. North," Mar. 25, 1911, File 53108/24-A, pp. 29–30, INSSC; Jensen, *Passage from India,* 104.

119. Angel Island Interviews, BL, Part II, p. 4.

120. Diaries of John Birge Sawyer, vol. 2, pp. 119–20, BL.

121. Giovinco, "California Career of Anthony Caminetti," 390–91, 361–72.

122. Lim P. Lee, "Sociological Data." My thanks to Judy Yung for sharing this article with me.

123. *AR-CGI* (1913), 10.

124. *AR-CGI* (1916), xvi; *AR-CGI* (1917), xxi.

125. Giovinco, "California Career of Anthony Caminetti," 371–72.

126. *AR-CGI* (1920), 177.

Part Two

1. Him Mark Lai, "Island of Immortals," 100.

Chapter Three

1. U.S. Congress, House, Select Committee, *Investigation of Chinese Immigration,* 298.

2. Rule 7, U.S. Dept. of Commerce and Labor, Bureau of Immigration, *Treaty, Laws, and Regulations* (1905), 47.

3. Ng, *Treatment of the Exempt Classes,* 1–2.

4. Recent studies have just begun to pay attention to immigration law enforcement. See Salyer, *Laws Harsh as Tigers,* and Calavita, "Paradoxes."

5. Here I borrow from the six "faces" of the Oriental that Robert Lee (*Orientals,* 8–10) has identified in American popular culture. See also Calavita, "Paradoxes," 14–18.

6. Lisa Lowe (*Immigrant Acts,* 14) writes that "the history of racial formation of Asian immigrants and Asian Americans have always included a 'class formation and a gender formation' that [were] mediated through such state apparatuses as the law."

7. "Immigration of Chinese Laborers Prohibited" (Scott Act) (25 Stat. 476).

8. On how "Chineseness" was similarly defined in Canada, see Anderson, *Vancouver's Chinatown,* 18. On the symbols of "Chineseness," see Robert Lee, *Orientals,* 2.

9. L. K. Kentwell to Victor H. Metcalf, Feb. 27, 1906, File 466-C, CAF, H.

10. On the racialization of Chinese in popular culture, see Robert Lee, *Orientals,* 1–14.

11. L. K. Kentwell to Victor H. Metcalf, Feb. 27, 1906, File 466-C, CAF, H.

12. Ibid.

13. L. K. Kentwell to Theodore Roosevelt et al., Nov. 20, 1905, ibid.

14. Robert Brown to CGI, Dec. 18, 1905, and Mar. 26, 1906, ibid.

15. F. M. Bechtel to Charles Mehan, Aug. 16, 1905, ibid.

16. Victor H. Metcalf to L. K. Kentwell, Mar. 9, 1906, ibid.

17. *San Francisco Chronicle,* June 21, 1904.

18. Rules 5–6, U.S. Dept. of Commerce and Labor, Bureau of Immigration, *Treaty, Laws, and Regulations* (1905), 42.

19. U.S. Congress, House, Select Committee, *Investigation of Chinese Immigration*, 279, 281, 297, 299.

20. Him Mark Lai, "Island of Immortals," 91; Lai, Lim, and Yung, *Island*, 8.

21. Act of Mar. 3, 1891 (26 Stat. 1084); Kraut, *Silent Travelers*, 2, 51, 54–55.

22. Y. Chen, *Chinese San Francisco*, 214.

23. Shah demonstrates that even the extensive reliance on new scientific methods such as bacteriology continued to be shaped by public health service physicians' racial assumptions (*Contagious Divides*, 179–203).

24. Confidential Dispatch to CGI, Jan. 24, 1907, File 51881/85, INSSC.

25. Judy Yung, interview with Mr. Jow, File 13, AIOHP.

26. On 1870s stereotypes, see Takaki, *Iron Cages*, 223, and Miller, *Unwelcome Immigrant*, 36, 83–94.

27. Collector of Customs to John Sherman, June 5, 1877, Press Copies of Letters from the Collector to the Secretary of the Treasury, 1870–1912, Port of San Francisco, Records of the U.S. Customs Service, San Francisco, RG 36, National Archives, Pacific Region, San Bruno, Calif.

28. Ralph, "Chinese Leak," 518.

29. *AR-CGI* (1903), 96–97; *AR-CGI* (1900), 46.

30. On the Bertillon system in general and its usage in Chinese exclusion, see Rhodes, *Alphonse Bertillon*, and U.S. Dept. of Commerce and Labor, Bureau of Immigration, *Facts Concerning the Enforcement*, 32. For a Chinese description of the Bertillon system, see K. Scott Wong, "Liang Qichao," 15. The Bertillon system became linked to early methods to advance eugenics in the United States. See Kevles, *In the Name of Eugenics*, 16, and Higham, *Strangers in the Land*, 149–57.

31. *AR-CGI* (1902); Act of June 30, 1903 (32 Stat. 1112); U.S. Dept. of Commerce and Labor, Bureau of Immigration, *Treaty, Laws, and Regulations* (1903); "Chinese Exclusion," *Outlook* 76 (Apr. 23, 1904): 964; Calavita, "Paradoxes," 21–24.

32. McKee, *Chinese Exclusion*, 74.

33. The editor was most likely Ng Poon Chew of the Chinese-language daily *Chung Sai Yat Bo*. Harold Bolce, Chinese Inspector, to Secretary of Commerce and Labor, May 29, 1905, File 53059/8, p. 47, INSSC.

34. *AR-CGI* (1900), 46.

35. John D. Nagle to T. Y. Tang, Aug. 17, 1927, File 55597/912, p. 5, INSSC.

36. U.S. Congress, House, Select Committee, *Investigation of Chinese Immigration*, 279–82, 297–300, 324–28.

37. Ibid., 324.

38. Coolidge, *Chinese Immigration*, 310–11.

39. U.S. Dept. of Commerce and Labor, Bureau of Immigration, *Treaty, Laws, and Regulations* (1906).

40. Him Mark Lai, "Island of Immortals," 94, 102 n. 28.

41. W. Chen, "Chinese under Both Exclusion and Immigration Laws," 99.

42. "Memorandum," Apr. 5, 1922, File 54261/147-A, p. 2, INSSC.

43. On the construction of the image of the Chinese coolie in popular culture, see Robert Lee, *Orientals*, 51–53.

44. "Memorandum," May 18, 1906, File 52600/48, INSSC.

45. Philip B. Jones to Inspector in Charge, Nov. 8, 1911, File 10508/151, CAF, SF.

46. John Endicott Gardner to Chinese Inspector in Charge, Sept. 21, 1912, File 11215, ibid.

47. Immigrant Inspector to Commissioner of Immigration, Jan. 12, 1916, File 14894/2-2, ibid.

48. Rules 5–6, U.S. Dept. of Commerce and Labor, Bureau of Immigration, *Treaty, Laws, and Regulations* (1905), 42.

49. Soo Hoo Fong to Kam Tong, Feb. 12, 1898, File 53108/9-B, INSSC.

50. H. H. North to CGI, Aug. 3, 1904, File 12811, CGC.

51. Interrogation of Lee Kwock Chow, May 31, 1903, File 37775/9-25, CAF, SF.

52. H. H. North to CGI, Aug. 3, 1904, File 12811, CGC.

53. Frank Sargent to H. H. North, Aug. 9, 1904, File 12811, CGC.

54. "McCreary Amendment to the Geary Act," 28 Stat. 7 (1893).

55. U.S. Treasury Dept. Circular 14877, Apr. 19, 1894; Chinese Partnership Case Files, 1894–1944, Records of the INS, San Francisco, RG 85, National Archives, Pacific Region, San Bruno, Calif.; U.S. Dept. of Commerce and Labor, Bureau of Immigration, *Treaty, Laws, and Regulations* (1906), 10, 23.

56. James Dunn to Collector of Customs, Apr. 20, 1901, File 6346, CGC. The Bureau of Immigration apparently reinstituted restaurant managers and proprietors as merchants around 1914, but the Immigration Act of 1924 redefined all persons connected with restaurants as laborers again.

57. Act of July 6, 1932 (47 U.S. Stat., 607); W. Chen, "Chinese under Both Exclusion and Immigration Laws," 140–41.

58. W. Chen, "Chinese under Both Exclusion and Immigration Laws," 141.

59. Rule 27, U.S. Dept. of Commerce and Labor, Bureau of Immigration, *Treaty, Laws, and Regulations* (1905), 50. In reading several hundred Chinese immigrant files, I did not come across a single case involving witnesses who were African American, Hispanic, non-Chinese Asian, or American Indian.

60. Chan, "Exclusion of Chinese Women," 95, 97.

61. McKeown, "Transnational Chinese Families," 74, 78, 83; McKeown, *Chinese Migrant Networks,* 30–32.

62. McKeown, "Transnational Chinese Families," 74, 78, 83.

63. On Chinese prostitution in general, see Cheng, "Free, Indentured, Enslaved," 3–29; Tong, *Unsubmissive Women;* Chan, "Exclusion of Chinese Women"; Peffer, *If They Don't Bring Their Women Here;* Edholm, "A Stain on the Flag"; and Grey, "Confession of a Chinese Slave-Dealer," 124–53, 159–70.

64. The court decision was *In re Chung Toy Ho and Wong Choy Sin.* Chan, "Exclusion of Chinese Women," 114; John Wise to A. L. Fitzgerald, Esq., Eureka, Nevada, Dec. 29, 1893, GCOCC.

65. See, for example, Correspondence to John Wise, Collector of Customs, Feb.-June 1895, GCOCC.

66. John Wise to W. F. Thompson, Feb. 26, 1895, ibid.

67. Ibid.

68. John Wise to R. R. Swain, Esq., Feb. 14, 1895, ibid.

69. See J. P. Jackson to Treasury Secretary, Nov. 24, 1899, File 987, CGC; Littleton, "Worse Than Slaves," 164–70; Pascoe, *Relations of Rescue,* 35–36.

70. John Wise to R. R. Swain, Esq., Feb. 14, 1895, and E. B. Johnson to R. S. Pena, Apr. 30, May 16, 1895, GCOCC.

71. John Wise to A. L. Fitzgerald, Esq., Dec. 29, 1893, ibid.

72. John D. Nagle to Mr. T. Y. Tang, Aug. 17, 1927, File 55597/912, p. 19, INSSC. The 1907 regulations do not list any requirement of white witnesses to marriages (U.S. Dept. of Commerce and Labor, Bureau of Immigration, *Treaty, Laws, and Regulations*).

73. On the influence of class and Victorian gender ideals on Chinese female immigration in general, see Chan, "Exclusion of Chinese Women," 138–39, and Pascoe, *Relations of Rescue*, 4.

74. File 10-23-85/180, CAF, SF.

75. John P. Jackson to the Treasury Secretary, Mar. 30, 1899, File 53108/9-B, INSSC. On campaigns to ban foot binding in China, see Ping, *Aching for Beauty*, 36–44.

76. Chan, "Exclusion of Chinese Women."

77. File 16327/3-3, CAF, SF.

78. Statement Sent to the San Francisco Chamber of Commerce, May 20, 1911, File 52961/24-C, INSSC.

79. Ng, *Treatment of the Exempt Classes*, 10.

80. W. Chen, "Chinese under Both Exclusion and Immigration Laws," 201.

81. Chan, "Exclusion of Chinese Women," 114.

82. Gabaccia, *From the Other Side*, 26.

83. File 10193, Chinese Exclusion Case Files, Seattle, Washington, Records of the INS, RG 85, National Archives, Pacific Alaska Region, Seattle, Washington; interview with Gladys Huie.

84. See Chapter 6.

85. *AR-CGI* (1925), 23.

86. File 14894/2-2, CAF, SF.

87. E. J. Sims to INS District Director, Apr. 21, 1942, File 38813/7-16, CAF, SF.

88. Act of Sept. 22, 1922 (42 Stat. 1021); Chan, "Exclusion of Chinese Women," 128–29.

89. *CR*, 43d Cong., 2d sess. (1875), 1082.

90. *CR*, 44th Cong., 2d sess. (1877), vol. 5, p. 3, 2005; U.S. Congress, Joint Special Committee, *Chinese Immigration*, vii.

91. U.S. Congress, Joint Special Committee, *Chinese Immigration*, vii.

92. *In re Look Tin Sing*, C.C.D. Cal., 21 Federal Reporter 905, 910 (C.C.D. Cal. 1884); U.S. Congress, Senate, Committee on Immigration, *Alleged Illegal Entry*, 153; Zhang, "Dragon in the Land of the Eagle," 313–18.

93. Interrogation of Wong Kim Ock [*sic*], July 16, 1890, 12017/42223, Box 458, RCCF.

94. Petition for Writ on Behalf of Petitioner, Nov. 11, 1895, Wong Kim Ark, Folder 11198, Box 594, Admiralty Case Files, Records of the U.S. District Court, RG 21, National Archives, Pacific Region, San Bruno, Calif.

95. Brief on Behalf of the U.S., Nov. 19, 1895, pp. 3–4, and Opinion Rendered *In the Matter of Wong Kim Ark*, Jan. 3, 1896, p. 5, ibid.

96. Brief on Behalf of the U.S., Nov. 19, 1895, pp. 4–5, ibid.

97. Petition for Writ on Behalf of Petitioner, Nov. 11, 1895, and Points and Authorities of U.S. District Attorney, Nov. 11, 1895, ibid.

98. Brief on Behalf of the U.S., Nov. 19, 1895, p. 6, ibid.

99. Points and Authorities of U.S. District Attorney, Nov. 11, 1895, ibid.

100. Opinion of Judge Morrow, Jan. 3, 1896, p. 14, ibid.

101. *United States v. Wong Kim Ark*, 169 U.S. 649, 694 (1898); Salyer, *Laws Harsh as Tigers*, 99.

102. On Asian Americans as "perpetual foreigners," see Lowe, *Immigrant Acts*, 4.

103. U.S. Congress, Senate, Committee on Immigration, *Alleged Illegal Entry*, 9.

104. Interrogation of Wong Kim Ock [*sic*], July 16, 1890, File 12017/42223, Box 458, RCCF.

105. File 10039/41, CAF, SF.

106. Collector of Customs to the Treasury Secretary, Mar. 30, 1899, File 53108/9-B, INSSC.

107. It is not clear when this regulation was formally dropped, but in his 1902 *Annual Report*,

the CGI noted that Chinese were gaining admission as citizens on a regular basis through Chinese testimony only (*AR-CGI* [1902], 76–77).

108. S. G. Carpenter to Charles Nagel, Sept. 23, 1910, File 52961/24-B, INSSC.

109. Report from Alfred W. Parker, Oct. 5, 1905, File 10079/6, CAF, SF.

110. Interrogation of Fon Toy, Jan. 25, 1905, File 10039/2, ibid.

111. Interrogation of Lim Tong, June 27, 1905, File 10062/19, ibid.

112. Interrogation of Lee Toy Mock, Feb. 7, 1930, File 12020/16793, Box 3, IF, SF.

113. Interrogation of Woo Wee Nuen, Aug. 22, 1905, File 10067/19, CAF, SF.

114. Interrogation of Lee Toy Mock, Feb. 7, 1930, File 12020/16793, Box 3, IF, SF.

115. July 26, 1934, deportation hearing, File 12020/23-401, IF, SF.

116. W. W. Husband to John D. Nagle, Apr. 26, 1924, File 55383/30, and Wallace R. Farrington to Secretary of Labor, Aug. 16, 1926, File 55383/30, INSSC.

117. Edna Lois Hing to Commissioner of Immigration, Jan. 25, 1923, File 14517/1-9, CAF, SF.

Chapter Four

1. Other studies that have emphasized the transnational character of Chinese migration include McKeown, *Chinese Migrant Networks*, 4–7, 19–23, 25–32, and "Transnational Chinese Families," 73–110; Y. Chen, *Chinese San Francisco*, 3, 7, 57, 145–47; and Hsu, *Dreaming of Gold*, 5–11.

2. See generally McClain, *In Search of Equality*, 3; Salyer, *Laws Harsh as Tigers*, xv; and Okihiro, *Margins and Mainstreams*, 151.

3. Chan, *This Bittersweet Soil*, 17, 19–21; Y. Chen, *Chinese San Francisco*, 20–22; Hsu, *Dreaming of Gold*, 18–23.

4. Chan, *This Bittersweet Soil*, 11–16; Y. Chen, *Chinese San Francisco*, 22. On the impact of Chinese remittances from America on families and villages in the district of Toisan, see Hsu, *Dreaming of Gold*, 31–54, 108–12.

5. Harold Bolce to Secretary of Commerce and Labor, May 29, 1905, File 53059/8, pp. 44–46, INSSC.

6. Hart Hyatt North to CGI, Mar. 24, 1910, File 53108/24, vol. 4, INSSC.

7. Victor H. Metcalf to Hart Hyatt North, Oct. 2, 1905, Folder 4, Box 2, H. H. North Papers, BL.

8. By the 1920s, 48 percent of Chinese in the United States worked in small businesses, laundries, restaurants, or stores. Twenty-seven percent were domestic workers. Only 11 percent worked in agriculture and 9 percent in manufacturing and skilled crafts. The occupations of the remaining 5 percent of workers is unknown (Chan, *This Bittersweet Soil*, 77).

9. Siu, *Chinese Laundryman*, 85.

10. Ibid.

11. Statement of Fong Ing Bong, Sept. 28, 1907, File 10209/77, CAF, SF.

12. Interview with Wallace Lee.

13. "Summary of Interview with Jeong Foo Louie," AIOHP.

14. *AR-CGI* (1890, 1897–1932); W. Chen, "Chinese under Both Exclusion and Immigration Laws," 206.

15. Siu, *Chinese Laundryman*, 107.

16. Chan, "Exclusion of Chinese Women," 95, 97; Yung, *Unbound Feet*, 55–63.

17. U.S. government statistics for Chinese immigrant admissions are highly inconsistent. When the U.S. Bureau of Immigration categorized immigrants by sex, it recorded 127,012 total Chinese immigrants (9,868 Chinese women) admitted from 1882 to 1943. These figures do not include citizens returning to the United States. When immigrants were categorized by immigration status, the total number of Chinese admitted for the same period, including Chinese in transit

through the United States as well as Americans of Chinese descent, was 422,908. From 1910 to 1924, when the number of Chinese immigrants was broken down by both sex and immigration status, Chinese women made up an average of 9.4 percent of the total pool. Taking this average percentage and multiplying it by the more complete figure of 422,908 Chinese admitted, the actual number of Chinese women (both immigrants and citizens) who entered or reentered from 1882 to 1943 was probably closer to 40,000. See tables "Immigrants Admitted" and "Summary of Chinese Seeking Admission to the U.S." in *AR-CGI* (1890, 1897–1932), and H. Chen, "Chinese Immigration," 181, 201, 206.

18. U.S. Congress, Joint Special Committee, *Reports of the Immigration Commissioner,* 384–85. On sojourning as a migration strategy in general, see Wang, "Sojourning," 1–3; Cinel, *National Integration,* 98, 104; Sánchez, *Becoming Mexican American,* 38–62; McKeown, *Chinese Migrant Networks;* and Hsu, *Dreaming of Gold.*

19. Nee and Nee, *Longtime Californ',* 16.

20. Wong Ngum Yin (a.k.a. Wong Hock Won), "Composition," enclosed in Inspector in Charge to CGI, Oct. 29, 1906, File 13928, CGC. A *mou* is a Chinese measurement for land.

21. Nakano, "Split Household," 38–39. See also Hsu, *Dreaming of Gold,* 90–123.

22. Translated Chinese Envelopes, June 10, 1918, File 2, Box 1, DIF, SF.

23. Hsu, *Dreaming of Gold,* 31–40.

24. Wong Cheung to Wong Jou, and Lee Shee to Wong Jou, 1926–38, Translated Chinese letters, File 37176/12-17, CAF, SF.

25. *Chung Sai Yat Po,* July 14, 1906.

26. Ibid., Mar. 24, 1906.

27. Ibid., Jan. 30, 1906.

28. Data compiled by author and derived from a random sample survey of immigration records of Chinese individuals who entered the United States through the port of San Francisco from 1884 to 1941. Return visits were documented by applicants' reentry papers (CAF, SF).

29. See, for example, Tung Pok Chin, *Paper Son,* 21.

30. Wong Cheung to Wong Jou, and Lee Shee to Wong Jou, 1926–38, Translated Chinese letters, File 37176/12-17, CAF, SF.

31. Wong Ngum Yin to Wong Sheong Yin, July 1906, enclosed in Inspector in Charge to CGI, Oct. 29, 1906, File 13928, CGC.

32. Lew Chew Mei to Lew Git, Oct. 1918, Jan. 1919, May 1919, File 19612/11-9, CAF, SF. On cycle of debt, see also Siu, *Chinese Laundryman,* 111, and Hsu, *Dreaming of Gold,* 40–53.

33. Nakano, "Split Household," 38; Leung, "Laundryman," 5–6; Nee and Nee, *Longtime Californ',* 17; Hsu, *Dreaming of Gold,* 108.

34. The formal name of the Chinese Six Companies was the Chinese Consolidated Benevolent Association. McClain, *In Search for Equality,* 156–57, 93; Chan, "Exclusion of Chinese Women."

35. Salyer, *Laws Harsh as Tigers,* 81–83.

36. *Fong Yue Ting v. United States,* 149 U.S. 698, 713 (1893); Salyer, *Laws Harsh as Tigers,* 47–58.

37. For Chinese diplomats and local elites, see Yow, "Chinese Exclusion," 314–30, and K. Scott Wong, "Cultural Defenders and Brokers," 8.

38. *San Francisco Morning Call,* Sept. 14, 1892, 8.

39. Oscar Greenhalgh to Walter S. Chance, Mar. 16, 1899, File 52730/84, INSSC.

40. Interview with Mr. Woo Gen, July 24, 1924, Document 183, SRR.

41. See Files 52363/14, 52961/26-B, 53620/115-C, INSSC.

42. Wu Ting-fang to John Hay, Dec. 26, 1900, Notes from the Chinese Legation in the U.S. to

the Dept. of State, Records of the U.S. Department of State, RG 59, National Archives, Pacific Region, San Bruno, Calif.

43. See Files 54152/75, 55597/912, 54152/75, 52961/24-B, INSSC.

44. "Report of the Special Committee," Chinese Chamber of Commerce and Chinese-American League of Justice of Los Angeles, California, Jan. 4, 1913, File 53620/115, INSSC.

45. Rhymes No. 12 and 10, in Hom, *Songs of Gold Mountain*, 85, 83.

46. F. H. Larned to Assistant Secretary of Commerce and Labor, Nov. 23, 1908, File 52270/21, INSSC; P. A. Surgeon to Collector of Customs, Jan. 13, 1909, File 52999/44, ibid.

47. Richard Taylor to CGI, Mar. 25, 1909, File 52270/21, ibid.

48. H. H. North to CGI, Sept. 20, 1909, File 52999/14, ibid.

49. See Rhyme No. 5, in Hom, *Songs of Gold Mountain*, 78. Apparently, conditions were no better at the detention houses at other ports. See R. J. Wilding, M.D., to E. V. Skinner, Jan. 18, 1904, File 52704/2, INSSC, and E. V. Skinner to James A. Towney, July 8, 1903, File 7902, CGC.

50. Huey Dow to Collector of Customs, Nov. 1902, File 9903/66, CAF, SF.

51. Wong Ngum Yin (a.k.a. Wong Hock Won), "Composition," enclosed in Inspector in Charge to CGI, Oct. 29, 1906, File 13928, CGC.

52. John Endicott Gardner to J. H. Barbour, Apr. 19, 1902, File 4862, CGC.

53. F. H. Larned to Secretary of Commerce and Labor, Jan. 28, 1909, File 5220/71, INSSC. See also *San Francisco Call*, Sept. 9 and Nov. 29, 1908.

54. *Chung Sai Yat Po*, Jan. 17, 1903. See File 5986, CGC; Daniel Keefe to Secretary of Commerce and Labor, Aug. 7, 1909, File 52270/21, INSSC; and William R. Wheeler to Secretary of Commerce and Labor, Jan. 28, 1909, ibid.

55. James Dunn to CGI, Feb. 1, 1901, File 2580, CGC.

56. "Memorandum," c. 1905, by Frank P. Sargent, File 52704/12, INSSC.

57. Frank P. Sargent to Secretary of Commerce and Labor, May 29, 1905, and Harold Bolce to Secretary of Commerce and Labor, May 29, 1905, File 53059/8, ibid.

58. Y. Chen, *Chinese San Francisco*, 148–61; Salyer, *Laws Harsh as Tigers*, 97–101, 139; Tsai, *Chinese Experience*, 77–79; Mei, Yip, and Leong, "*Bitter Society*," 46.

59. *AR-CGI* (1905), 78–81.

60. Ibid. (1907), 143–44.

61. "Enforcement of the Chinese Exclusion Laws—General Instruction," June 24, 1905, Dept. Circular No. 81, File 52423/40, INSSC.

62. Among the other changes in the rules and regulations concerning the enforcement of the Chinese exclusion laws were (1) the clause the "burden of proof shall be on the applicant" was omitted; (2) certificates that had heretofore been kept by immigration officials were now returned to all those immigrants who were admitted into the country; (3) the definition of merchant was liberalized; (4) no photographs of mercantile establishments were allowed to be used as evidence against the applicant; (5) the definition of student was liberalized; (6) Chinese who were admitted as members of the exempt class but who later became laborers were not to be arrested as before; (7) exempt-class Chinese who were waiting to enter the country were to be allowed to be released on $2,000 bond rather than required to serve detention until their cases had been determined. See U.S. Bureau of Immigration, *Facts Concerning the Enforcement*, 1906, 28–45, and Coolidge, *Chinese Immigration*, 297–301.

63. The CGI later rescinded this order in 1908, claiming that very few Chinese actually used this privilege, but after Secretary of Commerce and Labor Charles Nagel visited San Francisco in 1910, he reinstituted the rule (Salyer, *Laws Harsh as Tigers*, 221–22).

64. *AR-CGI* (1907), 141, 144.

65. H. H. North to George C. Perkins, Dec. 7, 1903, Box 1, H. H. North Papers, BL.

66. U.S. Congress, House, *Immigration Station on Angel Island*, cited in Him Mark Lai, "Island of Immortals," 91.

67. *Chinese World*, Jan. 22, 1910; *San Francisco Chronicle*, Jan. 23, 1910, as cited in Him Mark Lai, "Island of Immortals," 91.

68. *Chinese World*, Apr. 5, 1910, as cited in Him Mark Lai, "Island of Immortals," 91.

69. *AR-CGI* (1910), 126.

70. Feb. 3, 1910, circular found in San Francisco Chinatown, translated by John Endicott Gardner, File 52961/24, INSSC.

71. "Joint Report of Committee on Foreign Affairs," June 6, 1911, File 52961/24B, INSSC.

72. *Chung Sai Yat Po*, June 8 and Oct. 24, 1911, translated by John Endicott Gardner, File 52961/24 D-E, and "Transcript of Stenographic Notes," June 6, 1911, File 52961/24-D, INSSC.

73. "A Report of the Recent Position of American-Chinese Commercial Transaction," c. 1911, File 52961/24-B, INSSC.

74. Mr. T. Y. Tang to the U.S. Chamber of Commerce, Apr. 28, 1927, cited in McKenzie, *Oriental Exclusion*, 42–43.

75. McKenzie, *Oriental Exclusion*, 43–44.

76. Such class-based divisions also manifested themselves in the public health campaigns affecting Chinatown. See Shah, *Contagious Divides*, 115.

77. Ng, *Treatment of the Exempt Classes*, 1.

78. On Jewish and Mexican immigrants, see, for example, Cahan, *Yekl*, and Gutiérrez, *Walls and Mirrors*, 5.

79. Chinese merchants to Chester A. Arthur, Oct. 27, 1884, CCF.

80. Wu Ting-fang to John Hay, Dec. 26, 1900, File 2615, CGC.

81. Chinese merchants and students in Hong Kong to William Taft, Mar. 20, 1910, File 52961/24, INSSC.

82. Memorial to His Excellency the President of the United States of America, Sept. 20, 1911, File 52961/24-E, ibid.

83. Telegram to Woodrow Wilson, Oct. 10, 1918, File 53620/115-C, ibid.; McKenzie, *Oriental Exclusion*, 42–43.

84. McKenzie, *Oriental Exclusion*, 42–43, 127.

85. S. G. Carpenter to Charles Nagel, Sept. 23, 1910, File 52961/24-B, INSSC. On the history of the Native Sons, see Chung, "Fighting for Their American Rights."

86. C. P. Converse to Woodrow Wilson, June 8, 1916, File 54152/75, INSSC.

87. Ng Ah Ben to H. H. North, Dec. 3, 1909, File 28004/10-1, CAF, SF.

88. A. F. Haines to Secretary of Labor, Dec. 2, 1921, File 53620/115-C, INSSC.

89. CGI to Commissioner of Immigration, San Francisco, Mar. 17, 1910, File 52961/24-A, ibid.

90. See, for example, Telegram from the Chinese Consolidated Benevolent Association to President Woodrow Wilson, Oct. 10, 1918, File 53620/115-C, ibid., and Mears, *Resident Orientals*, 127.

91. See various letters, Box 4, CCF.

92. Wong Gong Kim to Wong Teung Kim, June 18, 1917, Box 1, DIF, SF.

93. Lee Young Sing to Lee Wooey Hong, Oct. 4, 1916, ibid.

94. Arthur Lem to Author, Jan. 13, 1996.

95. Wong Ngum Yin to cousins at Yuen Wo, July 1906, in Inspector to CGI, Oct. 29, 1906, File 13928, CGC.

96. Testimony of Fong Tim, Dec. 1, 1899, File 34240/8-19, CAF, SF.

97. Testimony of Wong Hong and Chew Dong Ngin, Dec. 6, 1899, File 34240/8-19, ibid.

98. Testimony of Lee Jung and Ching Bow, June 5, 1903, File 37775/9-25, ibid.

99. File 16327/3-13, ibid.

100. W. Chen, "Chinese under Both Exclusion and Immigration Laws," 402.

101. George Pippy to Treasury Secretary, July 24, 1899, File 624, CGC.

102. File 26002/1-9, CAF, SF; interview with Wallace Lee.

103. Lowe, *Immigrant Acts,* 9. See also, in general, Yung, *Unbound Feet.*

104. File 5-12-84/SS Oceanic, CAF, SF.

105. File 4098, Oct. 15, 1901, CGC.

106. Attorneys Stidger and Kennah to Commissioner of Immigration, Mar. 9, 1915, File 14144/5-6, CAF, SF.

107. See letters, 1889–91, to the Secretary of State and the Treasury Secretary, CCF.

108. File 9267/11, CAF, SF.

109. McConnell Jenkins to James Blaine, Jan. 3, 1890, CCF.

110. Report of Papers of Leong Fook On, Mar. 21, 1899, CGC.

111. Acting Treasury Secretary to John H. Wise, Sept. 7, 1895, GCC.

112. Frank B. Lenz to Charles Mehan, Jan. 25, 1915, File 14071/11-20, CAF, SF.

113. Ng Poon Chew to Samuel W. Backus, Jan. 26, 1915, File 14071/11-20, ibid.

114. Pascoe, *Relations of Rescue,* 78–79, 104, 106, 118, 167.

115. Yung, *Unbound Feet,* 66; Pascoe, *Relations of Rescue,* 96–98, 186–87.

116. Donaldina Cameron to Commissioner of Immigration, Jan. 26, 1916, File 14894/2-2, CAF, SF.

117. See, generally, McClain, *In Search of Equality.*

118. John Wise to Charles H. Page, 1895, GCOCC.

119. Oscar Greenhalgh to Walter S. Chance, Mar. 11, 1899, File 52730/84, INSSC.

120. W. Chen, "Chinese under Both Exclusion and Immigration Laws," 428–29, 6.

121. All data compiled by author and derived from a random sample survey of 608 immigration records of Chinese individuals who entered the United States through the port of San Francisco from 1884 to 1941 (CAF, SF).

122. Attorneys could examine only the stenographer's record of the hearing. They could not view the service's internal analysis of the case (Salyer, *Laws Harsh as Tigers,* 149).

123. See, for example, George McGowan in File 16288/14-15, CAF, SF.

124. John D. Nagle, "Comment on Proposed Chinese General Order No. 11," Aug. 1927, File 55597/912, INSSC.

125. McClain, *In Search for Equality,* 93, 336 n. 43, 345–46 n. 18.

126. Stidger's position is referred to in Fong Wing to Samuel Backus, May 6, 1915, File 14315/4-8, CAF, SF.

127. Stidger, "Highlights of Chinese Exclusion and Expulsion."

128. Around 1921, McGowan and Worley apparently disbanded, but each continued to represent Chinese immigrants (George A. McGowan to Edward White, Feb. 9, 1921, in File 19938/6-8, CAF, SF).

129. Papers of Wong Bing, Aug. 26, 1903, File 19981/4-29, ibid.

130. Henry Kennah served as an inspector from 1903 until 1912.

131. See firm letterhead in Thomas R. McGrath to Edward White, May 13, 1920, File 19034/16-17, CAF, SF.

132. O. L. Spaulding to Daniel Manning, Nov. 2, 1885, CCF.

133. *Chung Sai Yat Po,* Jan. 30 and 31, 1906.

134. Ibid., Feb. 27, 1906.

135. Ibid., Jan. 1, 1910; Nov. 22, 1906.

136. File 18703/13-5, CAF, SF.

137. The excludable classes under the general immigration laws included, among others: idiots, feeble-minded and insane persons, persons likely to become a public charge, persons afflicted with a contagious disease, prostitutes and other immoral aliens, procurers of prostitutes, contract laborers, illiterates, and alien enemies.

Part Three

1. Salyer, *Laws Harsh as Tigers*, 37. See also Wu, "Chinatowns," 102 and Hsu, *Dreaming of Gold*, 71–85.

2. Andreas writes: "Characterizing the state as simply reacting to a growing border problem fails to capture this dynamic. Even while failing to control illegal border crossings, law enforcement has shaped their location, routes, methods, and organizations." See Andreas, *Border Games*, 7, 12, 22–23, 25.

3. Gutiérrez, *Walls and Mirrors*, 254 n. 64.

4. See, for example, Ko-lin Chin, *Smuggled Chinese*, and Paul J. Smith, ed., *Human Smuggling*.

5. Haines and Rosenblum, *Illegal Immigration in America*, xi.

6. Gutiérrez, *Walls and Mirrors*, 254 n. 64.

7. Haines and Rosenblum, *Illegal Immigration in America*, xi.

Chapter Five

1. Testimony of Lim Wah, 12020/22130, Dec. 2, 1932, Box 13, IF, SF.

2. Since illegal immigration is, by nature, difficult to quantify and detect, this estimate is speculative. Government figures recorded only the numbers of immigrants caught while crossing the border and do not account for those who were successful in evading the authorities. Because no full record exists for both the northern and southern border, this estimate is also compiled from a number of sources. See *AR-CGI* (1903), 102; Paulsen, "Yellow Peril," 113–28; *AR-CGI* (1910), 146; and Fry, "Illegal Entry," 173–77.

3. Index to the *San Francisco Call*, 1894–1903.

4. The INS apprehended 450,152 individuals in the area surrounding the San Diego border during the fiscal year of 1994 alone. See U.S. Dept. of Justice, INS, "Operation Gatekeeper." On the regulation of immigration across the northern and southern borders, see Dunn, *Militarization of the U.S.-Mexico Border;* Andreas, *Border Games;* and Ramirez, *Crossing the 49th Parallel.* Studies that do acknowledge the significance of Chinese immigration and exclusion along the U.S.-Mexican or U.S.-Canadian border include Sánchez, *Becoming Mexican American;* Delgado, "In the Age of Exclusion"; and Sadowski-Smith, "Undocumented Border Crossings."

5. For studies related to the American West and to the northern and southern borderlands that use transnational and hemispheric frameworks, see Peck, *Reinventing Free Labor,* 1–7; Truett, "Neighbors by Nature," 3; and Sabin, "Home and Abroad," 308, 311, 333. See also Thelen, "Nation and Beyond," 965–75.

6. Resident Chinese laborers who had been in the United States at the time of the act's passage were allowed to reenter the country (David Lai, *Chinatowns*, 52).

7. "Chinese in B.C.," *Puget Sound Argus* (Port Townsend, Wash.), June 15, 1883; "More About the Chinese," ibid., July 9, 1883.

8. An Act to Restrict and Regulate Chinese Immigration into Canada, July 20, 1885, ch. 71, 1885 S.C. 207–12 (Can.); Roy, *White Man's Province*, 59–63; Wynne, "Reaction to the Chinese," 483; Con and Wickberg, *From China to Canada*, 55, 57.

9. *AR-CGI* (1903), 97.

10. Canadian Royal Commission on Chinese and Japanese Immigration, "Report," 271, cited in Zhang, "Dragon in the Land," 238; U.S. Congress, House, Select Committee, *Investigation of Chinese Immigration,* 1.

11. Ralph, "Chinese Leak," 517.

12. From 1901 to 1903, for example, the bureau reported that 3,445 Chinese crossed the Canadian border and entered the United States. Of those, 1,782 were released and 1,663 were eventually deported ("Arrests of Chinese Persons Crossing the Land Boundaries of the United States," *AR-CGI* [1903], 102).

13. An Act Respecting and Restricting Chinese Immigration, July 18, 1900, ch. 32, 1900 S.C. 215–21 (Can.); An Act Respecting and Restricting Chinese Immigration, ch. 8, 1903 S.C. 105–11 (Can.). For U.S. government complaints, see *AR-CGI* (1904), 138; *AR-CGI* (1910), 143; and *AR-CGI* (1911), 159.

14. Marcus Braun to CGI, "Report," Sept. 20, 1907, File 51630/44D, p. 31, INSSC.

15. Roy, *White Man's Province,* 67; Ralph, "Chinese Leak," 515.

16. David Lai, "Chinese Opium Trade," 23; Ralph, "Chinese Leak," 520–23; De Loreme, "United States Bureau of Customs," 77–88.

17. Kim and Markov, "Chinese Exclusion Laws," 16–30; *AR-CGI* (1903), 98–99.

18. U.S. Congress, Joint Special Committee, *Reports on Charge of Fraudulent Importation of Chinese,* 8.

19. Reynolds, "Enforcement of the Chinese Exclusion Law," 368; *AR-CGI* (1904), 137–41; *AR-CGI* (1909), 128.

20. Stanford, *Chinese Americans,* 106.

21. U.S. Dept. of Commerce and Labor, Bureau of Immigration, *Facts Concerning the Enforcement,* 63.

22. *AR-CGI* (1909), 130.

23. "Statements Made Before W. B. Howell, Assistant Secretary, in Reference to the Unlawful Admission of Chinese Persons into the United States," Nov. 26, 1898, File 53266/58-A, INSSC.

24. Richard H. Taylor, Immigrant Inspector, Buffalo, to Inspector in Charge, Niagara Falls, N.Y., Apr. 7, 1915, File 53788/1-V, ibid.

25. *United States v. Wong Kim Ark,* 169 U.S. 649, 694 (1898).

26. *AR-CGI* (1903), 96–97.

27. Salyer, *Laws Harsh as Tigers,* chs. 2–3.

28. John E. Gardner to F. P. Sargent, May 30, 1903, File 7808, CGC; U.S. Dept. of Commerce and Labor, Bureau of Immigration, *Facts Concerning the Enforcement,* 95–96.

29. Salyer, *Laws Harsh as Tigers,* ch. 3.

30. *AR-CGI* (1897), 758; *AR-CGI* (1904), 149, 626; U.S. Congress, Senate, Committee on Immigration, *Alleged Illegal Entry,* 153; Zhang, "Dragon in the Land," 349–50.

31. U.S. Dept. of Commerce and Labor, Bureau of Immigration, *McGettrick Certificates,* 1.

32. Ralph Izard to Walter S. Chance, Oct. 11, 1898, File 53266/588, INSSC.

33. John H. Clark to CGI, Oct. 27, 1911, File 52150/1, ibid.

34. *AR-CGI* (1903), 101.

35. Yen, *Coolies and Mandarins,* 292; Craib, "Chinese Immigrants," 8, 22, 24; Hu-DeHart, "Racism and Anti-Chinese Persecution," 2–4, 13.

36. Hu-DeHart, "Racism and Anti-Chinese Persecution," 2–3; Hu-DeHart, "Immigrants to a Developing Society," 276–82, 294; Craib, "Chinese Immigrants," 8; Cumberland, "Sonora Chinese," 195–96. Anti-Chinese sentiment in Mexico even turned to violence and all Chinese were expelled from Sonora in the 1930s.

37. John W. Dye, American Consul, Ciudad Juárez, Mexico, to Secretary of State, Nov. 4, 1926. My thanks to Grace Delgado for this information.

38. Hu-DeHart, "Racism and Anti-Chinese Persecution," 4, 13; Craib, "Chinese Immigrants," 22, 24.

39. Testimony of Law Ngim, May 17, 1931, File 12020/19153, Box 7, IF, SF.

40. Paulsen, "'Yellow Peril,'" 113–28; *AR-CGI* (1910), 146.

41. Hu-DeHart, "Immigrants to a Developing Society," 28.

42. F. W. Berkshire to CGI, June 23, 1909, File 52516/7, p. 2, INSSC.

43. Arthur G. Maggs to Officer in Charge, San Diego, June 9, 1912, and Charles E. Connell to Supervising Inspector, El Paso, June 12, 1912, File 54270/2, ibid.

44. *AR-CGI* (1906), 98; Marcus Braun to CGI, "Report," Feb. 12, 1907, File 52320/1, p. 11, INSSC. For estimates, see F. W. Berkshire to CGI, Apr. 16, 1910, File 52142/6, ibid.

45. F. W. Berkshire to CGI, Oct. 17, 1907, File 52212/2, pt. 1, p. 3, ibid.

46. *AR-CGI* (1907), 111.

47. Testimony of Law Ngim, May 17, 1931, File 12020/19153, Box 7, IF, SF.

48. S. E. Redfern to William W. Canada, Mar. 8, 1911, File 53161/2, INSSC.

49. Charles W. Snyder to CGI, Nov. 11, 1903, Folder 22, Box 2, H. H. North Papers, BL.

50. Marcus Braun to CGI, "Report," Feb. 12, 1907, File 52320/1, p. 29, INSSC; *AR-CGI* (1902), 75; *AR-CGI* (1907), 110; Ralph, "Chinese Leak," 524; Paulsen, "'Yellow Peril,'" 113–28; Testimony of Lim Wah, Dec. 2, 1932, File 12020/22130, Box 7, IF, SF.

51. Testimony of Jew Yick, Dec. 8, 1932, File 12020/22164, Box 13, IF, SF.

52. Perkins, *Border Patrol*, 17.

53. *AR-CGI* (1909), 127.

54. Ralph, "Chinese Leak," 524; *AR-CGI* (1907), 111; Craib, "Chinese Immigrants," 8.

55. *AR-CGI* (1907), 110.

56. Marcus Braun to CGI, "Report," Sept. 20, 1907, File 51630/44D, p. 3, INSSC; Burton Parker to Treasury Secretary, June 5, 1909, File 52516/7, ibid.

57. *AR-CGI* (1905), 95–96.

58. For late-twentieth-century descriptions of the U.S.-Mexican border region, see Anzaldúa, *Borderlands*, preface.

59. "Buffalo's Chinese Residents," *Buffalo Times*, Jan. 18, 1902, p. 5. See also "Chinese Exclusion Act Violations," *New York Times*, Nov. 29, 1896, p. 1, and "Exclusion Law Evaded by Traveling in Sleeping Cars," ibid., June 10, 1891, p. 1.

60. *AR-CGI* (1907), 110–11.

61. Marcus Braun to CGI, "Report," Feb. 12, 1907, File 52320/1, pp. 10, 30, 33, INSSC.

62. Feri F. Weiss to CGI, "Report of Inspector Feri F. Weiss In re: Cuban Smugglers," Apr. 4, 1925, and Feri F. Weiss to CGI, Feb. 25, 1925, File 55166/31, ibid. My thanks to Libby Garland for this source.

63. P. H. Shelton to CGI, Aug. 15, 1911, File 53161/2-A, ibid.

64. On the border as a "contact zone," see Saldívar, *Border Matters*, ix.

65. John H. Clark to CGI, Oct. 27, 1911, File 52150/1, INSSC.

66. Thomas M. Fisher to CGI, May 7, 1917, File 53788/3, ibid.

67. M. R. Snyder to Commissioner of Immigration, New Orleans, La., Feb. 2, 1911, File 53161/2, ibid.

68. F. W. Berkshire to CGI, Apr. 28, 1916, File 53788/6, ibid.

69. Richard H. Taylor to CGI, Oct. 24, 1908, File 52212/2, ibid.

70. Perkins, *Border Patrol*, 23.

71. *AR-CGI* (1910), 146.

72. F. W. Berkshire to CGI, Sept. 19, 1912, File 53507/32, INSSC.

73. F. W. Berkshire to CGI, May 7, 1910, File 52801/4A, p. 12, ibid.

74. Frank R. Stone to Supervising Inspector, El Paso, Tex., Apr. 23, 1910, p. 7, File 52801/4A, ibid.

75. H.R. 2915, "Preventing Immigration of Chinese Labor from Canada and Mexico," 1891, cited in Metz, *Border*, 365; Perkins, *Border Patrol*, 23.

76. On the construction of "John Chinaman," see Robert Lee, *Orientals*, 9, 22, 32. Mae Ngai ("Architecture of Race," 67–92) illustrates how the status of illegality became a racially inscribed category for Mexicans in the 1924 Immigration Act.

77. Both the Senate and the House passed the Fifteen Passenger Bill, demonstrating national and bipartisan support for Chinese exclusion. A presidential veto blocked its enactment. See Gyory, *Closing the Gate*, 3–6.

78. Unknown artist, "And Still They Come!," *Wasp: A Weekly Journal of Illustration and Comment* (San Francisco) 5, no. 227 (Dec. 4, 1880): 280.

79. Ralph, "Chinese Leak," 516. See also *AR-CGI* (1897), 758; U.S. Congress, Senate, Committee on Immigration, *Alleged Illegal Entry*, 153; Zhang, "Dragon in the Land," 349–50; and *AR-CGI* (1904) 149, 626.

80. Ralph, "Chinese Leak," 516–19, 522, 444.

81. "Wily Tricks Played by John Chinaman and His Smugglers," *Buffalo Express*, Mar. 4, 1904; "Three Chinamen Caught," *Buffalo Morning Express*, Jan. 29, 1901, p. 6; "Big Chinese Haul," ibid., Feb. 19, 1902, cited in "Scrapbook on Foreign Populations," vol. 1, Buffalo Public Library. On Bret Harte, see Robert Lee, *Orientals*, 39, 68–69, 91, and Takaki, *Iron Cages*, 223.

82. On statistics, see U.S. Senate, *Report of the Select Committee on Immigration and Naturalization*, 51st Cong., 1891, vii, cited in Ramirez, *Crossing the 49th Parallel*, 42, and *AR-CGI* (1902), 39. The illegal immigration of Europeans is further described in Marcus Braun to CGI, "Report," Feb. 12, 1907, File 52320/1, INSSC.

83. U.S. government officials' comments on Canadian immigration law can be found in *AR-CGI* (1902), 40–41, and *AR-CGI* (1909), 13.

84. *AR-ST* (1890), lxxv; *AR-ST* (1891), lxii; *AR-CGI* (1902), 40, 42.

85. *AR-ST* (1890), lxxvi; *AR-ST* (1891), lxiv–lxv; *AR-CGI* (1902), 71; Marcus Braun to CGI, "Report," Feb. 12, 1907, File 52320/1, INSSC.

86. Sánchez, *Becoming Mexican American*, 18–19. This attitude would change dramatically after 1924. As Mae Ngai has shown ("Architecture of Race," 91), Mexicans increasingly became characterized as dangerous foreigners and "illegal immigrants." On nativism directed toward Mexican immigrants, see Burnham, "Howl for Cheap Mexican Labor," 45, 48. On Mexicans as "birds of passage," see Cardoso, *Mexican Emigration*, 22; Sánchez, *Becoming Mexican American*, 20; and Hoffman, *Unwanted Mexican Americans*, 30–32.

87. U.S. Department of Justice, INS, "Early Immigrant Inspection."

88. Sánchez, *Becoming Mexican American*, 19–20; Hoffman, *Unwanted Mexican Americans*, 30–32; Reisler, *By the Sweat of Their Brow*, 8–13, 24–42.

89. Hart Hyatt North, Commissioner of Immigration, San Francisco to CGI, Mar. 9, 1905, File 13618, CGC; Metz, *Border*, 365.

90. For Chinese complaints from El Paso, see Ng Poon Chew to CGI, July 30, 1910, Folder 1, Box 3, NPCC. For Chinese described as "contraband," see F. H. Larned, "Memorandum for the Commissioner-General," Oct. 27, 1913, File 53371/2A, INSSC. On investigations of "chinks," see Letter from [signature illegible] to Brother Larned, Apr. 19, 1901, File 52730/53, ibid. The agree-

ment between the government and Edgar is outlined in F. H. Larned to Inspector in Charge, Seattle, Washington, Oct. 26, 1908, File 52214/1, pt. 4, ibid.

91. Perkins, *Border Patrol,* 9.

92. Rak, *Border Patrol,* 1.

93. Kaplan, "'Left Alone with America,'" 16–17.

94. Jacobson, *Barbarian Virtues,* 4, 6, 26–38.

95. *Chae Chan-ping v. United States,* 130 U.S. 606 (1889); *Fong Yue Ting v. United States,* 149 U.S. 698 (1893); Jacobson, *Barbarian Virtues,* 93. On the extension of Chinese exclusion to Hawaii and the Philippines, see Act of July 7, 1898 (30 Stat. 750); Act of Apr. 30, 1900 (31 Stat. 141); and Wu Ting-fang, Minister, Chinese Legation, to John Hay, Secretary of State, Dec. 12, 1898, Notes from the Chinese Legation in the U.S. to the Dept. of State, Records of the U.S. Department of State, RG 59, National Archives, Pacific Region, San Bruno, Calif.

96. Marcus Braun to CGI, "Report," Feb. 12, 1907, File 52320/1, and Frank P. Sargent, "Memorandum," c. 1905, File 52704/2, INSSC.

97. Descriptions of the U.S.-Canadian border as open and undefended can be found in Bennett and Kohl, *Settling the Canadian-American West,* 13; Gibbins, "Meaning and Significance of the Canadian-American Border," 315–32; Ralph, "Chinese Leak," 521; and De Loreme, "United States Bureau of Customs," 77–88.

98. McManus, "Their Own Country," 168–82; Ramirez, *Crossing the 49th Parallel,* 39.

99. For statistics on inspectors in 1902, see *AR-CGI* (1903), 46. For statistics for 1909, see Braun, "How Can We Enforce Our Exclusion Laws?," 140–42.

100. Harry E. Landis to U.S. Commissioner of Immigration, Montreal, Dec. 14, 1913, File 53371/72A, INSSC.

101. Ralph, "Chinese Leak," 516 (emphasis original).

102. Zhang, "Dragon in the Land," 373–76.

103. Falzone, *Terence V. Powderly,* 182.

104. The agreement underwent several revisions to permit additional transportation companies to become signatories and to perfect the implementation of its terms. At the same time, the U.S. government began to place inspectors along the border. Inspectors were stationed at Quebec, Montreal, Halifax, Vancouver, and Victoria beginning in 1895. On threats to close the border entirely, see *AR-CGI* (1904), 137. For the original Canadian Agreement, see Marian L. Smith, "Immigration and Naturalization Service," 127–47; "Canadian Agreement," Sept. 7, 1893, File 51564/4A-B, INSSC, and *AR-CGI* (1896), 13. Amended versions can be found in "Agreement Between the U.S. Commissioner-General of Immigration and Certain Transportation Lines of the Dominion of Canada," in *AR-CGI* (1902), 46–48, and Marcus Braun to CGI, "Report," Sept. 20, 1907, submitted by the Commissioner-General of Immigration, Oct. 9, 1907, File 51630/44D, p. 19, INSSC.

105. Marcus Braun to CGI, "Report," Sept. 20, 1907, File 51630/44D, pp. 30–34, INSSC.

106. *AR-CGI* (1902), 138; Marcus Braun to CGI, "Report," Sept. 20, 1907, File 51630/44D, pp. 29–30, INSSC; *AR-CGI* (1902), 52; U.S. Dept. of Commerce and Labor, Bureau of Immigration, *Facts Concerning the Enforcement,* 94.

107. On threats to close the border, see Marcus Braun to CGI, "Report," Sept. 20, 1907, File 51630/44D, p. 32, INSSC. Immigration officials cited the benefits of the agreement in "Memorandum in re Proposed Mexican Agreement" included in F. W. Berkshire, Supervising Inspector, San Antonio, Tex., to CGI, Jan. 15, 1908, File 51463/B, ibid.; *AR-CGI* (1904), 138; *AR-CGI* (1906), 94; and *AR-CGI* (1911), 159–60. On inland border inspection points, see Marian L. Smith, "Immigration and Naturalization Service," 127–35.

108. The term "induce" was first used in Marcus Braun to CGI, "Report," Feb. 12, 1907, File 52320/1, INSSC. Changes in immigrants' strategies at the border are described in Zhang, "Dragon in the Land," 323, and Marian L. Smith, "Immigration and Naturalization Service," 127–30. The discussion of the need for fuller cooperation from Canada can be found in *AR-ST* (1891), lxv.

109. For the 1903 Canadian law, see An Act Respecting and Restricting Chinese Immigration, ch. 8, 1903 S.C. 105–11 (Can.), and *AR-CGI* (1904), 138. On Canadian-U.S. negotiations, see, for example, John H. Clark, U.S. Commissioner of Immigration, Montreal, Canada, to U.S. CGI, July 16, 1912, File 51931/21, INSSC. On the 1923 Canadian law, see An Act Respecting Chinese Immigration, June 30, 1923, ch. 38, 1923 S.C. 301–15 (Can.), and Angus, "Canadian Immigration," 63–64.

110. Ward, *White Canada Forever*, 133; Wynne, "Reaction to the Chinese," 483.

111. U.S. Dept. of Commerce and Labor, Bureau of Immigration, *Facts Concerning the Enforcement*, 12–13.

112. McKinsey and Konrad, *Borderlands Reflections*, iii; Anzaldúa, *Borderlands*, 3; Hall and Coerver, *Revolution on the Border*, 7.

113. Marcus Braun to CGI, "Report," Feb. 12, 1907, File 52320/1, INSSC; Marcus Braun to CGI, June 10, 1907, File 52320/1-A, ibid.; Hu-DeHart, "Coolies, Shopkeepers, Pioneers," 92–98; Hu-DeHart, "Racism and Anti-Chinese Persecution," 16.

114. "Memorandum in re Proposed Mexican Agreement," included in F. W. Berkshire to CGI, Jan. 15, 1908, and "Memorandum" (Related to Mexican Agreement), Dec. 4, 1907, File 51463/B, INSSC.

115. Marcus Braun to CGI, June 10, 1907, p. 14, File 52320/1-A, ibid.

116. *AR-CGI* (1907), 112.

117. R. L. Pruett to Marcus Braun, May 11, 1902, File 52320/1-A, Exhibit "B," INSSC.

118. Grace Delgado ("In the Age of Exclusion," 241–42, 250–52) has found that inspectors regularly traveled into Sonora to obtain lists of Chinese entering Mexico through the port of Guaymas.

119. "Memorandum in re Proposed Mexican Agreement," included in F. W. Berkshire to CGI, Jan. 15, 1908, File 51463/B, INSSC.

120. Mexican historian Miguel Tinker Salas has described the Arizona-Sonora border during the Porfiriato as embodying "both the promise and peril of closer relations with the United States" (*In the Shadow of the Eagles*, 16, 161); see also Hall and Coerver, *Revolution on the Border*, 11, 15, and Delgado, "In the Age of Exclusion," 241–42, 250–52.

121. *AR-CGI* (1909), 142.

122. Ibid. (1907), 130.

123. Daniel J. Keefe to Supervising Inspector, El Paso, Tex., Nov. 26, 1909, File 52265/6; F. W. Berkshire to CGI, Feb. 15, 1910, File 52142/6; and Clarence A. Miller to Assistant Secretary of State, Washington, D.C., Oct. 11, 1909, File 52265/6, INSSC.

124. Marcus Braun to CGI, "Report," Feb. 12, 1907, File 52320/1, INSSC.

125. Frank R. Stone to F. W. Berkshire, Apr. 23, 1910, and F. W. Berkshire to CGI, May 7, 1910, File 52801/4A, ibid.

126. F. W. Berkshire to CGI, Aug. 22, 1907, File 52212/2, ibid.

127. Perkins, *Border Patrol*, 11, 23.

128. Richard H. Taylor to CGI, Oct. 24, 1908, File 52212/2, INSSC.

129. Inspector Miller to Inspector in Charge, Southern California, May 19, 1914, File 53788/1-D, ibid.

130. Perkins, *Border Patrol*, 9.

131. *AR-CGI* (1906), 95.

132. Marcus Braun to CGI, June 10, 1907, File 52320/1-A, INSSC.

133. H.R. 2915, "Preventing Immigration of Chinese Labor from Canada and Mexico," 1891, cited in Metz, *Border,* 364–65.

134. Myers, *Border Wardens,* 16–17; Rak, *Border Patrol,* 6; Perkins, *Border Patrol,* xii.

135. "The U.S. Border Patrol: The First Fifty Years," *I & N Reporter* (Summer 1974), 3.

136. Perkins, *Border Patrol,* 9; Myers, *Border Wardens,* 23; U.S. Department of Justice, INS, "Early Immigration Inspection."

137. Zhang, "Dragon in the Land of the Eagle," 372.

138. Perkins, *Border Patrol,* 9, 16, 18; *AR-CGI* (1910), 146.

139. *AR-CGI* (1907), 111.

140. Ibid. (1913), 255.

141. Ibid. (1906), 95.

142. Ibid. (1909), 132.

143. Ibid. (1904), 140.

144. "New Chinese Inspector," *El Paso Herald,* June 27, 1899, CGC.

145. Ibid.

146. Hart Hyatt North to CGI, Mar. 9, 1905, File 13618, ibid.

147. The exact figures in 1898 were 220 deported to 5,698 exempt-class immigrants admitted (excluding returning laborers and those in transit). In 1904, 783 Chinese were deported and 1,284 were admitted. A decrease in immigrants applying for admission should be factored in to this ratio of admissions to deportations (*AR-CGI* [1898–1904]).

148. U.S. Department of Justice, INS, "Early Immigration Inspection."

149. In an attempt to prevent the revolutionary violence in Mexico from "spill[ing] over," for example, the U.S. Army stationed soldiers every hundred yards between Nogales, Mexico, and Nogales, Arizona (Salas, *In the Shadow of the Eagles,* 171). Steamship passenger service between Asia and Mexico was also terminated during World War I and further decreased Chinese immigration to Mexico (Perkins, *Border Patrol,* 49).

150. *AR-CGI* (1905), 94; *AR-CGI* (1911), 146; Perkins, *Border Patrol,* 49.

151. The Act of Feb. 5, 1917, sec. 19, 39 Stat. 889; Frank P. Sargent, "Memorandum," c. 1905, File 52704/2, INSSC; Zhang "Dragon in the Land of the Eagle," 375–76.

152. McKenzie, *Oriental Exclusion,* 158.

153. Act of Feb. 27, 1925: Relating to the Border Patrol (43 Stat. 1049–50; 8 U.S.C. 110).

Chapter Six

1. Wu, "Chinatowns," 96. All names of individuals believed or proven to have entered the country illegally have been changed in this chapter.

2. *AR-CGI* (1909), 129.

3. Lucy Salyer concurs that government estimates are likely exaggerated. See Salyer, *Laws Harsh as Tigers,* 45.

4. North, "Chinese and Japanese Immigration," 343–50, and "Chinese Highbinder Societies in California," 19–31.

5. Interview nos. 45 and 12, SCCAOHP; Arthur Lem correspondence. See also Hsu, *Dreaming of Gold,* 71–72.

6. U.S. INS, *Annual Reports,* 1959–65, cited in H. Chen, "Chinese Immigration," 177.

7. *CR,* 52d Cong., 1st sess. (1892), p. 3567.

8. Harold Bolce to Commerce Secretary, May 29, 1905, File 53059/8, pp. 44–46, INSSC.

9. *AR-CGI* (1930), 1.

10. Siu, *Chinese Laundryman*, 106–21.

11. Data compiled by author and derived from a random sample survey of immigration records of Chinese individuals who entered the United States through the port of San Francisco from 1884 to 1941 (CAF, SF).

12. R. P. Schwerin to Acting Commerce Secretary, June 17, 1909, File 52270/21, INSSC.

13. Many contemporary migrants also seemingly justify illegal immigration in the face of laws that discriminate or long waiting periods to enter the U.S. through regular channels. See Martinez, *Troublesome Border*, 2–3.

14. Oscar Greenhalgh to Walter Chance, Mar. 16, 1899, File 52730/84, INSSC.

15. Interview with Mr. Henry A. Moore, Aug. 22, 1924, Document 219, SRR.

16. W. Chen, "Chinese under Both Exclusion and Immigration Laws," 437.

17. In 1906, a certificate cost over $100 (U.S. Dept. of Commerce and Labor, Bureau of Immigration, *Facts Concerning the Enforcement*, 53–55).

18. Ibid., 73–74.

19. *AR-CGI* (1909), 128.

20. M. R. Snyder to Commissioner of Immigration, New Orleans, Feb. 2, 1911, File 53161/2; Harry Davis to CGI, Sept. 7, 1909, File 52090/4; and George Baldwin to CGI, Apr. 6, 1909, File 52090/4, INSSC.

21. Richard Taylor to CGI, Apr. 20, 1912, File 52090/4D, INSSC; "Chinese Smuggling Trade Unearthed on Gulf Coast," *Daily Picayune* (New Orleans, La.), Jan. 5, 1909, in Daniel Keefe to the Assistant Commerce Secretary, Jan. 12, 1909, File 52229/1A, ibid.

22. Interview with Mr. Chew, No. 20, AIOHP; Hsu, *Dreaming of Gold*, 72.

23. Lum Bun Chong to Lau Ding Sing, Oct. 17, 1917, File 2, Box 1, DIF, SF.

24. Wong Bing Foon to Wong Som Gar, Oct. 6, 1914, ibid.

25. Interview with Gladys Huie; File 19586/43-12, CAF, SF.

26. Confession of Lee Wing Fon, July 12, 1968, in File 13861/13-3, ibid.

27. Confession of Chin Hing Kee, n.d., File 36715/8-28, ibid.

28. Confession of Lee Fong You, Sept. 6, 1968, in File 12832/8-18, ibid.

29. U.S. Congress, House, Select Committee, *Investigation of Chinese Immigration*, 271–72; Zhang, "Dragon in the Land of the Eagle," 320.

30. Interview with Mr. Chew, No. 20, AIOHP; Hsu, *Dreaming of Gold*, 91, 35–40, 150–51.

31. Soo Hoo Fong to Kam Tong, May 26, 1898, File 53108/9-B, INSSC.

32. Lo Yu Ting to Kam Tong, Oct. 23, 1898, ibid.

33. Angel Island Interviews, p. 21, BL.

34. Unsigned, undated coaching book, File 2, Box 1, DIF, SF.

35. Translated coaching book, in File 39262/11-6, CAF, SF.

36. Unsigned, undated coaching book, File 3, Box 1, DIF, SF.

37. Report to Treasury Dept., Mar. 21, 1899, File 52730/84, INSSC. See also Salyer, *Laws Harsh as Tigers*, 70.

38. Collector of Customs to Treasury Secretary, June 7, 1877, Press Copies of Letters from the Collector to the Secretary of the Treasury, 1870–1912, Records of the U.S. Bureau of Customs, RG 36, Port of San Francisco, National Archives, Pacific Region, San Bruno, Calif.

39. Report to Treasury Dept., Mar. 21, 1899, File 52730/84, INSSC.

40. *AR-CGI* (1906), 83–85.

41. O. L. Spaulding to Treasury Secretary, Nov. 2, 1885, CCF.

42. Yun Shang to Charlie Kee and Tsung Tseuk, no date, Box 1, H. H. North Papers, BL.

43. *San Francisco Call*, Mar. 9, 1899; File 52730/84, INSSC.

44. Report to Walter S. Chance, Mar. 21, 1899, File 52730/84, INSSC.

45. Albert H. Geffeney to H. H. North, Feb. 14, 1900, and Mar. 22, 1901, Folder 13, Box 1, H. H. North Papers, BL.

46. U.S. Dept. of Commerce and Labor, Bureau of Immigration, *Facts Concerning the Enforcement*, 20.

47. Mason S. Blackburn to H. H. North, Sept. 16, 1903, Folder 5, Box 1, H. H. North Papers, BL.

48. Report to Treasury Dept., Mar. 21, 1899, File 52730/84, INSSC.

49. Densmore's statistics are drawn from the confession of Agathon L. Hilkemeyer, Nov. 6, 1917, Box 1, DIF, SF.

50. Diaries of John Birge Sawyer, Aug. 15, 1917, vol. 2, pp. 159–61, BL.

51. Anonymous to J. B. Densmore, c. May 14, 1917, File 3, Box 3, DIF, SF; "Internal Memo," Nov. 10, 1917, File 9580/120, CAF, SF.

52. J. B. Densmore to the Attorney General, Dec. 26, 1917, File 54184/38, INSSC; Diaries of John Birge Sawyer, Aug. 15, 1917, vol. 2, p. 152, BL.

53. Interview with Wallace Lee.

54. Interview with Mr. Faris, Aug. 6, 1924, Document 190, SRR.

55. *AR-CGI* (1912), 57.

56. Oscar Greenhalgh to Treasury Secretary, Mar. 16, 1899, File 52730/84, INSSC.

57. See Zhang, "Dragon in the Land of the Eagle," 300, 304, 309–13; and Hsu, *Dreaming of Gold*, 76–77, 80–81.

58. U.S. Dept. of Commerce and Labor, Bureau of Immigration, *Facts Concerning the Enforcement*, 121–22.

59. "Memorandum," May 18, 1906, 5, File 52600/48, p. 5, INSSC.

60. Most Chinese who entered as citizens most likely steered away from registering to vote in order to avoid government scrutiny of their false papers.

61. Interview with Mr. Faris, Aug. 6, 1924, Document 190, SRR.

62. U.S. Dept. of Commerce and Labor, Bureau of Immigration, *Facts Concerning the Enforcement*, 122–24.

63. Ibid.; H. H. North to Chinese Inspector, Nov. 27, 1907, File 10211/192, CAF, SF; Interview with Paul Lee, "Love Letter to New York," New York Digital Design/New York Television, 2000.

64. U.S. Dept. of Commerce and Labor, Bureau of Immigration, *Facts Concerning the Enforcement*, 9.

65. *AR-CGI* (1931), 51. On the effects of the U.S. government's paper trail on the paper son system, see also Hsu, *Dreaming of Gold*, 74–85.

66. Interview with Mr. Yuen, Angel Island Interviews, BL.

67. Confession from Wong Jim Ping, File 34427/4-19, CAF, SF. See related files 34240/8-19, 34427/4-5, 23879/5-8, 22926/2-19, and 20828/102-2, ibid.

68. Some restrictions did apply. In the Supreme Court case of *Weedin v. Chin Bow*, 274 U.S. 657 (1927), the Court ruled that persons born to American parents who never resided in the United States were not of American nationality, thus not eligible for entry (*AR-CGI* [1928], 15–16).

69. *AR-CGI*, 1906–24, cited in Hsu, *Dreaming of Gold*, 79–80.

70. File 16431/5-8, INSSC. Madeline Hsu has also demonstrated the generational success of the paper son strategy. See Hsu, *Dreaming of Gold*, 81–83.

71. Confession of Ho Yin, Feb. 6, 1970, ibid.

72. Confession of Ho Gan Lit, Dec. 24, 1969, ibid.

73. Confession of Ho Hing, Nov. 30, 1971, ibid.

74. Interview with Immigration Inspector no. 3, File 49, AIOHP; McKeown, *Chinese Migrant Networks*, 32. Adam McKeown has found that the published rules and regulations governing Chinese admissions outline procedures that appear more lenient toward women. See U.S. Dept. of Labor, Bureau of Immigration, *Treaty, Laws, and Rules* (1915), 29, and McKeown, "Transnational Chinese Families," 85.

75. Chan, "Exclusion of Chinese Women," 118.

76. *AR-CGI* (1900), 46.

77. Edward Shaughnessy to the CGI, June 13, 1925, File 55452/385, INSSC.

78. Frank P. Sargent, "Memorandum," c. 1905, File 52704/2, ibid.

79. Rule 21, U.S. Dept. of Commerce and Labor, Bureau of Immigration, *Treaty, Laws, and Regulations* (1903); cited in Salyer, *Laws Harsh as Tigers*, 149. "Rules for the Government of Immigrant Inspectors and Boards of Special Inquiry," no date, H. H. North Papers, BL.

80. Smith and Herring, *Bureau of Immigration*, 35–36; untitled correspondence, Box 1, AIHF.

81. Chew, *Treatment of the Exempt Classes*, 1–2.

82. See, for example, the case of Louie Jung, in which immigrant inspector John Robinson made a special visit to the Oriental Public School in San Francisco to verify that he was in fact in attendance (John Robinson to Commissioner of Immigration, Sept. 29, 1917, File 16288/14-15, CAF, SF).

83. For details related to the board of special inquiry, see W. Chen, "Chinese under Both Exclusion and Immigration Laws," 101, and Him Mark Lai, "Island of Immortals," 98.

84. Wu, "Chinatowns," 105.

85. "Transcript of Stenographic Notes Taken on the Occasion of a Visit Paid the Angel Island Immigration Station," June 6, 1911, File 52961/24-D, INSSC.

86. *AR-CGI* (1926), 8; Lai, Lim, and Yung, *Island*, 113.

87. "Statement Sent to the San Francisco Chamber of Commerce by the Chinese Chamber of Commerce and the Six Companies," May 20, 1911, File 52961/24-C, INSSC.

88. File 34028/1923, CAF, SF.

89. Files 34427/4-19 and 34240/8-19, ibid.

90. "Transcript of Stenographic Notes Taken on the Occasion of a Visit Paid the Angel Island Immigration Station," June 6, 1911, File 52961/24-D, pp. 28–29, INSSC.

91. "Statement Sent to the San Francisco Chamber of Commerce by the Chinese Chamber of Commerce and the Six Companies," May 20, 1911, File 52961/24-C, ibid.

92. John D. Nagle, "Comment on Proposed Chinese General Order No. 11," Aug. 1927, File 55597/912, ibid.

93. Interrogation of Fong Hoy Kun, 1918, File A18485/7-97, CAF, SF.

94. The order was issued as a response to Chinese complaints about the length of interrogations. See Chinese General Order No. 11, Dec. 6, 1928, U.S. Dept. of Labor, Bureau of Immigration, "Chinese General Orders," courtesy of the INS History Office, Washington, D.C.

95. This procedure began as early as 1898. See, for example, File 9649/203, CAF, SF.

96. Files 10443/45, 34028/1923, and 34240/8-19, ibid.

97. See File 26002/1-8, ibid.

98. See Attorney George McGowan to the Commissioner of Immigration, San Francisco, July 3, 1917, in File 16288/14-15, ibid. For an extensive discussion of the "medical borders" created to process Chinese and other Asian immigrants on Angel Island, see Shah, *Contagious Divides*, 179–203.

99. File 23463/5-13, CAF, SF.

100. File 10079/6, ibid.

101. File 10442/137, ibid.

102. Connie Young Yu, "Rediscovered Voices," 127.

103. Chinese merchants and students in Hong Kong, China, to President William Taft, Mar. 20, 1910, File 52961/24, INSSC.

104. Chinese Chamber of Commerce and Chinese-American League of Justice, "Report of the Special Committee," File 53620/115, Jan. 4, 1913, ibid.

105. "Joint Report of Committee on Foreign Affairs of the Chamber of Commerce of San Francisco and of Committee on Trade and Commerce of the Merchants Exchange in the Matter of the Admission of Chinese at the Port of San Francisco," File 52961/24B, June 6, 1911, ibid.

106. *AR-CGI* (1909), 128–29.

107. Interview with Immigration Inspector at Angel Island, Felicia Lowe Collection, Asian American Studies Library, University of California, Berkeley; Interview with Ira Lee, Angel Island Interviews, BL.

108. Report to Treasury Dept., Mar. 21, 1899, File 52730/84, and Richard Taylor to CGI, Mar. 25, 1909, File 52270/21, INSSC.

109. File 55452/385, no date, INSSC.

110. Angel Island Interviews, pp. 3, 14, BL.

111. Interview with Mr. Tom, no. 23, AIOHP.

112. Interview with Mr. Chew, no. 20, and interview with Mr. Chan, no. 17, ibid.

113. Unfortunately for Yee You Tai, the letter was confiscated by immigration officials and used to deny entry to Yee (Translated Chinese letter, c. Feb. 6, 1905, File 10039-42, CAF, SF).

114. Unsigned, undated coaching note, File 3, Box 1, DIF, SF.

115. From File 12907/5-1, in File 4, Box 1, ibid.

116. Mary P. Corcoran (*Irish Illegals*, 143) discusses the normalization of illegal immigration among Irish immigrants in the 1990s.

117. Confession of Chew Lun Young, June 19, 1968, in File 10316/78, CAF, SF.

118. W. Chen, "Chinese under Both Exclusion and Immigration Laws," 426–27.

119. File 13043/3-24, CAF, SF.

120. Luther Steward to CGI, Jan. 9, 1911, File 52999/44-B, INSSC.

121. Him Mark Lai, "Island of Immortals," 98.

122. "Federal Immigration Conference," Mar. 26, 1928, cited in W. Chen, "Chinese under Both Exclusion and Immigration Laws," 403.

123. Yung, "Detainment at Angel Island"; W. Chen, "Chinese under Both Exclusion and Immigration Laws," 391–92.

124. W. Chen, "Chinese under Both Exclusion and Immigration Laws," 405, 476.

125. These poems are collected and translated in Lai, Lim, and Yung, *Island*.

126. Wu, "Chinatowns," 117–18.

127. Beginning in 1950, the U.S. government began to require Chinese emigrants to obtain travel documents from U.S. diplomatic agencies prior to the their arrival in the United States. Applicants were screened before a visa or passport was issued, but admission was not finally granted until immigration authorities of U.S. ports of entry also passed judgment on the applicant's claim to admission (Zhao, *Remaking Chinese America*, 153).

Part Four

1. Palumbo-Liu, *Asian/American*, 8, 38.

2. I borrow the concept of "disciplining the immigrant" from Earle, "Border Crossings," 407.

Chapter Seven

1. *AR-CGI* (1903), 90.

2. Act of May 6, 1882 (22 Stat. 58); W. Chen, "Chinese under Both Exclusion and Immigration Laws," 180–82; McKenzie, *Oriental Exclusion*, 164.

3. Aliens Act of June 25, 1798 (1 Stat. 570); Alien Enemy Act of July 6, 1798 (1 Stat. 577); Hutchinson, *Legislative History of American Immigration Policy,* 12–15, 80.

4. Hutchinson, *Legislative History of American Immigration Policy,* 80, 359–60.

5. Act of Sept. 13, 1888 (25 Stat., 476–77).

6. Act of May 5, 1892 (27 Stat. 25). The act also allowed for Chinese persons to be sent back to countries of which they were citizens. Prior to 1892, any Chinese person or person of Chinese descent who had been ordered deported had been automatically sent to China, regardless of their citizenship in another foreign country.

7. Rule 23, U.S. Dept. of Commerce and Labor, Bureau of Immigration, *Treaty, Laws, and Regulations* (1903), 39.

8. *Fong Yue Ting v. United States,* 149 U.S. 698 (1893). The decision in the case established three precepts: (1) The right of a nation to expel or deport foreigners as absolute and unqualified as the right to prohibit and prevent their entrance into the country. (2) Treaties establish no greater legal obligation than the acts of Congress, and Congress may exercise constitutional authority to pass an act even in contravention of the stipulations of a treaty. (3) The nature of expulsion is not a criminal proceeding but merely the removal of an alien from the country because his presence is deemed inconsistent with the public welfare. See W. Chen, "Chinese under Both Exclusion and Immigration Laws," 176–79, and McClain, *In Search of Equality,* 206–13.

9. W. Chen, "Chinese under Both Exclusion and Immigration Laws," 176; Palumbo-Liu, *Asian/American,* 24.

10. U.S. Dept. of Commerce and Labor, Bureau of Immigration, *Treaty, Laws, and Regulations* (1910), 53; Salyer, *Laws Harsh as Tigers,* 115.

11. W. Chen, "Chinese under Both Exclusion and Immigration Laws," 227–28.

12. U.S. Dept. of Commerce and Labor, Bureau of Immigration, *Treaty, Laws, and Regulations* (1905), 62; U.S. Dept. of Commerce and Labor, Bureau of Immigration, *Facts Concerning the Enforcement,* 62; W. Chen, "Chinese under Both Exclusion and Immigration Laws," 227–28.

13. U.S. Dept. of Commerce and Labor, Bureau of Immigration, *Treaty, Laws, and Regulations* (1910), 48–53.

14. Konvitz, *Alien and the Asiatic in American Law,* 55.

15. U.S. Dept. of Labor, Bureau of Immigration, *Treaty, Laws, and Rules* (1915), 42.

16. W. Chen, "Chinese under Both Exclusion and Immigration Laws," 179, 206–7.

17. Ibid., 176.

18. Life History and Social Document of Albert King, July 31, 1924, Document 193, SRR.

19. Wu, "Chinatowns," 135.

20. Chinese Chamber of Commerce and Chinese-American League of Justice, "Report of the Special Committee in Charge of Investigation of the Treatment of Chinese Residents and Immigrants by U.S. Immigration Officers," Jan. 4, 1913, File 53620/115, INSSC.

21. W. E. Howard to CGI, Mar. 27, 1903, File 6891, CGC.

22. J. H. Jenkins to Commerce Secretary, May 25, 1907, Folder 21, Box 1, H. H. North Papers, BL.

23. U.S. Dept. of Commerce and Labor, Bureau of Immigration, *Facts Concerning the Enforcement,* 128–29.

24. Foster, "Chinese Boycott," 122–23.

25. U.S. Dept. of Commerce and Labor, Bureau of Immigration, *Facts Concerning the Enforcement*, 129. See also K. Scott Wong, "'Eagle Seeks a Helpless Quarry,'" 81–103.

26. Coolidge, *Chinese Immigration*, 324.

27. "In Chinatown and China," *Nation* 121 (1925): 398, cited in Wu, "Chinatowns," 138.

28. Chinese Consolidated Benevolent Association to Woodrow Wilson, Oct. 10, 1918, File 53620/115-C, INSSC.

29. Native Sons of the Golden State to Julius Kahn, Oct. 24, 1923, File 55383/30, ibid.; see also Chinese Six Companies to the Secretary of Labor and to President Calvin Coolidge, ibid.

30. Hong Sling to Secretary of State, Oct. 20, 1900, File 2150, CGC; Testimony of J. W. Foster, U.S. Congress, House, Select Committee, *Investigation of Chinese Immigration*, 47–48.

31. U.S. Dept. of Commerce and Labor, Bureau of Immigration, *Facts Concerning the Enforcement*, 132.

32. Chinese Consul General to Inspector in Charge, Mar. 28, 1914, File 53620/115-A, INSSC (emphasis original).

33. See File 10277/45, CAF, SF.

34. See File 12020/21693, IF, SF. Wilkinson cited the 1933 case, *Haff v. Yung Poy*, in which the Northern California Circuit Court of Appeals ruled against the deportation of a merchant's son following his father's change in status. The court chastised the "absurdities and hardships" of a rule of law that would require deportation of the "hapless" and perchance "helpless" family of a merchant who, "because of illness, mishap, economic condition, or other misfortune," has been compelled to change his employment as a merchant and seek other employment. Later that year, the Bureau of Immigration eliminated its rule requiring maintenance of status.

35. Thomas D. Riordan to John H. Wise, Apr. 13, 1895, GCC.

36. Deposition of David A. Finn, Feb. 8, 1896, ibid.

37. U.S. Dept. of Commerce and Labor, Bureau of Immigration, *Facts Concerning the Enforcement*, 133.

38. Immigrant Inspector to Commissioner of Immigration, Aug. 5, 1922, File 20056/15-23, CAF, SF.

39. Collector of Customs to D. M. Pitts, Esq., July 13, 1896, GCOCC.

40. File 12020/13867, Box 1, IF, SF.

41. See File 12016/6339, CAF, SF.

42. File 12020/27145, IF, SF.

43. Anonymous to Commissioner of Immigration, June 9, 1919, File 2, Box 1, DIF, SF.

44. Inspector in Charge to Commissioner of Immigration, Oct. 25, 1923, File 55383/30, INSSC.

45. Unsigned Chinese letter to Charles Mehan, Jan. 11, 1910, File 10390/85, CAF, SF.

46. File 12020/18254, IF, SF.

47. File 10086/7885, CAF, SF.

48. Chinese Six Companies Announcement, Oct. 24, 1923, *Chinese World*, in File 55383/30, INSSC.

49. W. Chen, "Chinese under Both Exclusion and Immigration Laws," 213–14.

50. Siu, *Chinese Laundryman*, 199.

51. W. Chen, "Chinese under Both Exclusion and Immigration Laws," 459–60.

52. Siu, *Chinese Laundryman*, 123.

53. McKenzie, *Oriental Exclusion*, 167.

54. J. J. Davis, "A Century of Immigration," *Monthly Labor Review* 18 (1924): 13, cited in Wu, "Chinatowns," 81–82.

55. H. Chen, "Chinese Immigration," 188–90.

56. Lim P. Lee, "Sociological Data," *Chinese Digest*, Oct. 23, 1936.

57. Fong, "Asian Women Lose Citizenship," 12; Chan, "Exclusion of Chinese Women," 128–29.

58. Interview with Kaimon Chin, Nov. 13, 1995.

59. The alien and minor children of merchants were also deemed excludable because they were ineligible for citizenship. Chinese leaders and their lawyers eventually brought a case before the Supreme Court to challenge the new provisions of the 1924 act. On May 25, 1925, the Court affirmed that alien wives ineligible to citizenship—even those who were wives of American citizens—were excluded by the Act of 1924 (*Chang Chan et al v. Nagle* [69 L. ed. 642]). On the same date, the Court decided that the alien Chinese wives and minor children of domiciled alien Chinese merchants could enter the country for permanent residence as nonquota immigrants (*Charles sum Shee et al v. Nagle* [69 L. ed. 640]). One result of these decisions was that they gave greater rights to the alien Chinese residents in the United States than it accorded to American citizens of the Chinese race.

60. File 37775/9-25, CAF, SF.

61. On the history of the organization, which later renamed itself the Chinese American Citizens Alliance, see Chung, "Fighting for their American Rights," 95–126.

62. S. G. Carpenter to Secretary of Commerce, Sept. 23, 1910, File 52961/24-B, INSSC.

63. Native Sons of the Golden State to Honorable Julius Kahn, Oct. 24, 1923, File 55383/30, INSSC. The Chinese Six Companies sent a similar telegram to the secretary of labor. See Chinese Six Companies to the Secretary of Labor and to President Calvin Coolidge, ibid.

64. Louis King, "Study of American-Born and American-Reared Chinese in Los Angeles," 127.

65. Interview with unnamed Chinese American citizen, 1924, Document 186, SRR.

66. Wu, "Chinatowns," 288.

67. See also Zhang, "Dragon in the Land of the Eagle," 300.

68. Siu, *Chinese Laundryman*, 198.

69. Wong and Klein, "False Papers, Lost Lives," 368–74.

70. Interview with Kaimon Chin.

71. U.S. Department of Justice, Immigration and Naturalization Service, *Chinese Investigations;* Ngai, "Legacies of Exclusion," 3–35.

72. Arthur Lem correspondence.

73. Ibid.

74. U.S. INS, *Annual Reports*, 1959–65, cited in H. Chen, "Chinese Immigration," 177.

75. Wong and Klein, "False Papers, Lost Lives."

Epilogue

1. "An Act to Repeal the Chinese Exclusion Acts, To Establish Quotas, and For Other Purposes," Act of Dec. 17, 1943 (57 Stat. 600; 8 U.S.C. 212[a]).

2. Despite the small quota allocated to Chinese immigrants, Chinese could continue to enter as nonquota immigrants if they were returning U.S. citizens or residents returning from visits abroad. Members of certain professional classes were also allowed in outside of the quota. Ministers and professors and their wives and minor children were nonquota immigrants, as were students and the wives and minor children of U.S. citizens (Riggs, *Pressures on Congress;* Reimers, *Still the Golden Door*, 11–15).

3. Bennett, *American Immigration Policies*, 63–64, 79–80, 81, 86–87.

4. On the dramatic changes occurring in the Chinese American community following World War II, see Zhao, *Remaking Chinese America*, chs. 3 and 4, and Reimers, *Still the Golden Door*, 28.

5. Immigration and Nationality Act, Oct. 3, 1965 (79 Stat. 911).

6. Siu, *Chinese Laundryman*, 206.

7. Act of Aug. 3, 1882, ch. 367 (22 Stat. 214).

8. The Alien Contract Labor Law is also known as the Foran Act (23 Stat. 332).

9. Immigration Act of 1891 (26 Stat. 1084).

10. Immigration Act of 1903 (32 Stat. 1203, sec. 2); Immigration Act of 1907 (34 Stat. 898).

11. Quota Act of 1921 (42 Stat. 5, sec. 2); Immigration Act of 1924 (43 Stat. 153). See generally Higham, *Strangers in the Land*, 308–24; Ngai, "Architecture of Race"; and Hing, *Making and Remaking Asian America*, 30–36.

12. Divine, *American Immigration Policy*, 60; Melendy, "Filipinos in the United States," 115–16, 119–25. One recent estimate places the number of Mexicans, including their American-born children, returned to Mexico during the 1930s at one million (Balderrama and Rodriguez, *Decade of Betrayal*, 122).

13. Daniels, *Coming to America*, 338.

14. Reimers, *Still the Golden Door*, 84–90; Daniels, *Coming to America*, 340–41.

15. Chou and Dunn, "Simpson/Mazzoli." My thanks to Judy Yung for this citation. On the Simpson/Mazzoli provision in general, see Daniels, "Two Cheers for Immigration," 52.

16. *San Francisco Chronicle*, Dec. 17, 1993.

17. Hagan, "Commentary," 357.

18. Sánchez, "Face the Nation," 373.

19. Gary Imhoff, a former official of the INS, co-wrote *Immigration Time Bomb*—one of the most well-known nativist books of the 1980s—with Richard Lamm, governor of Colorado. Moreover, Harold Ezzell, who was an INS official in the 1980s, was co-author of California's Proposition 187, and Bill King, a former INS border patrol agent, was co-founder of the anti-immigrant organization called "Save our State" (Perea, *Immigrants Out*, 67).

20. Gotanda, "Race, Citizenship," 253.

21. Perea, *Immigrants Out*, 73.

22. Corcoran, *Irish Illegals*, 144.

23. Kwong, *Forbidden Workers*; Ko-lin Chin, *Smuggled Chinese*; Paul J. Smith, ed., *Human Smuggling*.

24. Johnson, "Race, the Immigration Laws," 1137.

25. Garcia, "Critical Race Theory"; Johnson, "Race Matters," 525–57.

26. The bill, known as the Citizen Reform Act of 1997, was introduced by Republicans in the House of Representatives led by Rep. Brian Bilbray (R.-San Diego). The bill also sought to deny U.S. citizenship to foreign students without immigrant visas and anyone else who was here legally but without permanent status, such as refugees. See Brian Bilbray, "Clarifying America's Citizenship Laws," *San Diego Union-Tribune*, Aug. 17, 1997; "Boxer Hits Bilbray Bill on Automatic Citizenship," *San Diego Union-Tribune*, July 4, 1997; and William Wong, "Editorial," *San Francisco Examiner*, Apr. 10, 1998.

27. "Congress Finishes Major Legislation," *Washington Post*, Oct. 1, 1996; "At the Justice Dept., Big Government Keeps Getting Bigger," ibid., Apr. 5, 1996; "Immigration Overhaul," *Migration News* 3, no. 10 (Oct. 1996), <http://migration.ucdavis.edu/mn/archive_mn/oct_1996-01mn.html> (Jan. 11, 2002); "Ambivalence Prevails in Immigration Policy," *New York Times*, May 27, 2001.

28. Andreas, *Border Games*, 347–50.

29. "In the Desert, A Drink of Mercy, Protest," *Washington Post*, June 11, 2001.

30. Associated Press, "US Border Patrol Crackdown."

31. National Network for Immigrant and Refugee Rights, "Portrait of Injustice."

32. "Doctors, Spaghetti and My American Wife," *New York Times,* June 7, 1993, cited in Salyer, *Laws Harsh as Tigers,* 247.

33. See Salyer, *Laws Harsh as Tigers,* 247.

34. *San Francisco Chronicle,* Nov. 6, 1990; *New York Times,* Nov. 11, 1990; *New York Times,* July 15, 1998.

35. *San Francisco Chronicle,* May 15, 1991; Dec. 17, 1993; June 14, 1999.

36. On America's ambivalence in contemporary immigration policy, see "Ambivalence Prevails in Immigration Policy," *New York Times,* May 27, 2001.

Afterword

1. "Swept up in Dragnet, Hundreds Sit in Custody and Ask, 'Why?,'" *New York Times,* Nov. 25, 2001; "Al Qaeda Link Seen in Only a Handful of 1,200 Detainees," *New York Times,* Nov. 29, 2001.

2. "Attacks and Harassment of Middle-Eastern Americans Rising," *New York Times,* Sept. 14, 2001; "Violence and Harassment: Victims of Mistaken Identity, Sikhs Pay a Price for Turbans," *New York Times,* Sept. 19, 2001; "Lax U.S. Visa Laws Give Terrorists Easy Entry — Immigrants Difficult to Track as They Blend into Ethnic Communities," *Detroit News,* Sept. 30, 2001.

3. "U.S. Has Covered 200 Campuses to Check up on Mideast Students," *New York Times,* Nov. 12, 2001.

4. "House Passes Terrorism Bill Much Like Senate's, but with 5-Year Limit," *New York Times,* Oct. 13, 2001.

5. "U.S. Makes It Easier to Detain Foreigners," *New York Times,* Nov. 28, 2001.

6. "Bush's New Rules to Fight Terror Transform the Legal Landscape," *New York Times,* Nov. 25, 2001.

7. The U.S. Border Patrol arrested 11,000 people for illegally crossing the U.S.-Canadian border in 2000. Approximately one million were arrested along the U.S.-Mexican border. See "11,000 Arrested Last Year Trying to Sneak into the U.S.," *National Post* (Ontario, Can.), Nov. 7, 2001; "Nation's Open Borders in Spotlight," *Chicago Tribune,* Sept. 26, 2001, 9; "Support for U.S. Security Plans Is Quietly Voiced across Canada," *New York Times,* Oct. 1, 2001; Dennis Bueckert, "Canadian Sovereignty Called into Question in Fight against Terrorism," Oct. 3, 2001, Canadian Press Newswire; "Border Painted as Magnet for Terror," *National Post* (Ontario, Can.), Oct. 4, 2001; "Vast U.S.-Canada Border Suddenly Poses a Problem," *New York Times,* Oct. 4, 2001; and "Bills Would Tighten U.S.-Canada Border," *Seattle Times,* Oct. 10, 2001.

8. "Bordering on Harmonization: Why Canada Faces Pressure," *National Post* (Ontario, Can.), Oct. 1, 2001; "Mexico's Security Advisor Gives Border Cooperation a Thumbs Up," Nov. 19, 2001.

BIBLIOGRAPHY

Unpublished Materials

Asian American Studies Center, University of California, Los Angeles
  Southern California Chinese American Oral History Project
Asian American Studies Library, University of California, Berkeley
  Angel Island Interviews, Felicia Lowe Collection
  Angel Island Oral History Project
  Ng Poon Chew Collection
Bancroft Library, University of California, Berkeley
  Angel Island Interviews
  Papers of Hart Hyatt North
  Diaries of John Birge Sawyer
  Correspondence and Papers of Frederick Stratton
Boston Public Library, Boston, Massachusetts
  Immigration Restriction League Scrapbooks, 1894–1912
Hoover Institution on War, Revolution, and Peace, Stanford University
  Survey of Race Relations: A Canadian-American Study of the Oriental on the Pacific Coast
National Archives, Northeast Region, New York, New York
  Records of the U.S. Bureau of Customs. RG 36. Correspondence, Port of Ogdensburg, New York, 1872–1928.
  Records of the U.S. Bureau of Customs. RG 36. Correspondence, Circulars, Telegrams, Reports, Port of Ogdensburg, New York, 1866–1919.

Records of the U.S. Immigration and Naturalization Service. RG 85. Chinese Exclusion Case Files, New York.

National Archives, Pacific Alaska Region, Seattle, Washington

Records of the U.S. Immigration and Naturalization Service. RG 85. Chinese Exclusion Case Files, 1895–1943, Seattle.

National Archives, Pacific Region, San Bruno, California

Records of the U.S. Bureau of Customs. RG 36. Correspondence from the Collector to Other Federal Agencies and the General Public, 1895–1915, Port of San Francisco.

Records of the U.S. Bureau of Customs. RG 36. General Correspondence from the Office of the Collector of Customs, 1869–1931, Port of San Francisco.

Records of the U.S. Bureau of Customs. RG 36. General Correspondence to the Office of the Collector, 1894–1928, Port of San Francisco.

Records of the U.S. Bureau of Customs. RG 36. Press Copies of Letters from the Collector to the Secretary of the Treasury, 1870–1912, Port of San Francisco.

Records of the U.S. Department of State. RG 59. Notes from the Chinese Legation in the United States to the Department of State, 1868–1906.

Records of the U.S. District Court. RG 21. Admiralty Case Files, 1851–1934, Northern District of California, San Francisco.

Records of the U.S. Immigration and Naturalization Service. RG 85. Angel Island Historical Files, 1894–1941, San Francisco.

Records of the U.S. Immigration and Naturalization Service. RG 85. Case Files of Investigations Resulting in Warrant Proceedings (12020), 1912–50, San Francisco.

Records of the U.S. Immigration and Naturalization Service. RG 85. Chinese Arrival Files, San Francisco and Honolulu.

Records of the U.S. Immigration and Naturalization Service. RG 85. Densmore Investigation Files (1917), San Francisco.

Records of the U.S. Immigration and Naturalization Service. RG 85. Return Certificate Application Case Files of Chinese Departing, 1913–44, San Francisco.

National Archives, Washington, D.C.

Records of the U.S. Department of State. RG 59. Notes from Foreign Consuls, 1789–1906.

Records of the U.S. Immigration and Naturalization Service. RG 85. Chinese General Correspondence, 1898–1908.

Records of the U.S. Immigration and Naturalization Service. RG 85. Customs Case File No. 3358d Related to Chinese Immigration, 1877–91.

Records of the U.S. Immigration and Naturalization Service. RG 85. Scrapbooks, 1902–5.

Records of the U.S. Immigration and Naturalization Service. RG 85. Subject Correspondence, 1906–32.

Author Interviews and Correspondence

Correspondence with Arthur Lem, January 13, 1996

Interview with Kaimon Chin, November 13, 1995

Interview with Gladys Huie, September 9, 1993

Interview with Mary Lee, February 20, 1990

Interview with Wallace Lee, February 20, 1990

Interview with Mr. Low, November 14, 1995

Dissertations, Theses, and Papers

Chen, Helen. "Chinese Immigration into the United States: An Analysis of Changes in Immigration Policies." Ph.D. dissertation, Brandeis University, 1980.

Chen, Wen-hsien. "Chinese under Both Exclusion and Immigration Laws." Ph.D. dissertation, University of Chicago, 1940.

Delgado, Grace. "In the Age of Exclusion: Race, Region and Chinese Identity in the Making of the Arizona-Sonora Borderlands, 1863–1943." Ph.D. dissertation, University of California, Los Angeles, 2000.

Gee, Jennifer. "Asian Immigrants and the Angel Island Immigration Station, 1910–1940." Ph.D. dissertation, Stanford University, 1999.

Giovinco, Joseph. "The California Career of Anthony Caminetti: Italian American Politician." Ph.D. dissertation, University of California, Berkeley, 1973.

Janisch, Hudson N. "The Chinese, the Courts, and the Constitution: A Study of the Legal Issues Raised by Chinese Immigration to the United States, 1850–1902." J.S.D. dissertation, University of Chicago, 1971.

King, Louis Kit. "A Study of American-Born and American-Reared Chinese in Los Angeles." Master's thesis, University of Southern California, 1931.

Liu, Fu-ju. "A Comparative Demographic Study of Native-Born and Foreign-Born Chinese Populations in the United States." Ph.D. dissertation, University of Michigan, 1953.

Masur, Kate. "Reconstructing the Nation's Capital: The Politics of Race, Citizenship, and Government in the District of Columbia, 1862–1878." Ph.D. dissertation, University of Michigan, 2001.

Ngai, Mae. "Illegal Aliens and Alien Citizens: United States Immigration Policy and Racial Formation, 1924–1945." Ph.D. dissertation, Columbia University, 1998.

Selig, Diana. "Lapses from Virtue: Immigrants, Authorities, and the Moral Exclusion Laws." Unpublished paper in possession of author.

Truett, Samuel. "Neighbors by Nature: The Transformation of Land and Life in the U.S.-Mexico Borderlands, 1854–1910." Ph.D. dissertation, Yale University, 1997.

Wong, Sandra. "'For the Sake of Kinship': The Overseas Chinese Family." Ph.D. dissertation, Stanford University, 1987.

Wu, Ching Chao. "Chinatowns: A Study of Symbiosis and Assimilation." Ph.D. dissertation, University of Chicago, 1928.

Wynne, Robert E. "Reaction to the Chinese in the Pacific Northwest and British Columbia, 1850–1910." Ph.D. dissertation, University of Washington, 1964.

Zhang, Qingsong. "Dragon in the Land of the Eagle: The Exclusion of Chinese from U.S. Citizenship." Ph.D. dissertation, University of Virginia, 1994.

Published Materials

Abbott, Edith. *Historical Aspects of the Immigration Problem.* Chicago: University of Chicago Press, 1926.

Almaguer, Tomás. *Racial Fault Lines: The Historical Origins of White Supremacy in California.* Berkeley: University of California Press, 1994.

Anderson, Kay J. *Vancouver's Chinatown: Racial Discourse in Canada, 1875–1980.* Montreal: McGill-Queen's University Press, 1991.

Andreas, Peter. *Border Games: Policing the U.S.-Mexico Divide.* Ithaca: Cornell University Press, 2000.

Angus, H. F. "Canadian Immigration: The Law and Its Administration." In *The Legal Status of*

Aliens in Pacific Countries, edited by Norman MacKenzie, 58–75. Toronto: Oxford University Press, 1937.

Anzaldúa, Gloria. *Borderlands: La Frontera; The New Mestiza.* San Francisco: Spinsters/Aunt Lute, 1987.

Asiatic Exclusion League of North America. "Proceedings of the Asiatic Exclusion League," February 1908. San Francisco: Allied Printing, 1908.

———. "Proceedings of the Asiatic Exclusion League," December 1908. San Francisco: Allied Printing, 1908.

———. "Proceedings of the Asiatic Exclusion League," July 1911. San Francisco: Allied Printing, 1911.

Associated Press. "US Border Patrol Crackdown Targets Immigrant Smugglers," March 13, 2001, *Migration News* 8, no. 4 (April 2001), <http://migration.ucdavis.edu>. May 1, 2001.

Balderrama, Francisco E., and Raymond Rodriguez. *Decade of Betrayal: Mexican Repatriation in the 1930s.* Albuquerque: University of New Mexico Press, 1995.

Barkan, Elliott, and Michael LeMay, eds. *U.S. Immigration and Naturalization Laws and Issues.* Westport, Conn.: Greenwood Press, 1999.

Barrett, James, and David Roediger. "Inbetween Peoples: Race, Nationality and the 'New Immigrant' Working Class." *Journal of American Ethnic History* 16, no. 3 (1997): 3–44.

Barth, Gunther. *Bitter Strength: A History of the Chinese in the United States, 1850–1870.* Cambridge: Cambridge University Press, 1964.

Behdad, Ali. "INS and Outs: Producing Delinquency at the Border." *Aztlan* 23, no. 1 (Spring 1998): 103–13.

Bennett, David. *The Party of Fear: From Nativist Movements to the New Right in American History.* Chapel Hill: University of North Carolina Press, 1988.

Bennett, John W., and Seena B. Kohl. *Settling the Canadian-American West, 1890–1915: Pioneer Adaptation and Community Building.* Lincoln: University of Nebraska Press, 1995.

Bennett, Marion T. *American Immigration Policies: A History.* Washington: Public Affairs Press, 1963.

Bernard, William S., ed. *American Immigration Policy: A Reappraisal.* New York: Harper, 1948.

Braun, Marcus. "How Can We Enforce Our Exclusion Laws?" *Annals of the American Academy of Political and Social Science* 34, no. 2 (September 1909): 360–62.

Burdette, Robert J. *American Biography and Genealogy, California Edition.* Chicago: Lewis Publishing Co., 191-.

Burnham, Frederick Russell. "The Howl for Cheap Mexican Labor." In *The Alien in Our Midst or Selling Our Birthright for a Mess of Pottage*, edited by Madison Grant and Charles Stewart Davison. New York: Galton Publishing, 1930.

Cahan, Abraham. *Yekl; A Tale of the New York Ghetto.* New York: Appleton, 1896.

Calavita, Kitty. "The Paradoxes of Race, Class, Identity, and 'Passing': Enforcing the Chinese Exclusion Acts, 1882–1910." *Law and Social Inquiry* 25, no. 1 (Winter 2000): 1–40.

California State Senate. Special Committee on Chinese Immigration. *Chinese Immigration: Its Social, Moral, and Political Effect.* Sacramento: State Office of Printing, 1878.

Canadian Royal Commission on Chinese and Japanese Immigration. *Report of the Royal Commission on Chinese and Japanese Immigration.* Ottawa, 1902. Reprint, Arno Press, 1978.

Cardoso, Lawrence. *Mexican Emigration to the United States, 1891–1931.* Tucson: University of Arizona Press, 1980.

Chan, Sucheng. *Asian Americans: An Interpretive History.* Boston: Twayne, 1991.

———. "The Exclusion of Chinese Women, 1875–1943." In *Entry Denied: Exclusion and the Chi-*

nese Community in America, 1882–1943, edited by Sucheng Chan, 94–146. Philadelphia: Temple University Press, 1991.

———. *This Bittersweet Soil: The Chinese in California Agriculture, 1860–1910.* Berkeley: University of California Press, 1986.

———. "The Writing of Asian American History." *Organization of American Historians Magazine of History* 10, no. 4 (Summer 1996): 8–17.

———, ed. *Entry Denied: Exclusion and the Chinese Community in America, 1882–1943.* Philadelphia: Temple University Press, 1991.

Chan, Sucheng, and K. Scott Wong, eds. *Claiming America: Constructing Chinese American Identities during the Exclusion Era.* Philadelphia: Temple University Press, 1998.

Chang, Robert. *Disoriented: Asian Americans, Law, and the Nation-State.* New York: New York University Press, 1999.

Chen, Yong. *Chinese San Francisco: A Trans-Pacific Community, 1850–1943.* Stanford: Stanford University Press, 2000.

Cheng, Lucie. "Free, Indentured, Enslaved: Chinese Prostitutes in 19th Century America." *Signs: Journal of Women in Culture and Society* 5 (1979): 23–29.

Chin, Ko-lin. *Smuggled Chinese: Clandestine Immigration to the United States.* Philadelphia: Temple University Press, 1999.

Chin, Tung Pok, with Winifred C. Chin. *Paper Son: One Man's Story.* Edited by K. Scott Wong. Philadelphia: Temple University Press, 2000.

Chou, Donald, and Patricia A. Dunn. "Simpson/Mazzoli: The Exclusion Act of 1982?" *Bridge* (Summer 1982): 15–17, 46.

Chung, Sue Fawn. "Fighting for Their American Rights: A History of the Chinese American Citizens Alliance." In *Claiming America: Constructing Chinese American Identities during the Exclusion Era,* edited by K. Scott Wong and Sucheng Chan, 95–126. Philadelphia: Temple University Press, 1998.

Cinel, Dino. *The National Integration of Italian Return Migration, 1870–1929.* Cambridge: Cambridge University Press, 1991.

Con, Harry, and Edgar Wickberg. *From China to Canada: A History of the Chinese Communities in Canada.* Toronto: McClelland and Stewart, 1982.

Condit, Ira M. *The Chinaman as We See Him and Fifty Years of Work for Him.* New York: F. H. Revell Co., 1900.

Coolidge, Mary Roberts. *Chinese Immigration.* New York: Henry Holt and Co., 1909.

Corcoran, Mary P. *Irish Illegals: Transients between Two Societies.* Westport, Conn.: Greenwood Press, 1993.

Craib, Raymond B. "Chinese Immigrants in Porfirian Mexico: A Preliminary Study of Settlement, Economic Activity and Anti-Chinese Sentiment." Research Paper Series No. 28. Albuquerque, N.Mex.: Latin American Institute, May 1996.

Crenshaw, Kimberlé, Neil Gotanda, Gary Peller, and Kendall Thomas, eds. *Critical Race Theory: The Key Writings That Formed the Movement.* New York: New Press, 1995.

Cumberland, Charles C. "The Sonora Chinese and the Mexican Revolution." *Hispanic American Historical Review* 40, no. 2 (May 1960): 191–211.

Daniels, Roger. *Asian America: Chinese and Japanese in the United States since 1850.* Seattle: University of Washington Press, 1988.

———. *Coming to America: A History of Immigration and Ethnicity in American Life.* New York: Harper Collins, 1990.

————. "No Lamps Were Lit for Them: Angel Island and the Historiography of Asian American Immigration." *Journal of American Ethnic History* 17, no. 1 (Fall 1997): 3–18.

————. *The Politics of Prejudice: The Anti-Japanese Movement in California and the Struggle for Japanese Exclusion.* Berkeley: University of California Press, 1962.

————. "Two Cheers for Immigration." In *Debating American Immigration, 1882–Present,* by Roger Daniels and Otis L. Graham, 5–72. Lanham, Md.: Rowman & Littlefield, 2001.

————. "Westerners from the East: Oriental Immigrants Reappraised." *Pacific Historical Review* 35 (1966): 373–83.

Delgado, Richard, and Jean Stefancic, eds. *Critical Race Theory: The Cutting Edge.* Philadelphia: Temple University Press, 2000.

De Loreme, Roland L. "The United States Bureau of Customs and Smuggling on Puget Sound, 1851 to 1913." *Prologue* 5, no. 2 (1973): 77–83.

Deverell, William. "Fighting Words: The Significance of the American West in the History of the United States." In *A New Significance: Re-envisioning the History of the American West,* edited by Clyde Milner, 29–55. New York: Oxford University Press, 1996.

Divine, Robert A. *American Immigration Policy, 1924–1952.* New York: Da Capo Press, 1957.

Dunn, Timothy J. *The Militarization of the U.S.-Mexico Border, 1978–1992: Low-Intensity Conflict Doctrine Comes Home.* Austin: University of Texas Press, 1996.

Earle, Duncan M. "Border Crossings, Border Control: Illegalized Migrants from the Other Side." In *Illegal Immigration in America: A Reference Handbook,* edited by David W. Haines and Karen E. Rosenblum, 396–411. Westport, Conn.: Greenwood Press, 1999.

Edholm, M. G. C. "A Stain on the Flag." *California Illustrated Magazine,* February 1892. In *Unbound Voices: A Documentary History of Chinese Women in San Francisco,* edited by Judy Yung, 159–70. Berkeley: University of California Press, 1999.

Evans, Peter B., Dietrich Rueschemeyer, and Theda Skocpol, eds. *Bringing the State Back In.* Cambridge. Cambridge University Press, 1985.

Falzone, Vincent. *Terence V. Powderly: Middle Class Reformer.* Washington, D.C.: University Press of America, 1927.

Fitzgerald, Keith. *Face the Nation: Immigration, the State, and the National Identity.* Stanford: Stanford University Press, 1996.

Foley, Neil. *The White Scourge: Mexicans, Blacks, and Poor Whites in Texas Cotton Culture.* Berkeley: University of California Press, 1997.

Fong, Kathryn M. "Asian Women Lose Citizenship." *San Francisco Journal,* December 29, 1976, 12.

Foster, John W. "The Chinese Boycott." *Atlantic Monthly* 97 (1906): 118–27.

Foucault, Michel. "Governmentality." In *The Foucault Effect: Studies in Governmentality,* edited by Graham Burchell, Colin Gordon, and Peter Miller, 99–102. Chicago: University of Chicago Press, 1991.

Friday, Chris. "'In Due Time': Narratives of Race and Place in the Western U.S." In *Race, Ethnicity, and Nationality in the United States: Toward the Twenty-first Century,* edited by Paul Wong, 102–52. Boulder, Colo.: Westview Press, 1999.

————. *Organizing Asian American Labor: The Pacific Coast Canned-Salmon Industry, 1870–1942.* Philadelphia: Temple University Press, 1994.

Fritz, Christian G. "A Nineteenth Century 'Habeas Corpus Mill': The Chinese before the Federal Courts in California." *American Journal of Legal History* 32 (October 1988): 347–72.

Fry, Luther. "Illegal Entry of Orientals into the United States between 1910 and 1920." *Journal of the American Statistical Association* 23, no. 162 (June 1928): 173–77.

Gabaccia, Donna. "Do We Still Need Immigration History?" *Polish American Studies* 55, no. 1 (1998): 45–68.

———. *From the Other Side: Women, Gender, and Immigration Life in the U.S., 1820–1990.* Bloomington: Indiana University Press, 1994.

———. "Is Everywhere Nowhere? Nomads, Nations, and the Immigrant Paradigm of United States History." *Journal of American History* 86, no. 3 (1999): 1115–34.

———. "The 'Yellow Peril' and the 'Chinese of Europe': Global Perspectives on Race and Labor, 1815–1930." In *Migration, Migration History, History: Old Paradigms and New Perspectives,* edited by Jan Lucassen and Leo Lucassen, 177–96. Bern, N.Y.: Peter Lang, 1999.

Garcia, Ruben J. "Critical Race Theory and Proposition 187: The Racial Politics of Immigration Law." *Chicano-Latino Law Review* 17 (Fall 1995): 118–54.

Gerstle, Gary. *American Crucible: Race and Nation in the Twentieth Century.* Princeton: Princeton University Press, 2001.

———. "Liberty, Coercion, and the Making of Americans." In *The Handbook of International Migration: The American Experience,* edited by Charles Hirschman, Philip Kasinitz, and Josh DeWind, 275–93. New York: Russell Sage Foundation, 1999.

Gibbins, Roger. "Meaning and Significance of the Canadian-American Border." In *Border and Border Regions in Europe and North America,* edited by Paul Ganster et al., 315–32. San Diego: San Diego State University Press, 1997.

Gjerde, Jon. "New Growth on Old Vines: The State of the Field: The Social History of Immigration to and Ethnicity in the United States." *Journal of American Ethnic History* 18, no. 4 (Summer 1999): 40–65.

Glazer, Nathan. *Clamor at the Gates: The New American Immigration.* San Francisco: ICS Press, 1985.

Glenn, Evelyn Nakano. "Split Household, Small Producer and Dual Wage Earner: An Analysis of Chinese American Family Strategies." *Journal of Marriage and the Family* (February 1983): 35–46.

Gompers, Samuel. "Some Reasons for Chinese Exclusion — Meat vs. Rice — American Manhood against Asiatic Coolieism — Which Shall Survive?" Washington: American Federation of Labor, GPO, 1902.

Gotanda, Neil. "Exclusion and Inclusion: Immigration and American Orientalism." In *Across the Pacific: Asian Americans and Globalization,* edited by Evelyn Hu-DeHart, 129–51. Philadelphia: Temple University Press, 1999.

———. "Race, Citizenship, and the Search for Political Community among 'We the People': A Review Essay on Citizenship without Consent." *Oregon Law Review* 76 (1997): 233–58.

Grant, Madison, and Charles Stewart Davison, eds. *The Alien in Our Midst or Selling Our Birthright for a Mess of Pottage.* New York: Galton Publishing, 1930.

Grey, Helen. "Confession of a Chinese Slave-Dealer." *San Francisco Call,* April 2, 1899. In *Unbound Voices: A Documentary History of Chinese Women in San Francisco,* edited by Judy Yung, 124–53. Berkeley: University of California Press, 1999.

Gutiérrez, David G. *Walls and Mirrors: Mexican Americans, Mexican Immigrants, and the Politics of Ethnicity.* Berkeley: University of California Press, 1995.

Gyory, Andrew. *Closing the Gate: Race, Politics, and the Chinese Exclusion Act.* Chapel Hill: University of North Carolina Press, 1998.

Hagan, Jacqueline. "Commentary." In *Crossings: Mexican Immigration in Interdisciplinary Perspectives,* edited by Marcelo M. Suarez-Orozco. Cambridge: Harvard University Press, David Rockefeller Center for Latin American Studies, 1998.

Haines, David W., and Karen E. Rosenblum. *Illegal Immigration in America: A Reference Handbook*. Westport, Conn.: Greenwood Press, 1999.

Hall, Linda B., and Don M. Coerver. *Revolution on the Border: The United States and Mexico, 1910–1920*. Albuquerque: University of New Mexico Press, 1988.

Haney-López, Ian F. *White by Law: The Legal Construction of Race*. New York: New York University Press, 1996.

Higham, John. "Instead of a Sequel, or, How I Lost My Subject." In *The Handbook of International Migration: The American Experience*, edited by Charles Hirschman, Philip Kasinitz, and Josh DeWind, 383–89. New York: Russell Sage Foundation, 1999.

———. *Strangers in the Land: Patterns of American Nativism, 1860–1925*. 2d ed. New York: Antheneum, 1978.

Hing, Bill Ong. *Making and Remaking Asian America through Immigration Policy, 1850–1990*. Stanford: Stanford University Press, 1993.

Ho, Yow. "Chinese Exclusion, a Benefit or a Harm?" *North American Review* 173 (1901): 314–30.

Hoffman, Abraham. *Unwanted Mexican Americans in the Great Depression: Repatriation Pressures, 1929–1939*. Tucson: University of Arizona Press, 1974.

Hom, Marlon K. *Songs of Gold Mountain: Cantonese Rhymes from San Francisco Chinatown*. Berkeley: University of California Press, 1987.

Howe, Frederic C. *Confessions of a Reformer*. New York: C. Scribner's Sons, 1925.

Hsu, Madeline. *Dreaming of Gold, Dreaming of Home: Transnationalism and Migration between the United States and South China, 1882–1943*. Stanford: Stanford University Press, 2000.

Hu-DeHart, Evelyn. "Coolies, Shopkeepers, Pioneers: The Chinese of Mexico and Peru, 1849–1930." *Amerasia Journal* 15, no. 1 (1989): 91–115.

———. "Immigrants to a Developing Society: The Chinese in Northern Mexico, 1875–1932." *Journal of Arizona History* 21 (Autumn 1980): 275–312.

———. "Racism and Anti-Chinese Persecution in Sonora, Mexico, 1876–1932." *Amerasia Journal* 9, no. 2 (1982): 1–28.

Hutchinson, E. P. *Legislative History of American Immigration Policy, 1798–1965*. Philadelphia: University of Pennsylvania, 1981.

Ignatiev, Noel. *How the Irish Became White*. New York: Routledge, 1995.

Imhoff, Gary, and Richard Lamm. *Immigration Time Bomb: The Fragmenting of America*. New York: Truman Talley Books, 1985.

Jacobson, Matthew Frye. *Barbarian Virtues: The United States Encounters Foreign Peoples at Home and Abroad, 1876–1917*. New York: Hill and Wang, 2000.

———. *Whiteness of a Different Color: European Immigrants and the Alchemy of Race*. Cambridge, Mass.: Harvard University Press, 1998.

Jensen, Joan M. *Passage from India: Asian Indian Immigrants in North America*. New Haven: Yale University Press, 1988.

Johnson, Kevin R. "Race, the Immigration Laws, and Domestic Race Relations: A 'Magic Mirror' into the Heart of Darkness." *Indiana Law Journal* 73 (1998): 1111–59.

———. "Race Matters: Immigration Law and Policy Scholarship, Law in the Ivory Tower, and the Legal Indifference of the Race Critique." *University of Illinois Law Review* 525 (2000): 525–57.

Jones, David D. *Surnames of the Chinese in America According to the David Jones System of Spelling Chinese Names*. San Francisco: Chinese Name Spelling Company, 1904.

Kaplan, Amy. "'Left Alone with America': The Absence of Empire in the Study of American Culture." In *Cultures of United States Imperialism*, edited by Amy Kaplan and Donald E. Pease. Durham, N.C.: Duke University Press, 1993.

Kelley, Ninette, and Michael Trebilcock. *The Making of the Mosaic: A History of Canadian Immigration Policy*. Toronto: University of Toronto Press, 1998.

Kevles, Daniel J. *In the Name of Eugenics: Genetics and the Uses of Human Heredity*. New York: Knopf, 1985.

Kim, Hyung-chan, and Richard W. Markov. "The Chinese Exclusion Laws and Smuggling Chinese into Whatcom County." *Annals of the Chinese Historical Society of the Pacific Northwest* (1983): 16–30.

King, Desmond. *Making Americans: Immigration, Race, and the Origins of the Diverse Democracy*. Cambridge: Harvard University Press, 2000.

Knobel, Dale T. *"America for the Americans": The Nativist Movement in the United States*. New York: Twayne, 1996.

Konvitz, Milton. *The Alien and the Asiatic in American Law*. Ithaca: Cornell University Press, 1946.

Kraut, Alan M. *Silent Travelers: Germs, Genes and the Immigrant Menace*. New York: Basic Books, 1994.

Kwong, Peter. *Forbidden Workers: Illegal Chinese Immigrants and American Labor*. New York: New Press, 1997.

Lai, David. *Chinatowns: Towns within Cities in Canada*. Vancouver: University of British Columbia Press, 1988.

———. "Chinese Opium Trade and Manufacture in British Columbia, 1858–1908." *Journal of the West* 38, no. 3 (1999): 21–26.

Lai, Him Mark. "Island of Immortals: Chinese Immigrants and the Angel Island Immigration Station." *California History* 57, no. 1 (Spring 1978): 88–103.

Lai, Him Mark, Genny Lim, and Judy Yung. *Island: Poetry and History of Chinese Immigrants on Angel Island, 1910–1940*. Seattle: University of Washington Press, 1980.

Lea, Homer. *The Valor of Ignorance*. New York: Harper and Brothers, 1909.

Lecker, Robert, ed. *Borderlands: Essays in Canadian-American Relations*. Toronto, Canada: ECW Press, 1991.

Lee, Erika. "Immigrants and Immigration Law: A State of the Field Assessment." *Journal of American Ethnic History* 18, no. 4 (1999): 85–114.

Lee, Lim P. "Sociological Data." *Chinese Digest*, October 23, 1936.

Lee, Robert. *Orientals: Asian Americans in Popular Culture*. Philadelphia: Temple University Press, 1999.

Lee, Rose Hum. *The Chinese in the United States of America*. Hong Kong: Hong Kong University Press, 1960.

LeMay, Michael C. *From Open Door to Dutch Door: An Analysis of U.S. Immigration Policy since 1920*. New York: Praeger, 1987.

———. *Gatekeepers: Comparative Immigration Policy*. New York: Praeger, 1989.

Leong, Karen J. "'A Distant and Antagonistic Race': Constructions of Chinese Manhood in the Exclusionist Debates, 1869–1878." In *Across the Great Divide: Cultures of Manhood in the American West*, edited by Laura McCall, Matthew Basso, and Dee Garceau, 131–48. New York: Routledge, 2000.

Leung, Sin Jang. "A Laundryman Sings the Blues." Translated by Marlon K. Hom. *Chinese America: History and Perspectives* (1991): 5–6.

Lipsky, Michael. *Street-Level Bureaucracy: Dilemmas of the Individual Public Services.* New York: Russell Sage Foundation, 1980.

Littleton, Louise A. "Worse Than Slaves: Servitude of All Chinese Wives." In *Unbound Voices: A Documentary History of Chinese Women in San Francisco,* edited by Judy Yung, 164–70. Berkeley: University of California Press, 1999.

Lodge, Henry Cabot. "The Restriction of Immigration." *North American Review* 152 (January 1891): 27–36.

Lombardi, John. *Labor's Voice in the Cabinet: A History of the Department of Labor from Its Origin to 1921.* New York: Columbia University Press, 1942.

Lowe, Lisa. *Immigrant Acts: On Asian American Cultural Politics.* Durham, N.C.: Duke University Press, 1996.

Martinez, Oscar. *Troublesome Border.* Tuscon: University of Arizona Press, 1988.

———. *U.S.-Mexico Borderlands: Historical and Contemporary Perspectives.* Wilmington, Del.: Scholarly Resources, 1996.

Massachusetts Bureau of Statistics of Labor. *Twelfth Annual Report of the Bureau of Statistics of Labor.* Boston: Wright and Potter, 1881.

Mazumdar, Sucheta. "Through Western Eyes: Discovering Chinese Women in America." In *A New Significance: Re-envisioning the History of the American West,* edited by Clyde Milner, 158–67. New York: Oxford University Press, 1996.

McClain, Charles, Jr. *In Search of Equality: The Chinese Struggle against Discrimination in Nineteenth-Century America.* Berkeley: University of California Press, 1994.

McClatchy, V. S. "Oriental Immigration." In *The Alien in Our Midst or Selling Our Birthright for a Mess of Pottage,* edited by Madison Grant and Charles Stewart Davison. New York: Galton Publishing, 1930.

McKee, Delber L. *Chinese Exclusion vs. the Open Door Policy, 1900–1906: Clashes over China Policy in the Roosevelt Era.* Detroit: Wayne State University Press, 1977.

McKenzie, Roderick Duncan. *Oriental Exclusion: The Effect of American Immigration Laws, Regulations, and Judicial Decisions upon the Chinese and Japanese on the American Pacific Coast.* Chicago: University of Chicago Press, 1928.

McKeown, Adam. *Chinese Migrant Networks and Cultural Change: Peru, Chicago, Hawaii, 1900–1936.* Chicago: University of Chicago Press, 2001.

———. "Transnational Chinese Families and Chinese Exclusion, 1875–1943." *Journal of American Ethnic History* 18, no. 2 (1999): 73–110.

McKinsey, Lauren, and Victor Konrad. *Borderlands Reflections: The United States and Canada.* Toronto: Borderlands Project, 1989.

McManus, Sheila. "Their Own Country: Race, Gender, Landscape, and Colonization around the 49th Parallel, 1862–1900." *Agricultural History* 73, no. 2 (1999): 168–82.

Mears, Eliot Grinnel. *Resident Orientals on the American Pacific Coast.* New York: Institute of Pacific Relations, 1927.

Mei, June, and Jean Pany Yip, with Russell Leong. "The *Bitter Society: Ku Shehui,* A Translation, Chapters 37–46." *Amerasia Journal* 8 (1981): 33–67.

Melendy, H. Brett. "The Filipinos in the United States." In *The Asian-American: The Historical Experience,* edited by Norris Hundley, 101–28. Santa Barbara, Calif.: American Bibliography Center, CLIO Press, 1976.

Merry, Sally Engle. *Colonizing Hawaii: The Cultural Power of Law.* Princeton, N.J.: Princeton University Press, 2000.

Metz, Leon C. *Border: The U.S.-Mexico Line.* El Paso: Mangan Books, 1989.

Meyer, George Homer, D. Wooster Taylor, and Arthur M. Johnson. *Municipal Blue Book of San Francisco.* San Francisco, 1915.

Miller, Stuart Creighton. *The Unwelcome Immigrant: The American Image of the Chinese, 1785–1882.* Berkeley: University of California Press, 1969.

Mink, Gwendolyn. *Old Labor and New Immigrants in American Political Development: Union, Party, and State, 1875–1920.* Ithaca: Cornell University Press, 1986.

Myers, John M. *The Border Wardens.* Englewood Cliffs, N.J.: Prentice-Hall, Inc., 1971.

National Network for Immigrant and Refugee Rights. "Portrait of Injustice: The Impact of Immigration Raids on Families, Workers, and Communities." Oakland, 1998.

Nee, Victor G., and Bret de Bary Nee. *Longtime Californ': A Documentary Study of an American Chinatown.* Stanford: Stanford University Press, 1972.

Neuman, Gerald L. "The Lost Century of American Immigration Law, 1776–1875." *Columbia Law Review* 93, no. 8 (December 1993): 1776–1875.

Ng, Poon Chew. *The Treatment of the Exempt Classes of Chinese in the United States: A Statement from the Chinese in America.* San Francisco: Chung Sai Yat Po, 1908.

Ngai, Mae. "The Architecture of Race in American Immigration Law: A Reexamination of the Immigration Act of 1924." *Journal of American History* 86, no. 1 (1999): 67–92.

———. "Legacies of Exclusion: Illegal Chinese Immigration during the Cold War Years." *Journal of American Ethnic History* 18, no. 1 (1998): 3–35.

North, Hart Hyatt. "Chinese and Japanese Immigration to the Pacific Coast." *California Historical Society Quarterly* 28, no. 4 (1949): 343–50.

———. "Chinese Highbinder Societies in California." *California Historical Society Quarterly* 27, no. 1 (1948): 19–31.

Okihiro, Gary. *Margins and Mainstreams: Asians in American History and Culture.* Seattle: University of Washington Press, 1994.

Omi, Michael, and Howard Winant. *Racial Formation in the United States from the 1960s to the 1990s.* New York: Routledge, 1994.

Palumbo-Liu, David. *Asian/American: Historical Crossings of a Racial Frontier.* Stanford: Stanford University Press, 1999.

Pascoe, Peggy. *Relations of Rescue: The Search for Female Moral Authority in the American West, 1874–1939.* New York: Oxford University Press, 1990.

Paulsen, George E. "The Yellow Peril at Nogales: The Ordeal of Collector William M. Hoey." *Arizona and the West* 13, no. 2 (Summer 1971): 113–28.

Peck, Gunther. *Reinventing Free Labor: Padrones and Immigrant Workers in the North American West, 1880–1930.* Cambridge: Cambridge University Press, 2000.

Peffer, George Anthony. *If They Don't Bring Their Women Here: Chinese Female Immigration before Exclusion.* Urbana: University of Illinois Press, 1999.

Perea, Juan. *Immigrants Out! The New Nativism and the Anti-Immigrant Impulse in the United States.* New York: New York University Press, 1997.

Perkins, Clifford. *Border Patrol: With the U.S. Immigration Service on the Mexican Boundary, 1910–1954.* El Paso: University of Texas at El Paso, 1978.

Perrot, Michelle, ed. *A History of Private Life, IV: From the Fires of Revolution to the Great War.* Cambridge, Mass.: Belknap Press of Harvard University Press, 1990.

Peters, Katherine McIntire. "Up Against the Wall—Operation Gatekeeper." *Government Executive Magazine* (1996), <http://www.govexec.com/archdoc/1096/1096s1.htm>. Jan. 3, 2001.

Ping, Wang. *Aching for Beauty: Footbinding in China.* Minneapolis: University of Minnesota Press, 2000.

Pitkin, Thomas M. *Keepers of the Gate: A History of Ellis Island.* New York: New York University Press, 1975.

Prince, Carl E., and Mollie Keller. *The U.S. Customs Service: A Bicentennial History.* Washington: Department of the Treasury, 1990.

Rak, Mary Kidder. *Border Patrol.* Boston: Houghton Mifflin, 1938.

Ralph, Julian. "The Chinese Leak." *Harper's New Monthly Magazine* 82, no. 490 (March 1891): 515–25.

Ramirez, Bruno. *Crossing the 49th Parallel: Migration from Canada to the United States, 1900–1930.* Ithaca: Cornell University Press, 2001.

Reagan, Leslie R. *When Abortion Was a Crime: Women, Medicine, and Law in the United States, 1867–1973.* Berkeley: University of California Press, 1997.

Reimers, David. *Still the Golden Door: The Third World Comes to America.* New York: Columbia University Press, 1985.

———. *Unwelcome Strangers: American Identity and the Turn against Immigration.* New York: Columbia University Press, 1998.

Reisler, Mark. *By the Sweat of Their Brow: Mexican Immigrant Labor in the United States, 1900–1940.* Westport, Conn.: Greenwood Press, 1976.

Reynolds, James. "Enforcement of the Chinese Exclusion Law." *Annals of the American Academy of Political and Social Sciences* 34, no. 2 (September 1909): 368–74.

Rhodes, Henry T. F. *Alphonse Bertillon: Father of Scientific Detection.* New York: Abelard-Schuman, 1956.

Riggs, Fred Warren. *Pressures on Congress: A Study of the Repeal of Chinese Exclusion.* New York: King's Crown Press, 1950.

Roediger, David. *The Wages of Whiteness: Race and the Making of the American Working Class.* New York: Verso, 1991.

Rowell, Chester H. "Chinese and Japanese Immigrants—A Comparison." *Annals of the American Academy of Political and Social Sciences* 34, no. 2 (September 1909): 3–10.

———. "Why Make Mexico an Exception?" *Survey,* May 1, 1931, 180.

Roy, Patricia E. *A White Man's Province: British Columbia Politicians and Chinese and Japanese Immigrants, 1858–1914.* Vancouver: University of British Columbia Press, 1989.

Sabin, Paul. "Home and Abroad: The Two Wests of Twentieth Century United States." *Pacific Historical Review* 66, no. 3 (August 1997): 305–35.

Sadowski-Smith, Claudia. "Undocumented Border Crossings and Theories of Diaspora." In *Globalization on the Line: Culture, Capital, and Citizenship at U.S. Borders,* edited by Claudia Sadowski-Smith. New York: Palgrave/St. Martin's, forthcoming.

Said, Edward. *Orientalism.* New York: Vintage, 1979.

Salas, Miguel Tinker. *In the Shadow of the Eagles: Sonora and the Transformation of the Border during the Porfiriato.* Berkeley: University of California Press, 1997.

Saldívar, José David. *Border Matters: Remapping American Cultural Studies.* Berkeley: University of California Press, 1997.

Salyer, Lucy. *Laws Harsh as Tigers: Chinese Immigrants and the Shaping of Modern Immigration Law.* Chapel Hill: University of North Carolina Press, 1995.

Sánchez, George J. *Becoming Mexican American: Ethnicity, Culture, and Identity in Chicano Los Angeles, 1900–1945.* New York: Oxford University Press, 1993.

———. "Face the Nation: Race, Immigration, and the Rise of Nativism in Late Twentieth-Century America." *International Migration Review* 31, no. 4 (Summer 1999): 1009–30.

————. "Race, Nation, and Culture in Recent Immigration Studies." *Journal of American Ethnic History* 18, no. 4 (1999): 66–84.

Sandmeyer, Elmer C. *The Anti-Chinese Movement in California.* Urbana: University of Illinois Press, 1939.

Saxton, Alexander. *The Indispensable Enemy: Labor and the Anti-Chinese Movement in California.* Berkeley: University of California Press, 1971.

Schiller, Nina Glick. "Transmigrants and Nation-States: Something Old and Something New in the U.S. Immigrant Experience." In *The Handbook of International Migration: The American Experience*, edited by Charles Hirschman, Philip Kasinitz, and Josh DeWind, 94–119. New York: Russell Sage Foundation, 1999.

Schiller, Nina Glick, Linda Basch, and Cristina Blanc-Szanton, eds. *Towards a Transnational Perspective on Migration: Race, Class, Ethnicity, and Nationalism Reconsidered.* New York: New York Academy of Sciences, 1992.

Shah, Nayan. *Contagious Divides: Epidemics and Race in San Francisco's Chinatown.* Berkeley: University of California Press, 2001.

Siu, Paul C. *The Chinese Laundryman: A Study in Social Isolation.* Edited by John Kuo Wei Tchen. New York: New York University Press, 1987.

Skocpol, Theda. "Bringing the State Back In: Strategies of Analysis in Current Research." In *Bringing the State Back In*, edited by Peter B. Evans et al., 3–43. Cambridge: Cambridge University Press, 1985.

Skowronek, Stephen. *Building a New American State: The Expansion of National Administrative Capacities, 1877–1920.* Cambridge: Cambridge University Press, 1982.

Smith, Darrell Hevenor, and H. Guy Herring. *Bureau of Immigration: Its History, Activities, and Organization.* Institute for Government Research Service Monographs of the United States Government, No. 30, Baltimore, 1924.

Smith, Marian L. "The Immigration and Naturalization Service (INS) at the U.S.-Canadian Border, 1893–1993: An Overview of Issues and Topics." *Michigan Historical Review* 26, no. 2 (Fall 2000): 127–47.

————. "Why Isn't the Green Card Green?" <http://www.ins.usdoj.gov/graphics/aboutins/history/articles/Green.htm>. January 3, 2001.

Smith, Paul J., ed. *Human Smuggling: Chinese Migrant Trafficking and the Challenge to America's Immigrant Tradition.* Washington: Center for Strategic and International Studies, 1997.

Solomon, Barbara Miller. *Ancestors and Immigrants: A Changing New England Tradition.* Cambridge: Harvard University Press, 1956.

Stanford, Lyman. *Chinese Americans.* New York: Random House, 1974.

Steiner, Edward. *On the Trail of the Immigrant.* New York: Fleming H. Revell Co., 1906.

Stidger, Oliver Perry. "Highlights of Chinese Exclusion and Expulsion: The Immigration Law of 1924 as It Affects Persons of Chinese Descent in the United States, Their Business Interests, Their Rights, and Their Privileges." San Francisco: Chinese Chamber of Commerce, 1924.

Stoddard, Lothrop. "The Permanent Menace from Europe." In *The Alien in Our Midst or Selling Our Birthright for a Mess of Pottage*, edited by Madison Grant and Charles Stewart Davison. New York: Galton Publishing, 1930.

Straus, Oscar S. "The Spirit and Letter of Exclusion." *North American Review* 187 (April 1908): 481–85.

Sung, Betty Lee. *Mountain of Gold: The Story of the Chinese in America.* New York: Collier Books, 1967.

Suro, Roberto. *Watching America's Door: The Immigration Backlash and the New Policy Debate.* New York: Twentieth Century Fund Press, 1996.

Takaki, Ronald. *Iron Cages: Race and Culture in Nineteenth Century America.* New York: Oxford University Press, 1979.

Tchen, John Kuo Wei. *New York before Chinatown: Orientalism and the Shaping of American Culture, 1776–1882.* Baltimore: Johns Hopkins University Press, 1999.

Thelen, David. "The Nation and Beyond: Transnational Perspectives on United States History." *Journal of American History* 86, no. 3 (1999): 966–69.

Tong, Benson. *Unsubmissive Women: Chinese Prostitutes in Nineteenth-Century San Francisco.* Norman: University of Oklahoma Press, 1994.

Torpey, John. *The Invention of the Passport: Surveillance, Citizenship, and the State.* New York: Cambridge University Press, 2000.

Tsai, Shih-Shan Henry. *The Chinese Experience in America.* Bloomington: University of Indiana Press, 1986.

U.S. Congress. House. *Immigration Station on Angel Island, Cal.* 59th Cong., 1st sess., H. Rept. 4640. Washington: GPO: 1906.

U.S. Congress. House. Select Committee on Immigration and Naturalization. *Investigation of Chinese Immigration.* 51st Cong., 2d sess., H. Doc. 4048, serial 2890. Washington: GPO, 1890.

U.S. Congress. Joint Special Committee to Investigate Chinese Immigration. *Chinese Immigration.* 44th Cong., 2d sess., S. Rept. 689. Washington: GPO, 1877.

———. *Immigration of Chinese into the United States.* 57th Cong., 1st sess. S. Doc. 106. Washington: GPO, 1901.

———. *Reports on Charge of Fraudulent Importation of Chinese.* 49th Cong., 1st sess. S. Exec. Doc. 103. Washington: GPO, 1886.

———. *Reports of the Immigration Commissioner.* 61st Cong., 3d sess., S. Doc. 756, Washington: GPO, 1911.

U.S. Congress. Senate. Committee on Immigration. *Alleged Illegal Entry into the United States of Chinese Persons.* 55th Cong., 1st sess., S. Doc. 120, Washington: GPO, 1897.

———. *Chinese Exclusion: Report and Testimony taken before the Committee on Immigration . . . on Senate bill 2960 and certain other bills before the Committee providing for the exclusion of Chinese laborers.* 57th Cong., 1st sess., S. Rept. 776, Washington: GPO, 1902.

U.S. Department of Commerce and Labor. *Annual Reports of the Commissioner-General of Immigration.* Washington: GPO, 1903–11.

———. *McGettrick Certificates: List of Chinese Cases Tried before Former United States Commissioner Felix W. McGettrick.* Washington: GPO, 1906.

———. Bureau of Immigration. *Compilation from the Records of the Bureau of Immigration of Facts Concerning the Enforcement of the Chinese-Exclusion Laws: Letter from the Secretary of Commerce and Labor, Submitting, in Response to the Inquiry of the House, a Report as to the Enforcement of the Chinese-Exclusion Laws.* Washington: GPO, 1906.

———. *Treaty, Laws, and Regulations Governing the Admission of Chinese.* Washington: GPO, 1903, 1905, 1906, 1907, 1909, 1910.

U.S. Department of Justice. Immigration and Naturalization Service. *Chinese Investigations: Investigator's Reference Bulletin No. 3.* Washington: GPO, 1957.

———. "Early Immigration Inspection along the United States/Mexican Border," <http://www.ins.usdoj.gov/graphics/aboutins/history/articles/MBTEXT3.htm>. January 3, 2001.

———. "Operation Gatekeeper: New Resources, Enhanced Results," <http://www.ins.usdog.gov/graphics/publicaffairs/factsheets/OpGateFS.htm>. August 1, 1998.

U.S. Department of Labor. *Annual Reports of the Commissioner-General of Immigration.* Washington: GPO, 1912–32.

U.S. Department of Labor. Bureau of Immigration. *Treaty, Laws, and Rules Governing the Admission of Chinese.* Washington: GPO, 1915, 1917, 1926.

U.S. Treasury Department. *Annual Reports of the Commissioner-General of Immigration.* Washington: GPO, 1894–1902.

———. *Annual Reports of the Secretary of the Treasury.* Washington: GPO, 1890–91.

———. Bureau of Immigration. *Laws, Treaty, and Regulations Relating to the Exclusion of Chinese.* Washington: GPO, 1900, 1902.

Van der Linden, Marcel. "Transnationalizing American Labor History." *Journal of American History* 86, no. 3 (1999): 1078–92.

Van Vleck, William C. *The Administrative Control of Aliens.* New York: Commonwealth Fund, 1932.

Wang, Gungwu. "Sojourning: The Chinese Experience in Southeast Asia." In *Sojourners and Settlers: Histories of Southeast Asia and the Chinese,* edited by Anthony Reid, 1–14. St. Leonards, Australia: Asian Studies Association of Australia and Allen and Unwin, 1996.

Ward, Peter. *White Canada Forever: Popular Attitudes and Public Policy toward Orientals in British Columbia.* Montreal: McGill-Queens University Press, 1978.

Warne, Frank Julian. *The Immigrant Invasion.* New York: Dood, Mead, and Co., 1913.

White, Richard. "Race Relations in the American West." *American Quarterly* 38 (1986): 396–416.

Widdis, Randy William. "Borders, Borderlands and Canadian Identity: A Canadian Perspective." *International Journal of Canadian Studies* 15 (Spring 1997): 49–66.

Wittke, Carl. *We Who Built America: The Saga of the Immigrant.* New York: Prentice-Hall, 1939.

Wong, Charles Choy, and Kenneth Klein. "False Papers, Lost Lives." In *Origins and Destinations: 41 Essays on Chinese America.* Chinese Historical Society of Southern California and UCLA Asian American Studies Center joint publication, 1994.

Wong, K. Scott. "Cultural Defenders and Brokers: Chinese Responses to the Anti-Chinese Movement." In *Claiming America: Constructing Chinese American Identities during the Exclusion Era,* edited by Sucheng Chan and K. Scott Wong, 3–40. Philadelphia: Temple University Press, 1998.

———. "The Eagle Seeks a Helpless Quarry: Chinatown, the Police, and the Press. The 1903 Boston Chinatown Raid Revisited." *Amerasia Journal* 22, no. 3 (1996): 81–103.

———. "Immigration and Race: The Politics and Rhetoric of Exclusion." In *Many Americas: Critical Perspectives on Race, Racism, and Ethnicity,* edited by Gregory Campbell, 231–44. Dubuque, Iowa: Kendall/Hunt, 1998.

———. "Liang Qichao and the Chinese of America: A Re-evaluation of His *Selected Memoir of Travels in the New World.*" *Journal of American Ethnic History* 11, no. 4 (1992): 3–24.

Wong, William. "Editorial." *San Francisco Examiner,* April 10, 1998, A-19.

Yen, Ching-Hwang. *Coolies and Mandarins: China's Protection of Overseas Chinese during the Late Ch'ing Period (1851–1911).* Singapore: Singapore University Press, 1985.

Yow, Ho. "Chinese Exclusion, A Benefit or a Harm?" *North American Review* 173 (September 1901): 314–30.

Yu, Connie Young. "Rediscovered Voices: Chinese Immigrants and Angel Island." *Amerasia Journal* 4, no. 2 (1977): 123–39.

Yu, Henry. "On a Stage Built by Others: Creating an Intellectual History of Asian Americans." *Amerasia Journal* 26, no. 1 (2000): 141–61.

Yu, Renqiu. *To Save China, to Save Ourselves: The Chinese Hand Laundry Alliance of New York.* Philadelphia: Temple University Press, 1992.

Yung, Judy. "Detainment at Angel Island: An Interview with Koon T. Lau." *Chinese America: History and Perspectives* (1991): 157–66.

————. *Unbound Feet: A Social History of Chinese Women in San Francisco.* Berkeley: University of California Press, 1995.

Zhao, Xiaojian. *Remaking Chinese America: Immigration, Family, and Community, 1940–1965.* New Brunswick, N.J.: Rutgers University Press, 2002.

Zolberg, Aristide. "Matters of State: Theorizing Immigration Policy." In *The Handbook of International Migration: The American Experience*, edited by Charles Hirschman, Philip Kasinitz, and Josh DeWind, 71–93. New York: Russell Sage Foundation, 1999.

Zucker, Norman L., and Naomi Zucker. *The Guarded Gate: The Reality of American Refugee Policy.* New York: Harcourt Brace Jovanovich, 1987.

ACKNOWLEDGMENTS

Writing this book has been a long and wonderful journey. Family, friends, and colleagues have all supported me over many years, and I have been looking forward to thanking them in these acknowledgments for as long as I have worked on this project. This book first began as a dissertation, and I have been extremely lucky to have had a number of mentors who supported and guided me from the very beginning. Jon Gjerde and Judy Yung read every version of this manuscript and helped shape my thinking at critical stages. I was the very fortunate recipient of their ideas and generosity and have learned how to be a mentor myself by following their example. K. Scott Wong took me under his wing during my first year of graduate school, and he has remained a wonderful adviser and friend. Sucheng Chan has also been a crucial supporter over many years, and I have benefited greatly from her suggestions and critiques.

The research that went into writing this book was truly a labor of love, made even more enjoyable by the camaraderie and valuable assistance from a number of archivists. Neil Thomsen, Waverly Lowell, and the entire staff at the National Archives, Pacific Region, in San Bruno, California, generously shared their own findings, greatly facilitated my research, and provided a second home to me. This book would not have been possible without their assistance and support. I know they will be as happy to see it in print as I will be. Betty Lee Sung guided me through the National Archives, Northeast Region, in New York City. Marian Smith, the historian at the U.S. Immigration and Naturalization Service, has been a tremendous resource throughout the course of this project. Librarians and archivists at the Bancroft Library at the University of California, Berkeley, the National Archives in Washington, D.C., the National Archives, Northeast Region, the Asian American Studies Library at the University of California, Berkeley, the Hoover Institution on War, Revolution, and Peace at Stanford University, the Asian American Studies Center at the University of California, Los Angeles, the Museum of the Chinese in the Americas, the California State Parks and Recreation Department, Catholic University of America, the San Francisco and Boston Public Libraries, the University of California at Berkeley, and the University of Minnesota were all enormously helpful. Kaimon Chin welcomed me into New York's Chinese American community and graciously allowed me to interview him and view his family papers. Arthur Lem and Mr. Lee also generously shared their exclusion-era experiences and memories. Jennie Lew helped my think about sharing this history with a larger audience.

A large community of colleagues helped in the research and writing of this book as well as with the exchange of ideas that shaped my perspective on many issues. Evelyn Nakano Glenn, David Roediger, Barbara Welke, George Anthony Peffer, Paula Fass, Catherine Ceniza Choy, Jigna Desai, Patrick McNamara, and Liping Wang all read parts or all of the manuscript closely and gave me useful suggestions for improving the text. They served as tough but extremely supportive critics. Josephine Fowler, Yuichiro Onishi, and Yuxin Ma contributed valuable research assistance and critiques. The book was also greatly influenced by the critical comments of publisher reviewers, including Sucheng Chan, an anonymous reader for the University of North Carolina Press, Bill Ong Hing, and K. Scott Wong. I also want to thank Him Mark Lai, Mae Ngai, Claudia Sadowski-Smith, Karen Leong, Madeline Hsu, David Igler, Grace Delgado, Donna Gabaccia, Rudolph Vecoli, Elliott Barkan, Matthew Frye Jacobson, Robert Lee, Patricia Limerick, George Sanchez, Joanne Meyerowitz, Adam McKeown, Richard White, Evelyn Hu-DeHart, Diana Selig, Henry Yu, Charles McClain Jr., the Comparative Women's History Workshop at the University of Minnesota, Libby Garland, Linda Ivey, FlorenceMae Waldron, and Margot Canaday, for helpful conversations, research suggestions, and comments. My undergraduate adviser, Reed Ueda, encouraged me to go to graduate school in the first place. Cheri Register helped edit the manuscript during the final stages of this project.

The University of Minnesota has been an especially wonderful place to complete this book. I have enjoyed and benefited from the intellectual exchange and cheerful support from numerous friends and colleagues in the Department of History and the Asian American Studies Program, including Sara Evans, Ann Waltner, Josephine Lee, Chris Isett, Allen Isaacman, Ted Farmer, David Good, Anna Clark, Kirsten Fischer, Lisa Norling, Sarah Chambers, Elaine and Lary May, MJ Maynes, Rich Lee, and Jeani O'Brien. Many friends, including Jeanne Tsai, Kevin Kinneavy, Greg Choy, and Sophie Huang, offered comfort and diversion when I needed it most.

The "U," the University of California at Berkeley, and the Bancroft Library provided generous research and fellowship support. The Social Science Research Council funded a sabbatical that allowed me to make crucial revisions. Portions of this book have appeared in different form in the *Journal of American Ethnic History,* the *Journal of American History,* and *The Human Tradition in California,* edited by David Igler and Clark Davis.

I owe special thanks to several individuals at the University of North Carolina Press who have guided this book through many stages. Lewis Bateman and Kate Torrey saw promise in this book when it was just a dissertation. Charles Grench and Amanda McMillan skillfully steered the manuscript toward its final production. Mary Caviness's keen eyes and sharp editorial skills helped me correct many errors of form and style and improved the manuscript immensely.

This book—and my initial interest in history—began with my family, and it is to them that I owe my deepest thanks. My parents, Fay and Howard Lee, and my sisters, Kristen Lee and Laurel Lee-Alexander, encouraged me at every step of the way, always believing in me and this project. They read my high school term papers, my college exams, my dissertation, and now this book. Their love, enthusiasm, and support have been most important. My mother deserves special recognition for taking me in as a roommate during my first arduous years of graduate school, when

I was not always a cheerful companion. Both she and my father instilled in me a sense of pride in my roots and a conviction that I could accomplish anything. My brother-in-law Todd Bontemps gave me a thesaurus for my high school graduation. He will be glad to know that it has been put to good use in the many years since then. My in-laws, Bill, Molly, Jenny, and Peter Buccella have embraced me as another daughter and sister. My father-in-law, in particular, has kept me on my toes with his tough questions on U.S. history. I still haven't figured out who is really buried in Grant's tomb.

My husband, Mark, has cared about this book almost as much as I have. He has been there from the very beginning, fully sharing in this journey of discovery and labor of love. His love, support, and understanding have made this and so many other things possible. Our son, Benjamin, arrived as I sent this book, my first "baby," off to the publisher. The joy he has brought to our lives has surpassed everything else, and I have gleefully left the computer to sing songs, roll around on the floor, and play peek-a-boo. My grandparents, who first inspired this initial journey of exploration, have all passed away. I hope and I believe that their stories have not died with them. I dedicate this book to their memory.

Minneapolis, May 2002

INDEX

Abbott, Edith, 32

African Americans, 7, 57; Chinese immigrants equated with, 27, 29, 31; illegal Chinese disguised as, 162

Aldrich, Thomas Bailey, 39

Alien and Sedition Acts of 1798, 224

Alien Contract Labor Law of 1885, 65, 246

Alien status, 5; and Asian immigrants, 2, 38, 103; and green cards, 10, 25, 42, 182, 250; "American-ness" vs., 22, 36; established by Chinese exclusion law, 25, 30, 38; and contract-labor law, 65, 246; and deportation of suspected radicals, 74; and marriage of Chinese American women, 100, 238; Supreme Court rulings on, 173–74, 225, 226; and arrests and deportations, 224–37; and Chinese Confession Program, 241–42; conflation of all Chinese into, 243; and California denial of benefits (1994), 249, 292 (n. 13)

American Federation of Labor, 26

American national identity ("American-

ness"), 6–7, 29; as defined by gatekeeping, 22; basis of "real American," 36; Chinese laborers as threat to, 64; as Chinese exclusion justification, 173–74. *See also* Nativism

Anarchists, 246

Andreas, Peter, 148, 278 (n. 2)

Angel Island (San Francisco), 4, 5, 48, 70–76, 81–87, 124–29; establishment of, 11–12, 126–28; poems carved on walls of, 17, 76, 111, 219; corruption on, 72, 200; contrasted with Ellis Island, 75, 82; symbolism of, 75–76, 126–28, 208, 251; historical preservation of, 76, 250–51; as National Historic Landmark, 76, 251; procedure at, 76, 81, 126–28; medical examinations on, 81–84, 87, 211–12; interrogation process, 95–96, 126, 210–13; detentions on, 126, 127, 213, 214–15, 217–20, 223; official opening of, 127; rejection-to-admissions ratio, 127; 1911 tour of, 127–28; miserable conditions of, 127–28, 217–20; Chinese merchants'

64, 69; broadening of, 66; Secretary of Commerce and Labor Oscar Straus's view of, 69; Angel Island as symbol of, 75–76, 126–28, 208, 251; and mixed-race Chinese, 80; gendered arguments in, 92–100; and U.S. labor shortage, 113; entrenchment of, 126; post-1910 response to, 129; Chinese adaptation to, 131–38; and attorney representation, 138–41; compared with treatment of other immigrant groups, 141; "John Chinaman" symbolizing message of, 165–66; and U.S. national sovereignty, 173–74; and Mexican immigrant screening, 180; and admission of other nationalities, 191; legacy of, 221, 222, 246–51; impact on Chinese Americans, 223–43; arrests and deportations, 224–37. *See also* Anti-Chinese movement; Chinese Exclusion Act of 1882

Chinese exclusion, enforcement of, 9, 49–74, 77; and illegal entries (*see* Illegal immigrants); interrogations as part of (*see* Interrogations); and surveillance of Chinese (*see* Deportation); and detention, 4, 56, 58, 84–85, 124–25, 127, 130, 217–19; and birthright citizens, 4, 68, 78, 103–9, 130–31, 135–36, 142, 201–4, 239; and class, 4–6, 20, 27, 30, 79, 87–97, 134–35, 201; and attitudes of immigration officials, 16, 50, 57, 58, 64–68, 72, 77, 84, 90, 208; as influence on national procedures, 40–43, 63–64; and documentation requirements, 41–42, 46, 49, 55, 74, 141, 199, 224, 226; and admissions decisions, 48, 55–56; by U.S. Bureau of Immigration, 49–50, 65–66, 68–74, 77, 265 (n. 3); and U.S. Customs Service, 49–54; and loose interpretations, 50; and anti-Chinese bias, 50–54, 58, 81–87, 100–109; and San Francisco as vigilancy model, 51–58; and humiliating procedures, 56, 58, 84–85, 124–25; role of Chinese interpreters in, 58–64; reforms in, 69, 85, 126, 226; and Chinese boycott, 69, 125–26; with restrictionist mind-set, 77; role of witnesses in, 85, 91–92, 106, 135–36; and attitudes of Chinese, 123–38; changes in, 126; detail and loopholes in, 131–32; imposition on Canada and Mexico, 152; and raids on Chinese communities, 185–86, 194, 230–32, 239; and cycle of exclusion, 207–13. *See also* Angel Island

Chinese Exclusion Act of 1882, 73; exemptions from (*see* Exempt classes); provisions of, 2, 4, 103, 246; significance of, 4, 5, 6, 8, 9, 24–25, 34, 40–44, 46, 246; repeal (1943), 4, 7, 13, 46, 220, 224, 241, 243, 245; deportation under, 4, 24, 43–44, 223, 224; legacy of, 7, 24–25, 30–39, 221, 222, 246–51; ease of evasion of, 12, 192; class-based restrictions in, 30; passage of, 30; definition of illegal immigration, 43; impact on Chinese immigration, 43–44; amendment proposals, 44–45; expansion of, 45–46, 64, 129, 174, 224; and birthright citizenship ruling, 103, 105; and Chinese railway workers in Canada, 152; and false citizenship claims, 155–56; groundwork for, 165; repeal attempts, 189; failed goal of, 221; precedents set by, 222; continued impact of, 243, 246; repeal anniversary celebration, 251

Chinese Exclusion Act of 1902 (and 1904 extensions), 46, 64, 129, 174

Chinese Exclusion Act of 1923 (Canada), 154, 179

Chinese Exclusion Convention of 1901, 33, 37, 45

Chinese immigrants: backdoor entrances for (*see* Canada; Mexico); barriers to returns by (*see* Returning residents); degrading characterizations of (*see* Stereotypes); and entry ports (*see* Ports of entry); illegal (*see* Illegal immigrants); transnational (*see* Transnationalism); reasons for emigration, 1, 2, 111, 112–15; prior to exclusion, 1–2; and alien status, 2, 38, 238; barred from naturalization, 2, 38, 103; arrival procedure for, 4–5, 124–25; numbers of (1849–82), 12; numbers of (1882–1943), 12, 48, 111; racialization of, 12, 20, 24–25, 76, 78–87, 187, 224; immigration service arrival files of, 14–16; first significant arrivals of, 25; home region of, 25, 112; as percentage of total numbers of immigrants (1870–80), 25; compared with African Americans, 27, 29, 31; compared with Mexican immigrants, 33–35; compared with southern and eastern European immigrants, 35; compared with all European immigrants, 37–38; documents of identity and, 41–42, 84–85; violence against, 44, 51; attorneys for, 56, 99, 123, 138–41; physical mistreatment of, 56, 57–58; derogatory terms for, 57, 169, 172; community raids and harassment of, 66, 185–86, 194, 230–32, 239; sex ratio of, 92, 97, 99, 115–16; and resistance to exclusion laws, 111–45; and economic incentives, 114; as sojourners, 116, 119, 120–23; mutual benefit organization of, 123; and adaptations to exclusion, 131–38; conflation of legal and illegal, 172–73, 216–17, 222; seen as threat to national sovereignty, 173–74; and chain migration pattern, 204–5; institutional suspicion of, 208; advance inspection of (1950), 220; and reform measures, 220; as deportable, 222, 223, 224–25; shadowed lives of, 228–37; harassment of, 230–32, 237–38, 242; as U.S. government informants, 235; numbers of (1908–23), 237; and psychology of fear, 237–43; and perpetuation of false identities, 240–41; and Confession Program, 241–42; percentage of women (1948–52), 245–46; occupations of, 273 (n. 8). *See also* Chinese Americans

Chinese immigration: changes in between 1854 and 1918, 2, 43–44; and paper son system, 4–5, 17, 194–95, 203–7, 211–12; patterns and pattern changes of, 9, 76, 112–16; U.S. processing costs, 87; decrease in, 237–38; and departure ratio, 237; and repeal of exclusion laws, 246; and symbolism of Angel Island, 251

Chinese interpreters. *See* Interpreters

Chinese laborers: Chinese Exclusion Act of 1882 barrier to, 2, 4, 45; California's efforts to exclude, 24; as first immigrants in California, 25; as threat to American workers, 25–26, 165, 234; and nativist rhetoric, 34; documentation requirements of, 41, 42, 85, 226; European immigrant workers vs., 64–65; and merchant distinctions, 89–90; U.S. demand for, 113, 191; as bulk of exclusion-era immigrants, 114–15; admittance numbers (1910–24), 115; as sojourners, 116, 120–23; legal challenges by, 123; exempt classes' view of, 131; illegal border crossings by, 152, 158, 171; Scott Act barrier to, 153; Canadian head tax on, 153, 154, 176, 178; Chinese Exclusion Act circumventions by, 189–220; fraudulent

citizenship claims by, 208; and deportation hearings, 225

"Chinese Leak" (Ralph), 166–67

Chinese litigation. *See* Courts

Chinese merchants. *See* Merchants, Chinese

Chinese Merchants Exchange (San Francisco), 129–30

"Chineseness," 61, 78–87; as argument against birthright citizenship, 105; in Canada, 269 (n. 8)

"Chinese problem," 57, 165

Chinese revolution (1911), 13

Chinese Six Companies, 236; challenges to exclusion procedures by, 123, 127, 130, 139, 231; and Confession Program, 241

Chinese students. *See* Students, Chinese

Chinese women. *See* Women, Chinese

Chinese World (newspaper), 127, 236

"Chink" terminology, 57, 169, 172, 266 (n. 42)

Chow, Paul, 250–51

Chung Sai Yat Po (Chinese-language newspaper), 77, 121, 127, 140

Citizen Reform Act of 1997, 292 (n. 26)

Citizenship: of U.S.-born Chinese (*see* Birthright citizenship); and U.S. bureaucracy, 22; denied to Asians, 38, 103, 237; definition of, 78, 100–109; unequal status of Chinese Americans, 100–109, 238; tests of, 106, 108–9, 203; false claims of, 155–56, 162; and Chinese naturalization eligibility, 241, 245

Civil service reforms, 68–69, 71

Class: in exclusion laws, 4, 24, 27, 30, 87–97; in immigration policy, 5–6, 20; and exclusion enforcement, 79, 87–97; and racial distinctions, 79, 91–92; overt markers of, 90, 94–95, 134–35, 201; of witnesses, 91–92, 137; and women immigrants, 92, 93, 94–95; and birthright citizenship cases, 106–7; and reasons for emigration, 115; and response to exclusion enforcement, 129–31, 133–38, 142, 201; and legal counsel, 139; and Mexican border crossings, 160–61

Clemens, George P., 33–34

Clement, H. N., 23, 29, 39

Cleveland, Grover, 52

Clonorchiasis (liver fluke), 83, 87

Closed gate metaphor. *See* Gatekeeping

Coaching books, 196–98, 213–15, 217

Cold War, 247

Collector of Customs. *See* Customs Service, U.S.

Commerce and Labor Department, U.S., 67–69, 80, 113; and Chinese boycott, 126; Chinese Americans formal complaint to, 130, 232, 239; Chinese immigrant appeals to, 212; and Chinese exclusion enforcement, 265 (n. 3). *See also* Bureau of Immigration, U.S.

Communist Party, Chinese, 113

Condit, Rev. Ira, 56, 62

Confession Program (1959–65), 17, 191, 241–42

Congress, U.S., 30, 64, 68; and Chinese exclusion testimony, 77, 166; Bertillon system approval, 84; power to expel aliens, 225; Chinese disenfranchisement bills, 238; and broadened immigration barriers, 246; and post–September 11, 2001, immigration controls, 254

Constitutional rights, 103, 104, 225, 226, 254

Contract laborers, 30, 33, 65, 246

Coolidge, Mary Roberts, 54, 55, 58, 231, 266 (n. 44)

Coolie, 26, 27, 30, 35, 57, 78, 90, 165, 166, 261–62 (n. 11)

Corruption: among government officials, 50, 72, 149, 195–96, 198–200; and Chinese interpreters, 60–61; and Chinese stereotype, 64, 156; on Angel Island, 72, 200; proliferation of, 148, 149, 156, 164, 195–96, 198–99, 216, 235, 236; J. B. Densmore investigation of, 200; and deportation threat, 233–34

Courts: and enforcement litigation, 4, 6, 8, 47, 123, 133, 156, 225; Chinese immigration decisions moved from, 11; and habeas corpus proceedings, 47–48, 103–4, 140, 156; immigration officials' decisions overturned by, 55; barring of Chinese access to, 66, 125; wives of Chinese U.S. citizens and, 92; birthright citizenship cases in, 103–6, 155, 202, 238; deportation rulings, 225–26, 234. *See also* Attorneys; Supreme Court, U.S.

Critical race theory, 260 (n. 31)

Cuba, 162, 193, 194

Customs Service, U.S.: Chinese immigration inspectors under, 41; and enforcement of exclusion laws, 49, 56, 58, 64, 68, 81, 84, 265 (n. 3); and local officials' biases, 50, 52,

53–54, 56; and corrupt officials, 50, 198; and Chinese interpreters, 58–64, 61–62; power transfer to Bureau of Immigration, 68, 74; and Chinese racialization, 84; and Mexican border patrol, 184; and Chinese paper identities, 201. *See also* Bureau of Immigration, U.S.; Immigration and Naturalization Service, U.S.; Immigration officials

Daniels, Roger, 24, 259 (n. 11)

Densmore, J. B., 200

Deportation, 25, 242–43; Chinese Exclusion Act establishment of, 4, 24, 43–44, 223, 224; as part of Chinese exclusion, 10, 45, 66, 67, 223, 224–37; of Mexicans and Filipinos, 39; first modern laws, 43; as shadow of exclusion, 53, 147, 224; of suspected alien radicals, 74; of Chinese from Mexico, 185–86, 187; and immigration raids, 194, 230–32; and corruption of U.S. marshals, 199; risks for merchants, 202; exploitation of threat of, 222, 233–34; expansion of system, 225; racist component of, 228; abuses of, 232; and Chinese informants, 235; and Great Depression, 246

Derogatory terms: for contract laborers, 30; for southern and eastern European immigrants, 31; for Chinese, 57, 169, 172; for illegal immigrants, 149, 172

Detentions, 4, 56, 58, 84–85, 124–27, 130, 213–15, 223; and habeas corpus cases, 47–48; "matrons," 71; Pacific Mail Steamship Company shed conditions, 124–25, 127, 214, 217; increased time of, 207, 217; Angel Island conditions, 217–20; of suspected terrorists, 254

Deverell, William, 260 (n. 24)

Díaz, Porfirio, 157, 158, 180

Diplomats, Chinese: as exempt class, 4, 50, 66, 78; document requirements, 41; protests of discriminatory treatment, 123; vulnerability to arrest, 225

Diseases, 81, 82–83, 262 (n. 33)

Documentation, 14–16, 41–42, 46, 49, 74; fraudulent, 13, 97, 99, 149, 160–62, 190–96, 199–207, 216–17, 232, 242, 250; for exempt classes, 41–42, 49, 52–53, 58, 115, 131, 225; purpose of, 58; and Bertillon system, 84–85; of marriages, 94; San Francisco earthquake and fire losses, 106, 201, 202; and birthright citizens, 106, 226; for sojourner returns, 122; character affidavits, 135; chain migration with, 190; and coaching book, 196–98; and paper identities, 200–207; of women immigrants, 206–7; and harassment of Chinese, 229–30, 232–34; and extortion, 233–34

Dollar, Robert, 127

Dollar Steamship Company, 127

Domestic service, 27, 273 (n. 8)

Double identities. *See* Paper identities and lives

Down Town Association of San Francisco, 129–30

Dress and appearance, Chinese, 27, 79, 89, 94–95; as factor in return admittance, 107, 108–9; as factor in merchants' wives admittance, 135; disguises as Mexicans, 161; and "John Chinaman" caricature, 166

Dunn, James, 55–57, 64, 125

Dye, Clarkson, 140

Earthquake, San Francisco (1906), 106, 201, 202

Eastern and southern European immigrants: restrictions on, 11, 30, 31, 38, 39, 246; racialization of, 21, 30, 31, 35, 37, 39; equated with Chinese, 35; nativist rhetoric against, 72; assertions of "whiteness" by, 263 (n. 65)

Ellis Island, 66–67, 203, 251; Angel Island contrasted with, 75, 82; immigrant inspection on, 81–82

El Paso, Texas: and border crossings, 150, 160–61; smuggling ring, 164, 182; and government corruption, 164, 199; and Chinese exclusion, 172, 186; and border inspectors, 180, 184–85; informants, 182–83; and contemporary gatekeeping, 249

Enfranchisement. *See* Voting rights

English language, 107, 108, 109, 239

Ethnicity: gatekeeping policy based on, 20, 221; and aftermath of September 11 attack, 253–54. *See also* Racialization

European immigrants: racialized hierarchy of, 11, 21, 36; and gatekeeping bureaucracy, 22; contrasted with Chinese, 29, 32, 46, 171; feared as cheap labor, 36; anti-Chinese sentiment of, 37–38; assertions of "white-

ness" by, 37–38, 263 (n. 65); restriction of, 39, 246; as preferred labor imports, 64–65; Ellis Island processing of, 75; as sojourners, 116, 119; illegal entry through Canada, 170–71; short detention time for, 217; U.S. preference for, 247. *See also* Eastern and southern European immigrants

Exempt classes, 2, 3, 4, 49; and birthright citizens, 4, 78, 103; document requirements of, 41–42, 49, 52–53, 58, 115, 131, 225; 1888 exclusions from, 45; strict construction of, 50, 52–53, 66, 192; interpretation and definition of, 66, 78; number of admittances (1898), 67; and interrogations, 85, 87; and women's status, 92, 95, 97, 99, 100, 238; and male child preference, 97, 99; and entrenchment of Chinese exclusion policy, 129–30; and women's strategies, 134–35; and illegal immigration, 192, 193; admission loopholes, 194; and paper identities, 200–203, 216–17; vulnerability to arrest, 225; and deportations, 225–26, 228

Extortion, 233–34

False identities. *See* Paper identities and lives

False papers. *See* Documentation: fraudulent

Families: remaining in China, 1–2, 114, 115–16, 119–23; and paper son system, 4–5, 17, 194–95, 203–7; effects of Chinese exclusion on, 6, 51, 240; transnational networks of, 8, 12, 132, 194–95; immigration of Japanese, 32; status of merchants', 78, 92–95, 97, 99, 131, 135, 206–7, 291 (n. 59); and male child preference, 97, 99; and dependent requirements, 99; and patriarchal values, 115–16, 121; immigration-facilitation networks, 132–33, 142; reunions as immigration incentive, 191–92; Chinese American sponsorship of, 202; and admittance interrogation, 209–13; coaching of detainees by, 215–16; illegal immigration effects on, 216–17; deportations of, 226; and Chinese American disillusionment, 240; and perpetuation of false identities, 240–41; and Chinese Confession Program, 241–42; post–World War II reunions of, 245–46; and Immigration Act of 1965, 247

Farm labor, 26, 32, 33–34, 38, 114–15, 171–72; California's shortage of, 113

Fifteen Passenger Bill of 1879, 165

50; corruption linked with, 148, 149, 156, 164, 195–96, 198–99, 216, 235, 236; and organized smuggling networks, 148–49, 154, 158–64, 169, 219; terminology of, 149–50, 172, 248–49; racialization of, 152, 171; numbers, 158, 171, 191; and disguises, 162, 194; Chinese contrasted with European, 169–70, 171–72; Chinese contrasted with Mexican, 171–72; and informant reward system, 172–73; and immigration raids, 185–86, 194, 230–32, 239; community network assistance to, 192–93; strategies of, 193–207, 213–19; male character of, 206; conflation with legal residents, 222; expanded definition of, 226; and harassment, 232; exploitation of, 233–34; and double identities, 240–41; contemporary increase in, 247–50

Illegal immigration; roots in Chinese exclusion laws, 6, 10, 13, 147–50; entrance doors, 13, 147–50 (*see also* Border crossing; Ports of entry); and federal government policies, 13, 25, 43, 46, 116; and smuggling terminology, 149, 248–49; costs of, 154, 195, 219–20; and U.S. sovereignty, 173; as lucrative business, 175–76, 176–77, 193–98, 212, 250; as survival strategy, 189; factors contributing to, 191–92; perpetuation of exclusion cycle by, 207–13; consequences of, 213–19; normalization of, 216–17; dangers of, 250

Illegal Immigration and Responsibility Act of 1996, 247

Immigrants: federal government documentation of, 14–16, 41, 42; Chinese percentage of total numbers, 25; treatment of Chinese vs. other groups, 78–89, 99, 123, 141; admission of non-Chinese nationalities, 191, 237–38; classes on deportation lists, 224; ratio of immigration to emigration, 237–38; equal footing of (1965), 246; American ambivalence toward, 251; and suspected terrorists, 254. *See also* Bureau of Immigration, U.S.; Immigration law; *specific nationalities*

Immigration Act of 1882, 246
Immigration Act of 1891, 31, 43, 262 (n. 33)
Immigration Act of 1903, 30
Immigration Act of 1917, 39, 172
Immigration Act of 1921, 39, 246

Immigration Act of 1924, 11; quota system, 9, 38, 39, 245, 246; Chinese merchant definition, 91; Oliver P. Stidger critique of, 139; deportation provisions, 225, 226–27, 233; citizenship provisions, 238

Immigration and Nationality Act of 1965, 246, 247

Immigration and Naturalization Service, U.S. (INS), 10, 248, 265 (n. 3); immigration arrival files, 14–16; Operation Gatekeeper, 19, 249; critics of, 250; and post–September 11, 2001, controls, 254. *See also* Bureau of Immigration, U.S.; Customs Service, U.S.; Immigration officials

Immigration brokers, 140, 195–96, 199, 203, 235

Immigration Bureau. *See* Bureau of Immigration, U.S.

Immigration law: anti-Chinese (*see* Anti-Chinese legislation); impact of Chinese Exclusion Act on, 4, 5, 6, 24–25, 32, 40–43, 222, 246; racial hierarchy in, 7, 21, 38; quota system, 9, 38, 39, 245, 246; barring contract laborers, 30; tightened restrictions in, 39, 46, 77–78; immigration inspectors' knowledge of, 69; interpretation in enforcement of, 77; barriers to single women immigrants, 97; Chinese exclusion entrenchment in, 126, 174; loopholes in, 147–48, 173; American imposition in Canada and Mexico, 148–49, 152; and illegal immigrant designation, 149, 173; Canadian, 153; Mexican, 157–58; and Canadian seaports, 176–77; reform of, 222, 246, 247; deportation provisions, 224–25; post-1943 provisions for Chinese, 245; overview of, 245–48; categories barred in, 246; abolishment of quota system, 246, 247; name changes of enforcement agencies, 265 (n. 3). *See also specific laws*

Immigration lawyers. *See* Attorneys

Immigration officials, 40–41, 46, 47–48; civil service examinations for, 17, 69; and fate of Chinese arrivals, 48; power of, 48; in enforcement hierarchy, 49–50; corruption among, 50, 72, 148, 149, 156, 195–96, 198–200; personal bias of, 52, 54, 55–58, 72; and Chinese interpreters, 62–63; post-1910 training of, 68–69; interpretation of exempt classes by, 78; interrogations

Lem, Arthur, 132, 191, 241, 242
Leong, Karen, 26
Ling, H. A., 53–54
Lipsky, Michael, 48
Li Sing v. U.S. (1901), 226
Literacy test, 39, 69, 74, 89, 172
Lodge, Henry Cabot, 35
Look Tin Sing, 103, 105
Lowe, Lisa, 134, 260 (n. 30)

Magnuson Bill (1943), 245
Marriage: and Chinese exclusion provisions, 45, 92, 94–95, 97, 99, 100; separation of couples on Angel Island, 76, 81; interrogation of couples, 95–96, 250; citizenship loss with alien partner, 100, 238; reasons for wives' non-emigration, 116, 240; treatment of merchants' wives, 131; War Brides Acts of 1945 and 1947, 245, 246. *See also* Children; Families
Mazumdar, Sucheta, 26
Mazzoli, Romano, 247
McClatchy, V. S., 34
McCreary Amendment of 1893, 42
McGettrick, Felix W., 156
McGowan, George A., 139–40, 141, 277 (n. 128)
McKee, Delber, 66, 85
McKenzie, R. D., 129, 237
McKeown, Adam, 92–93, 287 (n. 74)
Medical examinations, 4, 20, 81–85, 87; for manual labor evidence, 90; distrust of Chinese and, 207, 211–12
Mehan, Charles, 71, 186, 235, 268 (n. 112)
Men, Chinese: seen as sexually and racially ambiguous, 166; and Angel Island detention conditions, 217, 219
Merchants, Chinese, 1, 2, 3, 89–92, 115; as exempt class, 4, 45, 50, 78; documentation requirements, 41, 232–33; narrowing definition of, 52–53, 90–91; and Chinese boycott, 69, 125–26; status of wives and children of, 78, 92, 93, 94–95, 97, 99, 131, 135, 206–7, 291 (n. 59); and racialized class markers, 87, 89–92; and immigration officials, 89–90, 198; markers of status of, 91–92, 135, 135–36, 137–38; effects of exclusion laws, 112; percent of all admissions/readmissions, 114; admittance numbers (1910–24), 115, 207; legal challenges by, 123; exclusion enforcement protests, 129–31, 133–34, 135, 212–13; and white witnesses requirement, 135–36; evasion of exclusion laws, 192–93, 217; as paper identities, 200–201; deportation vulnerability of, 202, 225, 232–33; status compared with birthright citizens, 202–3
Metcalf, Victor, 67–68, 80, 115, 126, 212
Mexican Americans, 38, 39, 249
Mexican Border District, 186
"Mexican Exclusion Act," 247
Mexican immigrants: racialization of, 11, 21, 33–35, 38–39; illegal, 19, 38–39, 149, 171–72, 248–50; and gatekeeping bureaucracy, 22; suppression in U.S. West, 29; restriction of, 31, 222; compared with Chinese, 34, 46, 171–72; nativist rhetoric against, 34, 72; contrasted with southern/eastern European and Asian, 38–39; deportation and repatriation programs against, 39, 246; as sojourners, 116, 119; and legacy of Chinese exclusion, 222; contemporary campaigns against, 248–50
Mexican immigration: benign neglect of, 171–72
Mexicans: as Chinese border-crossing accomplices, 159–60; Chinese immigrant disguises as, 161–62; as immigration service informants, 164, 182–83
Mexico: Chinese illegal entry from (*see* Border crossings); U.S. relations with, 38, 148–49, 152, 157, 174, 180–86, 255; U.S. border policing and enforcing, 152, 179–87, 222, 255; anti-Chinese movement in, 157; revolutionary nationalism, 157; labor recruitment needs of, 157, 179–80, 181; Chinese immigration policies of, 157–58, 179–81; undefined U.S. border with, 158, 179; Chinese immigrant sea route to, 159; borderlands contact zones, 161–65; other illegal immigrant entries from, 169–70; as U.S. labor source, 172; lax immigration law enforcement by, 174, 179; border enforcement, 179–87; seaport controls, 180–81; immigration raids in, 185–86; decrease in Chinese immigration from, 187
Mexico-Canadian Steamship Company, 180–81
Middle Eastern Americans, 253–54
Milton, Jeff, 184

via Canadian border, 155; illegal border crossings by, 155–56, 192; via Mexican border, 158; and documents lost in San Francisco earthquake, 201. *See also* Sojourner migration; Transnationalism

Returns to China: ratio to emigration from, 237–38

Rickards, Carlton, 61, 77, 199

Riordan, Thomas, 103, 139, 233

Roediger, David, 31, 263 (n. 65)

Roosevelt, Franklin D., 245

Roosevelt, Theodore, 64, 66, 67, 69, 80, 199; and Chinese exclusion enforcement protests, 124, 126; and Mexican border patrol, 184

Rosenblum, Karen, 149–50

Rosencrans, W. S., 40

Rowell, Chester H., 34

Ruddell, S. J., 44, 195

Sacramento Bee (newspaper), 34

Saldívar, José David, 280 (n. 64)

Salyer, Lucy, 8, 44, 69, 147–48, 156, 250

Sánchez, George, 248

San Diego, Calif., 19, 64

San Francisco: as main port of entry for Chinese, 2, 7, 14, 48, 51; Chinese immigration entry process, 4–5; Chinese community, 7; local immigrant inspectors and interpreters, 11, 48, 50; Chinese immigration files, 14, 16; anti-Chinese movement, 23–24, 46, 50, 51; reasons for anti-Chinese sentiments, 25–26; newspapers, 32, 50, 67–68, 73, 165; anti-Asian movement, 32–33; Chinese immigrant registration policy, 44–45; as model for national gatekeeping, 45–46, 48, 63–64, 74; as most difficult processing center, 51–58; vigilant enforcers in, 52–58; Chinese interpreters, 61; Hart Hyatt North as commissioner of immigration, 69–70, 236; corruption scandals, 72, 199, 200; Chinese-language newspapers, 77, 121, 127, 236; prostitution investigation, 93; birthright citizenship cases, 103–8; earthquake and fire (1906), 106, 201, 202; Pacific Mail Steamship Company detention shed, 124–25, 127, 214, 217; Chinese kinship networks, 132–33; immigration attorneys, 139–40; Chinese community complaints, 231; extortion from Chinese

immigrants, 233. *See also* Angel Island; Chinese Bureau

San Francisco Call, 72

San Francisco Chamber of Commerce, 127

San Francisco Chronicle, 67–68

San Francisco Down Town Association, 127

Santa Barbara, Calif., 64

Sargent, Frank P., 57, 59–60, 67, 68, 80, 90; and Bertillon system, 84, 85; and Chinese exclusion enforcement protests, 125; and immigration raids, 185–86, 230; anti-Chinese sentiments of, 208; on deportation, 224

"Save our State," 292 (n. 19)

Sawyer, John Birge, 71, 73

Saxton, Alexander, 27

Sbarboro, A., 37–38

Schiller, Nina Glick, 259 (n. 16)

Schwerin, R. P., 51

Scott Act of 1888, 45, 153, 224–25

Scottish immigrants, 64–65

Seaports. *See* Ports of entry

Search and seizure, 226

Seattle, Wash., 14, 162, 164, 202

Section 6 certificates, 49, 55, 115, 131, 225

September 11, 2001, terrorist attack, 19, 253–55

Sex ratio, 92, 97, 99; reasons for imbalance in, 115–16

Sexuality. *See* Gender; Prostitution, Chinese

Shah, Nayan, 83, 270 (n. 23)

Shaler, Nathaniel, 35

Simpson, Alan, 247

Siu, Paul, 237, 240, 246

Slavery, 26, 27, 30, 31

Sojourner migration, 120–23; definition of, 1, 116; practice of by European, Asian, and Mexican immigrants, 116, 119, 171–72; and interrogations, 209; perpetuation of, 237

Sonora, Mexico, 157, 181

Soo Hoo Fong, 89–90

Southern Europeans. *See* Eastern and southern European immigrants

Southern Pacific Steamship Company, 199

Spanish language, 161–62

State-building, 10, 21–22, 74, 148, 225

Steamship companies, 49, 51, 159; immigration privileges of first- and second-class passengers, 134, 201; profit from illegal immigration, 176, 196, 199; and Canadian

on federal government by, 30; new immigrant racialization in, 31–34; anti-Asian movement in, 32–33, 37; anti-Mexican movement in, 33–34; depictions of Chinese illegal immigrants, 168

Wetbacks, 149, 172

White Chinese interpreters, 16, 58–64

"White man's burden" (term), 174

Whiteness, 37–38; class markers of Chinese merchants linked to, 92, 135–36, 137–38; European immigrants' assertion of, 263 (n. 65)

White supremacy, 27, 29, 30, 37, 46

White witnesses and references, 91–92, 106, 135–38, 201, 226

White workers, 20, 25–26, 30, 64–65, 165, 234

Wilkinson, W. H., 217, 233

Wilson, Woodrow, 74, 124, 130, 231

Winant, Howard, 10, 259–60 (n. 22)

Windom, William, 171

Wing, O'Malley, and McGrath, 140

Wise, John H.: anti-Chinese attitudes of, 52–54, 93–94, 95; enforcement practices of, 53–54, 58, 103; popularity of, 54; and Chinese interpreters, 62; on immigration attorneys, 138

Wittke, Carl, 32

Women, Chinese: and Orientalist ideology, 26; linked with prostitution, 26, 30, 76, 78, 93–96, 116; and Page Law, 41; as immigration detention "matrons," 71; as wives of citizens, 78, 92, 95–96, 131, 206, 207; as wives of merchants, 78, 93, 94–95, 97, 131, 206–7; and unequal sex ratio, 92, 99, 115–16; exclusion effects on, 92–93; and unequal immigration opportunities, 92–100, 206; dependent status of, 93, 96–97, 99–100; immigrant officials' treatment of, 94–95, 96; bound feet as status marker of, 94–95, 135; and birthright citizenship revocations, 100, 238; reasons for non-emigration of, 115–16; numbers admitted (1882–1943), 116; occupations and marital status, 116; higher admission rates of, 206–7, 245–56

Wong, Charles Choy, 241, 242

Wong Kim Ark, 103–5, 106, 238

Wong Lan Fong, 15, 134

Wong Ngum Yin, 119, 122, 124, 132

Working class. See Labor movement; White workers

Workingmen's Party of California, 26, 32, 37

World War II, 222, 245

Worley, Alfred L., 139–40, 141, 277 (n. 128)

Wu, Ching Chao, 189, 209, 220, 230

Wu Ting-Fang, 124, 129

Yellow Peril, 36, 73

Yong Chen, 125

Young Men's Christian Association, 137

Yu, Henry, 260 (n. 30)

Yung, Judy, 137